THEOLOGICAL INTERPRETATION OF THE OLD TESTAMENT

THEOLOGICAL INTERPRETATION OF THE OLD TESTAMENT

A Book-by-Book Survey

KEVIN J. VANHOOZER
GENERAL EDITOR

CRAIG G. BARTHOLOMEW
AND DANIEL J. TREIER
ASSOCIATE EDITORS

Baker Academic
a division of Baker Publishing Group
Grand Rapids, Michigan

© 2005, 2008 by Baker Book House Company

Published by Baker Academic
a division of Baker Publishing Group
P.O. Box 6287, Grand Rapids, MI 49516-6287
www.bakeracademic.com

Published in Great Britain by the Society for Promoting Christian Knowledge
36 Causton Street
London SW1P 4ST

Theological Interpretation of the Old Testament first published in 2008. Chapters for this volume previously appeared in Kevin J. Vanhoozer et al., eds., *Dictionary for Theological Interpretation of the Bible* (Baker Academic/SPCK, 2005).

Second printing, February 2009

Printed in the United States of America

Library of Congress Cataloging-in-Publication Data
Theological interpretation of the Old Testament : a book-by-book survey / Kevin J. Vanhoozer, general editor ; Craig G. Bartholomew and Daniel J. Treier, associate editors.
      p.   cm.
   Includes bibliographical references and index.
   ISBN 978-0-8010-3624-8 (pbk.)
   1. Bible—Criticism, interpretation, etc. I. Vanhoozer, Kevin J.
BS1171.3T493 2008
221.6—dc22   2008034059

British Library Cataloguing-in-Publication Data
A catalogue record for this book is available from the British Library.
UK ISBN 978-0-281-06101-3

Contents

List of Contributors 7
List of Abbreviations 9

Introduction: What Is Theological Interpretation of the
Bible? *Kevin J. Vanhoozer* 15
1 Genesis *Gordon J. Wenham* 29
2 Exodus *R. W. L. Moberly* 42
3 Leviticus *Paul L. Redditt* 52
4 Numbers *Kent L. Sparks* 59
5 Deuteronomy *Daniel I. Block* 67
6 Joshua *J. G. McConville* 83
7 Judges *J. Alan Groves* 92
8 Ruth *Murray D. Gow* 102
9 Samuel *Brian E. Kelly* 111
10 Kings *Richard S. Hess* 119
11 Chronicles *Mark A. Throntveit* 124
12 Ezra *John J. Bimson* 132
13 Nehemiah *John J. Bimson* 137
14 Esther *Paul L. Redditt* 142
15 Job *Lindsay Wilson* 148
16 Psalms *J. Clinton McCann Jr.* 157
17 Proverbs *Raymond C. Van Leeuwen* 171
18 Ecclesiastes *Craig G. Bartholomew* 179
19 Song of Songs *Tremper Longman III* 186
20 Isaiah *Richard L. Schultz* 194

21 Jeremiah *J. G. McConville* 211
22 Lamentations *Christian M. M. Brady* 221
23 Ezekiel *Thomas Renz* 226
24 Daniel *Ernest C. Lucas* 236
25 Hosea *Mary J. Evans* 244
26 Joel *Willem VanGemeren* 251
27 Amos *Karl Möller* 257
28 Obadiah *Paul R. House* 263
29 Jonah *John H. Walton* 268
30 Micah *Mignon R. Jacobs* 276
31 Nahum *Thomas Renz* 282
32 Habakkuk *Thomas Renz* 286
33 Zephaniah *Thomas Renz* 291
34 Haggai *Paul R. House* 295
35 Zechariah *Albert Wolters* 300
36 Malachi *Mignon R. Jacobs* 305

Scripture Index 313
Subject Index 327

Contributors

Craig G. Bartholomew (PhD, University of Bristol) is the H. Evan Runner Chair in Philosophy at Redeemer University College.

John J. Bimson (PhD, University of Sheffield) teaches Old Testament at Trinity College, Bristol.

Daniel I. Block (DPhil, University of Liverpool) is Gunther H. Knoedler Professor of Old Testament at Wheaton College.

Christian M. M. Brady (DPhil, University of Oxford) is director of the honors program and associate professor of classical studies and Jewish studies at Tulane University.

Mary J. Evans (MPhil, CNAA) is former vice principal of London School of Theology and currently lectures in Old Testament at the Ethiopian Graduate School of Theology in Addis Ababa.

Murray D. Gow (ThD, Australian College of Theology) is minister of St. Paul's Cooperating Parish in Kamo, New Zealand.

J. Alan Groves (PhD, Free University of Amsterdam) was professor of Old Testament at Westminster Theological Seminary.

Richard S. Hess (PhD, Hebrew Union College) is Earl S. Kalland Professor of Old Testament and Semitic Languages at Denver Seminary.

Paul R. House (PhD, Southern Baptist Theological Seminary) is associate dean and professor of divinity at Beeson Divinity School.

Mignon R. Jacobs (PhD, Claremont Graduate University) is associate professor of Old Testament at Fuller Theological Seminary.

Brian E. Kelly (PhD, University of Bristol) is dean of chapel at Canterbury Christ Church University College.

Tremper Longman III (PhD, Yale University) is the Robert H. Gundry Professor of Biblical Studies at Westmont College.

Ernest C. Lucas (PhD, University of Kent; PhD, University of Liverpool) is vice principal and teaches biblical studies at Bristol Baptist College.

J. Clinton McCann Jr. (PhD, Duke University) is Evangelical Professor of Biblical Interpretation at Eden Theological Seminary.

J. G. McConville (PhD, Queen's University, Belfast) is professor of Old Testament studies at the University of Gloucestershire.

R. W. L. Moberly (PhD, University of Cambridge) is reader in Old Testament in the department of theology and religion at the University of Durham.

Karl Möller (PhD, University of Gloucestershire) is lecturer in theology and religious studies at St. Martin's College.

Paul L. Redditt (PhD, Vanderbilt University) is professor and chair of the department of religion at Georgetown College.

Thomas Renz (PhD, University of Bristol) is lecturer in Old Testament at Oak Hill College.

Richard L. Schultz (PhD, Yale University) is Armerding Chair of Biblical Studies at Wheaton College.

Kent L. Sparks (PhD, University of North Carolina) is professor of biblical studies and special assistant to the provost at Eastern University.

Mark A. Throntveit (PhD, Union Theological Seminary, Virginia) is professor of Old Testament at Luther Seminary.

Willem VanGemeren (PhD, University of Wisconsin) is professor of Old Testament and Semitic studies at Trinity Evangelical Divinity School.

Kevin J. Vanhoozer (PhD, University of Cambridge) is research professor of systematic theology at Trinity Evangelical Divinity School.

Raymond C. Van Leeuwen (PhD, University of Toronto) is professor of biblical studies at Eastern University.

John H. Walton (PhD, Hebrew Union College; Jewish Institute of Religion) is professor of Old Testament at Wheaton College.

Gordon J. Wenham (PhD, King's College, London) teaches Old Testament at Trinity College, Bristol.

Lindsay Wilson (PhD, University of Melbourne) is vice principal and lecturer in Old Testament at Ridley College, Melbourne.

Albert Wolters (PhD, Free University of Amsterdam) is professor of religion, theology, and classical languages at Redeemer University College.

Abbreviations

Bible Texts and Versions

AT	Author's Translation
BHS	*Biblia Hebraica Stuttgartensia*. Edited by K. Ellinger and W. Rudolph. Deutsche Bibelgesellschaft, 1983
DH	Deuteronomic History
ET	English Translation
KJV	King James Version
LXX	Septuagint (Greek OT)
MT	Masoretic Text (Hebrew Bible)
NIV	New International Version
NRSV	New Revised Standard Version
NT	New Testament
OT	Old Testament
RSV	Revised Standard Version

Old Testament Books

Gen.	Genesis	Neh.	Nehemiah
Exod.	Exodus	Esther	Esther
Lev.	Leviticus	Job	Job
Num.	Numbers	Ps. (Pss.)	Psalms
Deut.	Deuteronomy	Prov.	Proverbs
Josh.	Joshua	Eccles.	Ecclesiastes
Judg.	Judges	Song	Song of Songs
Ruth	Ruth	Isa.	Isaiah
1–2 Sam.	1–2 Samuel	Jer.	Jeremiah
1–2 Kings	1–2 Kings	Lam.	Lamentations
1–2 Chron.	1–2 Chronicles	Ezek.	Ezekiel
Ezra	Ezra	Dan.	Daniel

Hos.	Hosea	Nah.	Nahum
Joel	Joel	Hab.	Habakkuk
Amos	Amos	Zeph.	Zephaniah
Obad.	Obadiah	Hag.	Haggai
Jon.	Jonah	Zech.	Zechariah
Mic.	Micah	Mal.	Malachi

New Testament Books

Matt.	Matthew	1–2 Thess.	1–2 Thessalonians
Mark	Mark	1–2 Tim.	1–2 Timothy
Luke	Luke	Titus	Titus
John	John	Philem.	Philemon
Acts	Acts	Heb.	Hebrews
Rom.	Romans	James	James
1–2 Cor.	1–2 Corinthians	1–2 Pet.	1–2 Peter
Gal.	Galatians	1–3 John	1–3 John
Eph.	Ephesians	Jude	Jude
Phil.	Philippians	Rev.	Revelation
Col.	Colossians		

Apocrypha

Add. Dan.	Additions to Daniel	2 Esd.	2 Esdras (= 4 Ezra)
Bel.	Bel and the Dragon	Jdt.	Judith
Pr. Azar.	Prayer of Azariah	Let. Jer.	Letter of Jeremiah (Bar. 6)
Song of Thr.	Song of the Three Young Men	1–4 Macc.	1–4 Maccabees
		Pr. Man.	Prayer of Manasseh
Sus.	Susanna	Ps. 151	Psalm 151
Add. Esth.	Additions to Esther	Sir.	Sirach (Ecclesiasticus)
Bar.	Baruch	Tob.	Tobit
1 Esd.	1 Esdras	Wis.	Wisdom (of Solomon)

OT Pseudepigrapha

1 En. *1 Enoch (Ethiopic Apocalypse)*
L.A.B. *Liber antiquitatum biblicarum* (Pseudo-Philo)
Liv. Pro. *Lives of the Prophets*

Dead Sea Scrolls and Related Texts

CD *Cairo Damascus Document* (cf. 4Q265–273; 5Q12; 6Q15)
1QIsa[a] Isa[a]
1QM *War Scroll*
1QS *Community Rule*
4Q174 *Florilegium* = 4QFlor
4QSam[a] 4Q51

Tractates of the Talmud
Jerusalem Talmud
y. 'Abod. Zar.   'Abodah Zarah

Babylonian Talmud

b. B. Bat.   Baba Batra
b. Ḥul.   Khullin/Ḥullin
b. Mo'ed Qat.   Mo'ed Qatan
b. Nid.   Niddah
b. Šabb.   Šabbat
b. Sanh.   Sanhedrin

Other Rabbinic Works

Gen. Rab.   Genesis Rabbah
Lev. Rab.   Leviticus Rabbah

Other Jewish Works
Josephus

C. Ap.   Contra Apionem (Against
            Apion)
A.J.   Antiquitates judaicae
            (Jewish Antiquities)

Apostolic Fathers

1 Clem.   1 Clement

Other Early Christian Literature
Augustine of Hippo

Civ.   De civitate Dei
            (The City of God)

Eusebius

Hist. eccl. Historia ecclesiastica
             (Ecclesiastical History)

Origen

Comm. Jo.   Commentarii in evangelium
            Joannis

Tertullian

Marc.   Adversus Marcionem
            (Against Marcion)

Additional Abbreviations

AB   Anchor Bible
ABD   Anchor Bible Dictionary. Edited by D. N. Freedman. 6 vols. Doubleday,
            1992
ACCSOT   Ancient Christian Commentary on Scripture: Old Testament
AJSL   American Journal of Semitic Languages and Literature
ANET   Ancient Near Eastern Texts Relating to the Old Testament. Edited by
            J. B. Pritchard. 3rd ed. Princeton, 1969
AThR   Anglican Theological Review
AUSS   Andrews University Seminary Studies
BA   Biblical Archaeologist
BBR   Bulletin for Biblical Research
BEATAJ   Beiträge zur Erforschung des Alten Testaments und des antiken
            Judentum
BETL   Bibliotheca ephemeridum theologicarum lovaniensium
BibInt   Biblical Interpretation
BKAT   Biblischer Kommentar, Altes Testament. Edited by M. Noth and H. W.
            Wolff
BLS   Bible and Literature Series

BSac	*Bibliotheca sacra*
BT	*The Bible Translator*
BZAW	Beihefte zur Zeitschrift für die alttestamentliche Wissenschaft
CBC	Cambridge Bible Commentary
CBQ	*Catholic Biblical Quarterly*
CCSL	Corpus Christianorum: Series latina. Turnhout, 1953–
CTJ	*Calvin Theological Journal*
CurBS	*Currents in Research: Biblical Studies*
DBSJ	*Detroit Baptist Seminary Journal*
EDBT	*Evangelical Dictionary of Biblical Theology.* Edited by W. Elwell. Baker Books/Paternoster, 1996
EvQ	*Evangelical Quarterly*
EvT	*Evangelische Theologie*
FC	Fathers of the Church. Catholic University of America, 1947–
FCB	Feminist Companion to the Bible
FOTL	Forms of the Old Testament Literature
HAT	Handbuch zum Alten Testament
HBT	*Horizons in Biblical Theology*
HS	*Hebrew Studies*
HSM	Harvard Semitic Monographs
HUCA	*Hebrew Union College Annual*
IBC	Interpretation: A Bible Commentary for Teaching and Preaching
ICC	International Critical Commentary
JAAR	*Journal of the American Academy of Religion*
JBL	*Journal of Biblical Literature*
JETS	*Journal of the Evangelical Theological Society*
JPS	Jewish Publication Society
JSNTSup	Journal for the Study of the New Testament: Supplement Series
JSOT	*Journal for the Study of the Old Testament*
JSOTSup	Journal for the Study of the Old Testament: Supplement Series
LCL	Loeb Classical Library
LWorks	Martin Luther. *Luther's Works.* Vols. 1–30 edited by J. Pelikan, 31–54 by H. Lehman. 55 vols. Concordia/Fortress, 1955–1986
NAC	New American Commentary
NCB	New Century Bible
NIB	*The New Interpreter's Bible.* Edited by L. Keck. 12 vols. Abingdon, 1994–2002
NIBCOT	New International Biblical Commentary on the Old Testament
NICOT	New International Commentary on the Old Testament
NIDOTTE	*New International Dictionary of Old Testament Theology and Exegesis.* Edited by W. A. VanGemeren. 5 vols. Zondervan, 1997
NIVAC	NIV Application Commentary
NovTSup	Novum Testamentum Supplements
NSBT	New Studies in Biblical Theology
OBT	Overtures to Biblical Theology
OTG	Old Testament Guides
OTL	Old Testament Library

RAC	*Reallexikon für Antike und Christentum*. Edited by T. Klauser et al. A. Hiersemann, 1950–
RACSup	*Supplements* to *RAC*. Edited by T. Klauser. A. Hiersemann, 1971–
RevQ	*Revue de Qumran*
RTR	*Reformed Theological Review*
SBL	Society of Biblical Literature
SBLDS	Society of Biblical Literature Dissertation Series
SBLMS	Society of Biblical Literature Monograph Series
SBLSP	*Society of Biblical Literature Seminar Papers*
SBT	Studies in Biblical Theology
SBTS	Sources for Biblical and Theological Study
SemeiaSt	Semeia Studies
SHS	Scripture and Hermeneutics Series
SJT	*Scottish Journal of Theology*
SSN	Studia semitica neerlandica
TJ	*Trinity Journal*
TOTC	Tyndale Old Testament Commentaries
TynBul	*Tyndale Bulletin*
VT	*Vetus Testamentum*
VTSup	Vetus Testamentum Supplements
WBC	Word Biblical Commentary
WC	Westminster Commentaries
WTJ	*Westminster Theological Journal*
WUNT	Wissenschaftliche Untersuchungen zum Neuen Testament
ZAW	*Zeitschrift für die alttestamentliche Wissenschaft*

Introduction

What Is Theological Interpretation of the Bible?

Kevin J. Vanhoozer

Of the making of books commenting on biblical books there would seem to be no end. There are now more *series* of biblical commentaries than there are books in the Bible. What, then, could possibly justify adding one more item to an already well-stocked inventory? Neither the editors nor the contributors are under the illusion that a new secondary text will change the world. Nevertheless, we believe that the time is ripe for a new kind of interpretation of Scripture that combines an interest in the academic study of the Bible with a passionate commitment to making this scholarship of use to the church. And we are not alone. The "theological interpretation of the Bible" has become a growth industry of late, spawning new journals, academic conferences, and commentary series.[1]

The race to recover a compelling mode of theological interpretation recalls the Oklahoma Land Rush of 1893 when settlers rushed into virgin territory to stake a claim. That event was, in the words of an eyewitness, one of the most noteworthy events of Western civilization. At that time there was an economic depression that made finding a habitable dwelling place especially urgent. The situation at the end of the twentieth century was not so different: for two centuries, biblical interpreters had been wandering in

---

1. For a good overview of the challenges that continue to attend this project, as well as a typology of the various ways in which people are responding to them, see D. J. Treier, *Introducing Theological Interpretation of Scripture: Recovering a Christian Practice* (Baker, 2008).

what Paul Ricoeur called the "desert of criticism," unable to find spiritual nourishment in speculations about likely historical backgrounds, sources of composition, or etymological footnotes. The recovery of theological interpretation of Scripture is about emerging from the desert to settle in and inhabit the promised land.

Theological interpreters want to inhabit the text, but even more they want to dig. Perhaps the better analogy, then, would be the 1848 California gold rush. News spread slowly at first, but eventually that event drew prospectors from around the world. Textual prospectors are currently mining both Scripture and tradition for theological gold: the knowledge of God. The chapters in the present work display different sorts of gold recovery; more importantly, they display the nuggets discovered in the process.[2]

What Theological Interpretation Is *Not*

As to the process itself, however, initially it is easier to say what theological interpretation of the Bible is *not* rather than what it is.

Theological interpretation of the Bible is not an imposition of a theological system or confessional grid onto the biblical text. In speaking of theological interpretation, we do not mean to encourage readers merely to read their own theologies into the text. While it may be true that exegesis without theological presuppositions is not possible, it is not part of the present volume's remit to take sides with a specific confessional or denominational tradition. (On the other hand, we do affirm the ecumenical consensus of the church down through the ages and across confessional lines that the Bible should be read as a unity and as narrative testimony to the identities and actions of God and of Jesus Christ.)

Theological interpretation is not simply what dogmatic theologians do when they use the Bible to support their respective doctrinal positions. Although so-called precritical interpretations took biblical authority seriously and sought to read for the church's edification, they may be vulnerable at three points: They may fail to take the text seriously in its historical context. They may fail to integrate the text into the theology of the OT or NT as a whole. They may be insufficiently critical or aware of their own presuppositions and standpoints (Wright).

2. It should be noted that the chapters in the present work originally appeared (in alphabetical order) in K. J. Vanhoozer et al., eds., *Dictionary for Theological Interpretation of the Bible* (Baker, 2005).

Theological interpretation of the Bible is not an imposition of a general hermeneutic or theory of interpretation onto the biblical text. Theological interpretation is also not simply a matter of imposing a *general* hermeneutic on the Bible as if the Bible could be read "like any other book." There are properly theological questions, such as the relationship of the OT and NT, that require more than what is typically offered in a general hermeneutic (Watson). Stated more strongly, there are some interpretative questions that require theological, not hermeneutical, answers: "The turn to hermeneutics as a general discipline . . . has not so much offered a resolution of older theological questions, historically considered, as it has changed the subject" (Seitz 42). There is something left for interpreters to do after reading the Bible like any other book. At the same time, we believe that certain biblical and theological themes have implications not only for biblical interpretation, but for general hermeneutics as well.

Theological interpretation of the Bible is not a form of merely historical, literary, or sociological criticism preoccupied with (respectively) the world "behind," "of," or "in front of" the biblical text. Those who seek to renew biblical interpretation will incorporate whatever is true, noble, right, admirable, and useful in the various historical, literary, and sociological approaches used to describe the world "behind" the text (e.g., in the past), the world "of" the text (e.g., its plot and literary form), or the world "in front of" the text (e.g., the way in which readers receive and react to it). Theological interpretation may not be reduced to historical or to literary or to sociopolitical criticism, but it is not less than these either. For God has been active in history, in the composition of the biblical text, and in the formation of a people to reveal and redeem. Yet each of these disciplines, though ancillary to the project of interpreting the church's Scripture, stops short of a properly theological criticism to the extent that it brackets out a consideration of divine action.

Why "Theological" Interpretation of the Bible?

The present book of essays responds to two crises precipitated by Enlightenment and post-Enlightenment developments in biblical interpretation respectively: to the modern schism between biblical studies and theology, and to the postmodern proliferation of "advocacy" approaches to reading Scripture where each interpretative community does what is right in its own eyes. The primary purpose of the present volume is to provide biblical interpreters with examples of best interpretative practice: a display ranging across the canon of the state of the theological interpretative art. Our hope is that this work will encourage others to recover biblical studies as a properly theological discipline.

The "ugly ditch" in modern biblical interpretation: between exegesis and theology. The critical approach to biblical interpretation that has come to dominate the modern study of the Bible, especially in the university but also in seminaries, was developed in order to protect the Bible from what was thought to be its "dogmatic captivity" to confessional and theological traditions. For some two hundred years now, Christian faith has not been thought to be either necessary or relevant in the attempt to discover "what it meant." Theology thus came to be of only marginal importance for biblical studies as practiced in university and divinity school settings. Indeed, modern biblical studies has become a virtual "theology-free zone." Even scholars who identify themselves as Christians have to check their theological convictions at the door when they enter the academy (Fowl xii–xxx).

The divide separating biblical studies and theology was nothing less than Lessing's famous "ugly ditch": the gap between reason and faith, between publicly ascertainable history on the one hand and privately valued belief on the other. The goal of biblical studies for the typical modern scholar was to understand the texts by restoring them to their original historical contexts and by reading them on their own terms, namely, as (human) products of particular times and places, cultures and societies. In this interpretative framework, the Bible tended to be studied as evidence of a historically developing "religion," as evidence of how ancient Israelites—and later, Jesus and his followers—tended to think about God, the world, and themselves. To study "religion," however, is to study human beings and human history—in contrast to "theology" as the study of God and the mighty acts of God.

The problem was not so much with modern biblical scholarship's interest in reconstructing historical contexts and the history of the text's composition. The bigger problem was its tendency to treat the biblical texts as sources for reconstructing human history and religion rather than as texts that testify to God's presence and action in history. To treat the Bible as a source—as evidence for some natural phenomenon "behind" it—is to deflect attention away from what the texts are saying (as testimony) in favor of a hypothetical reconstruction of "what actually happened." History here trumps exegesis.

Further, it is likely that modern critics are working with an overly "thin" conception of history, as a self-enclosed, linear set of temporal events whose causal explanation is to be found in the relation of earlier to later events in the same horizontal space-time spectrum. The Bible, however, announces events that partake of the "fulness" of time, events that are the result of divine as well as human agency, events in which the future breaks in, as it were, from above. This way of viewing the ugly ditch posits a gap between thin (reductionist) descriptions of biblical history and thick descriptions that take account of the text's own appeals to divine agency.

Interpreted theologically, the ugly ditch may be nothing less than the perceived gap between "nature" and "grace." Reason, together with its many critical children—source, form, tradition, redaction criticism, and so on—is qualified to interpret the Bible as a historical and human text. But to read the Bible as the word of God is to make a leap into the realm of "grace" that either opposes, crowns, or outflanks reason (Wolters).

The "muddy ditch" in postmodern biblical interpretation: between exegesis and ideology. The Bible-theology relation in the late modern or postmodern era is less an ugly ditch, across which it is impossible to leap, than it is a "muddy ditch"—the quagmire of history, language, tradition, and culture—out of which it is impossible ever to extricate oneself. Postmoderns typically deny that we can escape our location in history, culture, class, and gender. Our readings of the biblical text will be shaped, perhaps decisively so, by our particular location and identity. The goal of interpretation is therefore to discover "what it means to my community, to those with my interpretative interest." Postmodern readers come to Scripture with a plurality of interpretative interests, including (perhaps) the theological, though no one interest may claim more authority than another. The postmodern situation of biblical interpretation gives rise to a pluralism of interpretative approaches and hence to a legitimation crisis: Whose interpretation of the Bible counts, and why?

Biblical interpretation in postmodernity means that independent standards and universal criteria for determining which of many rival interpretations is the "right" or "true" one will be met with no little suspicion. A host of postmodern thinkers has slain the giant assumption behind much modern biblical scholarship that there can be objective, neutral, and value-free reading of biblical texts. Postmodern thinkers have charged modernity's vaunted historical-critical method with being just one more example of an ideologically motivated approach. The critical approach only pretends to be objective, neutral, and value free. Modern biblical critics are as rooted in the contingencies of history and tradition as everyone else. Indeed, biblical criticism is itself a *confessional* tradition that begins with a faith in reason's unprejudiced ability to discover truth. The question postmoderns raise for historical critics is whether, in exorcising the spirit of faith from biblical studies, they have not inadvertently admitted even more ideological demons into the academic house.

Whereas the temptation of historical criticism is to offer only thin descriptions of the world behind the text or of the process of the text's composition, the temptation of ideological criticism is to offer only thinly veiled echoes of one's own voice. To be distracted by what is "behind" or "before" the text, however, is to miss its message; such nontheological biblical criticism is like music criticism by the deaf and art criticism by the blind.

What Is Theological Interpretation of the Bible?

Theological Interpretation of the Old Testament and its companion *Theological Interpretation of the New Testament* attempt to provide models for proceeding toward a more constructive engagement with Scripture. While the authors are not working from a single methodological template, three premises undergird the approaches represented herein.

The theological interpretation of the Bible is not the exclusive property of biblical scholars but the joint responsibility of all the theological disciplines and of the whole people of God, a peculiar fruit of the communion of the saints. It was Gerhard Ebeling who once declared that church history is essentially the history of biblical interpretation. To the extent that this is so, the present crisis in biblical interpretation—the confusion not only over what the Bible means but also over how to read it—is also a crisis for the church. The study of church history can itself be a theological discipline insofar as it helps the present church to learn from previous ways of interpreting Scripture. Indeed, one reason for the increased interest in theological interpretation of the Bible is the recent rehabilitation of the reputation of the church fathers as profound exegetes. Some have even touted "the superiority of pre-critical exegesis" (Steinmetz).

Is biblical studies a theological discipline? By and large, the resounding answer, at least in the setting of the modern university, has been *Nein!* Modern biblical scholars insist that biblical studies must be autonomous in order to be critical (Barr). Yet some degree of involvement with theology seems to be inevitable, for three reasons. First, biblical scholars must have recourse to theology in order to make sense of the Bible's main subject matter, God (Jeanrond). Readings that remain on the historical, literary, or sociological levels cannot ultimately do justice to what the texts are actually about. Second, biblical studies needs theology (especially the latter's analysis of contemporary culture) in order to be aware of the aims, intentions, and presuppositions that readers invariably bring to the biblical text (Wright). Third, biblical studies needs theology in order to provide a sufficient reason for the academy's continued engagement with the biblical text. Only the assumption that these texts say something of unique importance can ultimately justify the depth of the exegete's engagement (Levenson).

A word about biblical theology is in order, for on the surface this discipline seems a likely candidate to mediate the divide between biblical studies and theology. However, some (e.g., Barr; Fowl) see biblical theology as one more symptom of modern biblical scholarship's assumption that it is possible neutrally and objectively to describe the religious beliefs of the biblical writers. The results of this study—"what it meant" to *them*, back then—are of more antiquarian than ecclesial interest and are offered to the academy, not the church. Yet others (e.g., Watson; Rosner) view biblical theology as an activity that is practically identical with the theological interpretation of the Bible in its concern for hearing the word of God in the church today.

If exegesis without presuppositions is impossible, and if some of these presuppositions concern the nature and activity of God, then it would appear to go without saying that biblical interpretation is always/already theological. One's view of God, for instance, will influence which biblical statements about God one considers literal and which statements one takes as figurative. The inevitability of employing theological categories, however, does not automatically license a wholesale appropriation of any one theological system. Nevertheless, readers with a theological interest, whether in the academy or the church, will at least seek to go further than describing what *others* have said or thought about God. Theological interpreters want to know, on the basis of Scripture and in light of contemporary concerns, what *we* should say and think about God.

Finally, practical theology takes part in biblical interpretation when it inquires into how the people of God should respond to the biblical texts. The way in which the church witnesses, through its language and life, is perhaps the most important form of theological interpretation of the Bible.

The theological interpretation of the Bible is characterized by a governing interest in God, the word and works of God, and by a governing intention to engage in what we might call "theological criticism." Can theological interpretation be "critical," and if so, in what sense? Historical

21

and literary criticism we know, but with regard to theological criticism, we may be tempted to ask, "Who are you?"

A theological interpretation of the Bible is more likely to be critical of readers than of biblical authors or biblical texts. It is not that text criticism and other forms of criticism have no role; it is rather a matter of the ultimate aim of reading. Those who seek to interpret Scripture theologically want to hear the word of God in Scripture and hence to be transformed by the renewing of their minds (Rom. 12:2). In this respect, it is important to note that God must not be an "afterthought" in biblical interpretation. God is not simply a function of a certain community's interpretative interest; instead, God is prior to both the community and the biblical texts themselves. A properly theological criticism will therefore seek to do justice to the priority of the living and active triune God. One way to do so is to guard against idols: images of God manufactured by the interpretative communities.

We believe that the principal interest of the Bible's authors, of the text itself, and of the original community of readers was theological: reading the Scriptures therefore meant coming to hear God's word and to know God better. Our aim therefore is not to impose yet another agenda or ideology onto the Bible, but rather to recover the Bible's original governing interest. On this view, biblical interpretation takes the form of a *confession* or acknowledgment of the work and word of God in and through Scripture.

One should not abandon scholarly tools and approaches in order to interpret the Bible theologically. On the contrary, modern and postmodern tools and methods may be usefully employed in theological interpretation to the extent that they are oriented to illumining the text rather than something that lay "behind" it (e.g., what actually happened) or "before" it (e.g., the ideological concerns of an interpretative community). At the same time, a theological vantage point calls into question the autonomy of the realm of "nature," and the autonomy of so-called critical approaches to reading the Bible, in the first place. Neither "nature" nor "knowledge" is ever religiously neutral; from the standpoint of Christian doctrine, "nature" is a divine creation, and "knowledge" is inseparable from some kind of faith. The challenge, therefore, is to employ critical methods, but not uncritically. Critical tools have a ministerial, not magisterial, function in biblical interpretation. The aim of a properly "confessional criticism" (Wolters) is to hear the word of God; theological criticism is governed by the conviction that God speaks in and through the biblical texts.

The strongest claim to be made for theological interpretation is that only such reading ultimately does justice to the subject matter of the text itself.

Because biblical texts are ultimately concerned with the reality of God, readers must have a similar theological interest (Jeanrond). Theological *text* genres (e.g., Gospels, prophecies, apocalyptic, etc.) call for theological *reading* genres, for styles of reading that proceed from faith and yet seek theological understanding. To read the biblical texts theologically is to read the texts as they wish to be read, and as they should be read in order to do them justice.

The theological interpretation of the Bible names a broad ecclesial concern that embraces a number of academic approaches. At present, no one model of theological interpretation of the Bible holds sway in the church.[3] The contributors to the present work recognize that there is more than one way of pursuing an interest in theological criticism. Because we are only in the initial stages of recovering a distinctly theological interpretation of Scripture, it would be unwise to preempt discussion of how best to read the Bible in the church. In choosing the various contributors, the editors were careful to invite representatives of different theological backgrounds, denominations, and interpretative approaches. Nevertheless, it is possible to discern at least three distinct emphases, more complementary than contradictory, that help us begin to distinguish types of theological interpretation.

Some interpreters have an interest in divine authorship, in the God-world relation "behind" the text as it were. This first type recognizes that our doctrine of God affects the way we interpret the Scriptures, while simultaneously acknowledging that our interpretation of Scripture affects our doctrine of God. Indeed, this two-sided problematic has been designated a matter of "first theology" (Vanhoozer). The focus here is less on establishing "what actually happened" than on reading the Bible in terms of divine authorship or as divinely appropriated human discourse (Wolterstorff). Interpreting Scripture as divine discourse opens up interesting possibilities for discerning the unity among the diversity of biblical books and for relating the two Testaments. Theological assumptions about God's involvement with the production of Scripture play an important role in how interpreters take or construe the text and in how they deal with thematic developments as well as apparent historical inconsistencies.

A second group of theological interpreters focuses on the final form of the text rather than on questions of human or divine authorship. For these interpreters, it is the text as a finished literary work or narrative that serves as the prime theological witness. One discovers who God is

---

3. See Davis and Hays pp. 1–5 for a statement of the Princeton Scripture Project's "Nine Theses on the Interpretation of Scripture."

by indwelling the symbolic world of the Bible. Proponents of this second approach seek to interpret the Bible on its own terms, whether these terms be literary (e.g., narrative) or properly religious (e.g., canon). Theology is a matter of "intratextual" reading (Lindbeck) that patiently unfolds the world of the text in order to learn what God was doing in Israel and in Jesus Christ. The God-world relation as depicted in the text thus becomes the framework for understanding today's world too.

Still other interpreters of Scripture identify the theologically significant moment with the reading and reception of the Bible in the believing community today. The divine action that counts for these interpreters is the work of the Holy Spirit, which they locate as much in the present as, if not more than, in the past. What makes biblical interpretation theological is a function of the aims and interests of the community of readers for which the Bible is "Scripture" (Fowl). The focus here is on the world of the Christian community and its members, who seek to live before God and to worship faithfully. The theological interpretation of Scripture is a distinct practice *of the church,* and hence it is regulated by the goods at which that practice aims. The primary concern with the *outcome* of biblical interpretation affords an interesting vantage point from which to assess the relative contribution of various types of biblical criticism and interpretative approaches.

The Purpose of a Book-by-Book Survey

Theological Interpretation of the Old Testament and its companion *Theological Interpretation of the New Testament* are intended as resources for all readers interested in the theological interpretation of Scripture, not merely for those who advocate a particular approach. The three emphases mentioned above are by no means mutually exclusive. One purpose of these books is to heal the debilitating breach that all too often prevents biblical scholars and theologians from talking to each other, or even from using the same reference books. If these books, together with their original host, the *Dictionary for Theological Interpretation of the Bible*, accomplish the purpose for which they were originally commissioned, they should appeal to biblical scholars, theologians, pastors, and laypeople alike.

The present work may prove an indispensable resource for any serious student of the Bible who also regards it as Scripture—a word from God about God. And this leads to the second purpose: to provide a resource for scholars in other disciplines to employ as they seek to promote biblical wisdom in and for their own disciplinary domains. The theological interpretation of Scripture is as important for scientists and sociologists as it is for exegetes and theologians proper—for all of us need a biblically and theologically informed framework for understanding God, the world, and ourselves.

The chapters of *Theological Interpretation of the Old Testament* and *Theological Interpretation of the New Testament* interpret every book of the Bible, focusing on the message rather than the historical background or process of composition that often make up the bulk of biblical commentaries. Each author was asked to discuss something of the history of interpretation, the theological message of the book, its relation to the whole canon, its unique contribution to the people of God, and to provide a brief bibliography for readers who may wish to probe further. Not all authors answered this editorial call in the same way. Some highlight special problems and/or contributions that particular books of the Bible make with regard to doctrine and theology. By and large, however, what is of special value in these pages is "canon sense" and "catholic sensibility." First, canon sense: authors are keen to discuss what each book contributes to Scripture as a whole and how its place in the canon affects its interpretation. Second, catholic sensibility: a bird's-eye view of the history of interpretation of a particular book provides a wealth of ecclesial wisdom in a nutshell.

Truth be told, our contributors are not representative of the whole width and breadth of the one true church. With some notable exceptions, they represent different shades of North American and British Protestant evangelicalism. It would therefore be interesting to read this book in conjunction with, say, the *Africa Bible Commentary* (Adeyemo).

Finally, let me repeat my initial point: the present volume is less a manifesto for a single way of interpreting the Bible theologically than it is a call to theological interpretation and a display of its best practice. Yet no single "best practice" is defined nor is one method mandated. Instead, the authors set about the various tasks of theological interpretation—tracing the history of interpretation, putting the text in canonical context, analyzing what the text says about God, reflecting on the text in light of the Rule of Faith—without saying which task is most important. Again, this is intentional; we are only at the beginning stages of recovering this complex practice. What this book presents is not a seamless garment, then, so much as a coat of many methodological colors.[4]

4. My reference to "seamless garment" alludes to M. J. Gorman's review of the *Dictionary for Theological Interpretation of the Bible* ("A 'Seamless Garment' Approach to Biblical Interpretation?" *Journal of Theological Interpretation* 1 [2007]: 117–28).

Conclusion: Reading to Know and Love God

Of the making of books about the Book there is no end. Quite so! Yet the "end" of the present work, its most important raison d'être, is to help promote the knowledge of God, the good, and the gospel via a recovery of the practice of theological interpretation. The ultimate justification for yet another book about the Bible is its utility in helping to promote the knowledge of what God has done in Israel and in Jesus Christ for the good of the world.

The principal thrust of theological interpretation is to direct the interpreter's attention to the subject matter of Scripture—God, the acts of God in history, the gospel—rather than to a particular theological tradition or, for that matter, to some other topic (e.g., the history of the text's composition, the secular history "behind" the text, the structure of the text, etc.). These other elements are included, however, to the extent that they help the reader grow in the knowledge of God.

Theological interpretation of the Bible, we suggest, is biblical interpretation oriented to the knowledge of God. For much of their history, biblical studies, theology, and spirituality were all aspects of a single enterprise, that of knowing God (McIntosh). Knowing God is more than a merely academic exercise. On the contrary, knowing God, like theological interpretation of the Bible itself, is at once an intellectual, imaginative, and spiritual exercise. To know God as the author and subject of Scripture requires more than intellectual acknowledgment. To know God is to love and obey him, for the knowledge of God is both restorative and transformative. The saving knowledge of God results in the transformation of the reader into the likeness of Jesus Christ. In the final analysis, theological interpretation of the Bible may be less a matter of knowing God than of engaging with the living God and being known by God (Gal. 4:9).

Theological interpretation of the Bible achieves its end when readers enter into the world of the biblical texts with faith, hope, and love. When we make God's thoughts become our thoughts and God's word become our word, we begin to participate in the world of the text, in the grand drama of divine redemption. This is perhaps the ultimate aim of theological interpretation of the Bible: to know the triune God by participating in the triune life, in the triune mission to creation.[5]

5. Matthew Levering is even more succinct: "the goal of exegesis is union with God" ("Principles of Exegesis: Toward a Participatory Biblical Exegesis," *Pro Ecclesia* 17 [2008]: 50).

No one denomination, school of interpretation, or hermeneutical approach has a monopoly on reading the Bible for the word of God. Insights from the whole body of Christ—a body animated and guided by the Spirit of Christ—are needed if Christians are to display the mind of Jesus Christ.

In sum, the aim of this book-by-book survey is to provide the resources necessary to respond to what for Johann Albrecht Bengel (1687–1752) was the biblical interpreter's prime directive: "Apply yourself wholly to the text; apply the text wholly to yourself." Interpreting Scripture theologically is the way to read the Bible "for a blessing" (Kierkegaard), for the sake of human flourishing, for the individual and social "good." Commentaries are not schools of sanctification, of course; yet the ultimate aim of the present work is to commend ways of reading Scripture that lead to the blessing of knowing God and of being formed unto godliness.

Bibliography

Adeyemo, T., ed. *Africa Bible Commentary*. Zondervan, 2006.

Barr, J. *The Bible in the Modern World*. SCM, 1973.

Davis, E. F. and Hays, R. B., eds. *The Art of Reading Scripture*. Eerdmans, 2003.

Fowl, S., ed. *The Theological Interpretation of Scripture*. Blackwell, 1997.

Jeanrond, W. *Text and Interpretation as Categories of Theological Thinking*. Crossroad, 1988.

Levenson, J. *The Hebrew Bible, the Old Testament, and Historical Criticism*. Westminster John Knox, 1993.

Levering, M. *Participatory Biblical Exegesis: A Theology of Biblical Interpretation*. University of Notre Dame Press, 2008.

Lindbeck, G. "Postcritical Canonical Interpretation: Three Modes of Retrieval." Pages 26–51 in *Theological Exegesis*, ed. C. Seitz and K. Greene-McCreight. Eerdmans, 1999.

McGrath, A. *The Genesis of Doctrine*. Eerdmans, 1990.

McIntosh, M. *Mystical Theology*. Blackwell, 2000.

Rosner, B. "Biblical Theology." Pages 3–11 in *New Dictionary of Biblical Theology*, ed. T. D. Alexander and B. Rosner. InterVarsity, 2000.

Seitz, C. "The Theological Crisis of Serious Biblical Interpretation." Pages 40–65 in *Renewing Biblical Interpretation*, ed. C. Bartholomew et al. SHS. Zondervan/Paternoster, 2000.

Steinmetz, D. "The Superiority of Pre-Critical Exegesis." Pages 26–38 in *The Theological Interpretation of Scripture*, ed. S. Fowl. Blackwell, 1997.

Treier, D. J., *Introducing Theological Interpretation of Scripture: Recovering a Christian Practice*. Baker, 2008.

Vanhoozer, K. *First Theology*. InterVarsity, 2002.

Watson, F. *Text, Church, and World*. T&T Clark, 1994.

Wolters, A. "Confessional Criticism and the Night Visions of Zechariah." Pages 90–117 in *Renewing Biblical Interpretation*, ed. C. Bartholomew et al. SHS. Zondervan/ Paternoster, 2000.

Wolterstorff, N. *Divine Discourse*. Cambridge University Press, 1995.

Wright, N. T. *The New Testament and the People of God*. SPCK, 1993.

1

Genesis

GORDON J. WENHAM

Introduction

By its very position as the first book of the Bible, Genesis (Greek: "origin") has been the focus of more attention than most other parts of the OT. It sets the scene for the rest of Scripture and is one of the books most quoted in the NT. Genesis orients the Bible reader to study the following books with appropriate assumptions about their context and theology. Its narratives have been an inspiration to countless authors and artists. Even in today's secular West, its stories and themes are still familiar.

But familiarity is no guarantee of interpretative integrity. Texts used out of context are liable to be misunderstood and misused, so here, as elsewhere in this dictionary, the aim is to understand Genesis both as a text of its time and as a key witness in the canon of Holy Scripture.

History of Interpretation

"The early chapters of Genesis had arguably a greater influence on the development of Christian theology than did any other part of the Old Testament" (Louth xxxix). Early Christian writers, following the lead of the NT, drew heavily on the opening chapters of Genesis to explain the doctrines of creation and the fall. The typology of Christ as the second Adam, who triumphed where the first Adam failed, was very important in patristic theology. Vital too was the understanding of humanity created in the image of God. Though this image was marred in the fall, God's ultimate purpose was its restoration in the new creation.

Symbolism was important in early Christian interpretation of Genesis, but that is not to say that they took the stories allegorically. They were accepted as literal accounts of the origin of the cosmos, just as the patriarchal narratives that follow them were understood historically. The problems posed by modern science did not trouble Christian interpreters till the nineteenth century. The Reformers and their immediate successors continued the same essentially literal approach to Genesis, with less emphasis on the symbolic dimensions of the book. Throughout this time it was assumed that Moses was the author of Genesis.

From the seventeenth century and the dawn of the Enlightenment, however, these traditional views began to be questioned. Spinoza in his *Tractatus theologico-politicus* (1670) suggested that Ezra had compiled the Pentateuch from Mosaic materials. A landmark for the discussion of Genesis was Astruc's *Conjectures on the Memoires Used by Moses to Compile Genesis* (1753), which proposed that Genesis was compiled from several parallel sources. This idea that Genesis and the other books of the Pentateuch were composed of various sources was intensely debated throughout the nineteenth century. Thanks to the brilliant advocacy of Julius Wellhausen in *Prolegomena to the History of Israel* (1878), a form of the documentary hypothesis came to be widely accepted by biblical scholars. This approach distributes Genesis into three main sources, J (Yahwist, 950 BCE), E (Elohist, 850 BCE), and P (Priestly, 500 BCE). These three sources were combined successively, so that Genesis reached its final form in the fifth century BCE, about 800 years after Moses. This entailed a quite skeptical approach to the content of Genesis. The accounts of the patriarchs do not reflect their own historical situation, "but only of the time when the stories about them arose. . . . This later age is here unconsciously projected . . . into hoar antiquity, and is reflected there like a glorified mirage" (Wellhausen 319).

While historical skepticism was battering the patriarchs, scientific discovery was undermining the traditional understanding of Gen. 1–11. Early Christian writers read these chapters more as narrative theology than as history, but nevertheless tended to assume that the chronology of Genesis was credible. But the development of geology indicated that the earth originated much earlier than 4004 BCE, as Archbishop Ussher had supposed in the seventeenth century. This made the interpretation of the genealogies of Gen. 5 and 11 problematic. Further discovery showed that the processes of creation had probably taken many millions of years, not six days. And Darwin's *Origin of Species* (1859) led many to conclude not only that the timescale of Genesis was wrong, but also that its ultimate assertion, "God created the heavens and the earth" (1:1), was misleading. Chance mutation was a sufficient explanation of the diversity of life on earth: the idea of a creator was superfluous and indeed just the superstition of a less-enlightened era.

This dismissal of Genesis and its theology as just the misguided notions of an ignorant age seemed to be confirmed by texts from ancient Nineveh of a flood story similar to Gen. 6–9. G. A. Smith deciphered and announced the Gilgamesh tablet 11 in 1872 and published it the next year. Though Smith was no skeptic, works by him and others led many to regard Gen. 1–11 as just another ancient oriental myth, with no more credibility or authority than the creation myths of any other people. The nineteenth-century intelligentsia concluded that Western science is the source of real truth.

The twentieth century was kinder to Genesis. Although for most of the century the documentary hypothesis with its late dating of the sources reigned supreme, there was a concerted attempt by scholars to find early authentic elements in these sources. Alt and Westermann argued that elements of the promises to the patriarchs went back to very early times. Scholars well-versed in archaeology and comparative Semitics (Albright; Speiser; de Vaux) found many parallels between the names and customs of Genesis and those of early-second-millennium Mesopotamia. This allowed them to argue that the stories of Genesis contain more historical information than their date of composition might have led one to expect. Though more skeptical voices (Van Seters; Thompson) have been raised in the late twentieth century, the archaeological evidence still tends to speak in support of Genesis (Millard and Wiseman).

The discovery of yet more ancient texts paralleling Gen. 1–11 (Sumerian King List, Flood Story, and the Atrahasis epic, among others) has led to the recognition that Genesis is not simply reproducing the ideas of surrounding cultures. At least at the theological level, it is contesting them fiercely (see below on "The Message of Genesis").

Finally, the last quarter of the twentieth century has witnessed many assaults on the documentary hypothesis (e.g., Whybray), so that it is now widely agreed that a better explanation of the growth of the Pentateuch ought to be found. Meanwhile, a vogue for final-form canonical readings has swept through biblical studies, including work on Genesis. This has bypassed much of the debate about sources and led to scholars asking about the structure and message of the books in their extant form. Though some of this work is driven more by literary concerns than by theological interest, it has often revealed some very instructive points about the theology of the book.

The Message of Genesis

Like many other books, Genesis has suffered from attempts to read its parts separately. This is most obvious among commentators who accept the documentary hypothesis. The Yahwist's (J) love of simple anthropomorphic descriptions of God is contrasted with the Priestly writer's (P) lofty transcendental approach. Whereas P tells of God speaking, in the Elohistic (E) source God tends to reveal himself in dreams. In commentators wedded to this theory of distinct sources, it is unusual to find much attempt to describe the theology of the book as a whole, to see these different emphases in polyphonic harmony as opposed to clashing dissonance.

More traditional readers of Genesis have also been guilty of directing more attention to one portion of the book than another. Christian commentators tend to devote disproportionate attention to Gen. 1–11 because of its importance in NT and later theologies. Jewish readers, on the other hand, are more interested in the stories of the patriarchs because they tell of the origins of the Jewish people and their claim to the land of Israel.

If we are to be fair to the text, however, we must be wary of privileging one part of the book over another. We should look at individual parts, but it is necessary to integrate the message of one part into the overall picture.

The Structure of Genesis

The coherence of the book is demonstrated by its carefully articulated structure. The opening creation account (1:1–2:3) is followed by ten sections, each headed by the same (*toledoth*) title: "These are the generations/descendants of" (2:4; 5:1; 6:9; 10:1; 11:10, 27; 25:12, 19; 36:1; "story," 37:2 NRSV). The sections alternate between extended narratives, such as chapters 2–4 and 37–50, and terse genealogies, such as chapters 5 and 36. If extended narratives are compared, such as the career of Abraham (chs. 12–25) alongside that of Jacob (chs. 25–35), certain similarities emerge, suggesting a typological reading. This is particularly evident in the comparison of Adam and Noah, where the latter is clearly a second-Adam figure. Like Adam, he is the father of the whole human race; and like Adam, he sins (9:20–27).

Keywords form another device linking and unifying the book of Genesis. The terms "bless" and "blessing" are used more often in Genesis than in any other book of the Bible. At creation, God blesses birds, fish, humankind, and the Sabbath, but it is preeminently the patriarchs who are blessed. Indeed, Abraham's name contains two of the three consonants in the word "bless" (*barakh*), suggesting that he is the incarnation of blessing. A second key term in Genesis is "seed" or "offspring" (*zera'*), first used of human seed in 3:15 and then frequently in the promises to the patriarchs. The third important word is "land/earth," first occurring in 1:1 and often again in the patriarchal promises.

These keywords tie the introductory eleven chapters to the following stories about the patriarchs. They cluster thickly in 12:1–3: "bless/ing" occurs five times, "land/earth" three times, and the whole passage revolves round the promise of descendants: "a great nation." Genesis 1–11 tells of the disarray between the nations; 12:3 declares that in Abraham all the nations will find blessing. The call of Abraham is the answer to the problems of the world.

The Sections of Genesis

To grasp the message of Genesis more exactly, however, we need to examine the contribution of each section in more detail. It falls into three distinct sections:

1. First Exposition: The Hexaemeron, 1:1–2:3
2. Second Exposition: The Protohistory, 2:4–11:26
3. The Core: The Patriarchs, 11:27–50:26

The opening expositions not only give the background to the core; they also foreshadow its themes.

The Hexaemeron

The magnificent overture tells of God creating the cosmos in six days (hence the Greek title "Hexaemeron," "six days [of creation]") and gives the first exposition of the theology of Genesis. Its first verse, "In the beginning God," mentions not a pantheon but only one God, who takes the initiative and orders the whole of creation. Implicitly, this rules out polytheism, the general belief of antiquity.

Second, this one God is sovereign. There is no fight with competing deities, as in other creation myths. God simply speaks, and there is light, dry land appears, and fish swarm in the sea. This is a God whose word effects what is spoken. The God who spoke in creation is the God who spoke to the patriarchs and who will do what he promised them.

Third, not only is this one God almighty, but also the celestial bodies—such as the sun, moon, and stars, worshipped by much of the ancient world—are merely creatures. Indeed, the significance of the attention given to the creation of these bodies and the dry land is that they are vital for human existence.

Fourth, the Hexaemeron climaxes with the creation of human beings in the image of God. Everything builds to this point, and God himself draws the attention of the rest of creation to it by inviting the heavenly host to watch the creation of the human race: "Let us make man in our image" (1:26). Humankind is not only blessed but also encouraged to propagate: "Be fruitful and multiply" (1:28 NRSV).

Here the contrast with Babylonian thought is again evident. In the Atrahasis epic, the creation of humanity is an afterthought, to supply the gods with food; later the gods regret making humans and therefore curb human fertility. Genesis, on the contrary, sees God supplying human beings with food and encouraging their proliferation.

Finally, the Hexaemeron concludes with God resting on the seventh day, another unique feature of this account. The implication is clear: since human beings are made in God's image, they too should rest on the seventh day. The erratic patterns of ancient pagan festivals and holidays are replaced by a weekly Sabbath, on which not only God rests but also his creatures, humankind and beasts (Exod. 20:8–11; Deut. 5:14), must rest as well. The goal of creation is thus rest and peace, not ceaseless activity: this is a vision reaffirmed in Jacob's blessing (Gen. 49).

The Protohistory

The second exposition, or Protohistory (2:4–11:26), simultaneously reaffirms the ideals of Gen. 1 and explains how the present sin-dominated world emerged. The Garden of Eden was a place of harmony, where a benevolent Creator provided all humankind's needs: water, food, animals, and companionship. First, 1:28 urges humankind to be fruitful and multiply; then, 2:21–25 portrays the archetypal marriage, in which God creates the perfect bride and presents her to Adam. Yet in a world where humanity lacks nothing, Adam and Eve break the one injunction given to them, and their cosmos turns to chaos.

Their relationship of mutual help and companionship turns sour. The harmony between humankind and beast now becomes a deadly struggle: "He shall bruise your head, and you shall bruise his heel" (3:15 RSV). Since the serpent will suffer in the head and the man only in his heel, the text clearly predicts the eventual triumph of man over beast, of humankind over the power of evil; but the focus of the text is on the ongoing violence within creation. Humankind will battle not just with animals, but also with plant life while struggling to grow food rather than weeds (3:18). And the result of it all is death (3:19).

Death comes quickly in chapter 4: Cain kills Abel, and Lamech promises seventy-sevenfold vengeance on those who attack him. Fratricidal strife will characterize the families of the patriarchs too (Jacob-Esau in chs. 25–33, and Joseph in ch. 37). But the avalanche of sin continues in Gen. 3–11, culminating in God's remark that "the earth is filled with violence" (6:11, 13). This state of affairs prompts God to send the flood to wipe out all flesh, both humans and animals.

Again, this is an example of Genesis rejecting the theology of the Near East. The Gilgamesh and Atrahasis epics tell of the gods sending a flood simply because there were too many people making too much noise! In Genesis, however, sin, not pique, motivates the divine judgment. Gilgamesh portrays the gods as scared by the catastrophe they have unleashed and as quite unable to halt it; Genesis presents matters as always under God's sovereign control. When God remembered Noah, the flood started to subside (8:1).

The flood is portrayed as a great act of decreation. Not only are all living creatures destroyed, but the water also covered the earth, just as it did before God declared, "Let the dry land appear" (1:2, 9 RSV). This act of decreation is followed by an act of re-creation. Once again, the dry land appears, plants and trees are seen, and the animals and Noah leave the ark to repopulate the earth. Indeed, like Adam and Eve, Noah is told to "be fruitful and multiply" (8:17; 9:1, 7 RSV). He is the new Adam, who by his obedience and sacrifice has transformed divine wrath into mercy (8:21; cf. 6:5–6).

Unfortunately, Noah, the one perfectly righteous man, also falls (9:20–21), and his sin is compounded by his son's behavior (cf. Cain). So the world enters a downward spiral again, which culminates in another universal act of judgment at the Tower of Babel (11:1–9).

The Patriarchs

The stories of the patriarchs (Gen. 12–50) are five times as long as the opening chapters of the book. This clearly shows where the author's interests lie: he wants to trace the origins of Israel and the twelve tribes. However, he wants to show more than that. He is putting forward the call of Abraham and his offspring as the answer to the problems of humankind set out in Gen. 3–11. The promises in 12:1–3 are more than a conglomeration of keywords such as "blessing"; they declare God's intention to deal with the effects of sin on the human race.

There are four elements to the promises in Gen. 12 and following chapters. First, a land is promised (12:1, 7; 13:14–17). Second, this land will be inhabited by numerous descendants of Abraham (12:2; 13:15–16; 17:4–6). Third, Abraham and his descendants will enjoy a special covenant relationship with God (12:3; 17:4–13). Fourth, through Abraham and his descendants all the families of the earth will be blessed (12:3; 18:18; 22:18). A close reading of all the promise passages shows how the promises develop each time they are repeated. These repetitions make the promises more detailed and specific: "a land" (12:1) becomes "this land" (12:7) and "all the land . . . forever" (13:15). Similar developments are discernible in the other elements of the promise.

The promises are so central to the message of Genesis that David Clines (29) is right in defining the theme of the Pentateuch: "the partial fulfillment—which implies the partial non-fulfillment—of the promise to or blessing of the patriarchs." Nearly all the episodes in Gen. 12–50 may be related to these promises. The patriarchs gradually acquire land rights in Canaan (21:22–33; 23:1–20; 33:19). Slowly and with difficulty they have children (21:1–7; 25:21; 30:1). God's blessing is evident in his protection of the patriarchs despite their folly (12:10–20; 20:1–18; 28:1–22; 34:1–35:5). Finally, through them some foreigners are blessed (14:15–24; 20:17–18; 21:22–24; 39:3–23; 47:13–25). As Clines observes, the fulfillment of these promises within the book of Genesis is but partial: subsequent books of the Pentateuch show a yet more complete fulfillment, and it is not until the book of Joshua that the Israelites eventually acquire the land. Running through the story line is openness to the future, a mood alternating between hope and disappointment.

The promises announce God's solution to the problems painted so graphically in Gen. 3–11. They also reaffirm his original intentions for creation. Abraham, like Noah before him, is a second-Adam figure. Adam was given the Garden of Eden; Abraham is promised the land of Canaan. God told

Adam to be fruitful and multiply; Abraham is assured that God will make his descendants as numerous as the dust of the earth (13:16) and the stars of heaven (15:5). In Eden, God walked with Adam and Eve; Abraham is told to walk before God and be perfect (3:8; 17:1; cf. 6:9). Through his obedient and faithful response to these promises, the promise is turned into a divine oath guaranteeing its ultimate fulfillment (22:16–18; cf. 50:24).

The length and detail of the patriarchal narratives show that the origin of Israel and the twelve tribes is the chief concern of Genesis. However, this analysis of the promises and their relationship to the story line shows that Israel's special relationship with God—and through that relationship their connection with land and to the nations—is even more important. It justifies Israel's claim to the land: God promised it to them, and the Canaanites forfeited their right to it through their misbehavior (Gen. 19).

However, a subsidiary theme is particularly apparent in the second half of the book. The two longest stories are about feuds between Jacob and Esau in chapters 25–33 and between Joseph and his brothers in 37–50. Fratricidal strife is also prominent in the Cain and Abel episode of the Protohistory (4:1–16). There is no resolution of the conflict in chapter 4; indeed, the situation degenerates until the whole earth is filled with violence (6:11, 13). But in the case of the later patriarchs, there are quite different endings. Both stories present moving scenes of reconciliation. Esau runs to meet Jacob and throws his arms around him. Joseph declares he has forgiven his brothers: "You meant evil against me, but God meant it for good. . . . So do not fear; I will provide for you and for your little ones" (33:4; 50:20–21 RSV). On a number of occasions Abraham and Isaac act as peacemakers in disputes (13:8–10; 26:17–33).

In all these episodes the patriarchs are depicted as being anxious to make peace and forgive past wrongs. This goodwill shines all the more brightly when set against the unrepentant callousness of Cain and Lamech. The experience of the patriarchs, on the other hand, suggests that forgiveness and reconciliation within families and between nations is not only possible but also desirable. It is an appeal to its readers to forgive and make up with their enemies, whether they be close relatives or people of other races, for it is by so doing that the fulfillment of the promise comes that "through your offspring all nations on earth will be blessed" (22:18).

Genesis in the Canon

As the first book of the Hebrew and Christian canon, Genesis inevitably occupies a most important place. It sets the tone and agenda for the rest of

Scripture. The book sets out in clear and simple terms some of the basic affirmations of the Bible. Direct allusion and quotation from it are rare in the OT, but its ideology is pervasive. In the NT direct quotation from it is quite frequent, and its ideas are treated as even more fundamental than the law.

Within the OT canon it heads the first section, the Torah, which is often translated as "the Law." But this English term is too narrow a rendering of the Hebrew: "Instruction" would be better. The narratives of Genesis are profoundly instructive: they explain the nature of God, the role of humankind, God's ideals for human behavior, and so on. Similarly, in the following books of the Pentateuch, it is not just the laws that instruct, but also the narratives in which the laws are given.

There is a particularly close relationship between Genesis and the next four books of the canon: Genesis gives essential background information for readers of Exodus to Deuteronomy. Without Genesis the plot of Exodus to Deuteronomy would be difficult to follow. In particular, the frequent references to the patriarchs and the promises made to them would be most obscure. However, it is difficult to define the relationship between the books of the Pentateuch more decisively.

Exodus to Deuteronomy does look like a biography of Moses. Exodus 2 tells of his birth, and Deut. 34 of his death, while in between he is the most important human character in the story. But Genesis seems almost superfluous to a biography of Moses. On closer reading more connections emerge between Genesis and the following books. The promises to the patriarchs constitute the foundation of Moses' ministry (Exod. 3:6–22). Other experiences of the patriarchs foreshadow episodes in Moses' life. For instance, Abraham's expulsion from Egypt is described in terms suggesting that it was like the exodus. The patriarchal encounters with their future brides at wells prefigure Moses' meeting with his future wife (Gen. 12:20–13:3; 24:15–28; 29:1–14). These features make Genesis more than mere background to the life of Moses: they show his continuity with Israel's founding fathers.

In other ways Genesis sheds light on the teaching of the later books and complements them. Sacrifice figures quite importantly in Exodus to Deuteronomy, and in Genesis the patriarchs are depicted as offering sacrifice at various turning points in their careers. Furthermore, the sacrifices of Cain and Abel, Noah, and Isaac (Gen. 4; 8; 22) serve to teach key principles of sacrifice through narrative, just as the later books of the Law make similar points through precept. Genesis 1 teaches monotheism: the later laws insist that Israelites may worship only "the LORD." Genesis 2 sets out the Pentateuch's approach to relations between the sexes: passages such as Lev. 18 and 20 and Deut. 22 show how these ethical principles apply in some controversial situations.

Themes and personalities from Genesis reappear in many parts of Scripture. Psalms celebrate creation (e.g., 104), lament the sinfulness of God's people (e.g., 106), and retell the patriarchal story (e.g., 105). The same themes reappear in the prophets, who also occasionally mention the patriarchs (Isa. 41:8; Hos. 12). The whole book of Ecclesiastes is a reflection on the state of humankind after the fall, which has made death universal and inevitable (Gen. 3:19).

The NT's debt to Genesis is also huge. In defining his views on marriage, Jesus appeals to Gen. 1:27 and 2:24 (Matt. 19:5). In a similar way Paul uses Gen. 3 to explain the nature of sin and to develop his doctrine of Christ as the second Adam (Rom. 3; 5; 7). Several writers hold up Abraham as a model of faith and obedience (Rom. 4; Heb. 11:17–22; James 2:21–23). And the Bible ends with Revelation's vision of the new Jerusalem, some of whose most notable features—a river, tree of life, gold, and jewels—all hark back to the original Garden of Eden (Rev. 21:1–22:5).

Genesis and Theology

The pervasive influence of Genesis on the rest of Scripture and on early Christian theology has already been mentioned, and it can hardly be explored further here. Suffice it to say that the themes of Genesis are both fundamental and central to biblical theology. That there is but one sovereign God, who created the world and continues to rule it by his power, is apparent from Gen. 1 and is foundational to the whole of Scripture and the theologies that have sprung from it.

Also apparent in the early chapters of Genesis is God's concern for humankind. Inverting the beliefs of the ancient world that humans were designed to supply the gods with food, Genesis declares that God provides both the human and the beast with food. His concern for human well-being is also apparent in Gen. 2. This divine care for God's creatures runs through the OT and in the NT climaxes in the incarnation.

Contrasting with the immorality of ancient deities and the permissiveness of modern gods, however, the God of Genesis is stern in his moral demands. Humanity's sinfulness and particularly its violence lead to three massive acts of judgment: the flood, the scattering of the nations at Babel, and the destruction of Sodom. The rest of Scripture affirms God's moral character: "You are of purer eyes than to see evil and cannot look on wrong" (Hab. 1:13 AT). This divine intolerance of sin is at once both the hope of the world and its greatest problem. It is its hope, in that God will not permit evil ultimately to triumph. It is its greatest problem: Genesis shows that even the most righteous are liable to sin, with disastrous consequences.

Yet Genesis looks forward in hope; the promise to the patriarchs comes to its climax: "In you all the families of the earth shall be blessed" (12:3 NRSV). The book affirms that the offspring of Abraham will ultimately bruise the serpent's head. From pre-Christian times this verse (3:15) has rightly been read messianically. The grim realism of Genesis about the present human condition is lightened by the firm hope of redemption in the future.

Finally, through its accounts of forgiveness and reconciliation in chapters 33 and 50, Genesis points the way forward for human societies. It anticipates our Lord's demand that we should forgive our enemies and demonstrate our discipleship by loving one another.

Bibliography

Alt, A. "The God of the Fathers." In *Essays on Old Testament History and Religion*. Blackwell, 1966.

Brueggemann, W. *Genesis*. Interpretation. John Knox, 1982.

Calvin, J. *Commentary on Genesis*. 1554, ed. and trans. J. King. 2 vols. Calvin Translation Society, 1847, 1965. Reprint, Banner of Truth Trust, 1975.

Cassuto, U. *A Commentary on the Book of Genesis*. 2 parts. Magnes, 1961–64.

Clines, D. J. A. *The Theme of the Pentateuch*. JSOT, 1978.

Dalley, S. *Myths from Mesopotamia*. Oxford University Press, 1989.

Driver, S. R. *The Book of Genesis*. WC. Methuen, 1904.

George, A. *The Epic of Gilgamesh*. Penguin, 2000.

Gunkel, H. *Genesis*. 3rd ed. Göttinger Handkommentar zum Alten Testament. Vandenhoeck & Ruprecht, 1910.

Hamilton, V. *The Book of Genesis*. 2 vols. NICOT. Eerdmans, 1990–95.

Hartley, J. *Genesis*. NIBCOT. Hendrickson/Paternoster, 2000.

Kitchen, K. *The Bible in Its World*. Paternoster, 1977.

Louth, A., ed. *Genesis 1–11*. ACCSOT 1. InterVarsity, 2001.

Millard, A., and D. Wiseman, eds. *Essays on the Patriarchal Narratives*. InterVarsity, 1980.

Moberly, R. W. L. *The Old Testament of the Old Testament*. OBT. Fortress, 1992.

Rad, G. von. *Genesis*, trans. J. Marks. Rev. ed. OTL. SCM, 1972.

Speiser, E. A. *Genesis*. AB 1. Doubleday, 1964. 3rd ed., 1979.

Van Seters, J. *Abraham in History and Tradition*. Yale University Press, 1975.

Vaux, R. de. *The Early History of Israel*. 2 vols. Darton, Longman & Todd, 1978.

Wellhausen, J. *Prolegomena to the History of Ancient Israel*. 1878. Meridian, 1957.

Wenham, G. *Genesis*. 2 vols. WBC. Word, 1987–94.

———. *Pentateuch*. Vol. 1 of *Exploring the Old Testament*. SPCK, 2003.

———. *Story as Torah*. T&T Clark, 2000.

Westermann, C. *Genesis,* trans. J. Scullion. 3 vols. SPCK/Fortress, 1984–86.

Whybray, R. N. *The Making of the Pentateuch*. JSOT, 1987.

Williamson, P. *Abraham, Israel and the Nations*. Sheffield Academic Press, 2000.

Young, D. *The Biblical Flood*. Eerdmans, 1995.

2

Exodus

R. W. L. MOBERLY

The book of Exodus—traditionally ascribed to Moses, the central human figure in the book, but in itself anonymous—is foundational for the biblical understanding both of God, Yahweh, and of the people of God, Israel. Its content sets out parameters for understanding God and Israel, parameters that have always played a major role in the thought and practice of both Jews and Christians, though these differing religious traditions have tended to appropriate the material in markedly different ways. Of enormous significance for Christian theology is God's self-revelation to Moses at the burning bush (Exod. 3); for ethics, the Ten Commandments (Exod. 20); and for spirituality, the pattern of Egypt, exodus, sea, and wilderness read metaphorically in terms of sin, redemption, baptism, and discipleship.

The book is in two main parts, strikingly depicted in its own words. First, Yahweh delivers Israel from Egypt: "You have seen what I did to Egypt and how I bore you upon eagles' wings and brought you to myself" (19:4 NRSV). Second, Yahweh gives torah, a moral and ritual constitution for Israel to enable them to realize their unique vocation: "So now, if you truly obey my voice and keep my covenant, you shall be my special treasure among all peoples. Although the whole earth is mine, you shall be for me a priestly kingdom and a holy nation" (19:5–6 AT).

The preliminary question of the genre(s) of the text, and the difference this might make to its theological interpretation, is complex. What it might mean to take seriously the received form of the text, and yet to recognize its intrinsic diversity and its likely lengthy underlying processes of transmission and discernment, can here only be briefly suggested, rather than argued. First, divine self-revelation and its faithful human recognition could as well take place over an extended period as at a single point of time. Second, the shape and sequence of the material may be meaningful in its own right, even if it does not correspond straightforwardly to the historical development of Israel's religion. Third, there need be no intrinsic reason why the Spirit should not appropriate any meaningful form of human communication. If ancient Israel's genres do not correspond to those of "history" as articulated in modern Western thought, they need be none the worse for that. The challenge is learning to recognize and appreciate the ancient conventions, and to relate them appropriately to our modern ones.

Exodus is well served by modern, theologically oriented commentaries. The outstanding volume remains the one by Childs, both for its reflection on the text and for its giving access to the great Jewish and Christian commentaries down through the centuries. Fretheim and Brueggemann each offer sophisticated but easily readable interpretation. From a Jewish perspective, Sarna is accessible and fascinating, while Jacob is more comprehensive though more polemical.

The richness and complexity of Exodus suggest an approach to its theological interpretation section by section.

1. Setting the Scene, Exod. 1:1–2:22

The growth of Israel into a people has clear resonances with God's mandate at creation and with his promise to Abraham (Exod. 1:7; cf. Gen. 1:28; 12:2), thus clearly contextualizing all that follows within God's overall purposes for his world. Yet human opposition directly threatens this outworking of God's purposes, and the patient overcoming of this opposition is a major concern of the book.

It is striking that the first characters to play a positive role are all women—the midwives, Moses' mother and sister, Pharaoh's daughter—

and unsurprisingly, feminist interpreters have engaged suggestively with this (Bellis and Kaminsky 307–26).

Moses means well, but his act of violence exposes the double-edged nature and unpredictable consequences of such acts (Childs 27–46).

2. God Calls and Commissions Moses, Exod. 2:23–7:7

The burning bush story is one of the most discussed passages in the whole OT (for an introduction to its symbolic interpretations, see Levine). Fire that burns without consuming is a prime symbol of God; perhaps because fire, as in Otto's famous characterization of holiness as *mysterium tremendum et fascinans*, both attracts (by its movement and color) and repels (by its heat if one gets too close). The hearing of God's voice from the fire will characterize Israel's encounter with God at Sinai (Deut. 4:9–13).

God calls Moses to be a "prophet," one who will speak and act for God; God will deliver Israel (3:7–8), which means that Moses is to deliver Israel (3:9–10). Moses feels overwhelmed at the enormity of this and produces a series of excuses, mainly expressing a sense of inadequacy; God takes these difficulties seriously, thereby implying genuine space in relationship with himself (3:11–4:12). Only when Moses tries to decline altogether does God become angry (4:13–14).

Moses' second difficulty relates to the name of God, which God then gives—Yahweh (3:13–15). The wordplay on the verb "to be" (*hayah*), which indicates something of the meaning of the divine name (3:14), has been a focus for Christian theologizing about the nature of God down through the ages, not least in relation to the LXX's rendering: "I am the One who is" (see LaCocque and Ricoeur 307–61). In both Hebrew and Greek, the text envisages a Deity whose nature is not dependent upon other than self—yet who graciously engages with, and indeed commits to, Moses and Israel. The self-revelation that makes God known also in no way removes the intrinsic mystery of God, but rather establishes the principle that, with God, "the more you know, the more you know you don't know." (On the vocalization of the divine name and the appropriate form for Christian use, see Seitz 131–44.)

Moses' initial encounter with Pharaoh is disappointing—far from heeding Moses, Pharaoh responds with cynical brutality; Moses needs to learn that God's ways are not his ways (5:1–23). God reaffirms his new self-revelation as Yahweh, a God who will deliver his people, and a reluctant Moses prepares to try again.

(On the much-discussed technical problem of how Yahweh giving his name to Moses relates to the extensive use of the divine name in Genesis, see Moberly, *Old Testament*.)

3. The Plagues, Exod. 7:8–11:10

Moses' confrontation with Pharaoh and his magicians—who initially can exercise the same kind of power that Moses exercises—raises numerous theological issues. First, why such an extended sequence? Why does not Yahweh, through Moses, simply sweep away the opposition? This is explicitly addressed in 9:14–16, in terms of the plagues serving to enhance recognition of Yahweh. Implicitly also, God's action is appropriately encountered within the familiar constraints of a long struggle.

Second, why does God harden Pharaoh's heart? This is clearly related to the first issue. At least it is clear that Pharaoh also hardens his own heart; thus it is not the case that Pharaoh is wanting to respond positively but is being prevented, but that God confirms him in the course he embraces for himself, and uses this to heighten the significance of Israel's deliverance.

Third, what if one reads this text (and the crossing of the sea) from an Egyptian perspective? Does this not show Yahweh to be, in some sense, a tribal or national deity, less than the one God of all? Interestingly, this question, sharply posed by those who have suffered oppression that has justified itself by appeal to God (Warrior), tends not to bother liberation theologians who are inclined to see an oppressor receiving just deserts. The underlying issue is election, Yahweh's call of Israel, with God consequently making a distinction in how he treats Israel (9:4, 26). Yet election is not just a privilege, for the OT principle is that (in the words of Jesus, Luke 12:48 AT) "much is expected of those to whom much is given" (cf. Amos 3:2).

4. Passover, Exodus, and Crossing the Sea, Exod. 12:1–15:21

The Passover texts have usually been of greater interest to Jews, who have still sought to enact what is prescribed, than to Christians, who have seen them as prefiguring Christ and so have tended to read the texts in a metaphorical mode (cf. 1 Cor. 5:7–8).

The use of the exodus by liberation theologians raises important hermeneutical issues (see Bellis and Kaminsky 215–75). On the one hand, a general OT case can be made that Israel is a model for the nations, and that therefore what applies to Israel can be applied to others also; and deliverance from unjust oppression is clearly a major concern within the text. On the other hand, God is said to be motivated explicitly by his antecedent commitment to the patriarchs (2:24; 6:2–8). The particularity of Israel's election should not be ignored, as also the purpose of the exodus, to make Israel servants/slaves to Yahweh. In general, any responsible Christian use of the material should be refracted through the lens of Christ, where the judgment and redemption of God are definitively revealed. To take the OT seriously both in its own right and in the light of Christ is demanding, but that is the task of Christian theology.

5. Learning in the Wilderness, Exod. 15:22–18:27

The wilderness narratives of Exodus are continued in Numbers, where some of the stories are clearly similar so as to draw a contrast (manna/quails, Exod. 16//Num. 11; rebellion at Meribah, Exod. 17:1–7//Num. 20:2–13). Israel's failings are treated more lightly in Exodus, before the giving of torah at Sinai, than in Numbers, where the post-Sinai context implies that more is expected of those to whom more is given.

In the wilderness Israel has to learn new ways of living—what it means to be Yahweh's people. Exodus 16 is paradigmatic, presenting a form of "Give us each day our daily bread." The hardships of the wilderness lead Israel to complain and to remember Egypt selectively (16:1–3). Yahweh's response is not only to provide for them, but explicitly to test their obedience (16:4–5). After Israel is reprimanded for complaining (16:6–12), God's provision is given (16:13–14) and initiates a didactic sequence. First, when God provides food, the people do not even realize it without Moses' explanation (16:15). Second, God's provision is strictly according to need (not strength)—neither more nor less (16:16–18). Third, it cannot be hoarded, so God's gift must be collected fresh each day (16:19–21). Fourth, the regular daily pattern varies on the Sabbath, for on Sabbath eve double can be collected and some kept; but the people are tempted to disbelieve this just as much as the regular pattern (16:22–30). Finally, some manna is solemnly preserved, presumably as a reminder of its lesson and meaning even in the promised land, where manna no longer needs to be provided (16:31–36).

6. The Covenant at Sinai, Exod. 19–24

As Israel gathers at Sinai, we have the keywords that sum up Exodus as a whole (19:4–6). The awesome nature of Yahweh's presence at Sinai is depicted by the language of storm, earthquake, volcano, fire, and trumpet (19:16–19). The argument that this depicts a live volcano, and therefore attempts to locate Mt. Sinai should search for a volcano, seriously misconstrues the purpose of the language. The text seeks to convey the overwhelming nature of the divine presence by appealing to the most shaking and moving of known phenomena.

In this awesome scene, Moses has uniquely privileged access to God (19:19–20; cf. 19:9; 14:31). Sinai in Exod. 19:24 is like a temple with restricted access: the people stay off/outside; selected leaders, such as priests, come into the holy place and encounter God (24:1, 9–11); Moses, like the high priest, goes alone to God as into the holy of holies (24:2, 15–18). Among other things, this underlines the parallels between Israel's regular worship and its foundational engagement with God; also, it stresses the implicit authority of the legislation associated with Moses. (In a different vein, Moses' ascent of the mountain into the fire and darkness of the divine presence was taken as a model of spiritual life in the suggestive typological interpretation of the early church; see Gregory of Nyssa.)

Yet even Moses is off the mountain when God speaks the Ten Commandments (19:21–20:1), which are presented as the direct, and overwhelming, address of God himself (20:18–19, 22), so as to suggest the conformity of their content to the very nature of God. Moses interprets the giving of the commandments in a key verse, 20:20: they are to *test* Israel, so as to bring about the *fear of God* and *diminish sin*. Obedience to the commandments is demanding but will make Israel into the upright people they are meant to be. "Fear of God" is the prime OT term for appropriate human responsiveness to God. The combination of "test" and "fear" recurs in Gen. 22, in a way suggesting that Abraham's costly obedience in being willing to relinquish Isaac in some way models what Israel's responsiveness to the Ten Commandments should be (Moberly, *Old Testament,* 144–45).

The detailed laws of Exod. 21–23 are, by contextual implication, outworkings in everyday, mundane situations of the fundamental concerns of the Ten Commandments. The Israelites then commit themselves to the covenant explicitly in terms of obedience to the Ten Commandments and the detailed laws (24:3) in a ritual where the blood perhaps symbolizes consecration (24:4–8; cf. 29:20–21), thus marking Israel as Yahweh's holy people (Nicholson 172). On this basis Israel's representatives "see" God (24:9–11). The proximity of access to God that is now possible, on the basis of consecrated covenantal obedience to the will of God, contrasts sharply with the earlier distance from the holy place of God that was enjoined upon Israel (19:10–15, 21–24).

7. Tabernacle and Priesthood, Exod. 25–31

The purpose of the tabernacle is to mediate the presence of Yahweh, so that as Israel moves on from Sinai, the divine presence that came upon Sinai can continue to accompany Israel in this "sacramental" shrine. The ark and the mercy seat are where Yahweh will meet with Moses (25:22), and the regular daily sacrifices will set the context for Yahweh's sanctifying presence in Israel (29:38–46, a key interpretative passage). Subsequent Jewish and Christian practices of morning and evening prayer seek to perpetuate this basic pattern of enabling openness to the divine presence in differing contexts.

The images and symbols within the tabernacle resonate with a wider ancient Near Eastern context (Keel 111–76). Since royal thrones were regularly flanked by fabulous creatures, the flanking cherubim above the ark implicitly indicate the presence of Yahweh's royal throne (25:17–22). The symbolism also acquires meaning from its Israelite context. It is likely that the seven-branch lampstand (25:31–40) is meant to be understood as a stylized representation of the burning bush—a perpetual symbolization of the fundamental encounter at Sinai/Horeb.

8. Covenant Breaking and Renewal, Exod. 32–34

Israel's impatient making of the golden calf is presented as, in effect, a breaking of the first two commandments, and this while Israel is still at the mountain of God; it is rather like committing adultery on one's wedding night. Even if this was not the specific intention of the people (which is open to various less-heinous construals), the text's account of their action is explicit (32:7–10). Aaron's self-exculpatory evasiveness—compare his account to Moses (32:21–24) with the narrator's own account (32:1–6)—suggests deception of self and/or others in a way indicative of a gap between appearance and reality.

Israel's faithlessness almost terminates the covenant at the outset. But Moses remains faithful, and his intercession makes a difference within God's purposes (32:10–14; cf. the importance attached to the role of faithful intercessor in Ezek. 22:30; Isa. 62:6–7). When Yahweh offers to make of Moses another Abraham (32:10b; cf. Gen. 12:2–3), Moses shows his true stature by declining the offer. The intercessory role of Moses is further developed in Exod. 33:11–20. The pattern here is that initially Moses speaks much and Yahweh little; but as the intercession continues, Moses speaks less and Yahweh more, until finally Yahweh alone speaks and Moses recedes from view. Overall, Moses uses his privileged position before God to seek a fuller revelation of God, which is granted in terms of what stiff-necked Israel most needs—grace and mercy (33:19). Yet this deeper engagement with God brings out the intrinsic limits of such engagement: the one with whom Yahweh speaks "face-to-face" (33:11) "cannot see my [Yahweh's] face" (33:20) (cf. Eph. 3:19, where Paul prays for Christians *to know* the love of Christ *that surpasses knowledge*). And the following provisions for Moses' safety in the rock (33:21–23), which stress the limited and partial nature of what Moses will see, paradoxically prepare for the greatest self-revelation of the nature of God, upon Yahweh's own lips, in the whole Bible (34:6–7).

Despite its intrinsic importance for the character of God, 34:6–7 has received less attention in Christian theology than 3:14. By contrast Jewish theology has given prime weight to 34:6–7, even designating it as a revelation of "the thirteen attributes" of God (for enumeration, see Jacob 985). Together the two passages are complementary in a foundational way for the OT understanding of Yahweh. In the context of Israel's sin, the strong emphasis is on divine mercy (see Moberly, "How?" 191–201). The reaffirmation of judgment in 34:7b is striking—since, in context, there is a sense in which Yahweh *is* clearing the guilty—and is most likely meant to safeguard Yahweh's moral nature and requirements, to clarify that the mercy is not leniency or moral indifference. In other words, Yahweh's mercy is meant to lead to renewed practices of faithfulness and integrity (cf. Ps. 130:4), not to a sense that Israel can "get away" with things because God will let them off. If Exod. 19–24 emphasizes God's searching moral demand, Exod. 32–34 stresses his searching grace. Theologically, it is vital to hold these two emphases in tension, and to resist all attempts to play off one against the other.

As a unit Exod. 32–34 offers a fundamental construal of Israel's existence before God, analogous to the construal of the world's existence in the flood narrative (Gen. 6–9). At their very beginnings the world in general and the chosen people in particular commit sin and face destruction (Gen. 6:5–13; Exod. 32:7–10). One person, Noah/Moses, remains faithful, is uniquely said to have "found favor" with Yahweh (Gen. 6:8; Exod. 33:12), and becomes a mediator of God's grace for the future. Faithful Noah and Moses are mentioned at the turning point of the narratives from judgment to renewal (Gen. 8:1; Exod. 33:11). Noah offers sacrifice and Moses prays (Gen. 8:20; Exod. 33:12–18), each to elicit a climactic pronouncement of divine mercy and forbearance toward sin (Gen. 8:21; Exod. 33:19; 34:6–7).

And each narrative strikingly emphasizes that the sinful qualities that brought judgment in the first place remain unchanged (humanity's sinful inclinations, Gen. 6:5; 8:21; Israel's being stiff-necked, Exod. 32:9; 33:3, 5; 34:9). So God deals with the world in general, and the chosen people in particular, in the same way (without partiality). And each should know that their continuing existence is because of divine grace toward the unfaithful, grace paradoxically mediated by one who is faithful.

9. The Tabernacle Established and Inaugurated, Exod. 35–40

Israel brings extensive freewill offerings (implicitly a response to grace), and the skilled craft that enables the tabernacle to be constructed is explicitly an endowment from God (35:4–36:7). Everything for the tabernacle and for the vestments of its priests is made as prescribed (39:32–43). Moses is obedient in exactly the same way that Noah was obedient (40:16; Gen. 6:22).

At the end of the book the cloud and glory of Yahweh's presence come to the tabernacle as they earlier came to Mt. Sinai (40:34; 24:15–16). So the one who met with Israel at Sinai will accompany Israel through the wilderness, and will also come to the temple in Jerusalem (1 Kings 8:10–11).

Conclusion

One possible way of reading the book as a whole is to see Exodus as probing the meaning of servitude and freedom, which can be focused on the differing implications of the Hebrew root 'bd (slave/servant). Israel is delivered from slavery to Egypt (esp. 1:13–14, 'bd, 5x), a slavery of heartless oppression, so as to become a slave to Yahweh instead. The first of the specific "ordinances" at Sinai is about the Hebrew slave ('ebed) who (remarkably) loves his master and chooses to serve him for life in preference to gaining independence (21:2–6). This may well be put in this prime position so as to metaphorically picture Israel in relation to Yahweh, who later says, "For it is to me that the Israelites are slaves" (Lev. 25:55 AT). Such servitude is one of justice and holiness. It is the highest honor elsewhere in the OT for a person to be designated as "servant ['ebed] of Yahweh" (so, e.g., Abraham, Moses, David [Gen. 26:24; Josh. 1:7; 1 Kings 11:13]). Likewise, Paul calls himself the servant/slave (doulos, the regular LXX rendering of 'ebed) of Christ (Rom. 1:1; etc.). The thought underlying all this is well captured in the famous (Book of Common Prayer) words,

"His service is perfect freedom." Compare the psalmist's linking obedience to torah with living in freedom (Ps. 119:44–45), and Paul's emphasis that Christian freedom is not for self-gratification but for loving service of others (Gal. 5:1, 13). The basic point is the intrinsic conceptual connection between freedom from alien oppression and obedient service to God—a conceptuality that, in a contemporary culture that rather too easily appeals to "freedom" as self-evident in value and meaning, requires careful and sustained attention.

Bibliography

Bellis, A., and J. Kaminsky. *Jews, Christians, and the Theology of the Hebrew Scriptures*. SBL, 2000.

Brueggemann, W. "The Book of Exodus." *NIB* 1:675–981.

Childs, B. *Exodus*. OTL. SCM, 1974.

Fretheim, T. *Exodus*. IBC. John Knox, 1991.

Gregory of Nyssa. *The Life of Moses*, trans. A. Malherbe and E. Ferguson. Classics of Western Spirituality. Paulist, 1978.

Jacob, B. *The Second Book of the Bible,* trans. W. Jacob. Ktav, 1992.

Keel, O. *The Symbolism of the Biblical World*, trans. T. Hallett. SPCK, 1978.

LaCocque, A., and P. Ricoeur. *Thinking Biblically*. University of Chicago Press, 1998.

Levine, E. *The Burning Bush*. Sepher-Hermon, 1981.

Moberly, R. W. L. "How May We Speak of God? A Reconsideration of the Nature of Biblical Theology." *TynBul* 53 (2002): 177–202.

———. *The Old Testament of the Old Testament*. OBT. Fortress, 1992. Reprint, Wipf & Stock, 2001.

Nicholson, E. *God and His People*. Oxford University Press, 1986.

Otto, R. *The Idea of the Holy,* trans. J. Harvey. Oxford University Press, 1924.

Sarna, N. *Exodus*. JPS Torah Commentary. JPS, 1991.

Seitz, C. *Figured Out*. Westminster John Knox, 2001.

Warrior, R. "Canaanites, Cowboys, and Indians: Deliverance, Conquest, and Liberation Theology Today." Reprinted in pages 188–94 of *The Postmodern Bible Reader,* ed. D. Jobling et al. Blackwell, 2001.

3

Leviticus

Paul L. Redditt

In the first five books of the OT, Genesis narrates events before the life of Moses, while Deuteronomy repeats the law given on Mt. Sinai for the generations after Moses. The middle three books detail the career of Moses, with Exod. 1–19 tracing it from his birth until he receives the law and Num. 10:11–36:13 tracing it afterward until just before his death. The account of the giving of the law runs from Exod. 20:1 to Num. 10:10. The book of Leviticus, therefore, stands in the center of the law and contains many of its most striking provisions.

History of Interpretation

One early interpreter of Leviticus was Jesus, who cited Lev. 19:18: "You shall love your neighbor as yourself" (NRSV). Likewise, the NT book of James makes frequent positive allusions to Lev. 19 (Johnson). Often, though, the NT has to deal with issues from Leviticus that were problematic for the early church: sacrifice (Lev. 1–7), circumcision (12:3), and dietary regulations (ch. 11). Led by Paul, early Christians determined that such works were unnecessary for salvation. In addition, the early church perhaps preserved Mark 5:25–34 because it remembered the church's break with the purity rules found in Lev. 15:19–20.

Jewish interpreters also commented on Leviticus. After the destruction of the temple in 70 CE, the rabbis emphasized prayer and substituted the *study* of the sacrificial laws for performing the *ritual*. Indeed, the medieval scholar Maimonides argued that sacrifice was a concession to human frailty (to give Jews a rite similar to rites practiced by the worshippers of other deities) and never really God's intention.

Post-temple Jews had to address three other issues emphasized in Leviticus: the purity of priests, the Jewish family, and dietary regulations (Levine). Even though there was no further use for priests as officials at sacrifices, priestly families continued to hold to Levitical laws of purity, especially in regard to marriage and contact with the dead. Priests could not marry divorcees, harlots, or daughters born to forbidden unions. Adultery by the wife was the only grounds for divorce. In addition, priests were still to avoid contact with the dead, though members of the immediate family were exempted from this restriction. Preserving the purity of the Jewish family involved observing the ban on a woman's having intercourse for seven days (for her monthly period) and circumcising male babies. The dietary laws in Lev. 11 were not only retained but also carried out strictly in traditional families.

Within Christianity, Origen articulated a theory of Scripture interpretation that distinguished the literal from the more important spiritual meaning discerned by typology. Hence, the sacrifices described in Lev. 1–7 constituted a typology and prediction of Christ, whose sacrifice was superior to and fulfilled the system outlined in Leviticus.

Similar views dominated for over a millennium, but in the last few centuries the interpretation of Leviticus has come under the influence of historical, sociological, and literary theory. Based on stylistic and theological differences, scholars have for years pointed to various alleged sources for the Pentateuch (JEDP) and assigned them different dates, running from the tenth to the fifth centuries BCE. The law codes of the Pentateuch perhaps grew up independently, though often scholars identify their theology with that of a given source. Scholars adhering to this theory generally argue that Leviticus belongs to the postexilic P, or Priestly source, but think Leviticus was comprised of smaller codes, particularly the so-called Holiness Code (chs. 17–26). Among these scholars there has often been a noticeable denigration of Leviticus because of its perceived legalism and ritualism in favor of the prophets, who are thought to have better prepared the way for Jesus and the gospel.

The twentieth century witnessed an explosion of interpretative developments. Hermann Gunkel began a new form of study called form criticism, which utilized an approach to the study of oral literature developed in Germany. For Leviticus, this meant that the original setting for some laws was understood to be priestly judgments on cases brought to them, which became precedents for other people. Other laws or narratives were said to have grown up to regularize sacrifices or in defense of priestly prerogatives. That approach divided biblical books into such small units; however, reaction against it came in the form of attention to the work of editors or redactors and to the rhetorical devices that supply cohesion to books.

Other scholars have taken their cue from sociologists and anthropologists, seeking to interpret Leviticus against the backdrop of societies thought to be comparable to ancient Israel. So, for example, Douglas has subjected the dietary regulations to sociological scrutiny and observes that animals seem to be grouped into what one may call—for a lack of better terms—species and subspecies (not Douglas's terms). If a subspecies conformed wholly to the requirements of the species, it was considered clean and could be eaten. For example, Israel seems to have thought of a species of cloven-footed, cud-chewing farm animals. Subspecies that conformed to both characteristics (e.g., sheep) could be eaten. Subspecies with only one of these characteristics were considered unclean and were not to be eaten: e.g., swine did not chew the cud and camels did not have cloven feet. Similarly, water animals should have scales and fins; those that did were clean, and those that did not were unclean. Animals that died on their own were to be considered unclean; if alive, they could be slaughtered or sacrificed and eaten. Thus, scavengers should be avoided because of their consumption of dead animals. She argues that these distinctions reflect and make specific the worldview of the priestly creation account in Gen. 1:1–2:4a.

Still other scholars advocate abandoning such enterprises altogether and approaching the text of Leviticus simply as a literary product of the postexilic period. For them, it can supply no information about the preexilic period, but can give insights into the thinking of the postexilic author(s) of the Pentateuch and the worship practices current then.

In light of these divergent interpretations, one might approach Leviticus as a book with many laws that no longer apply literally in either a Jewish or a Christian context. Nevertheless, it still retains relevance for its insistence on the worship of God and on moral living in response to God's holiness.

The Message of Leviticus

From the book of Exodus, Leviticus presupposes God as the One who has delivered Israel from bondage in Egypt and covenanted with Israel to be their God. Hence, it conceives of God as somehow resident among the Israelites in their camp (Lev. 1:1). For Israel, the implications of that residency revolve around two pairs of terms: "holy" and "profane," "clean" and "unclean." What is holy has been marked off or set aside for God. In Leviticus, the holy include people (the Aaronic priesthood), space (the tabernacle, which has the peculiar feature that it can be moved), implements used in worship (priestly garb, vessels of various sorts, the altar), and time (festivals, the Day of Atonement). Laws pertaining to these items appear in Lev. 1–10, 16, 23–25, and 27. In addition, things in the world are either clean or unclean. What is holy is supposed to be clean, but can be polluted by what is unclean. Hence, both sacred and nonsacred people have to be careful how they approach the holy, lest they pollute it and bring danger upon themselves and/or others. So, the book of Leviticus contains numerous laws about dealing with impurity, including diet, the purification of women after childbirth, the purification of lepers, and proper sexual relations (Lev. 11, 12, 13–15, and 18, respectively). Either priests or the people can be rendered unholy, with the result that they have to be sanctified before they can again approach the holy (Lev. 18–20; ch. 21 for priests only). Jenson has argued that this worldview actually amounted to a system running from the very holy through the holy, the clean, the unclean, to the very unclean.

One should note, however, that the term "holy" is also used of God, and not only as what is set apart for God (Lev. 19:2 et passim). God is both the source of life and the only being worthy of worship. Hence, idolatry is wrong. Moreover, to be holy as God is holy involves morality in the sense of living in proper communion with God and humans, of recognizing one's dependence upon God and limits to one's desires and rights, and thus the necessity for justice in human affairs. The message of Leviticus, therefore, can be summarized under four sentences that spell out the implications of the residence of the holy God among the people.

First, *the people are to worship God* (Lev. 1–7). This worship will take the form of a variety of sacrifices. In the "burnt offering" (1:1–17), the priests burn the entire carcass of the animal. Reasons for making this offering might include dedicating new altars or worship sites, expressing thankfulness, imploring God's help in times of difficulty, and covering sin.

The "grain offering" (2:1–16) can accompany the burnt offering, honor God, or express thanksgiving for the grain crop. In the "peace" or "well-being offering" (3:1–17 NRSV), the worshippers consume a large portion of the animal and share the best parts (fat parts and kidneys) with God. Passover seems to be such an occasion. The "sin offering" (4:1–5:13) atones for inadvertent errors in cultic practice and other inadvertent sins. It is accompanied by confession. The "guilt offering" (5:14–6:7) atones for inadvertent actions where restitution is called for. The sacrificial system does not cover intentional sins (see Num. 15:30), though God nevertheless can forgive people for such behavior.

Second, *the Aaronic priests are to direct the worship* (Lev. 8–10). Leviticus 8 narrates the selection, anointing, and purification of the Aaronic priesthood, while Lev. 9 describes the commencement of Aaron's priesthood. Two of Aaron's sons, however, violate the altar entrusted to the Aaronites and pay for their sin with their lives. Mediating between God and the people is serious business.

Third, *the people are to avoid ritual impurity and make atonement when they fail* (Lev. 11–16). Avoiding ritual impurity covers various aspects of family life, even including, for example, what to do about household mold (14:34–53), which is discussed in connection with leprosy. Actions that render one impure include coming into contact with the dead or with blood. According to Lev. 16, the Day of Atonement arises upon the death of Aaron's two sons, but it becomes a time for public repentance and community cleansing. The liturgy for the day calls upon the high priest to offer a sacrifice for his own sins, and a second one for the people. Then he is to lay his hands upon the scapegoat, symbolically laying the sins of the people upon it. He then sends the scapegoat away into the wilderness, symbolically carrying the sins of the people with it.

Fourth, *the people are to be holy* (Lev. 17–26). The book reaches its pinnacle in the Holiness Code. It derives its name from the oft-repeated phrase "You shall be holy, for I the LORD your God am holy" (as in 19:2). These laws forbid misdeeds ranging from sacrificing in the wrong places to committing incest to worshipping foreign deities. It prescribes the three annual feasts (Passover/Unleavened Bread, Weeks, Tabernacles). One law deserves particular attention. The so-called *lex talionis* (the law of the talon or claw) seems cruel to moderns who see in it "an eye for an eye, a tooth for a tooth" (24:20). Actually, however, it limits revenge and takes the first step toward leaving revenge to God and ultimately to forgiving one's enemies.

Leviticus and the Canon

The canonical status of Leviticus was established by virtue of its central place in the Pentateuch. The later OT books Chronicles, Ezra, and Nehemiah cited it. A few examples must suffice. Second Chronicles 7:9–10 describes the dedication of Solomon's temple at the festival of Booths as sacrifices offered in accordance with laws such as those in Lev. 23:23–43. It also explains the fall of Jerusalem and the destruction of the temple as the consequence of Israel's failure to observe the Sabbath years as commanded in Lev. 25:1–7 (see 26:27–39 for a warning; 2 Chron. 36:21). Also Ezra 9:11, part of Ezra's penitential prayer, seems to be a fair summary of Lev. 18:24–30 and Deut. 7:1–6 combined. Ezra 3:5 appears to have in view Lev. 23, and Neh. 8:14–15 refers to the commandment in Lev. 23:42 that the Israelites live in booths during the fall festival.

The author of Hebrews dialogued with the book in his discussion of Jesus' superiority to the old law. First, Jesus the Son of God is superior to Moses, the servant of God who received the law (Heb. 3:1–6). Second, Jesus belongs to a line of priests descended from Melchizedek, which is superior to the Levitical priests. This superiority manifests itself in a number of ways. Jesus is the perfect high priest because he is without sin (2:17–18; 4:15) and did not have to offer sacrifices to cleanse himself as the OT priests did (5:3; cf. Lev. 9:7; 16:2–14). Jesus did not simply offer an animal sacrifice; he offered himself as the perfect sacrifice (Heb. 5:7–8). That sacrifice was superior to the Levitical sacrifice because it was given once for all and did not need to be repeated (9:13–14, 25–26). Finally, Jesus is superior to Levitical priests because he has been raised to the right hand of God, to mediate an eternal covenant superior to the one given at Sinai (8:1–2; 9:15).

Leviticus and Theology

The book of Leviticus (particularly chs. 17–26) emphasizes the holiness of God as the most important theological motif. The holy is *mysterium tremendum et fascinans*, to use Otto's terms. Worshippers confront God as an overwhelming and yet appealing mystery, and then recognize themselves as creaturely. Regardless of the characteristic of God by which worshippers might measure themselves (e.g., power, knowledge, love, moral purity), God is always superior.

Leviticus is about worship. The sacrificial system is the means it outlines by which penitent sinners can express their contrition to God. It is never intended as the vehicle to buy forgiveness, as the prophets made clear (cf. Isa. 1:12–15; Amos 5:21–24). Nevertheless, it speaks the word of God that in worship people should express contrition and ask forgiveness (Lev. 1:1–2:16; 4:1–5:13), share with others and with God (3:1–17), and be prepared to make restitution for losses inflicted on others (5:14–6:7). It has a healthy appreciation for the role of ritual in living the holy life and the possibility of forgiveness when God's people fail.

Bibliography

Budd, P. *Leviticus*. NCB. HarperCollins/Eerdmans, 1996.

Douglas, M. "The Abominations of Leviticus." Pages 41–57 in *Purity and Danger*. 2nd ed. Routledge & Kegan Paul, 1969.

Elliger, K. *Leviticus*. HAT 1.4. Mohr, 1966.

Gerstenberger, E. *Leviticus*. OTL. Westminster John Knox, 1996.

Grünwaldt, K. *Das Heiligkeitsgesetz Leviticus 17–26*. De Gruyter, 1999.

Hayes, J. "Atonement in the Book of Leviticus." *Int* 52 (1998): 5–13.

Jenson, P. P. *Graded Holiness*. JSOTSup 106. JSOT, 1992.

Johnson, L. T. "The Use of Leviticus 19 in the Letter of James." *JBL* 101 (1982): 391–401.

Levine, B. *Leviticus*. JPS Torah Commentary. JPS, 2003.

Milgrom, J. *Leviticus*. AB 3, 3A, 3B. Doubleday, 1991–2001.

Noth, M. *Leviticus*. OTL. Rev. ed. Westminster, 1977.

Origen. *Homilies on Leviticus 1–16*, trans. G. Barkley. FC 83. Catholic University of America Press, 1990.

Otto, R. *The Idea of the Holy*, trans. J. Harvey. 2nd ed. Oxford University Press, 1923.

Rendtorff, R. *Leviticus*. BKAT. Neukirchener Verlag, 1985.

Wenham, G. *Leviticus*. NICOT. Eerdmans, 1979.

4

Numbers

KENT L. SPARKS

According to Jewish and Christian tradition, Numbers is the fourth book of Moses, relating the history of Israel's desert journey from Mt. Sinai to the dawn of the conquest, a chronological span stretching from the second to the fortieth year after the exodus. Parsed geographically, the book begins with Israel's stay at Sinai (1:1–10:10), chronicles its travels from Sinai to the plains of Moab (10:11–22:1), and then narrates a series of events in Moab (22:2–36:13). The book is known by two Hebrew titles, *Khomesh happequddim* ("the fifth of the census totals") and the more common *Bamidbar* ("in the wilderness" [1:1 MT/NRSV]). The first title, from the Talmud, corresponds to the Greek and Latin names (*Arithmoi* and *Numeri*), from which comes "Numbers." But both Hebrew titles reflect an important feature in the book: the story's setting in the wilderness (hence, *Bamidbar*) and the two censuses that frame the narrative in Num. 1 and 26 (hence, *Khomesh happequddim*).

A Survey of the Book

The book of Numbers is organized around a story that begins with one generation of Israelites (the "exodus generation") and ends with the next (the "conquest generation"). At issue for both generations is their willingness to undertake military operations against stronger, better-equipped forces living in the land that Yahweh has promised Israel. The first generation undertakes a military census in preparation for this engagement and even travels to Kadesh Barnea, a good staging point for the attack. However, after a gloomy reconnaissance report from twelve scouts sent into the land, the Israelites elect not to invade. As a result, God forbids that generation of Israelites from entering the land and condemns them to death in the wilderness. After forty years of nomadic life, during which these Israelites continually make trouble for Moses and thanklessly murmur against God, the last remnants of the exodus generation are destroyed after committing idolatry at Peor in Moab (Num. 25). This final act of disloyalty occasions no surprise since it follows their earlier idolatries at Mt. Sinai (see Exod. 32).

The next generation of Israelites, the conquest generation, immediately took another military census (Num. 26) and made preparations for an invasion of the land, which includes their initial successful military operations in Transjordan. At the same time, Joshua is appointed to succeed Moses as Israel's leader because of Moses' impiety at Kadesh Barnea (cf. Num. 20, 27). So, Numbers concludes with Israel on the plains of Moab in Transjordan, poised to enter the land under Joshua's leadership.

Numbers in Canonical Context

Because Numbers is only one chapter in the biblical story of Israel, its theological import cannot be properly appraised apart from its narrative context in the "Primary History," which runs from the book of Genesis through 2 Kings. This story has two beginnings, one that focuses on the estrangement between God and humanity (Gen. 1–11), and a second that introduces Yahweh's redemptive plan for humanity through his covenant with Abraham. Because Abraham was a man of faith in word and deed, he received a divine promise of land, progeny, and blessing, blessings that would extend not only to his own children but also to all nations (Gen. 12, 15, 17). The remainder of the Primary History highlights the sometimes happy and sometimes stormy relationship between God and Abraham's children, focused through Yahweh's additional covenants with Israel at Sinai (the Mosaic covenant in Exodus) and with Israel's king, David (2 Sam. 7). The people and their kings eventually broke these covenants, receiving in return the double punishment of exile in Babylon and the destruction of Jerusalem and its temple (2 Kings 25).

If the Primary History is a story of the "ups and downs" in Israel's capricious faith, then the books of Exodus and Numbers vividly portray one of these fickle cycles. According to Exodus, Yahweh has prospered and multiplied the people in Egypt, miraculously delivering them from slavery, providing for them in the desert, and speaking to them in a mighty theophany at Sinai. Israel's response to God's graciousness appears in the book of Numbers, and the response is neither faithful nor pretty. Israel responds no better to God's blessings than does humanity as a whole in the primeval history of Gen. 1–11. So, it appears that the editor of the Pentateuch wishes us to perceive the religious disposition of Israel and of humanity along the same lines: both Jews and Gentiles are rebels (cf. Rom. 1–3). God responds to Israel's rebellion in the wilderness by preserving the nation, but he does not prosper them as in Genesis and Exodus. The count of people in the first census of Numbers (603,550; see 1:46) is actually greater than in the second census taken forty years later (601,730; see 26:51). Numbers, then, is a story that juxtaposes the faithfulness of God with Israel's faithless rebellion.

While the narrative contours of Numbers are clear enough, the unfolding story is generously interspersed with a broad range of ritual and legal materials, which seem to continue the priestly rules found in the book of Leviticus. Indeed, Leviticus also juxtaposes story with law, but its narratives invariably relate to the rituals and so do not seem like an interruption. In Numbers, however, these materials do seem to interrupt the book's narrative flow. The rites and laws are presented as divine prescriptions (Num. 5–10, 15–16, 18–19, 28–30, 35) or in narrative episodes that either illustrate these legal prescriptions (e.g., 15:32–36) or describe the occasion that prompts their creation (e.g., 17; 27:1–11; 36). While these materials cannot be easily integrated with the narrative of Numbers, they share a common focus on the concept of holiness, the special concern being to preserve Israel's purity, and hence to protect its sacred nexus with God.

Numbers presents readers with impressions of narrative unity as well as with diverse ritual and legal materials that do not easily satisfy our hermeneutical thirst for coherence. A good theological reading of this interesting book will need to account for this. Fortunately, our efforts can benefit from the penetrating exegetical and theological work done by our Jewish and Christian forebears.

The Theology of Numbers in Historical Purview

Our earliest theological readings of Numbers, or at least of the traditions now found in Numbers, appear in the Hebrew Bible itself. Deuteronomy relates a summary of Israel's wilderness experience in its first few chapters (1–3). This historical review implicitly accentuates God's faithfulness to Israel in the face of the nation's unfaithfulness, and it explicitly warns Israel not to duplicate the failures of the exodus generation—especially its idolatry—and so reap similar dire consequences (4:1–4). Nevertheless, in Deuteronomy, the piety of the conquest generation shines no brighter than that of its fathers (9:6), and the book predicts a gloomy future for the idolatrous people of Israel (4:30; 30:1–10; 31:14–32:47). The Hebrew prophetic books also allude to Israel's wilderness experience, but in strikingly different ways. Hosea and Jeremiah recall the wilderness with pleasant nostalgia (Hos. 2:14–15 [2:16–17 MT]; Jer. 2:1–7), while Ezekiel remembers it as the first in a litany of Israel's religious rebellions (ch. 20). These positive and negative appraisals of the wilderness also appear in the three psalms that relate Israel's history in hymnic style. Psalm 105 reads the wilderness as an example of God's kind provision for Israel, in contrast to Pss. 78 and 106, where Israel's desert wanderings are a period of ongoing mutiny. The later apocryphal book of 2 Esdras combines these contrasting images of the wilderness experience: "Thus says the Lord Almighty: When you were in the wilderness, at the bitter stream, thirsty and blaspheming my name, I did not send fire on you for your blasphemies, but threw a tree into the water and made the stream sweet" (1:22–23 NRSV).

Thus, the authors of the Hebrew Bible and Apocrypha attend to the wilderness story of Numbers and largely ignore its extensive ritual and legal material. This pattern of exegetical bifurcation, in which interpreters treat the two major genres of Numbers differently by ignoring one or the other, appears in later Jewish exegesis. Philo's work *On the Life of Moses* (first century CE) offers an extensive paraphrase of the wilderness story but touches on the rituals only briefly and under a separate heading (Colson 277–595). His preferred strategy for drawing out the implications of Moses' life is allegory, an interpretative method that suits not only his Hellenistic audience but also his own identity as a Hellenistic Jew. By way of contrast, *Midrash Sifre*, an early commentary on Numbers (second century CE), virtually ignores the narrative in favor of halakic (legal) interpretations of its ritual and legal prescriptions (Levertoff). The few instances of haggadah (illustrative narrative commentary) in *Sifre* only confirm this rule. Rashi's medieval Jewish commentary treats the entire book of Numbers, blending literal interpretation (*peshat*) with free homiletical exegesis (*derash*). But here again one detects an underlying theological concern to show how Numbers informs Jewish traditions of ritual and law.

Early Christian interpreters in the NT allude to Numbers rather sparingly. Two notable exceptions were Paul and the writer of Hebrews, for whom the faithless exodus generation illustrates the ever-present threat of Christian apostasy (Heb. 3–4; 1 Cor. 10:3–14). In briefer allusions, Acts remembers the wilderness as a time of God's divine provision for Israel (7:36), while John's Gospel sees in Moses' bronze serpent an image of the coming Christ (cf. 3:14; Num. 21:4–9). Similar exegetical patterns appear in the patristic evidence, where christological and tropological (moral/behavioral) insights were derived from Israel's story in Numbers (see Lienhard). Not surprisingly, neither the NT nor the church fathers gave much attention to the ritual and legal materials in Numbers.

Two general observations can be culled from early Jewish and Christian readings of Numbers. First, Jewish and Christian interpreters were generally interested in different portions of Numbers. Jewish readers focused on its ritual and legal materials, while Christian readers drew moral and ethical content from its stories. As we will see, in certain respects this generic distinction anticipates modern critical readings of Numbers. Second, in spite of their differing generic interests, both Christian and Jewish commentators viewed Numbers as a manual for achieving holiness in their respective communities. Judaism expressed its holiness through ritual purity (hence the interest in ritual law), and Christian interpreters used Numbers as a guide for moral living (hence their tropological readings of the book's narrative).

Numbers in Modern Biblical Scholarship

Because of the book's ostensible disorganization, modern scholars have been preoccupied with the composition of Numbers rather than with its theology. Although there is continuing debate about the details (Sparks, *Pentateuch*, 22–36), the consensus is that the book was not composed by Moses, as tradition might suggest, but rather by several authors and editors working over a lengthy period of time and at some remove from the so-called Mosaic period. The standard theory is that Numbers owes much of its present shape to at least two major writers, the preexilic or exilic Yahwist (J) and the postexilic priestly writer (P). It is further believed that the basic narrative contours of Numbers were laid down by J (see 10:29–12:15; 20:14–21; 21:12–32; 22:2–25:5), while much of the remaining ritual, legal, and narrative materials—over three-quarters of the book—derives from P. This two-source theory explains the odd combination of law and narrative in the book. It has in its favor both critical and precritical evidence. Critical scholars find similar J/P distinctions elsewhere in the Pentateuch, and precritical Jewish and Christian interpreters focused on one or the other of these two generic segments of Numbers.

Some modern scholars, such as Douglas, Olsen, and Lee, have attempted to peer behind the putative structural confusion in Numbers to discern an underlying coherence in the book's stories and law. Douglas believes that she has discovered a ring structure that alternates between law and story in order to teach a theology of holiness and defilement.

Olsen argues that the final theological shape of Numbers reflects the coherent design of an editor, who has skillfully combined the narrative of J with the rituals, laws, and narratives of P. The resulting structure uses the two censuses in Num. 1 and 26 to frame the story as a tale of two generations, the disobedient exodus generation and the new generation of hope. This tale has as its central themes that God does not tolerate rebellion and that, on the other hand, Israelite rebellions would not frustrate God's plan to bless them according to his promises. Olsen avers that the legal and ritual materials in Numbers do not disrupt the presentation of these themes but rather are editorially integrated into the book to illustrate and reinforce them.

Lee's reading of Numbers is similar to Olsen's, inasmuch as it uses the narrative plot as its organizing principle. According to Lee, the book's conceptual structure is determined by God's responses to Israel, first in punishing the exodus generation because of its disobedience, and then in forgiving Israel and granting the conquest generation success against the Canaanites.

While it is indeed worthwhile to pursue a coherent understanding of the book's combination of law and story, one wonders whether our pursuit of coherence does not apply a modern, post-Enlightenment literary expectation to an ancient anthology of Jewish stories, law, ritual, and priestly lore.

Conclusions

As we have seen, there is a long-standing exegetical tradition in ancient and modern scholarship that either explicitly or implicitly bifurcates the book of Numbers along generic lines, focusing either on the narrative or the legal material. Christians have been interested predominantly in the narrative material because they naturally find themselves tropologically in its powerful story. Whether Israel lived in sin (the exodus generation) or in obedience (the conquest generation), God in all respects was faithful to his people and to his promises to Abraham, Isaac, and Jacob. So, God can be counted on, but we must choose our road. Healthy Christian living does not take the difficulties of life's "wilderness" as evidence for God's absence; rather, we notice God's power as he carries us through it.

Turning to the laws and rituals of Numbers, Christian interpreters have generally neglected this material, largely because of the uniquely Christian viewpoint that the people of God are no longer subject to the minutiae of Jewish law and ritual. Consequently, early Christians did not attempt to directly integrate Jewish rituals and laws into their theology so much as they sought a theological explanation for this conundrum: Why would God command the Jews to observe rites and keep laws that would become obsolete? The standard explanation of the church fathers was that God had accommodated primitive and errant viewpoints of law and ritual in his revelation to Israel, viewpoints that were naturally subject to obsolescence and hence to elimination (Sparks, "Sun"). In some respects this solution only goes halfway, for it fails to assess the function of the laws and rituals in the life of ancient Israel and then to ask what import this function might have for Christians. The most obvious theme that appears in the laws and rituals is God's holiness, which is vividly expressed in these portions of Numbers. Appreciation of divine holiness is, of course, essential to a healthy theological appraisal of what God has done for humanity—and for us—in the person of Jesus Christ.

Bibliography

Ashley, T. *The Book of Numbers.* NICOT. Eerdmans, 1993.

Colson, F. H., trans. *Philo.* 10 vols. LCL. Harvard University Press, 1984.

Davies, E. W. *Numbers.* NCB. Eerdmans, 1995.

Douglas, M. *In the Wilderness.* JSOTSup 158. JSOT, 1993.

Drazin, I. *Targum Onkelos to Numbers.* Ktav, 1998.

Lee, W. W. *Punishment and Forgiveness in Israel's Migratory Campaign.* Eerdmans, 2003.

Levertoff, P. P., trans. *Midrash Sifre on Numbers.* SPCK, 1926.

Levine, B. *Numbers.* 2 vols. AB. Doubleday, 1993–2000.

Lienhard, J., ed. *Exodus, Leviticus, Numbers, Deuteronomy.* ACCSOT 3. InterVarsity, 2001.

Olsen, D. *The Death of the Old and the Birth of the New.* Scholars Press, 1985.

Rashi. *The Metsudah Chumash,* trans. Y. Rabinowitz. Simcha, 2000.

Sparks, K. *The Pentateuch.* IBR Bibliographies 1. Baker, 2002.

———. "The Sun Also Rises: Accommodation in Inscripturation and Interpretation." In *Evangelicals and Scripture,* ed. D. Okholm et al. InterVarsity, 2004.

Vaux, J. de. *Les Nombres.* Gabalda, 1972.

Wenham, G. *Numbers.* OTG. Sheffield Academic Press, 1997.

5

Deuteronomy

DANIEL I. BLOCK

The theological significance of Deuteronomy can scarcely be overestimated. Inasmuch as this book offers the most systematic presentation of truth in the entire OT, we may compare it to Romans in the NT. On the other hand, since Deuteronomy reviews Israel's historical experience of God's grace as recounted in Genesis–Numbers, a comparison with the Gospel of John may be more appropriate. Having had several decades to reflect on the significance of Jesus, John produced a profoundly theological Gospel, less interested in the chronology of the life of Christ, and more concerned with its meaning. Similarly, according to Deuteronomy's internal witness, Moses has had almost four decades to reflect on the exodus from Egypt and Yahweh's establishment of a covenant relationship with Israel. Like John, Deuteronomy functions as a theological manifesto, calling Israel to respond to God's grace with unreserved loyalty and love.

History of Interpretation

Deuteronomy is the fifth and final book of what Jewish tradition knows as the Torah, and Christians refer to it as the Pentateuch. In popular Hebrew tradition, the book is called *Sefer Devarim*, "Book of Words," which is an adaptation of the official Hebrew name, *'Elleh Haddebarim*, "These are the Words," the first two words of the book. In the third century BCE the LXX translators set the course for its history of interpretation. Instead of translating the Hebrew *To Biblion tōn Logōn*, "The Book of Words," or more simply *Logoi*, "Words," they replaced this with *To Deuteronomion*, "Second Law" (Latin: *Deuteronomium*). The form of the name seems to be derived from Deut. 17:18, where Hebrew *mishneh hattorah*, "a copy of the Torah," is misinterpreted as *to deutero-nomion*. This Greek heading probably became determinative because the book reiterates many laws found in Exodus–Numbers, and in chapter 5 cites the Decalogue almost verbatim. But the name "Deuteronomy" overlooks the fact that the book presents itself not primarily as law but as a series of sermons. Much of the book reviews events described in the earlier books. Where laws are dealt with (e.g., the central sanctuary law in ch. 12), the presentation is often exposition rather than recital of the laws themselves.

Prior to source criticism, both Jewish and Christian readers assumed Mosaic authorship, a fact reflected in the common designation of the pentateuchal books outside the English world as the Five Books of Moses. For the former, as the work of Moses it came with profound authority (cf. Mark 10:3; 12:19; Luke 20:28; John 5:45; 9:28; etc.). Observing Jesus' manner, some looked upon him as the eschatological prophet like Moses, whom Yahweh would raise up (Deut. 18:15; cf. Matt. 11:9; John 1:21, 25; 6:14; 7:40). While Jesus himself rejected this role (John 1:21), judging by his number of quotations, Deuteronomy was Jesus' favorite book. This impression is reinforced by his distillation of the entire law into the simple command to love the Lord with one's whole being and to love one's neighbor as oneself. In the Pentateuch, although appeals for loving one's neighbor and the stranger occur earlier (Lev. 19:18, 34), the command to love God appears only in Deuteronomy (6:5; 11:1; 11:13; 13:3; 30:6).

Paul repeatedly cites Deuteronomic texts (Rom. 10:19; 11:8; 12:19; 1 Cor. 5:13; 9:9; Eph. 6:2–3; etc.). However, it is clear that Paul interpreted the entire history of God's revelation and also Deuteronomy in light of Christ and the cross (Rom. 10:6–8; 1 Cor. 8:6; Gal. 3:13). He seems to have functioned as a second Moses, not only providing a profoundly theological interpretation of God's saving actions in Christ, but also reminding readers that salvation comes by grace alone. In Romans and Galatians Paul's argumentation addresses those who would pervert the "law" (a narrow legalistic interpretation of Hebrew *torah*) into a means of salvation, rather than treating it as a response to salvation (cf. Schreiner; N. T. Wright). While on the surface Paul's responses to this heresy often appear to contradict

Moses, such statements should be interpreted in context and as rhetorical responses to opponents. In his disposition toward the "law," he was in perfect step with Moses. There is nothing new in Paul's definition of a true Jew as one who receives the praise of God because he is circumcised in the heart (Rom. 2:28–29; cf. Deut. 10:16–21; 30:6), nor in his praise of the law as holy, righteous, and good (Rom. 7:12; cf. Deut. 6:20–25), nor in his distillation of the whole law into the law of love (Rom. 13:8–10; cf. Deut. 10:12–21). Elsewhere, Peter's characterization of Christians as a privileged people, "a chosen race" and "God's own possession" (1 Pet. 2:9), echoes Moses' understanding of Israel (Deut. 4:20; 10:15; 14:2; 26:18–19).

Insofar as the early church used Deuteronomy, on the one hand the fathers and other spiritual leaders tended to follow Paul's christological lead, but in application of the laws often resorted to spiritualizing the details. By marshaling the Shema (Deut. 6:4–5) to defend trinitarian doctrine (Lienhard 282–83), they obscured the original contextual meaning (Block, "How?"). In the Reformers we witness two different dispositions toward the laws of Deuteronomy. Luther tended to read them through Paul's rhetorical and seemingly antinomian statements (Rom. 7:4–9; 2 Cor. 3:6; Gal. 3:10–25) and his own debilitating experience of works-righteousness within the Roman Catholic church. Hence, he saw a radical contrast between the law (which kills) and the gospel (which gives life). His emphasis on the dual function of the law (civic—to maintain external order on earth; theological—to convict people of sin and drive them to Christ; cf. Lohse 270–74) missed the point of Deuteronomy. This book presents the law as a gift to guide the redeemed in righteousness, leading to life (cf. Deut. 4:6–8; 6:20–25). Like Luther, Calvin insisted that no one can be justified by keeping the law. But through the law, Israel is instructed on how to express gratitude for their redemption and bring glory to God (Calvin 363).

These two approaches tended to dominate until the Enlightenment, when the attention of critical scholars shifted from the theological value of Deuteronomy to hypotheses concerning its origin. By the second half of the nineteenth century, the documentary approach to pentateuchal studies was firmly entrenched. Deuteronomy had been isolated as a source separate from J, E, and P. Julius Wellhausen proposed that chapters 12–26 represent the original core, written by a prophet (some suggest Jeremiah) ca. 622 BCE (cf. 2 Kings 22–23) to promote reform of Israel's religious practices (2 Chron. 34–35) and centralize the cult in Jerusalem. The prophet presumably hid the book in the temple so as to be found; it was completed after the exile and combined with Genesis–Numbers (an amalgam of J, E, and P sources).

69

Convinced that Joshua completed the story of the Pentateuch, Wellhausen and others preferred to interpret Deuteronomy within the context of the Hexateuch. Deuteronomy was crucial for von Rad's OT theology, which found in 26:5–9 an ancient credo confessing the essentials of Israelite faith (e.g., "The Form-Critical Problem," in *Problem*). Martin Noth went in the opposite direction, cutting Deuteronomy from Genesis–Numbers and treating this book as the paradigmatic theological prologue to the Deuteronomistic History (Joshua–Kings). Its purpose is to provide a theological explanation for the events surrounding 722 BCE and 586 BCE, now viewed as the result of Israel's persistent apostasy and worship of strange gods.

Some scholars attribute the bulk of Deuteronomy to country Levites writing shortly before 701 BCE (von Rad, *Studies*), prophetic circles of northern Israel (Nicholson 58–82), or sages in the Jerusalem court (Weinfeld). Recent scholarship tends to interpret the book as a manifesto, written in support of Josiah's efforts to centralize the religion of Israel in Jerusalem. According to Weinfeld, Deuteronomy is not only a remarkable literary achievement but also represents a profound monument to the theological revolution advocated by the Josianic circles. This revolution involved attempts to eliminate other shrines and centralize all worship of Yahweh in Jerusalem, as well as to "secularize," "demythologize," and "spiritualize" the religion. It sought to replace traditional images of divine corporeality and enthronement in the temple with more abstract, spiritual notions reflected in its "name theology." In this new religious world, sacrifices were no longer institutional and corporate but personal expressions of faith, and the tithe was no longer "holy to Yahweh" but remained the owner's (14:22–27; Weinfeld, *ABD* 2:177).

Recognizing the strengths of each position, most recently some have proposed that dissidents (scribes, priests, sages, aristocrats) originally produced Deuteronomy. According to Richard D. Nelson (4–9; cf. Albertz 194–231), the book has roots in crisis (seventh century), when loyalty to Yahweh was undermined by veneration of other gods. The well-being of many was jeopardized by exploitative royal policies, and the prophetic institution was out of control, calling for tests of authenticity and limitation of influence. The inconsistencies and ambiguities in the Deuteronomic legislation reflect the varying interests of the dissident groups. On the one hand, virtually all critical scholars agree that Deuteronomy either provides the occasion for or is the result of the Josianic reform. On the other hand, they agree that its speeches are pseudepigraphical, fictionally attributed to Moses in support of the parties whose interests are represented (cf. Sonnet 262–67).

Not all are willing to date Deuteronomy this late. J. G. McConville (*Deuteronomy*, 33–40) and others argue that its religious and political vision does not fit the Josianic period as described in 2 Kings. On the contrary, "Deuteronomy, or at least a form of it, is the document of a real political and religious constitution of Israel from the pre-monarchic period" (34). As such, it challenges prevailing ancient Near Eastern royal-cultic ideology, replacing this with a prophetic vision of Yahweh in direct covenant relationship with his people governed by torah. Through the torah the prophetic authority of Moses, the spokesperson for Yahweh, extends to the community. The "Book of the Torah," deposited next to the ark and formally read before the assembly, provides a constant reminder of the will of the covenant Lord. As for the theological revolution envisioned by Weinfeld, this interpretation is coming under increasingly critical scrutiny (Wilson; Richter; Vogt).

Deuteronomy presents itself as a record of addresses delivered orally by Moses on the verge of Israel's crossing over into the promised land, speeches immediately committed to writing (31:9; cf. Block, "Recovering"). However, in accordance with ancient Near Eastern literary convention, strictly speaking, the book as we have it is anonymous. We can only speculate when the individual speeches of Moses were combined, arranged, and linked with their present narrative stitching. Certain stylistic and literary features, the content of historical notes in the book, and the resemblances of the present structure to second millennium BCE Hittite treaty documents suggest that this happened much earlier than many critical scholars admit.

Hearing the Message of Deuteronomy

Because of a pervasive latent Marcionism and adherence to theological systems that are fundamentally dismissive of the OT in general and Deuteronomy in particular, its message has been largely lost to the church. This is a tragedy, not only because—more than any other OT book—the message of Deuteronomy lies right on the surface, but also because few OT books proclaim such a relevant word. How can readers today rediscover the message?

First, it is important to "hear" Deuteronomy. At significant junctures Moses appeals to his people to "hear" the word he is proclaiming (5:1; 6:3–4; 9:1; 20:3). In 31:9–13 he charges the Levitical priests to read the torah that he has just transcribed (i.e., his speeches) before the people every seven years at the Feast of Booths. This statement not only assumes canonical status for the torah Moses has just proclaimed; it also highlights the critical link between hearing his words in the future and the life of the people of God. This link may be represented schematically as follows:

Reading → Hearing → Learning → Fear → Obedience → Life

A similar relationship between reading/hearing the words of "this torah" and future well-being is expressed in 17:19, where Moses explicitly charges future kings to read the torah so that they may embody the covenant fidelity he has espoused on the plains of Moab.

Second, to hear the message of Deuteronomy, we must recognize its genre and form. At one level, Deuteronomy represents the final major segment of Moses' biography that began in Exod. 1 (cf. Knierim 355–59, 372–79). Accordingly, Deuteronomy may be interpreted as narrative in which lengthy speeches have been embedded.

At another level, the manner in which the first two speeches have been arranged is reminiscent of ancient Near Eastern treaty forms, especially the second millennium BCE Hittite suzerainty treaties (see Thompson; Craigie). Recognition of the fundamentally covenantal character of Deuteronomy has extremely significant implications. Yahweh is the divine suzerain, who graciously chose the patriarchs and their descendants as his covenant partner (4:37; 7:6–8). He demonstrated his commitment (*'ahab*, "he loved") by rescuing them from Egypt (4:32–40), entering into an eternal covenant relationship with them at Sinai (4:9–32), revealing his will (4:1–8), and providentially caring for them in the desert (1:9–3:29). He is now about to deliver the promised land into their hands (1:6–8; 7:1–26). As a true prophet of Yahweh, Moses challenges Israel to respond by declaring that Yahweh alone is its God (6:4), and by demonstrating unwavering love for him through obedience (6:5–19; 10:12–11:1; etc.). Moses realistically anticipates Israel's future rebellion, leading ultimately to banishment from the land. Yet, Yahweh's compassion and the irrevocable nature of his covenant mean that exile and dispersion among the nations cannot be the last word; Yahweh will bring them back to himself and to the land (4:26–31; 30:1–10). Indeed, Moses perceives the covenant that he is having them renew with Yahweh as an extension of Sinai (29:1), and ultimately an extension and fulfillment of the covenant made with the ancestors (29:10–13).

At a third level, Deuteronomy presents itself as a series of addresses by Moses to Israel immediately before their entrance into Canaan and his own death. The narrative preamble (1:1–5) should determine how we hear its message. Although in later chapters Moses will integrate many prescriptions given at Sinai and afterward into his preaching, contrary to prevailing popular opinion Deuteronomy does not present itself as legislation. Rather, this is prophetic preaching at its finest. The preamble identifies Moses' words as *hattorah hazz'ot*, "this torah" (1:5 AT). The word *torah* should be primarily understood not as "law" (for the book includes much that is not legal), but as "instruction." *Torah* is derived from the verb *yarah*, "to teach," and from the expression *sefer hattorah* (e.g., Deut. 29:21 [20 MT]; Josh. 1:8; etc.): "Book of the Instruction," rather than "Book of the Law." *Torah* was applied to specific aspects of Yahweh's will revealed earlier (e.g., Exod. 12:49; 24:12; Lev. 7:1; Num. 19:14; etc.). Nevertheless, the torah that Yahweh commanded Joshua to read and obey fully (Josh. 1:7–8) and read to the people of Israel as part of the covenant-renewal ceremony at Shechem (8:30–35) was likely the collection of Moses' sermons that constitute the bulk of the present book. Eventually, the scope of torah was expanded to include the narrative sections (Deut. 1:1–5; 27:1–10; 34:1–12; etc.), that is, the entire book of Deuteronomy more or less as we have it. It is widely accepted that the document referred to as "the book of the torah" (*sefer hattorah*, 2 Kings 22:8; 2 Chron. 34:15) and "the book of the torah of Yahweh by the hand of Moses" (2 Chron. 34:14), discovered by Josiah's people in the course of renovating the temple, was some form of Deuteronomy. It represents the heart of the torah, which the priests were to teach and model (Deut. 33:10; 2 Chron. 15:3; 19:8; Mal. 2:6, 9; cf. Jer. 18:18; Ezek. 7:26; Ezra 7:10). Psalmists praised it (Pss. 19:7–14; 119), the prophets appealed to it (e.g., Isa. 1:10; 5:24; 8:20; 30:9; 51:7), faithful kings ruled by it (1 Kings 2:2–4; 2 Kings 14:6; 22:11; 23:25), and righteous citizens lived by it (Ps. 1). In short, Deuteronomy provides the theological base for virtually the entire OT and the paradigm for much of its literary style.

Deuteronomy obviously incorporates prescriptive and motivational material deriving from Sinai (in the Decalogue, 5:7–21; the so-called Deuteronomic Code, 12:1–16:15; the covenant blessings and curses, 28:1–29:1). Yet, specific prescriptions analogous to other ancient Near Eastern law codes tend to be concentrated in only seven chapters (19–25; on legal lists as a genre, see Watts 36–45). But even these are punctuated by strong rhetorical appeals and a fundamental concern for righteousness rather than merely legal conformity. The remainder, even of the second address, bears a pronounced homiletical flavor. Both Deuteronomy and the word *torah* are represented more accurately by Greek *didaskalia* and *didachē*, as used in the NT, than by *nomos*.

This does not mean that what Moses declares in these speeches is any less authoritative than the laws given at Sinai. In 1:3 the narrator declares that Moses functions as the authorized spokesman for Yahweh. Nevertheless, here Moses' role is that of pastor, not lawgiver. Like Jacob in Gen. 49, Joshua in Josh. 24, and Jesus in John 13–16, knowing that death is imminent, Moses gathers his flock and delivers his final homily, pleading with the Israelites to remain faithful. Deuteronomy is therefore to be read primarily as discourse on the implications of the covenant for a people about to enter the promised land (cf. Gen. 15:7–21; 26:3; Exod. 6:2–8).

But hearing the message of Deuteronomy involves more than hearing the words and correctly identifying the genre; it also involves interpreting the book correctly, grasping its theology, and making appropriate application. According to the internal witness, with these addresses Moses sought to instill deep gratitude in the generation that was about to claim the promised land. At the same time he guided them in applying the covenant made at Sinai to the new situation on the other side of the Jordan. While the Canaanites posed a formidable military threat, the spiritual threat was more serious. Accordingly, throughout the book emphasis is on exclusive devotion to Yahweh, demonstrated in grateful obedience. If they would do so, Moses envisioned the people of Israel and the land they would occupy as flourishing.

How are Christians to read the book today? The following principles may guide in the face of this challenge. First, rather than beginning with what the NT has to say about Deuteronomy, we should read the book as an ancient Near Eastern document that addressed issues current a thousand years before Christ, in idioms derived from that cultural world. Although the NT church accepted this book as authoritative Scripture, Deuteronomy sought to govern the life of Israel, composed largely of ethnic descendants of the patriarchs.

Second, we should recognize the book as a written deposit of eternal truth. Some of these verities are cast in explicit declarative form, as in "Yahweh is God; there is no other [god] besides him" (4:35, 39 AT). Others are couched in distinctive Israelite cultural dress, for which we need to identify the underlying theological principle. For example, "When you build a new house, you shall make a parapet for your roof" (22:8 NRSV). This represents a specific way of demonstrating covenantal love for one's neighbor. The validity of specific commands for the Christian may not be answered simply by examining what the NT explicitly affirms. On the contrary, unless the NT explicitly declares a Deuteronomic ordinance passé, we should assume minimally that the principle underlying the command remains valid.

Third, after we establish the meaning of a passage in original context, we must reflect on its significance in light of Christ, who has fulfilled the law (and the prophets, Matt. 5:17). This means not only that he is the perfect embodiment of all the law demands, and its perfect interpreter, but also that he represents the climax of the narrative. The message of the NT is that the One who spoke on the plains of Moab is none other than Jesus Christ, Yahweh incarnate in human form.

Deuteronomy and the Canon

The written copies of Moses' last addresses to Israel were recognized as authoritative from the very beginning. Not only did Moses prohibit addition to or deletion from his words (4:2), but he also commanded the Levites to place the written torah beside the ark of the covenant. There it was to remain perpetually as a witness against Israel, as the norm by which the nation's conduct in the promised land would be measured. The fact that this torah was placed *beside* the ark, rather than *in* it (unlike the tablets containing the Decalogue [10:1–9], written down by God himself [5:22; 10:2]), does not suggest lesser authority, but different significance. The Decalogue represented the actual covenant document (4:13; 10:1–4), placed in the ark as a reminder to God of his covenant with Israel. The Deuteronomic torah was Moses' commentary on the covenant, whose terms included not only the Ten Principles, declared directly by God himself, but also the statutes and ordinances (*khuqqim* and *mishpatim*) revealed to Moses at Sinai and then passed on to the people (4:1). Moses' instructions on the covenant were fully inspired and authoritative, for he spoke to Israel "according to all that Yahweh had commanded him [to declare] to them" (1:3 AT).

The theological stamp of Deuteronomy is evident throughout the OT canon and into the NT. If in Deuteronomy the term *torah* applies expressly to the speeches of Moses, eventually it was applied to the entire Pentateuch, for which Deuteronomy represents the conclusion. Many treat Deuteronomy as a dangling legal appendix to the narratives of the patriarchs, Israel's exodus from Egypt, the establishment of covenant at Sinai, and the desert wanderings; yet, some (e.g., Noth) divorce the book from the Pentateuch altogether. However, critical scholars are increasingly recognizing a Deuteronomic flavor in many of the preceding narratives, so that in some the classical JEDP source hypothesis of pentateuchal origins has collapsed into a theory of two sources. One would be Deuteronomic (including most of what was previously attributed to Yahwist and Elohist sources), and the other the reactive P source (Albertz 464–93).

The stamp of Deuteronomy on the so-called Deuteronomistic History (Joshua–Kings) is evident not only in the style of these books (many of the embedded speeches sound like Deuteronomy—Josh. 23, 24; 1 Sam. 12; etc.), but also especially in its theology (cf. McConville, *Grace*). Specifically, Solomon's emphasis on the temple as a place for the "name of Yahweh" to dwell (1 Kings 8) harks back to Deut. 12 et passim. More generally, if and when the nation of Israel and her monarchy are destroyed, it is because they have failed in covenant with Yahweh as outlined in Deuteronomy. The influence of Deuteronomy is less obvious on Chronicles and Ezra-Nehemiah, but in the Latter Prophets one hears echoes of Moses' orations throughout. In Hosea and Jeremiah, the links are so direct that scholars often debate which came first, Deuteronomy or the prophet. Prophetic pronouncements of judgment and restoration appear often to be based on the covenant curses of Deut. 28 and promises of renewal in chapter 30. Indeed, the canonical prophets as a whole and Malachi specifically (Mal. 4:4–6) end with a call to return to the "torah of my servant Moses" (AT), which has its base in the revelation at Sinai but, strictly speaking, refers fundamentally to Moses' exposition.

In the Psalms, Deuteronomic influence is most evident in the so-called torah psalms (1, 19, 119), which highlight the life-giving purpose of the law, but also in the "wisdom" psalms, with their emphasis on fear of Yahweh (111:10; cf. 34:8–12). Weinfeld has argued that Deuteronomy bears many verbal and conceptual affinities with Proverbs (e.g., emphasis on fear of Yahweh and presentation of two ways—life/blessing and death/curse)—which point to wisdom influence (*Deuteronomy 1–11*, 62–65; *School*, 244–319). However, it seems more likely that the influence was in the opposite direction.

NT texts like Luke 24:44 suggest that by the time of Christ the expression *Torat Mosheh* ("Law of Moses," as in Josh. 8:31) served as the standard designation for the first part of the Jewish canon (alongside "the Prophets" and "the Psalms"). As noted earlier, the pentateuchal location of Deuteronomy, which serves as a theological exposition of the events narrated in the previous books, may have influenced the canonical location of John. However, whereas Christ himself is presented as Yahweh incarnate, the person whose role most closely resembles Moses in Deuteronomy is Paul. This apostle was specially called not only to lead the community of faith in mission, but also to interpret God's saving actions and instruct God's people in the life of covenant faith. In so doing he responded sharply to those who insisted that adherence to the law of Moses was a prerequisite to salvation. Like Deuteronomy, often Paul's Epistles each divide readily into two parts, the first being devoted to theological exposition (cf. Deut. 1–11), and the second to drawing out the practical and communal implications of the theology (cf. Deut. 12–26).

Deuteronomy and Theology

As an overall theme to Deuteronomy, we propose the following: A call to Israel for faithfulness in the land, in response to the grace Yahweh has lavished on them (cf. 6:20–25). In developing this theme, Moses presents a theology that is remarkable for both profundity and scope.

First, Israel's history begins and ends with God. Deuteronomy instructs Israel and all subsequent readers on his absolute uniqueness (4:32–39; 6:4; 10:17; 32:39; 33:26), eternality (33:27), transcendence (7:21; 10:17; 32:3), holiness (32:51), justice and righteousness (32:4; cf. 10:18), passion (jealousy) for his covenant and relationship with his people (4:24; 5:9; 6:15; 9:3; 32:21), faithfulness (7:9), presence (1:45; 4:7; 6:15; 7:21; 31:17), compassion (4:31), and especially covenant love (4:37; 7:7–8, 13; 10:15, 18; 23:5). But none of these are mere abstractions. Yahweh lives in relationship with humans, which explains why Moses never tired of speaking of God's grace—expressed in many different concrete actions toward Israel. Examples include election of Abraham and his descendants (4:37; 7:6), rescue of Israel from the bondage of Egypt (4:32–36), establishment of Israel as his covenant people (4:9–31; 5:1–22; 26:16–19), providential care (1:30–33; 8:15–16), provision of a homeland (6:10–15; 8:7–14), provision of leadership (16:18–18:22), and victory over their enemies (7:17–24).

Second, Deuteronomy offers a comprehensive picture of the community of faith. Externally, the community that stands before Moses consists largely of the descendants of Abraham and the first-generation offspring of those who had experienced the exodus from Egypt. In Deuteronomy, the doctrine of divine election plays a prominent role. The book speaks of the divine election (*bakhar*, choose) of the place for Yahweh's name to be established and to which the Israelites are invited for worship and communion (12:5; et passim). It also tells of the divine election of Israel's king (17:15), whose primary function is to embody covenant righteousness, and of the Levitical priests (18:5; 21:5), who were to promote righteousness. However, Yahweh's election of Israel to be his covenant people receives special attention. Deuteronomy 4:32–40 places Yahweh's rescue of Israel within the framework of cosmic history, declaring this event to be unprecedented both as a divine act and as a human experience. Lest hearers have any illusions about the grounds of election, Moses emphasizes that Yahweh's election of Israel was based on neither exceptional physical nor spiritual qualifications. Israel was not granted favored status with Yahweh because of its significance as a people, for it was the least (7:6–8), or because of its superior behavior vis-à-vis the nations, for her past is characterized by rebellion (9:1–23). On the contrary, election was an act of sheer grace, grounded in Yahweh's love for the ancestors (4:32–38) and in his inexplicable love for their descendants (7:6–8). In so doing, Deuteronomy presents Israel as an incredibly privileged people. They alone have experienced the strong redeeming hand of Yahweh (4:32–40), have participated in a covenant ceremony (4:9–31), and enjoy vital communion with Yahweh. Thereby he not only hears them whenever they cry out, but in an unprecedented act of revelation he also has made his will known to them (4:1–8; 6:20–25). Their standing with God is characterized directly as that of covenant partners (26:16–19) and a holy people belonging to him alone (7:6; 14:2; 26:19; 28:9). Metaphorically, they are counted as his adopted sons (14:1; cf. the portrayal of God as their father in 1:3 KJV/MT; 8:5; 32:5–6, 18) and his treasured possession (*segullah*, 7:6; 14:2; 26:18). However, although Yahweh had called the nation as a whole to covenant relationship, the true community of faith consists of persons who love Yahweh with their entire being. They demonstrate that love through righteousness (*tsedaqah*, 6:25), which includes repudiating all other gods and compassionately pursuing justice toward others (10:16–20).

Third, no other book in the OT presents as thorough a treatment of covenant relationship as Deuteronomy. Though some draw sharp lines of distinction between the Abrahamic covenant and the covenant that Yahweh made with Israel at Sinai, Deuteronomy perceives these to be organically related. The Sinai/Horeb covenant represents the fulfillment of the covenant Yahweh had made with Abraham and an extension of his commitment to Abraham's descendants (cf. Gen. 17:7). In Deuteronomy, Moses propounds an exposition of the covenant to which the present generation binds itself (26:16–19). Chapters 29–30 do not envision a new covenant, but the present generation's recommitment to and extension of the old.

It is within this covenantal context that we must understand the role of the law. Deuteronomy stresses obedience within that relationship: (1) Obedience was not to be viewed as a burden but as response to the unique privilege of knowing God's will (Deut. 4:6–8), in contrast to the nations who worshipped gods of wood and stone (4:28; Ps. 115:4–8). (2) Obedience is not a way of salvation, but the grateful response of those who had already been saved (6:20–25). (3) Obedience is not primarily a duty imposed by one party on another, but an expression of covenant relationship (26:16–19). (4) Obedience is the external evidence of the circumcision of one's heart and the internal disposition of fearing God (10:12–11:1; 30:6–9). (5) Obedience involves a willing subordination of one's entire being to the authority of the gracious divine suzerain (6:4–9; 10:12–13). (6) While obedience is not the prerequisite to salvation, it is the evidence of righteousness, which is a precondition to Israel's fulfillment of her mission and blessing (4:24–25; chs. 11, 28). (7) Obedience is both reasonable and achievable (30:11–20).

The last point demands further comment, especially since the book seems to view Israel's failure as inevitable (4:24; 5:29; 29:14–30:1; 31:16–21; 32:14–27). Part of the answer to this dilemma may be found in the frequent alternation of singular and plural forms of direct address. The shifts between "you" singular and "you" plural serve a rhetorical function, recognizing that though Yahweh entered into covenant relationship with the nation, in the end fidelity cannot be legislated and must be demonstrated at the personal level. Yet, this device also recognizes the existence of two Israels. On the one hand, there was a physical Israel, consisting of descendants of Abraham, Isaac, and Jacob. On the other hand, there was a spiritual Israel, consisting of those persons (like Moses and Joshua and Caleb) who demonstrated unqualified devotion to Yahweh. For the latter, obedience was not only possible; it was a delight. But Deuteronomy is both pessimistic and realistic about the former, anticipating a future of rebellion that will lead eventually to the destruction and exile of the nation. According to 30:6–10 this problem of national infidelity will only be resolved in the distant future, when Yahweh brings the people back and circumcises their hearts.

Fourth, Deuteronomy presents a highly developed theology of land. Moses' cosmic awareness is expressed by his appeal to heaven and earth to witness Israel's renewal of the covenant (4:26; 30:19; 31:28). But corresponding to Yahweh's love for Israel within the context of the nations, in 11:12 he declares that the land currently occupied by the Canaanites, set aside for Israel, is the special object of Yahweh's perpetual care (*darash*). Yahweh is delivering this land to the Israelites as their special grant (*nakhalah*, 4:21 et passim), in fulfillment of his oath to the ancestors (1:8 et passim). Yet, the Israelites are challenged to engage the Canaanites, drive them out (9:3), and utterly destroy them and their religious installations

(7:2–5; 12:2–3). However, this land is not given to Israel because the people have earned it (9:1–24), but as an act of grace.

Deuteronomy describes the nation's relationship to the land within the context of the tripartite association of Deity-land-people. Accordingly, the response of the land to Israel's occupation will depend entirely upon the people's fidelity. If they are faithful to Yahweh, the land will yield bountiful produce (7:11–16; 11:8–15; 28:1–14). But if they prove unfaithful, not giving Yahweh the credit for their prosperity and going after other gods, then the land will stop yielding its bounty, and he will sever the tie with it (4:25–28; 8:17–20; 11:16–17; 28:15–26). When the Israelites will be removed from the land because of their sin (which in Moses' mind appears inevitable), this will not represent a cancellation of the covenant, but the application of its fine print (cf. Dan. 9:4–16). Because of Yahweh's immutable covenant commitment to Abraham (Deut. 4:31), he must and will bring Israel back to the land and to himself (30:1–10). Accordingly, within their present literary contexts and the history of God's covenant relationship with Israel, the "new" covenant of which Jeremiah speaks in Jer. 31:31–34 and the eternal covenant of which Ezekiel writes in 16:60 (cf. 34:25–31) should not be interpreted as absolutely new. Instead, they are anticipations of the full realization of God's original covenant made with Abraham (ratified and fleshed out at Horeb), when the boundaries of physical and spiritual Israel will finally be coterminous. (The NT development of this theme in the context of the Lord's Supper [Luke 22:20; 1 Cor. 11:25] and in Hebrews [8:8–13; 9:15; 12:24] recognizes that ultimately God's covenant relationship with his people is possible only because of the mediatorial and sacrificial work of Christ.) Accordingly, Israel's exile cannot be the final word on the land. Because of Yahweh's compassion and the irrevocability of his covenant with Israel (Deut. 4:31), when the people repent he will regather them (30:1–5). However, the book is clear: Israel's occupation of the land and her prosperity are contingent on fidelity to Yahweh.

Fifth, Deuteronomy presents a remarkable approach to government. From beginning to end, Israel is presented as a theocracy, with Yahweh as her divine suzerain (though the kingship of Yahweh receives scant explicit attention; cf. 33:5). The book provides for judicial officials appointed by the people (1:9–15; 16:18), and kings, priests, and prophets appointed and/or raised up by Yahweh (17:14–18:22). Indeed, many scholars interpret 16:18–18:22 as a sort of state "constitution" for Israel, designed to reinforce the centralization of power in Jerusalem under Josiah (cf. McConville, *Deuteronomy*, 78–79). However, this interpretation is extremely problematic, because 17:14–20 presents the monarchy as optional, and interest in the king's real power over the people is eclipsed by concern for his role as a paradigm of covenant faithfulness. This disposition is quite at odds with the nature of Israelite kingship historically. The "constitution" interpretation of 16:18–18:22 also is especially problematic because it tends to overlook the primary concern of the book—to establish a people under the authority of torah and governed by "righteousness" (*tsedaqah*).

Conclusion

For modern readers plagued by a negative view of the OT in general and OT law in particular, Deuteronomy offers a healthy antidote. Through the work of Christ not only is Israel's relationship made possible, but also the church, the new Israel of God, is grafted into God's covenant promises. As with Israel, access to these promises remains by grace alone, through faith alone. However, having been chosen, redeemed, and granted covenant relationship with God, Yahweh's people will gladly demonstrate wholehearted allegiance with whole-bodied obedience (Rom. 12:1–12). Deuteronomy remains an invaluable resource for biblical understanding (1) of God, especially his grace in redeeming those bound in sin; (2) of appropriate response to God, entailing love for God and for our fellow human beings; and (3) of the sure destiny of the redeemed. More than any other book in the OT (if not the Bible as a whole), Deuteronomy concretizes faith for real life. Inasmuch as the NT identifies Jesus Christ with the God of Israel's redemption, in the spiritual and ethical pronouncements of Deuteronomy we find fleshed out both the first and great commandment (Matt. 22:34–40) and "the law of Christ" (Gal. 6:2). A church that has discovered this book will have its feet on the ground, resisting the tendency to fly off into realms of Platonic ideas and inward subjectivity so common in Western Christianity.

Bibliography

Albertz, R. *A History of Israelite Religion in the Old Testament Period*. 2 vols. Westminster John Knox, 1994.

Block, D. "How Many Is God? An Investigation into the Meaning of Deuteronomy 6:4–5." *JETS* 47 (2004): 193–212.

———. "Recovering the Voice of Moses: The Genesis of Deuteronomy." *JETS* 44 (2001): 385–408.

Calvin, J. *The Four Last Books of Moses.* Vol. 1. Eerdmans, 1950.

Craigie, P. *The Book of Deuteronomy.* NICOT. Eerdmans, 1976.

Knierim, R. "The Composition of the Pentateuch." Pages 351–79 in *The Task of Old Testament Theology.* Eerdmans, 1995.

Lienhard, J., et al., eds. *Exodus, Leviticus, Numbers, Deuteronomy.* ACCSOT 3. InterVarsity, 2001.

Lohse, B. *Martin Luther's Theology.* Fortress, 1999.

Luther, M. *Lectures on Deuteronomy. LWorks* 9. Concordia, 1960.

McConville, J. G. *Deuteronomy.* Apollos/InterVarsity, 2002.

———. *Grace in the End.* Zondervan, 1993.

———. *Law and Theology in Deuteronomy.* JSOTSup 33. JSOT, 1984.

McConville, J. G., and J. G. Millar. *Time and Place in Deuteronomy.* JSOTSup 179. Sheffield Academic Press, 1984.

Millar, J. G. *Now Choose Life.* Eerdmans, 1998.

Nelson, R. *Deuteronomy.* OTL. Westminster John Knox, 2002.

Nicholson, E. W. *Deuteronomy and Tradition.* Fortress, 1967.

Noth, M. *The Deuteronomistic History.* JSOTSup 15. JSOT, 1981.

Olsen, D. *Deuteronomy and the Death of Moses.* Fortress, 1994.

Rad, G. von. *Deuteronomy.* OTL. Westminster, 1966.

———. *The Problem of the Hexateuch and Other Studies.* SCM, 1966.

———. *Studies in Deuteronomy.* SBT 9. SCM, 1953.

Richter, S. *The Deuteronomistic History and the Name Theology.* De Gruyter, 2002.

Schreiner, T. *The Law and Its Fulfillment.* Baker, 1993.

Sonnet, J.-P. *The Book within the Book.* Brill, 1997.

Thompson, J. A. *Deuteronomy,* TOTC. InterVarsity, 1974.

Tigay, J. *Deuteronomy.* JPS Torah Commentary. JPS, 1996.

Vogt, P. *Deuteronomic Theology and the Significance of the Torah.* Eisenbrauns, 2006.

Watts, J. *Reading Law.* Sheffield Academic Press, 1999.

Weinfeld, M. *Deuteronomy 1–11.* AB 5A. Doubleday, 1991.

———. "Deuteronomy, Book of." *ABD* 2:168–83.

———. *Deuteronomy and the Deuteronomic School.* Clarendon, 1972.

Wenham, G. "Deuteronomy and the Central Sanctuary." *TynBul* 22 (1971): 103–18.

Wilson, I. *Out of the Midst of the Fire.* SBLDS 151. Scholars Press, 1995.

Wright, C. J. H. *Deuteronomy.* NIBCOT. Hendrickson, 1996.

Wright, N. T. *The Climax of the Covenant.* Fortress, 1993.

6

Joshua

J. G. McConville

Joshua gives the account of Israel's taking possession of the land promised by God, the division of the land among the tribes, and finally a renewal of the covenant at Shechem (Josh. 24).

History of Interpretation

In precritical Christian interpretation, Joshua was read in light of theology. Since the name Joshua is close to Jesus (identical in the Greek forms in LXX and NT), the figure was readily taken as a type of Christ. In Heb. 4:8–11 the "rest" into which Joshua led Israel is seen as temporary and inferior to the "rest" that still awaits God's people in Christ. Allegorical readings persisted into medieval times (Sæbø 184). In the Reformation it was read with the perspective that God's historical dealings and covenant with Israel were both preparatory for and analogous to his dealings with the Christian church and Christian nations (O'Donovan and O'Donovan 715). Joshua's actions in Canaan could then be exemplary for contemporary rulers (86, 605).

Critical interpretation, no longer looking for Christian doctrine, saw the book rather as evidence of the historical emergence of Israel. Because

Joshua relates the taking of the land that was promised in the Pentateuch (Exod. 23:20–33; Deut. passim), early critics thought that the sources they found in the Pentateuch could be traced into Joshua, within a so-called Hexateuch (von Rad 296–305; Fohrer 197). The strength of this view is its recognition of Joshua's continuities with the pentateuchal books prior to Deuteronomy (e.g., Num. 13–14; 34:17). This kind of approach found links with Israel's actual early history, for example, in memories of conquest kept alive at the sanctuary at Gilgal (Fohrer 200–201).

Recent critical study has placed Joshua within the Deuteronomistic History (Deuteronomy–Kings; Noth). This view rightly observes close affinities between Deuteronomy and Joshua, for example, in the "Deuteronomic" terms in which Joshua succeeds Moses, especially the importance there of "the Book of the Law" (Josh. 1:1–9; cf. Deut. 28:61; 31:26), and also in specific correspondences between the two books (e.g., Deut. 27 and Josh. 8:30–35). Yet there are also contrasts between Deuteronomy and Joshua and, conversely, continuities with Numbers. For example, Joshua has a larger role for the priests than Deuteronomy (Josh. 4:10; cf. Num. 4:1–15). Noth's answer to this was to postulate priestly additions to the Deuteronomistic work. But this underrates the extent to which Joshua follows Numbers as well as Deuteronomy. The role of Joshua himself is prepared for throughout Exodus–Deuteronomy (Exod. 33:11; Num. 27:12–23; Deut. 3:23–29; 31:1–8, 23; 34:9).

Smend's reading of Josh. 1:1–9 found evidence of an exilic "nomistic," or conditional, redaction (1:7–9) of the basic Deuteronomistic account, which had stressed complete victory. A different line derives from the now-dominant view that the basic Deuteronomistic edition stems from the time of Josiah. Here, Joshua is deliberately portrayed as a type of Josiah, and the issue in the book is the need to affirm Yahwistic faith in the context of religious pluralism in late monarchic Judah; this is the condition of Josiah's expansionistic policies (Nelson 21–22).

Form-critically, Joshua has been compared with ancient Near Eastern conquest accounts. Younger has shown that Joshua broadly fits within patterns of such accounts from 1300 to 600 BCE. However, the book may also include other forms, such as toponym lists and boundary descriptions (cf. Nelson 9–11).

Regarding historicity, it is widely argued that Joshua's account of the conquest does not match what is known from archaeology about the patterns of occupation and destruction of the cities in Canaan, such as Ai (Jericho is less of a problem in this respect than sometimes claimed [Mazar 283]). Conservative explanations for these disharmonies include redating the conquest from the generally accepted thirteenth century to the fifteenth century BCE (Bimson), reexamining the identifications of cities in the account (including Ai), and exegetical strategies (e.g., Joshua may not always imply the total destruction of a city; Hess 141, cf. 158–59). In general, the provisional nature of archaeological results is stressed, "etiological" explanations of traditions avoided, and the basic historicity of the text affirmed.

Modern literary approaches draw attention to the dangers of oversimplified readings. Most significantly, a tension is perceived between the claims in the text that Joshua conquered the entire land (11:23; 21:44–45) and the perspective that, even in Joshua's old age, much of the land remained to be conquered (13:1) and certain enclaves still held out (15:6). It is the latter perspective that gave credence to Smend's nomistic redactional layer. The literary approach tends to see the discrepancy as having a function in the meaning of the book, such that, for example, Israel is depicted as undeserving and yet taking the land (Polzin 90).

Finally, sociological readings understand Joshua, not as the history of an actual conquest, but as the delineation of cultural, ethnic, and religious boundaries. Mullen's work provides this new paradigm, and for him the setting is, once again, the time of Josiah, the need being to define carefully who counts as "Israel" (Mullen 87–119).

Hearing the Message of Joshua

The book may be divided into four sections: entry to the land (1:1–5:12), its conquest (5:13–12:24), its division among the tribes (13:1–21:45), and the worship of Yahweh in it (22:1–24:33).

The opening verses of Joshua announce that the time has come for the promises made to Israel through Moses to be fulfilled. The words "After the death of Moses the servant of the LORD" (1:1) not only function as a structural marker of a new beginning, but also recall that Joshua, not Moses, would lead Israel into the land (Deut. 3:23–29). The vision of the land that awaits is reaffirmed (1:4; cf. Deut. 11:24), God's promise of his presence is transferred from Moses to Joshua (1:5), and Joshua is called to "be strong and very courageous" (as Moses had already commissioned him; Deut. 31:7). This courage is to be directed in two ways: first to the battles ahead (v. 6), and second to the keeping of God's commandments, in the form of the "Book of the Law" (1:7–8), which thus stands over the whole action of the book. Joshua is both like and unlike Moses. With respect to

God's call and enabling, he is like Moses in taking responsibility to put Israel in possession of the promised land (Moses had begun this with the settlement of the Transjordanian tribes; Deut. 3:12–17), and in his loyalty to Yahweh alone and his obedience to "the Book of the Law." Joshua is unlike Moses in that he is not himself *lawgiver* (but see Josh. 24:25–26), and that his leadership is specifically orientated to the task of land possession. His role as successor to Moses is thus limited, since in a certain sense Moses is succeeded by the "Book of the Law" itself (the written form of his spoken words), and in another sense by the "leaders of the congregation," who make decisions alongside Joshua concerning the status of the Gibeonites (Josh. 9:15, 18 NRSV; see also 23:2). The succession to Moses as prophet (Deut. 18:15–18) is not directly raised in Joshua.

The first section of the book (1:1–5:12) focuses on the crossing into the land. The mission of the spies (ch. 2) recalls a previous, unsuccessful mission (Num. 13–14), but here the cooperation of the Canaanite Rahab and her confession of faith give hope of a better sequel. The crossing of the Jordan (Josh. 3–4) has echoes of that of the Reed Sea at the exodus (Exod. 15). The first Passover in the land (5:10–12) signals the completion of the journey from Egypt to Canaan. Passover structurally marks the departure and the arrival, and theologically the passage from slavery to freedom.

The freedom has yet to be realized in the conquest itself, however. The narrative of this follows in 5:13–12:24. The taking of Jericho furnishes the paradigm for the conquest of a city within the promised land, with the destruction of every living creature in it (6:21), in accordance with the law of Deut. 20:16–18. That this is a victory of Yahweh alone is emphasized by the means by which the city falls. The qualifications of totality in this action are, first, the sparing of Rahab, in fulfillment of the spies' promise to her (2:14), and second, the offense against the ritual proscription of the goods of the city by Achan, which is then nullified by his execution along with his family.

The taking of Jericho is followed by further victories over cities both north and south, these victories being specifically over *kings* (Josh. 12:7–24). In this way a triumph is suggested, not only over enemies as such, but also of a new kind of society over one based (like Egypt) on tyranny. This is another example of the full circle from the exodus.

The account of the conquest is presented first as a clean sweep (11:23), but then as an ongoing work, likely to overspill Joshua's own life (13:1; cf. Judg. 1:1). In the account of the division of the land that follows, there are several indications that this corresponds to reality (15:63; 16:10; 17:12). The stage is thus set for a continuing struggle.

The third section relates the division of the land among the tribes (13:1–21:45). An exception is made for the Levitical (priestly) tribe, who receive towns within the other tribes' territories (14:3–4; ch. 21), following the principle in Deut. 18:2 that "the LORD is their inheritance" (where "inheritance" otherwise entails territory). In practice, they would have towns and land, and in that limited way hold property. But their particular role in relation both to Yahweh and to Israel as a whole is highlighted by this special treatment.

Finally, the commitment of Israel to worship Yahweh alone is reaffirmed, first in a charge by Joshua to "all Israel," represented by its elders, judges, and officers (23:2; cf. Deut. 16:18), then in a formal covenant renewal at Shechem (Josh. 24). This follows a reaffirmation of the obligation of Israel to worship Yahweh alone, including the tribes who had settled in Transjordan (ch. 22). The people are unified within one land, and the unrivaled place of Yahweh in it is symbolized by the acknowledgment of only one place of worship, which at this stage is Shiloh, by virtue of the presence of the tabernacle there (18:1).

Can this story of Israel's liberation into its own land have relevance today? The answer lies neither in treating the book's message in a purely spiritualizing way (where, for example, crossing the Jordan is a metaphor for death) nor in finding direct mandates for the warlike behavior of contemporary nations. If there is a mandate for godly nationhood in Joshua, what form does it take? A reading of the NT, with its proclamation of the gospel to all nations, apparently precludes the application of Joshua narrowly to historic Israel and the land it once occupied. On the contrary, the idea of a "Christian nation," which has appeared frequently in the history of Christian thought, in widely differing places (Grosby 213–33), has more credibility. Yet that too has been capable of abuse, to the point of justifying repressive nationalisms and landgrabs. If the dangerous theology of Joshua is to be appropriated somehow for political theology, it must be in such a way as to avoid such extreme and self-regarding realizations.

Joshua and Theology

Joshua continues, in one sense, Deuteronomy's blueprint for nationhood. This consists in an ordering of people under Torah, which is in turn given by God. Joshua himself is called to show the right attitude to this Torah (Josh. 1:7–8), in terms similar to those required of the king (Deut. 17:18–20). And when he comes to pass on responsibility for leadership to "elders and heads, their judges and officers," he urges them in turn to adhere rigorously to it (Josh. 23:2, 6 NRSV). In the covenant renewal at Shechem, Joshua establishes a "statute and ordinance" with the people (24:25 AT; cf. Deut. 5:31), and then writes in the "Book of the Law [Torah] of God" (v. 26). This suggests that the "Book of the Law" is open to allow reaffirmations of Israel's allegiance to God to be added to it (this in qualification of Deut. 4:2). Joshua shows that Torah always informs the people's true leadership.

It is Torah obedience, furthermore, that legitimates the people's possession of territory. The close connection of law and territory is established in Deuteronomy, in which the gift of land is consistently predicated on the people's obedience to Torah (Deut. 17:14–20 is an example). The same connection is made at the outset of Joshua, when Joshua is exhorted to "be strong and courageous" in respect of both law-keeping and land-possession (Josh. 1:6–9). The book of Joshua, therefore, enacts in principle the concept of a people living in a territory, subject to a law that operates within its borders.

Such possession, however, must be legitimate. An important function of Joshua is to demonstrate the legitimacy of Israel's possession of the land of Canaan. The issue is confronted directly, because the land to be possessed is no "land without a people." On the contrary, it is inhabited by peoples who are firmly bedded down in their own places, and who base their own claims, we suppose, on their actual possession, their culture, and their religion. The claim to legitimate possession entails the assertion of the right to take and keep by force, and in principle the need to press the claim against others. This is what is asserted in Yahweh's victory over the peoples of Canaan. It is not only a victory but also an act of judgment, a claim that it is right that Israel and not others should possess this land. The nature of the war against the Canaanites as a judgment is signaled in several texts outside Joshua (Gen. 15:16; Lev. 20:23; Deut. 9:4–5), and in the frequent characterization of them as acting abominably in God's eyes (Deut. 12:29–32). (For the nexus of victory, judgment, and possession, see also O'Donovan and O'Donovan 36–45.)

The confrontation between Israel and the nations, therefore, is between a nation that lives under Yahweh in obedience to Torah and others that do not. This fundamental difference between Israel and the Canaanite nations is fully present in Joshua only by virtue of the knowledge that Deuteronomy and the Pentateuch generally lie behind it. But it appears at certain points, one hint being in the categorization of the Canaanite enemies repeatedly as "kings" (Josh. 12), a feature that seems to pitch the type of power in the city-states against the kingship of Yahweh, much like the power of Pharaoh in Exodus.

It is against this background that we have to consider the greatest stumbling block for modern readers of Joshua, notwithstanding the rationale just offered. This is the "ban of destruction," or the *kherem*, the command from God to put the inhabitants of Canaan to the sword (6:17). In modern commentary it is common to explain this command as a metaphor for rigorous adherence to Yahweh and separation from other forms of religion (Moberly). This is supported by the historical assessment that in all probability Israel never did to Canaan what the book of Joshua depicts it as having done. The language of *kherem* was borrowed from the conventions of ancient Near Eastern religious war (also known from the famous ninth-century BCE Moabite Stone, on which the Moabite King Mesha claimed to have put *Israel* to the *kherem*).

The problem with a metaphorical understanding is that Joshua speaks about real peoples, land, and politics. The plain force of the language has been felt by those in every age who have used the conquest of Canaan as grounds, by identifying themselves with Israel, for their own subjugation of peoples by war in order to possess land (Collins). The use of a warlike metaphor to speak of a God who abhors war would have to be regarded as a failed strategy!

The issue must be approached differently, by asking whether the book of Joshua as a whole really portrays Israel as matching the criteria of legitimate possession. We have begun to see that the story of the book is not as straightforward as it appears at first glance. Israel permits first Rahab (Josh. 2) and then the Gibeonites (ch. 9) to live alongside themselves in the land. And the picture of total possession is called in question by the perspective that possession remains to be accomplished (13:1), and has in some cases been frustrated. There are thus questions as to boundaries: what are the actual boundaries of the people? As Hawk (xxii–xxiii) has put it, outsiders (Rahab, Gibeon) become insiders, while insiders (Achan's family) become outsiders. And even the geographical boundary of the Jordan is put in question by the issue of the settlement of some tribes in Transjordan, producing the conflict related in Josh. 22 (Jobling).

On this view the careful constructions of Israelite identity are not finally affirmed in Joshua, but precisely put in question. While the building blocks for a national identity may be put in place here (and thus for nations generally, not just Israel), the picture of Israel in Joshua is part of the wider portrayal in Genesis–Kings of a people that fails to become what it is called to be. Joshua proclaims at Shechem: "You cannot serve the LORD" (24:19

NRSV), a jarring note that corresponds to Deuteronomy's view (9:4–7), ensuring that the story of Israel's possession becomes a critique of the violence that subjugates others without rightly possessing a mandate to do so. In Israel's failure to occupy the land of Canaan in obedience lies the warning that none might claim to make war and dispossess others in the name of God. In Hawk's words: "Joshua should be studied, not shunned, precisely because it holds the mirror up to all who regard themselves as the people of God" (xxxii). Joshua is the counterpart of the prophetic vision for Israel, which consistently resists the identification of "Israel" with an ethnic people and with power that relies on force (see also Jewett and Lawrence). The legitimate possession of warrants to be a nation depends not on unbreakable historic guarantees, but on ongoing commitment to true freedom from tyrannies and idolatries of whatever kind. Joshua, as a document for Israel in its own place and time, offers a remit for peoples today to conceive their specific traditions of culture and place anew, in light of God's law of liberty.

In the NT, Israel finds its true self in Christ (O'Donovan and O'Donovan 131), and so in the supranational church. This does not mean that God's action of judgment on the nations is revoked, nor the enactment of judgment within political structures (Rom. 13:1–5), both of which can be said to be proposed by the book of Joshua, the latter with warrants that extend to all political authorities. But it does mean the renunciation of all claims to be the people of God in ways that equate with ethnic or national entities.

Bibliography

Bimson, J. *Redating the Exodus and Conquest*. JSOTSup 5. Almond, 1981.

Collins, J. "The Zeal of Phinehas: The Bible and the Legitimation of Violence." *JBL* 122 (2003): 3–21.

Fohrer, G. *Introduction to the Old Testament*. SCM, 1970.

Grosby, S. *Biblical Ideas of Nationality*. Eisenbrauns, 2002.

Hawk, L. *Joshua*. Liturgical Press, 2000.

Hess, R. *Joshua*. TOTC. InterVarsity, 1996.

Jewett, R., and J. Lawrence. *Captain America and the Crusade against Evil*. Eerdmans, 2003.

Jobling, D. "'The Jordan a Boundary': Transjordan in Israel's Ideological Geography." Pages 88–134 in *The Sense of Biblical Narrative, II*. JSOTSup 39. JSOT, 1986.

Mazar, A. "The Iron Age I." Pages 258–301 in *The Archaeology of Ancient Israel*, ed. A. Ben-Tor. Open University of Israel, 1992.

Moberly, R. W. L. "Theological Interpretation of an Old Testament Book: A Response to Gordon McConville's *Deuteronomy*." *SJT* 56 (2003): 516–25.

Mullen, E. *Narrative History and Ethnic Boundaries*. SemeiaSt. Scholars Press, 1993.

Nelson, R. *Joshua*. OTL. Westminster John Knox, 1997.

Noth, M. *The Deuteronomistic History*. JSOTSup 15. JSOT, 1981.

O'Donovan, O. *The Desire of the Nations*. Cambridge University Press, 1996.

O'Donovan, O., and J. Lockwood O'Donovan, eds. *From Irenaeus to Grotius*. Eerdmans, 1999.

Polzin, R. *Moses and the Deuteronomist*. Seabury, 1980.

Rad, G. von. *Old Testament Theology*. Vol. 1. Oliver & Boyd, 1962.

Sæbø, M. *Hebrew Bible/Old Testament: The History of Its Interpretation*. Vol. 1, part 2, *The Middle Ages*. Vandenhoeck & Ruprecht, 2000.

Smend, R. "The Law and the Nations: A Contribution to Deuteronomistic Tradition History." Pages 95–110 in *Reconsidering Israel and Judah*, ed. G. Knoppers and J. G. McConville. SBTS 8. Eisenbrauns, 2000.

Younger, K. L. *Ancient Conquest Accounts*. JSOTSup 98. Sheffield Academic Press, 1990.

7

Judges

J. ALAN GROVES

On the surface Judges seems a straightforward account of Israel's history between the conquest of Canaan and the rise of David, focused on the role of Israel's leadership with respect to the people's increasingly sinful behavior. Along these lines the book breaks quite neatly into three parts:

- an overview story of the failure to complete the conquest (1:1–2:5);
- stories of various judges, which collectively portray a downward spiral of repeated cycles of sin, judgment, distress, and deliverance (2:6–16:31); and
- two final stories of religious and moral depravity (chs. 17–21).

Below the surface, the book is more than simply a negative account of this particular period. The writer of Judges was using past events and experiences of the community of faith and its leadership to exhort his contemporary audience to follow the Lord. Based on theology drawn from Deuteronomy, Judges argued that Israel's leaders were to be constantly reminding Israel to remember the Lord's covenant faithfulness demonstrated by his past action in the exodus and conquest, as well as his ongoing and continued acts of compassion in repeated deliverances of Israel. Therefore, they were to fear the Lord and follow him by keeping covenant (Deut. 4:9–12; cf. Judg. 2:6–10, 20–23; 3:1–6; 6:13). Judges understood this leadership as coming from Judah (1:2–20) and through a king (e.g., 17:6; 18:1; 19:1; 21:25). Judges was pointing, in other words, to King David as the ideal, covenant-keeping leader. For the writer, the right kind of leader—exemplified by King David—was essential for transforming the people of God.

History of Interpretation

Among the historical books in the OT, Judges has perhaps received the least attention in the history of interpretation, except in the modern period.

The events and personages from the period of the judges are barely mentioned in the rest of the OT (only a dozen times outside the book of Judges). The references are of three types: (1) General historical overviews reflect the same negative view (in language similar to Judges) of Israel's covenantal failings in the period of the judges (1 Sam. 12:8–12; Neh. 9:22–37; Pss. 78:54–72; 106:34–46). (2) There are particular accounts of events in Judges (e.g., the victory over Midian [chs. 7–8; Ps. 83:9–12; Isa. 9:4; 10:26], the moral failure of Gibeah [ch. 19; Hos. 9:9; 10:9], and Abimelech's ignominious death [ch. 9; 2 Sam. 11:21]). And (3) there is one positive allusion to the period of the judges (Isa. 1:26), where Isaiah sees the future Zion, purified of sin, as a time of the restoration of judges "as in days of old."

Jewish interpretation in the Second Temple period and Christian interpretation in the NT (and early church period) also show relatively little use of the book, especially in light of much more substantial treatment of other portions of the OT. In the Second Temple period, only a few of the various historical reviews covered the period of the judges. Pseudo-Philo (first century CE) reviewed the period of the judges (L.A.B. 25.1–48.5), and spoke of Kenaz, rather than Judah, as the one to lead Israel. (Kenaz is mentioned only in passing in Judges but receives extensive treatment in Pseudo-Philo.) Ben Sirach (175 BCE), as part of a brief review of Israel's history, spoke briefly of the judges in positive tones, suggesting that they did not yield to idolatry (Sir. 46:11–12). During this period the tendency to idealize important figures from Israel's past (e.g., Abraham, Moses, Jacob) was part apologetic against those opposing the Jews of the Second Temple period, and part support for a positive history to encourage national Jewish identity. Not all comments were positive, however. In a passing remark,

The Lives of the Prophets (early first century CE) refers to the period of the judges as "days of the anarchy" (*Liv. Pro.* 16.3).

In the NT, Acts 13:19–20 and Heb. 11:32–34 are the only clear reflections on the period of the judges. In Acts 13, as Paul reviews Israel's history in a sermon leading up to Christ, he mentions only that the conquest took about 450 years and that God gave Israel judges. (None of the similar sermons in Acts—by Peter, Stephen, and Paul—where a historical review is used even mention the judges; in Acts 7:45–47 Stephen jumps from Joshua to David.)

Hebrews 11:32–34 mentions four judges:

> And what more shall I say? I do not have time to tell about Gideon, Barak, Samson, Jephthah, David, Samuel and the prophets, who through faith conquered kingdoms, administered justice, and gained what was promised; who shut the mouths of lions, quenched the fury of the flames, and escaped the edge of the sword; whose weakness was turned to strength; and who became powerful in battle and routed foreign armies.

This passage comes at the end of the so-called honor roll of faith, where the writer of Hebrews extols the faith of Abraham, Moses, and significant others. The remark in verse 32—"*I do not have time to tell about* Gideon, Barak, Samson, Jephthah"—sums up (unintentionally) what seems to have been the prevailing attitude among interpreters, that one can pass over Judges quickly, if not skip it altogether.

Between the ancient church and the present day, relatively little has been done with the book of Judges as a whole. Yet in 1615, during the Reformation, Richard Rogers wrote a thousand-page commentary on the book of Judges. He saw the period through the lens of Heb. 11, with his commentary as being for the benefit of "all such as desire to grow in faith and Repentance, and especially of them, who would more cleerely [*sic*] understand and make use of the worthie [*sic*] examples of the Saints, recorded in divine history." Rogers saw the various judges as positive examples of faith. What other work was done on Judges seems to share Rogers's approach of interpreting particular judges as illustrations of theological points. A century later, for example, Jonathan Edwards reflected on Jephthah's vow (Judg. 11:32–40) at length, while addressing issues of his day concerning making vows and covenants.

In the modern period, Judges has been treated as part of a larger, single body known as the "Deuteronomistic History," comprised of Deuteronomy, Joshua, Judges, Samuel, and Kings. Within this grouping of books, scholars have spent more time with Joshua, Samuel, and Kings than with Judges. Only in the contemporary period, where literary—particularly feminist—readings of the Bible have been the focus, has Judges become the object of more intense theological and interpretative scrutiny. In particular, the stories of Acsah, Deborah, Jael, Jephthah's daughter, and the Levite's concubine have received much attention.

When studying any OT passage or book, one should "read the text twice." A "first reading" seeks to understand the text in its own historical setting and on its own terms, without reference to later scriptural or historical developments (e.g., the life, death, and resurrection of Christ). What was the situation of the original audience? How did the author address their concerns and struggles? What did he want them to learn about God and about themselves? How did he want them to respond? A "second reading" looks at how the text fits into the broader picture of the whole sweep of redemptive history, how it appears in light of the climax of the OT story in Christ, and then how it contributes to theology and application.

The book of Judges is not merely a showcase of examples of behavior or belief to imitate or avoid. Rather, it reveals God's plan, purpose, and character (e.g., faithfulness to his covenant and to his people; his patience and compassion in delaying the ultimate judgment of exile from the land). It also reveals the human heart (e.g., its inability to serve God faithfully; its ongoing need to know who God is and what he has done for his people). Judges lays bare the community of faith's need in a certain place and time—the need for godly leadership to lead them in keeping covenant by faith. But like all OT Scripture, it also points forward to Christ, the perfect leader who alone can truly redeem, change hearts, and reveal God.

The Message of Judges

This section reflects a "first reading," as described above, concerned with the message of Judges to its original OT audience. Under the later section entitled "Judges and Theology," a "second reading" of Judges in the light of Christ will come into play.

Written *after* the time when David became king, Judges has provided the only extant account of the historical events between the conquest and the rise of David. But the recounting of that history was not its primary purpose. Rather, most simply put, the message of Judges addresses the difficulty that Israel's leadership (the judges) had in leading the people of God to fear the Lord and keep covenant. Failure to follow the Lord by fearing him and keeping his covenant threatened Israel's continued peace and presence in the land. Judges calls the Israelites to consider whom they would follow in terms of both human and divine leaders.

More particularly, Judges' purpose is (1) to demonstrate the failure of Israel's leadership to pass on the knowledge of God to the next generation or to lead them in covenant-keeping (2:10 as it leads into 2:11ff.) and (2) to argue for a better leader: a covenant-keeping king, not a judge; from Judah, not Benjamin; David, not Saul. (David and Saul are never explicitly mentioned in Judges, but the character and behavior of the tribes of Judah and Benjamin are contrasted several times, serving to contrast the character of the leadership of the most famous sons of each tribe—David and Saul.) For Judges, the answer to the crisis in leadership and the increasing Canaanization of Israel was David, the king from Judah, who would lead the people of God in fearing the Lord and keeping covenant.

Judges opens by noting the crisis in leadership created by Joshua's death and God's answer that Judah would lead Israel in completing the conquest (1:1–2). Judges 1 continues by outlining the general success of the tribe of Judah in taking their allotted inheritance (1:2–20) and the almost universal failure of the other tribes to do likewise (1:21–36). Judah is presented as keeping covenant and as a result being the tribe to lead Israel. David, to whom Judges' focus on Judah is pointing, ultimately completed the conquest of Canaan by taking the stronghold of Zion from the Jebusites (2 Sam. 5:6–10). Moreover, he decisively defeated the Philistines (5:17–25), something that even Judah was unable to do in the period of the Judges (Judg. 1:19).

The heart of the book recounts the stories of twelve judges: six are extended accounts and six are short (3:7–16:31). In the extended narratives the problem of the particular leadership of the judges themselves is elaborated. Significantly, the first judge, Othniel, is from Judah, and there is nothing negative recounted about his leadership (3:7–11), both details pointing positively to the role of Judah in leadership, and hence to David. Judges concludes with the accounts of two sordid episodes of religious and moral failure (chs. 17–21). The refrain "in those days Israel had no king; everyone did as he saw fit" (17:6; 21:25; cf. 18:1; 19:1) punctuates the message of Judges, pointing to a king—David in particular—as the solution to Israel's covenant-keeping woes.

Judges showed that not just any king would do. Appealing to the theology of kingship found in Deut. 17:14–20, the writer of Judges is arguing for a covenant-keeping king who would read the Law daily and lead the people in faithful acknowledgment of God (Deut. 4:9, 32–40).

Throughout Deuteronomy that obedience is presented as a faith response (fearing the Lord). As Israel knew God, experienced his care and lordship, meditated on his amazing acts on their behalf (particularly the exodus), and rejoiced in being his children, they would *want* to honor him. Hence, it was essential to recall regularly, and teach their children, these things so that each new generation of Israelites would know the Lord and live as his obedient covenant children.

Judges tells repeated tales of what happens when that knowledge of the Lord is not passed on to subsequent generations (e.g., the story of Gideon, who has heard of the Lord from his father; but his father has also built an altar of Baal—Judg. 6:11ff., esp. vv. 13, 25). By focusing on the judges, the book emphasizes the integral role of *leaders* in this process.

Judges 2:16–19 states that Israel will *not listen to their judges* but prostitute themselves after other gods, thus suggesting that the judges may serve prophetic roles (although the accounts portray them almost exclusively as military leaders). And 2:17, read by itself, seems to imply that the judges are righteous and that the problem is simply with Israel at large. The individual stories, however, give more complex accounts of the judges' faith and failure, elaborating on the problems of their leadership and indicating that their own behavior and struggles with belief have made it difficult for them to remind and teach Israel. They do bring about mighty victories and deliver the people, and they do exercise faith; they are not simply failures. But they fall short and do not establish permanent peace (e.g., 2:19; 3:11; 8:33).

Judges recounts a downward spiral in the pattern of Israel's belief and behavior. The people become increasingly "Canaanized" (Block 58), as shown preeminently in their idolatry, but also in religious (chs. 17–18) and moral (chs. 19–21) failure. The pattern of sin, judgment, crying out in distress, and then deliverance by means of Spirit-anointed judges is not effecting any lasting change. God shows compassion again and again by not sending the nation into exile and by continually delivering the people. But the foreshadowing is there: Israel has to change, or the downward spiral of sin and judgment is going to lead to loss of the land and of God (18:30–31). The judges are not getting that job done. Israel needs to have changed hearts, as Deuteronomy calls for (10:16; 29:2–4; 30:6). They desperately need the right kind of leader—who will remind them of who the Lord is, who will lead them in obeying, and who will help them pass that knowledge on to their offspring. According to Judges, they need a king—from Judah.

By providing mixed accounts of the judges—faith and failure—with the repeated refrain in the closing chapters—"In those days Israel had no king;

everyone did as he saw fit" (17:6; 18:1; 19:1; 21:25)—Judges is arguing that a king is a better kind of leader. Not just any king would accomplish this, of course. It is essential that he be a God-fearing, covenant-keeping king, who would help the people themselves keep covenant.

Judges was not written to the people who lived during the time of the judges. It was an account of that time period for a later audience of God's people. For its contemporary audience, Judges is an account of what happens when one generation fails to pass on the knowledge and fear of the Lord, and it is therefore an exhortation to correct that problem among themselves. Its message is to seek and embrace God-fearing, covenant-keeping leadership, which would lead Israel in keeping covenant.

The original setting has been much debated: Was it during David's reign? In the divided kingdom? During the reign of Josiah? In the exile? After the exile? A subtle polemic against Benjamin (and by implication Saul) is found throughout. Benjamin was first in the list of tribes who failed to complete their part of the conquest (1:21). Gibeah in Benjamin (Saul's hometown) was portrayed as a new Sodom (Judg. 19 vs. Gen. 19). Benjamin was the source of a civil war in Israel (Judg. 20), in which all Israel fought against Benjamin. In contrast, Judah, the tribe chosen to lead (1:1–2; 20:18) against Israel's enemies, is the tribe that successfully keeps covenant by driving out the Canaanites (1:2–20). Together the anti-Benjamite polemic and the pro-Judahite apology suggest that Judges may well have been written in the period when there were two viable candidates for the throne—one from the house of David and the other from the house of Saul. That is the period when David was king in the south in Hebron, and Ish-Bosheth, the son of Saul, was king of the ten northern tribes in Ephraim (2 Sam. 2:8–5:10).

In that context, the writer of Judges was encouraging his fellow Israelites to choose and follow King David. One senses the writer hoping that under the leadership of a godly king like David, the people's hearts would at last be changed, they would fear the Lord and keep covenant, and they would avoid the covenant curse of the loss of the land that the Lord had given them.

Judges and the Canon

While Judges may not be reflected upon in great detail elsewhere in the history of interpretation, it does have several important canonical functions. First of all, if not for the book of Judges, almost nothing would be known of this period between the initial entry into the land and the time of Samuel. In that context it provides the first extended picture of problems with covenant-keeping in Israel. It sets a quite different tone than Joshua. Judges repeats the conclusion of Joshua (24:27–31) virtually verbatim rather early (Judg. 2:6–9). Yet, this passage, which served to conclude Joshua on a positive and hopeful note, is used by Judges to introduce the decline of Israel.

The second canonical contribution concerns a particular accent in Deuteronomic theology. As mentioned above, more recent OT scholarship has most often treated Judges as part of a larger Deuteronomistic History. This DH reflects the particular theological concerns of the late preexilic and exilic periods as refracted through certain key themes: God dealt with Israel by means of the covenant he had made with them (Deut. 4:31). Worship was to be centralized in Jerusalem (ch. 12). Idolatry was the key sin that represented covenant-breaking (4:15–28). And blessing for obedience or judgment for disobedience was the primary expression of covenant in action (ch. 28). It is arguable, however, that Judges was written earlier than the late preexilic period and stands as a unique witness to an earlier Deuteronomic theology with a somewhat different focus. One generation is proclaiming the great and mighty deeds of God to the next and teaching the next generation to fear the Lord (Deut. 4:9–12; Judg. 2:6–10). Judges then becomes an account of what happens when one generation fails to pass on the knowledge and fear of the Lord.

A third canonical contribution concerns the land of inheritance that the Lord had given to Israel. The land's theological significance was underscored by (1) the use of the refrain that "the land had peace" to conclude narratives of deliverance (3:11, 30; 5:31; 8:28) and (2) the recollection of the Lord's gift of the land in covenant lawsuit contexts (2:1–4; 6:7–10). The Lord (appropriately) punished the Israelites for their covenant disobedience by letting them experience captivity to foreigners while they were still in the land, which foreshadowed the eventual captivity of Israel outside it.

A fourth canonical contribution concerns kingship, about which Deuteronomy was reticent (17:14–20). David brought kingship into a prominent position in the theology and tradition of Israel. Judges, written after David had become king, argued for covenant-keeping kingship like David's as a means for leading people in spiritual transformation (echoed by Ps. 78—see esp. vv. 65–72 in light of 56–64). This would help Israel to avoid a continual falling into sin, and instead to enjoy lasting peace. From a perspective of leadership in the community of faith, Judges is perhaps the strongest canonical argument for kingship, although the focus is not on political structure but on spiritual transformation.

Judges and Theology

As has been noted, Judges took its theology primarily from Deuteronomy. Its theology was covenantal. That is, whatever happened to Israel, for good or for ill, was in the hands of the Lord, according to the covenant that he had made with them. When they were oppressed, it was the Lord who sold Israel into the hands of oppressors on account of their sin. When they were delivered, it was the Lord who raised up the judge to deliver them because of his compassion. Both judgment and deliverance (compassion) flowed from God's absolute covenant faithfulness (cf. Deut. 4:31; Judg. 2:18–19).

For the writer of Judges, the immediate hope on the horizon was a king, in particular, David, the king after God's own heart. In later OT history, however, it became obvious that most of the kings were no better at leading the people in keeping covenant than the judges had been. In fact, their perpetual unfaithfulness eventually caused Israel to be cast out of the land. Even the few outstanding, godly kings like David, who brought peace that lasted beyond their own reigns, were not able to change their own hearts or the hearts of the people. Books written by those standing further down the stream of OT history paint substantially the same bleak picture of covenant unfaithfulness on the part of the Lord's people. The OT story as a whole still cries out, like the book of Judges, for a leader who would be faithful to God and lead his people in keeping covenant.

That cry is answered in Christ, who was from the tribe of Judah, descended from David. Deuteronomy shows that Israel's faithfulness would flow from knowing the Lord. Jesus, God himself, became a man and dwelt among the Israelites, revealing the Lord to humankind in an unprecedented way (e.g., John 1:14; 1 John 1:1–2), being the exact radiance of God's glory (Heb. 1:3). Israel was to remember the great deliverance event of the exodus as the ultimate expression of God's care. Jesus brought about an even greater deliverance, saving his people even from sin and death by his own death on the cross. The unfaithfulness of the Israelite kings cost the nation the promised land. Jesus' faithfulness secures heaven itself for his people. The judges did not bring about permanent peace. Jesus, David's son, brought an enduring kingdom and peace that lasts even into eternity. Judges urged the need for a king, from Judah, who would fear God, live in covenant faithfulness, and lead the people in doing the same. Jesus, who was from the tribe of Judah, feared God and lived in perfect obedience to the Father (e.g., Phil. 2:5–8), giving his people an example to follow. Even more, by sending the Holy Spirit, he was able to do what David could not do: break the cycle of sin, judgment, crying out, and deliverance, and actually change the hearts of God's people, enabling them to be faithful to God.

God's compassion during the period of the judges pointed to the greater compassion and permanent peace he would bring through Jesus, the better deliverer. In Jesus, God's repeated acts of compassion in the OT have a foundation; God's mercy, grounded in the cross, extends "backward" as the basis for his compassion in Judges.

Furthermore, in Christ the judges are viewed from a new perspective. As recognized in the history of interpretation, Heb. 11 focuses on the judges as examples of faith, not as examples of failed covenantal leadership. Hebrews is not simply idealizing these characters the way interpreters in the Second Temple period did. Rather, Hebrews' interpretation is grounded in a "second reading," as described earlier, in rereading the OT in light of what has happened in Christ. In the setting of a first reading, the judges are complex characters, sometimes acting in faith, sometimes falling short. But once Christ had come, the struggling faith of the judges was understood as looking forward to Christ. In the end, in Christ, they were seen not as bringing the solution, but as acting in faith that God would bring the solution. Which he did, in Christ.

The book of Judges called its original audience to follow a king who would lead them in knowing and fearing the Lord. In its place in the Christian canon, it issues the same call, except that the king to follow is no longer David but Jesus.

Bibliography

Block, D. *Judges, Ruth*. NAC 6. Broadman & Holman, 2002.

Brettler, M. Z. "The Book of Judges: Literature as Politics." *JBL* 108 (1989): 395–418.

Davis, D. R. "A Proposed Life Setting for the Book of Judges." PhD diss., Southern Baptist Theological Seminary, 1978.

Klein, L. R. *The Triumph of Irony in the Book of Judges*. Almond, 1988.

O'Connell, R. H. *The Rhetoric of the Book of Judges*. Brill, 1996.

Rogers, R. *A Commentary upon the Whole Booke of Iudges*. T. Man, 1615.

Webb, B. G. *The Book of Judges*. JSOT, 1987.

8

Ruth

MURRAY D. GOW

The book of Ruth tells how a Bethlehemite family of Elimelech and
Naomi, with sons Mahlon and Chilion, migrates to Moab to escape fam-
ine. All the males die there, leaving Naomi with two widowed daughters-
in-law. The story develops around the return of Naomi with Ruth to
Bethlehem, the events leading to Ruth's marriage to Elimelech's kinsman,
Boaz, and the birth of Obed, forming part of David's genealogy.

History of Interpretation

Various theories for the book's purpose have been proposed, several of
which will be considered briefly in what follows.

In Praise of Khesed

This has ancient rabbinic support; according to R. Ze'ira, it was written to "teach how great is the reward of those who do deeds of *kindness*"
(*Ruth Rabbah* 2.14). Some modern scholars concur (such as Würthwein;
Rebera, "Ruth"; Bush). If *khesed* were the main theme, however, then the
word might be expected at more focal points, particularly 2:11–12; 4:14–15.

God is petitioned to do *khesed* (1:8), while Boaz (2:20) and Ruth (3:10) are praised for showing it. The actors are praised for behavior conforming to an accepted ideal, rather than the ideal itself being encouraged or praised. *Khesed* is an important but auxiliary motif to the purpose of the story.

To Encourage Performance of the Levirate

This is unlikely. Regardless of whether the story of Ruth is truly an instance of levirate marriage, we observe that the social customs are neither evaluated nor praised but are simply background to the story.

As a Defense of Mixed Marriage

This would counter the exclusiveness of Ezra and Nehemiah by showing that even the great David had Moabite ancestry—suggested as long ago as 1816 by Bertholdt (Rowley 173n1) and widely accepted in the early twentieth century, but rarely today. Lacocque is a modern exponent (84–116). If this view were correct, then Ruth must be dated late; but many scholars believe the book is preexilic. Rowley explains that Ruth might as easily be read as supporting Ezra and Nehemiah, since Ruth is shown to be a true convert.

To Support Inclusion of Gentiles

Ruth is viewed not as a defense of mixed marriage per se, but as encouraging acceptance of believing Gentiles. Though it was considered important to uphold the exclusiveness of Israel's monotheism, the book of Ruth demonstrates the possibility of Gentiles truly converting to Yahwism (cf. Herbert 271). Sakenfeld (4) sees the story as "legitimizing an inclusive attitude towards foreigners, perhaps especially towards foreign women." Irrespective of whether we accept an inclusivist purpose for the book, Ruth's ethnicity and inclusion are clearly significant motifs. But it should be recognized that in contexts where her Moabite ancestry receives mention, it is followed by a corresponding note, either of her relationship as daughter-in-law of Naomi (Ruth 2–3 passim), or, in Ruth 4:5, 10, that she is wife of Mahlon. So, while Ruth's Moabite ancestry *is* seen as a problem, her marriage to Boaz is legitimized by its intention to continue Mahlon's lineage. Rather than defending mixed marriages in general, the book of Ruth is defending one particular marriage. Hence, the inclusion motif is important but is not the central purpose of the book.

To Demonstrate Divine Providence

The book may intend to show God's hand in events giving rise to the Davidic monarchy. Theological elements are certainly found in the story, such as the providential answering of prayer, the reversal motif, the practice of *khesed*, and so on (see "Theological Aspects of Ruth," below). But the paucity of *narrative* theological statements suggests that the theological dimension is in some respects auxiliary to the purpose.

Nontheological Readings

Various literary readings have appeared in the last quarter century, such as Sasson's formalist-folklorist approach, focusing on the literary artistry of Ruth while playing down "theology" (qualified in the foreword to Sasson's second edition). It is true that narrative statements of Yahweh's activity are rare in Ruth and the exceptions (1:6; 4:13) could be interpreted as part of Israelite belief in Yahweh's general providence over matters of fertility. Thus, Rebera's discourse analysis (esp. "Ruth," 181–244) shows that Ruth, like the author of the succession narrative, prefers to embed theological evaluation in dialogue. The author appears reluctant to show his or her own *tendenz*, if there is one.

"Realistic" Readings

Against a long tradition of interpreting Naomi, Ruth, and Boaz as "ideal" characters worthy to be emulated, some recent studies have highlighted the gritty realism of the story (e.g., Fewell and Gunn). Naomi is viewed as a self-centered character, whose silence after Ruth's magnificent vow of loyalty indicates her hardness of heart. Moreover, she ignores Ruth when lamenting her emptiness before the women of Bethlehem, thus showing that she considers Ruth a liability. Likewise, Boaz has been portrayed as protective of his own interests in a self-righteous manner, needing a push before he is prepared to act as redeemer.

However, while the story *is* realistic, Naomi's behavior in the first chapter conforms better to the effects of depression. It may be Naomi's concern for Ruth that leads to her attempt to persuade her to stay in Moab, recognizing that a Moabite might not be welcome in Bethlehem. As for Boaz, he treats Ruth kindly enough, but in view of the age difference, he may have considered himself an unlikely candidate for Ruth's amour. When she did signal her availability, he responded with alacrity, but also with restraint, out of respect for the nearer kinsman.

As an Apology for David

This may be necessary because of David's Moabite ancestry. According to Deuteronomy, Moabites were prohibited from entering the congregation till the tenth generation (Deut. 23:3–6). However, Ruth shows that despite her Moabite ancestry, she was a person of great worth, loyal to Mahlon's kinsfolk, loyal to his memory in seeking marriage to his kinsman Boaz, and a true believer in the God of Israel. Moreover, the events leading to the marriage of Boaz to Ruth, followed by the birth of Obed, were providential. The portrayal of the marriage as leviratic also served as part of its justification. The information that this concerned David's ancestry is kept to the end so as not to arouse audience prejudice prematurely (cf. 2 Sam. 12:1–7).

The advantages of interpreting Ruth as "Davidic apologetic" are that it incorporates and accounts for the focus on *khesed* and explains the preponderance of kin terms, especially where Ruth's Moabite ancestry receives mention. Thus, in Ruth 2 the inclusion motif is emphasized, and Ruth 4 settles the legal basis of the marriage. Further, it accounts for the inclusion of theological elements, including providential answers to prayer and Ruth's conversion, as well as the restraint of the author in making narrative theological statements. Finally, the apologetic interpretation accounts for a feature unique in Hebrew narrative—a genealogy placed at the end rather than the beginning.

Canonical Context

Ruth's canonical position was fluid. The MT locates Ruth in the *Ketubim* (Writings) but with divergent order. The Babylonian Talmud (*B. Bat.* 14b) places Ruth ahead of Psalms. The Ben Asher family of Masoretes (see *BHS*) place Ruth at the head of the Megillot, directly after Proverbs, perhaps answering the question, "Who can find a worthy woman?" (Prov. 31:10 AT). A later tradition found in the Ben Hayyim family of manuscripts has Song of Songs first, since it is read at Passover, followed by Ruth, read at the Feast of Weeks/Pentecost.

The LXX, followed by the Latin Vulgate and Christian tradition, sets Ruth between Judges and Samuel. This appears to be supported by Josephus (*C. Ap.* 1.8), who speaks of a twenty-two-book Hebrew canon. Jerome in his prologue to Samuel and Kings knows of a twenty-four-book canon but claims a twenty-two-book canon was accepted by most Jews, this being achieved by combining Judges with Ruth and Lamentations with Jeremiah.

By contrast, the Babylonian Talmud (*B. Bat.* 14b–15a) and 2 Esd. 14:44–46 hold to a twenty-four-book canon; Ruth and Lamentations are separated from Judges and Jeremiah respectively and included with the Megillot.

These two traditions—one setting Ruth in the Former Prophets (so Moore 294–95; Linafelt xviii–xxv), the other among the Writings (so Campbell 32–36; Bush 5–9)—each have ancient support. Any preference must be tentative, but it is worth recognizing the interpretative consequences. The setting in the Writings would attribute to Ruth a liturgical purpose, including a fertility motif. Placing Ruth between Judges and Samuel sets Ruth in the transition from tribal federation to monarchy, emphasizing Ruth's role in salvation history.

The sorry tale of Judg. 17–18 is set in Ephraim, the territory of Jeroboam, and the terrible events of 19–21 relate to Gibeah, the home of Saul. Both stories are replete with cultic elements, but cult gone awry. By contrast, Ruth, set in Bethlehem, lacks cultic elements. Instead, we find a community of ordinary people serving Yahweh as they go about the business of everyday life and showing *khesed* to those in need. This reflects favorably on the origins of David, while showing us a better way.

Theological Aspects of Ruth

Prayer and Blessing

Ruth has been thought theologically sparse since only 1:6 and 4:13 provide narrative statements of Yahweh's activity, but as Rebera observes, Ruth mostly embeds theological evaluation in dialogue ("Ruth," esp. 181–244). This has significance for seeing that prayer constitutes a significant part of the "theology." Prayers or blessings include 1:8–9; 1:20–21; 2:11–12; 3:10 (compare Gen. 15; 30:16, 18; and Ps. 127:3, where reward is linked with progeny); 2:19–20; 3:10–11; 4:11–12; and 4:14–15. All these prayers/blessings have fulfillment in the marriage of Ruth to Boaz, and a lineage leading to David. The author of Ruth expected readers to be alert to the work of God in answering prayer, as should we today. Like Boaz, we too may be called to participate in answering our own prayers.

Providence

As well as the divine activity suggested by answered prayer, providence is discerned in the reversal of the famine (1:6), leading to Naomi's return with Ruth. While chapters 2 and 3 lack overt narrative theological statements, chapter 2 first introduces us to Boaz and tells us that Ruth "happened" upon the field of Boaz, hinting at divine overruling. This echoes the meeting of Abraham's servant and Rebekah (Gen. 24, also overruled by Yahweh). There is *concurrence* between divine and human activity. Although God is the unseen actor, this is very much a human story, about "people, living as they are to live under God's sovereignty, who proceed to work it out" (Campbell 29). Thus, Naomi counsels Ruth to act boldly to achieve marriage with Boaz. Ruth plays her part, but after she returns home in the morning, Naomi counsels her to wait to see how the matter falls out. While Boaz can be relied on, ultimately the result is in the hand of God. Chapter 4 likewise points to concurrence. Boaz does his part by marrying Ruth, but we are told that it is Yahweh who gives conception (4:13).

Reversal Motif

In the OT, it is Yahweh who "sends poverty and wealth," who "lifts the needy from the ash heap" (1 Sam. 2:7). In the book of Ruth, there is a movement from emptiness to fulfillment. Elimelech migrates to escape famine, but dies; his sons marry, and die. Naomi, widowed and childless, is left with two childless widows. News of Yahweh's providence prompts her return, commencing a movement from deprivation to restoration. In the remainder of the story, Naomi's immediate needs are met through Ruth's industry and Boaz's generosity. The levirate marriage of Boaz and Ruth plus the birth of Obed restores the lineage.

Conversion/Inclusion

Ethnicity is first mentioned when the sons of Elimelech marry Moabite women (1:4). Once Ruth arrives in Bethlehem, it becomes a key issue because there she is a foreigner (Rebera, "Ruth," 156–59), being mentioned at 1:22; 2:2, 6, 10, 21; and twice during the legal case (4:5, 10). But it is important to observe a countermovement for Ruth's inclusion. When Naomi counsels Ruth to return to her god(s) and people, Ruth vows allegiance to Naomi in life and death, declaring, "Your people shall be my people and your God my God" (1:16 NRSV), showing that she is a convert to Yahwism. Whenever Ruth's Moabite origins are mentioned in the remainder of the story, there are kin terms linking her to her Judahite family. She is described as "daughter-in-law of Naomi," and by both Naomi and Boaz as "my daughter" (2:2, 8). Chapter 2 highlights Boaz's actions to include Ruth; he approves her actions and gives her protection (2:8–16). Ethnicity is not an issue in chapter 3 but arises again in 4. Twice in the legal case, Ruth is described as Moabite, but the countering fact of her marriage to Mahlon is then immediately mentioned. Hence, the marriage of Boaz and Ruth is viewed as leviratic and legally justified. When the women give their final blessing at the birth of a son, Ruth's inclusion is complete. Now she is "your daughter-in-law who loves you, who is [worth] more to you than seven sons" (4:15 NRSV).

Kindness (Khesed)

This motif has long been recognized (1:8; probably 2:11; definitely 3:10; 2:20, supported by Rebera ["Yahweh or Boaz?"]). Earlier studies of the Hebrew word *khesed* pointed to the loyalty expected in reciprocal relationships, implying obligation. But in the OT *khesed* contains a gracious element: in human relationships it "mainly describes exceptional acts of one human to another, meeting an extreme need outside the normal run of perceived duty, and arising from personal affection or goodness" (Andersen 81). The KJV comes close to this sense with "loving-kindness." God in his grace and mercy shows such kindness to humans; he does not owe salvation but gives it freely. The nature of the divine-human relationship means we cannot give *khesed* to God. But if we have experienced God's loving-kindness, we can, like Ruth and Boaz, demonstrate it in our relationships with others (cf. Mic. 6:8; Matt. 25:34–40; 1 John 4:7–12).

The Place of Women

Whether or not we posit a female author (cf. Campbell 22–23), Ruth's story is unique among ancient literature in celebrating female friendship (cf. Daube 35–37). The power of the story lies largely in the hands of female characters. Elimelech, his wife, and sons commence the story, but the males soon die. Thereafter, Ruth and Naomi are the main characters, with Boaz being given third place. In a sense, his is a supporting role, and the heroine receives the larger role, highlighted by the fact that it is Ruth, not Boaz, who proposes marriage in 3:9. Boaz has the lead role in the legal case, but it is the women who again take the lead in 4:13–17. In the patrilineal genealogical material (4:18–22), Ruth drops from view, but this should not be viewed negatively. The outsider has now been integrated into Israelite history. The story of Ruth is a reminder of how much women with chutzpah can achieve even in a society that restricts their roles.

Davidic Messianic Role

The marriage of an Israelite to a Moabite and the genealogy of David are key elements in understanding the book of Ruth. The book seeks to justify the marriage of Boaz to Ruth, a believing Gentile, and hence to defend the claim of the Davidic line to the throne. There is a move in recent scholarship to favor some such view (e.g., Gerleman; Gow; Hubbard; Nielsen; Block), although with a variety of views as to the possible historical setting for such an apologetic. As part of the lineage of the Davidic king, the story becomes messianic in character, partially fulfilled in the Davidic monarchy, but widened out to bring blessing to the whole world through a future descendant of David (cf. Gen. 12:1–3; Matt. 1; Rom. 1:3).

Bibliography

Andersen, F. I. "Yahweh, the Kind and Sensitive God." Pages 41–88 in *God Who Is Rich in Mercy*. Anzea, 1986.

Atkinson, D. *The Message of Ruth*. InterVarsity, 1983.

Block, D. *Judges, Ruth*. NAC. Broadman & Holman, 1999.

Bush, F. *Ruth, Esther*. WBC 9. Word, 1996.

Campbell, E. F. *Ruth*. AB 7. Doubleday, 1975.

Daube, D. *Ancient Jewish Law*. Brill, 1981.

Farmer, K. *The Book of Ruth*. NIB. Abingdon, 1998.

Fewell, D. N., and D. M. Gunn. "'A Son Is Born to Naomi': Literary Allusion and Interpretation in the Book of Ruth." *JSOT* 40 (1988): 99–108.

Fisch, H. "Ruth and the Structure of Covenant History." *VT* 32 (1982): 425–37.

Gerleman, G. *Ruth*. Biblischer Kommentar, Altes Testament Bd. 18. Neukirchener Verlag, 1981.

Gow, M. *The Book of Ruth*. Apollos, 1992.

———. "Prayer and Providence in the Book of Ruth." *Journal of the Christian Brethren Research Fellowship* 101 (1985): 9–25.

Hals, R. M. *The Theology of the Book of Ruth*. Fortress, 1969.

Herbert, A. "Ruth." Pages 271–72 in *Peake's Commentary on the Bible,* ed. M. Black and H. Rowley. T. Nelson, 1962.

Hubbard, R., Jr. *The Book of Ruth*. NICOT. Eerdmans, 1988.

———. "Ruth, Theology of." *NIDOTTE* 4:1153–57.

Lacocque, A. *The Feminine Unconventional*. Fortress, 1990.

Larkin, K. J. A. *Ruth and Esther*. OTG. Sheffield Academic Press, 1996.

Linafelt, T. *Ruth*. Berit Olam. Liturgical Press, 1999.

Merrill, E. "The Book of Ruth: Narration and Shared Themes." *BSac* 142 (1985): 130–41.

Moore, M. S. *Ruth*. NIBCOT 5. Hendrickson, 2000.

Nielsen, K. *Ruth*. OTL. SCM/Westminster John Knox, 1997.

Porten, B. "The Scroll of Ruth: A Rhetorical Study." *Gratz* 7 (1978): 23–49.

Prinsloo, W. S. "The Theology of the Book of Ruth." *VT* 30 (1980): 330–41.

Rebera, B. "The Book of Ruth." PhD diss., Macquarie University (Sydney, Australia), 1981.

———. "Yahweh or Boaz? Ruth 2.20 Reconsidered." *BT* 36 (1985): 317–27.

Rowley, H. H. "The Marriage of Ruth." Pages 171–94 in *The Servant of the Lord and Other Essays on the Old Testament*. Blackwell, 1965.

Sakenfeld, K. D. *Ruth*. Interpretation. John Knox, 1999.

Sasson, J. M. *Ruth*. 2nd ed. JSOT, 1989.

Trible, P. *God and the Rhetoric of Sexuality*. Fortress, 1978.

Van Wolde, E. *Ruth and Naomi*, trans. J. Bowden. SCM/Smyth & Helwys, 1997.

Wegner, P. "Ruth." *EDBT*, 694–96.

Younger, K. L., Jr. *Judges, Ruth*. NIVAC. Zondervan, 2002.

9

Samuel

BRIAN E. KELLY

Samuel was originally one book that was divided into two when the Hebrew text was translated into Greek, to accommodate the work to the length of scrolls typically used in classical antiquity. The books of Samuel are concerned primarily with the establishment of the monarchy in Israel under Saul, followed by the rise and reign of David. The prophet Samuel oversees the introduction of the monarchy, as kingmaker to both Saul and David. Through the actions of these three, the order of Israel's life and faith is fundamentally changed, with reverberations felt throughout the rest of the Bible.

Highlights in the History of Interpretation

A dominant approach of patristic and medieval exegesis was to seek out the "spiritual" senses of Scripture as a strategy for reading the OT as a prophetic Christian book. These methods entailed imaginative typological and eschatological interpretations of the text. Thus, David's career and rejection, then subsequent elevation as king in Jerusalem, were seen as prefiguring Christ, who was crucified, then enthroned in glory in heaven.

Reformation exegesis was much more restrained in any typological comparisons it drew between David and Christ. The Reformers essentially affirmed the Antiochene approach to Scripture, insisting that "the literal sense *is* the spiritual sense." Thus, in Calvin's *Sermons on 2 Samuel* the moral and theological meaning of the text is deduced primarily from historical exegesis and close attention to the literary context. For Calvin, of course, the OT's witness was to Christ, and the NT authoritatively interpreted the OT. David's kingdom and God's promises to him had their proper meaning within that context and anticipated their fulfillment in Christ's kingdom.

Much scholarly work in the nineteenth and twentieth centuries concentrated on literary source-critical approaches as a way of dealing with perceived tensions and doublets in the text. Thus, Wellhausen (1871) argued that an early promonarchic stratum (1 Sam. 9:1–10:16; chs. 11, 13–14) had been combined with a postexilic, antimonarchic stratum (1 Sam. 8; 10:17–27; chs. 12, 15) to produce a hybrid text of conflicting attitudes. The view that the present text has arisen from numerous expansions and elaborations of earlier sources has remained influential up to recent years (see, e.g., McCarter's commentary).

Rost (1926) strongly advocated the view that older, originally separate documents had been combined to produce the present work. Rost identified 1 Sam. 4:1b–7:1 + 2 Sam. 6 as an independent "Ark Narrative," 1 Sam. 16:14–2 Sam. 5 as an original "History of David's Rise," and 2 Sam. 9–20 + 1 Kings 1–2 as a "court history" (the "Succession Narrative" [SN]) detailing how Solomon became king. This last work Rost considered to be one of the world's earliest examples of eyewitness historiography.

Noth's (1943) hypothesis of a "Deuteronomistic History" (DH) understood 1–2 Samuel to be part of a continuous narrative (Deuteronomy–2 Kings) composed by a single exilic writer using traditional materials. The extent of pre- and postexilic redactions of DH and additions thereto (and even the existence of such a work) remains a hotly debated subject. In Noth's view, the underlying documents of 1–2 Samuel were incorporated into DH with comparatively little redaction. Noth held that 2 Sam. 21–24 was an "appendix" of miscellaneous Davidic materials added to the narrative after DH was divided into separate books.

Rost's basic identification of documents is still broadly accepted, although the precise boundaries, dating, genre, and theme of these postulated documents (especially SN) are now much more disputed. Gunn, for example, defines SN as a novella rather than historiography. Keys rejects the inclusion of 1–2 Kings in the narrative on grounds of style and content, and holds that the real theme of 2 Sam. 9–20 is not succession but David's sin and punishment. Complementary observations are made by Stoebe (2 Sam. 9–20 shows that despite David's failings, the kingship perdured under God's hand) and Provan (the narrative unmasks pretensions to "wisdom" that are not rooted in God and the divine Torah).

Gunn's work signaled a turn from a concern with source criticism and historiography to final-form literary approaches concentrating on the poetics and ideology of the book. Brueggemann's postliberal commentary follows this approach in focusing on the imaginative force and rhetoric of the presentation, and the relationship between religious faith and political power. More adventurous is Jobling's postmodern handling of 1 Samuel, which presents an eclectic set of subversive readings engaged with contemporary issues (including class, polity, gender, ethnicity).

Recent writing in a more conservative vein argues against the older documentary theories (that differing outlooks in the text arose from the untidy growth and conflation of various traditions over time), holding instead that 1–2 Samuel should be read as a complex, intentional unity with a coherent theological message.

Long's study of Saul's reign rejects Wellhausen's thesis of conflicting pro- and antimonarchic documents underlying 1 Sam. 8–15 by distinguishing the narrator's voice from that of the characters (some of whom express anti-Saul rather than antimonarchic views). Following Halpern and Edelman, Long argues next that the complex account(s) of Saul's election as king is comprehensible and not confused, once we grasp the different stages involved in king-making in the ancient world. Finally, Saul's rejection as king makes sense as well, when we adopt the appropriate reading strategy for deducing the author's intent. Saul's rejection arises from his unwillingness to submit to the new authority structure of the theocracy, whereby the king must obey the word of the Lord mediated through God's prophet (cf. 1 Sam. 12:13–15, 24–25).

On the structural level, Klement concentrates on the ending (2 Sam. 21–24), arguing that it is no "appendix" or miscellany but a carefully composed conclusion to the work as a whole. The conclusion provides the key to the grand, chiastic structure of the book and its basic theological message. Klement identifies other structural patterns throughout the book as evidence of a sophisticated and intentional artistic design.

The advantage of these recent approaches is that they support a final-form reading of the text that is not arbitrary but takes seriously the original literary integrity of the Samuel scroll. (In contrast, it must be remembered that DH is a scholarly postulate without any manuscript basis.) This allows the message of 1–2 Samuel to be heard on its own terms, and not just as an episode within a larger narrative.

Message of 1–2 Samuel

The two major themes of the work are monarchy and Yahweh's word. The offices of king and prophet (along with the priesthood in its oracular activity) exist by God's election and call (1 Sam. 2:28; 3:4; 10:24; 13:14; 2 Sam. 6:21; 7:8) for the protection and rule of his people.

On monarchy, Klement identifies the message at the center of the chiasm of 2 Sam. 21–24 (and thus the summative message of the book) as an affirmation of Yahweh's covenant with David as an institution for Israel's good. David utters the two poems in this section (2 Sam. 22:2–51; 23:1–7), which celebrate Yahweh's "everlasting covenant" and "steadfast love to David and his descendants forever." At its outset this work shows Israel to be afflicted both by the corrupt priesthood in Shiloh and the oppression of the Philistines. Yahweh acts to reverse the unhappy state of his people, first by answering Hannah's prayer for a son. The birth of Samuel, the faithful prophet and kingmaker, sets in train the course of actions that will culminate in David's kingship. Hannah's song of thanksgiving (1 Sam. 2:1–10), with its prayer that Yahweh "will give strength to his king and exalt the horn of his anointed one," has close verbal and thematic correspondences with the concluding poems. Thus, these two poetic sections function as chiastic bookends for the whole work.

Hannah's prayer is fulfilled in the achievements of David's reign at its best (2 Sam. 5–10; cf. 23:3–4), where he appears as the ideal ruler. Monarchy as such is not really faulted in the book (cf. Deut. 17:14–20). The issue turns rather on the *type* of king. Shall he be a figure of human political conceiving and choice ("a king for ourselves," 1 Sam. 8:18–20; 12:19 NRSV), or one of Yahweh's choice and for his purpose ("I have provided for myself a king [David]," 1 Sam. 16:1 NRSV)? Saul is rejected as king because of his failure in the fundamental matter of obedience to God's word as mediated by his prophet Samuel. (A parallel theme to this is the rejection of the priestly family of Eli for dishonoring God; 1 Sam. 2:31.) With the departure of Yahweh's spirit (1 Sam. 16:14), Saul declines into depression and madness. David, on the other hand, is presented as Yahweh's chosen king, Spirit-endowed and Saul's "better" (1 Sam. 13:14; 15:28; 16:13). Pious, brave, and innocent of treachery against Saul, David gains the throne through Yahweh's choice and

Israel's willing assent (2 Sam. 5:1–3). He subjugates the neighboring states, thus securing "rest" for the people (2 Sam. 5:17–25; 8:1–14). David's conquest of Jerusalem provides a capital for his kingdom and a final resting place for the ark of the covenant, uniting in one place the religious and political symbols of the nation (2 Sam. 5:6–14; 6:1–23). In turn, Yahweh's commitment to David extends to his descendants in the gracious promise of a secure and enduring dynasty and kingdom (2 Sam. 7:16; 23:5).

David thus appears as a worthier and more effective ruler than Saul, whose reign ends in apostasy and national disaster (1 Sam. 28, 31). The apogee of David's obedient reign (and the sign of divine blessing upon it) is indicated in 2 Sam. 8:15–18, the brief note on his administration, and in 2 Sam. 9, his exemplary treatment of Mephibosheth. Overall, however, David's reign has an ambiguous character. Blessing turns to curse in the following chapters, where David's later disobedience and decline are candidly revealed, along with the destructive consequences these have, both for his family and for the nation (2 Sam. 11–20). Thus, David in his later years fails to realize the blessings promised to his own kingship. His rule is beneficial only insofar as he submits himself to Yahweh and his commands. The various intrigues involving a wayward David and his equally wayward sons indicate that politics (both sexual and power) posited on a calculating worldly wisdom leads only to disaster. Nevertheless, Yahweh's covenant grace prevails. Unlike Saul, David himself is not rejected (cf. 1 Sam. 15:26), nor is Yahweh's promise done away with.

The theme of Yahweh's word is presented in two major ways. First, the narrative shows that Yahweh's word, mediated by his prophets or the priestly oracle, determines the course of history, in declaring blessing or judgment. We are informed that early in this period "the word of Yahweh was rare" (1 Sam. 3:1 AT), but everything is changed for Israel by the time Samuel reaches adulthood (1 Sam. 3:19–4:1a). What Yahweh's messengers declare will surely happen (cf. Deut. 18:21–22). Thus, Samuel first anoints Saul as "leader" (*nagid*) in obedience to Yahweh's word, with confirming signs to follow (1 Sam. 9:16; 10:1–9), then David as his successor, again as Yahweh directs (1 Sam. 16:12, fulfilled in 2 Sam. 5:1–3). Through Nathan, David also receives the promise of a dynastic line and the assurance that his successor will build a temple (2 Sam. 7:11–16), matters whose fulfillment lies outside this book (1 Kings 2:12; ch. 6).

Conversely, the word of divine judgment is given in the declarations against Eli's house and descendants and is fulfilled in subsequent events (1 Sam. 2:31–36; 3:11–14; cf. 4:11; 22:18–19); in the rejection of Saul (15:26, specifically for spurning Yahweh's word, v. 23; cf. 31:6; 2 Sam. 6:21); and against David (2 Sam. 12:10–12; 24:13; cf. chs. 13–20; 24:15).

Second, Yahweh's word is given to admonish and guide. Samuel reproaches the sinful people in Yahweh's name (1 Sam. 8:10; 10:18–19), as well as giving specific instructions to Saul (9:27; 10:3–8; 15:2–3, 17–19). Nathan and Gad are also specifically sent by Yahweh to counsel David or rebuke him with God's word (2 Sam. 7:4–5; 12:1; 24:11–12, 18), and David responds fittingly on each occasion. In addition, David inquires of God through the oracles given by Ahimelech and Abiathar (1 Sam. 22:10; 23:2, 4; 30:8; 2 Sam. 2:1; 5:19, 23), and enjoys success. By contrast, a disobedient Saul is denied a word from God and has recourse instead to necromancy (1 Sam. 28:6–7). In these ways, the book teaches that the exercise of kingship within Israel must be subject to Yahweh's word.

Notwithstanding its final canonical location (within a history extending from Genesis to 2 Kings), 1–2 Samuel can be read on its own terms as a reflection of the early days of the Judahite monarchy (cf. 1 Sam. 27:6). The work holds up the Davidic covenant as the grounds for national and dynastic confidence, along with the necessity of royal obedience to the prophetic word. Hence, it perhaps sought to inculcate a similar response from the first descendants of David and his people, in the difficult days that followed the division of the kingdom (cf. 1 Kings 14:8).

1–2 Samuel and the Canon

The book has close connections with many other parts of the canon. First, whatever we make of Noth's hypothesis (DH), 1–2 Samuel is the natural narrative bridge from Judg. 17–21, when "there was no king in Israel" (21:25 NRSV), to the history of the monarchy in 1–2 Kings. Kings also reflects many of the themes in Samuel, such as the fulfillment of the dynastic promise (cf. 1 Kings 2:4; 8:25; 9:4–5), Solomon as the appointed temple builder (5:5), and the backward look to David as the standard for evaluating his successors (3:14; 11:6, 38; 2 Kings 14:3; 15:3; 18:3; 22:2).

The closest canonical connection is with 1 Chron. 10–21, which is directly dependent on 1–2 Samuel in recounting the narratives of Saul and David. The Chronicler significantly recast and modified his sources, omitting most of the material on Saul and on David's rise to power and subsequent family problems. The Chronicler's chief interest here was to extol the public role of David as king and cofounder with Solomon of the Jerusalem cult. At the same time, David's sinful census, with its disastrous consequences for Israel (2 Sam. 24) has a pivotal place in the Chronicler's presentation (1 Chron. 21)—recognition that David could be a source of ill for the nation as well as good.

The presentation of David as musician and composer of psalms (1 Sam. 16:18, 23; 18:10; 2 Sam. 22:1–51; 23:1–7) was no doubt a fountainhead of the tradition that ascribes large parts of the Psalter to David (whether by or about him). The superscriptions on many of the psalms (3, 7, 18, 34, 51, 52, 54, 56, 57, 59, 60, 63, 142) associate these compositions with incidents in 1–2 Samuel and indicate how these psalms were anciently understood and related (perhaps midrashically) to David as the model worshipper of Yahweh.

1–2 Samuel and Theology

The historical development of messianism is especially dependent on this work. In its presentation of David and the Davidic covenant, the book provided the soil for later messianic hopes and conceptions. As Yahweh's "anointed" (*mashiakh*, 1 Sam. 2:10; 2 Sam. 22:51; 23:1), David is elected and upheld by God for the blessing of his people. As the ideal king and recipient of the promise, David becomes the archetype of prophetic hopes for a successor in the troubled later centuries of Judah's existence (Mic. 5:2–5; Isa. 11:1–2; Jer. 23:5; Ezek. 37:24). That trajectory continues throughout the NT in its expectation of a Messiah in David's line (cf. Matt. 1:1; 21:9; Luke 1:32; John 7:42; Rom. 1:3; Rev. 5:5). However, the NT goes beyond comparisons, emphasizing that Jesus as Messiah also surpasses and *contrasts* with David, a great but flawed human being (cf. Acts 2:25–36).

Historically speaking, 1–2 Samuel has played a significant role in the articulation of political theology, especially in medieval and early modern reflection on the meaning of Christian kingship. In portraying the (Davidic) king as the representative and mediator of God's own kingship, charged with securing the continued identity of the people through military leadership against external threats and by ensuring justice and right worship at home, 1–2 Samuel presents data on the political task with which Christians must constantly reckon. Yet the book is also skeptical (at least) about human kingship, which is not fundamental to Yahweh's rule or Israel's identity, and is sometimes inimical to these, especially when the prophetic word is spurned. Similarly, while no state today understands itself as a Christian theocracy, the exercise of political and judicial power must always be tempered by the church's proclamation of the gospel (which centers on the present and coming kingship of Christ). Otherwise, the state will lose sight of its own identity and the concept of right that it exists to defend.

Bibliography

Brueggemann, W. *First and Second Samuel*. John Knox, 1990.

Edelman, D. *King Saul in the Historiography of Judah*. Sheffield Academic Press, 1991.

Gordon, R. P. *1 and 2 Samuel*. Zondervan, 1986.

Gunn, D. *The Story of King David*. Sheffield Academic Press, 1978.

Halpern, B. *The Constitution of the Monarchy in Israel*. Scholars Press, 1981.

Jobling, D. *1 Samuel*. Liturgical Press, 1998.

Keys, G. *The Wages of Sin*. Sheffield Academic Press, 1996.

Klement, H. *II Samuel 21–24*. P. Lang, 2000.

Long, V. P. *The Reign and Rejection of King Saul*. Scholars Press, 1989.

McCarter, P. K. *I Samuel*. Doubleday, 1980.

———. *II Samuel*. Doubleday, 1984.

McConville, J. G. "Law and Monarchy in the Old Testament." Pages 69–88 in *A Royal Priesthood?*, ed. C. Bartholomew et al. SHS. Zondervan/Paternoster, 2002.

Provan, I. "On 'Seeing' the Trees While Missing the Forest: The Wisdom of Characters and Readers in 2 Samuel and 1 Kings." Pages 153–73 in *In Search of True Wisdom*, ed. E. Ball. JSOTSup 300. Sheffield Academic Press, 1999.

Rost, L. *The Succession to the Throne of David*, trans. M. D. Rutter and D. M. Gunn. Sheffield Academic Press, 1982.

Stoebe, H. J. *Das zweite Buch Samuelis*. Chr. Kaiser, 1994.

10

Kings

RICHARD S. HESS

The books of 1 and 2 Kings provide a theologically laden interpretation of the history of the Israelite monarchy from the death of King David until the end of the monarchy itself. Although some chapters contain administrative records (1 Kings 4), building descriptions (chs. 6–7), rituals (ch. 8), and prophecies and prayers (2 Kings 19), the dominant genre is narrative. For this reason, the primary theological exposition of the text is indirect, through narrative rather than clear exhortative forms. Major theological themes lie behind the narratives and also inform the other types of literature. They concern the nature of God and his relation to his people, including matters such as divine sovereignty and human responsibility, judgment, covenant, worship of God alone, and the Messiah.

Foremost in the books of Kings is the reign of the single God of Israel. Along with it is the habitual practice of God's people, who turn from him to worship other gods. The centers of contrast between the one true God of Israel and the other gods of the nations appear in 1 Kings 11 and 18 and 2 Kings 17. In 1 Kings 11 Solomon reaches the low point of his reign. The king's many foreign wives entice him to leave his devotion to the God who had given him his power, and they divert him to the worship of other gods. This brings about divine judgment: the division of the kingdom and the capitulation to compromise the sole worship of the LORD God in the northern kingdom. A few of the oldest members from that time of division may still have been alive when Elijah challenged the wholesale worship of Baal by Jezebel and Ahab (1 Kings 18). The absolute victory of Israel's God over Baal in the contest and the subsequent execution of all the priests of Baal (and Asherah) demonstrated the uncompromising nature of God's demand for sole worship by his people. The final grand statement of God's sovereignty is that of 2 Kings 17, where the author reflects on the fall of the northern kingdom, attributing it to the worship of other deities and the abandonment of the one true God of Israel. As the writer observes, the consequence of these actions, begun before the time of Solomon, was to bring other nations into the land (through Assyrian deportation and resettlement) so that the countryside became even more polytheistic. This result would contrast with the practice of southern kings, such as Hezekiah and Josiah, who to varying degrees sought to abolish idolatry. The author of Kings praises them for doing so. Nevertheless, the preponderance of kings in the south tolerated the worship of other deities and at times even supported it. Thus, even the righteousness of Josiah was unable to prevent God's judgment for the worship of other deities, as announced by his prophetess (2 Kings 22:17).

Perhaps nowhere is the contrast more vivid between Israel's God and those of other nations than in the verbal challenges that the invading Assyrian king Sennacherib and his representatives raise against Hezekiah and the inhabitants of Jerusalem. In 2 Kings 18:22, 32–35; 19:10–12, 18 appears the Assyrians' charge that the God of Israel cannot deliver the Israelites from their hand. They suggest that this is the reason Hezekiah closed the outlying worship centers (high places) and brought all formal worship into Jerusalem. The Assyrians point to the inability of all the other national gods to deliver their countries from this superpower. However, it is the response of Hezekiah and of the prophet Isaiah that seals the fate of the enemy. In particular, 19:18–19 brings the matter to a conclusion: "They have thrown their gods into the fire and destroyed them, for they were not gods but only wood and stone, fashioned by men's hands. Now, O LORD our God, deliver us from his hand, so that all kingdoms on earth may know that you alone, O LORD, are God." Thus the collapse of the northern kingdom demonstrates the failure to worship God alone, while the survival of Judah shows how faith in God can bring about unexpected miracles.

It also ties together the theology of God as one, and of God alone with absolute sovereignty over all nations of the world. That power is able to bring the greatest nation of the era, Assyria, to its knees. God's majesty becomes worthy of the greatest of structures that the wealthiest of the kings can build (1 Kings 6–7). The form and structure of this temple, as well as the multitude of sacrifices, represent imports from the surrounding lands—a transformation of the forms and style of the media of worship toward the honoring of the one true Deity.

Solomon's prayer of dedication for the temple sets forth another key theological principle of God's dealings with his people and their kings. In 1 Kings 8:44–53 Solomon prays to God that the nation might receive forgiveness when it sins. If at that time it turns back to God, even if it has been deported to a foreign land, God will forgive and restore the nation to his blessing. This possibility is based upon the sense of Israel as specially chosen by God. God affirms this promise to Solomon in 1 Kings 9:3–10. There he promises that Solomon and his descendants will be treated according to the degree to which they wholeheartedly worship God and refrain from worshipping other gods. God has entered into covenant with them, and their responsibility is to remain faithful to him and refuse the worship of foreign deities. Thus, God promises retribution—punishment for those who turn away from him and blessing for those who follow him. Solomon himself becomes a model of both elements and, in the sequence of blessing followed by judgment, a foreshadowing of the experience of the nation (both northern and southern kingdoms) through the remainder of its history to the exile. Solomon's early search for wisdom from God (1 Kings 3), organization of his kingdom and palace (ch. 4; 7:1–12), and above all his construction and dedication of Yahweh's temple (chs. 5–6; 7:13–9:9)—all indicate a king in obedience to the divine will, leading his people to great prosperity and devotion to God. Nevertheless, his success with other nations, and the consequent diplomatic marriages, compromise his faith and lead to prophecies of judgment (11:1–13). At Solomon's death, the kingdom is divided. Thus, the mixture of some faithfulness with apostasy, characteristic of Solomon's reign and the beginning of the book, anticipates the subsequent history of the monarchy.

Although the title of the books suggests the dominant focus, and the doctrine of retribution is most pronounced with the leaders of the two kingdoms, the prophetic stories that lie in the heart of the books also depict encounters of personal faith and the responses of God. Unlike earlier and especially later prophets, Elijah and Elisha, along with others of their generation, are gifted with amazing abilities to work miracles that complement their verbal messages. Their miracles most often provide life for those to whom they minister. This could include the miraculous provision of food. As with the story of Solomon, many of these are anticipated in the initial words and acts that introduce the prophet Elijah. In 1 Kings 17, where he first appears, he is kept alive by ravens that feed him. In the same chapter, he preserves alive the widow of Zarephath in Sidon and resurrects her son from death. These miracles would be repeated again and again by Elijah and other prophets who represent living signs of God's power for life. Indeed, even in death the body of the prophet can remain a source of life for others (2 Kings 13:21). The best-known event of Elijah is his challenge of the prophets of Baal, a challenge that ends in their execution (1 Kings 18). This, however, is the other side of the story. God provides signs through his prophets. For those who believe and respond, these are life-giving. For those who reject the signs and turn away from God, they lead to death. The lives of the prophets and the people with whom they deal, kings and commoners, illustrate the love of God for all people (even outside Israel, as at Zarephath), and the need to respond with personal faith. It is this ministry of life that forms the closest living model of Jesus' life and work in the NT. Again and again the miracles that Jesus performs are anticipated by prophets' works in the books of Kings. Further, Elijah ministered in Sidon, outside Israel, and Elisha assisted Naaman the Syrian; these episodes anticipate the mission of Jesus to the Gentiles (Luke 4:25–27).

The theology of the prophetic movement also provides a critique of simple assumptions of retribution. The prophetic word of 1 Kings 13:2, proclaimed against the apostasy of the northern kingdom at the time of the division, names King Josiah, three centuries into the future, as a figure who will bring to an end the sacrifices of the unauthorized northern kingdom altars. Thus the fulfillment of judgment is postponed for three hundred years. In addition, this prophet, one of the first to appear in Kings, is duped by a northern prophet to disobey God's word. As a result, he pays for it with his life. An even greater indictment of the prophets as a group is 1 Kings 22:19–38, which depicts God orchestrating a lying spirit to mislead the court prophets. The prophet Micaiah tells this story, which demonstrates the universal effects of the sin nature on all humanity—even on the prophets (cf. also Gehazi in 2 Kings 5:20–27). No one group or individual is without sin, and the book of Kings makes this clear among kings, commoners, and prophets.

The role of the Lord's anointed, the Messiah, provides a key theological theme throughout the books and ties the whole together. It plays a dominant role in the three great sections of the text: the Solomonic era from David's last days to the division of the united monarchy (1 Kings 1–11); the prophetic challenge from Elijah's conflict with Ahab until the death of Athaliah and the rise of Joash (1 Kings 17–2 Kings 11); and the downfall of the northern kingdom followed by the last kings of Judah (from Hezekiah to Zedekiah) and the destruction of Jerusalem (2 Kings 17–25). The Messiah, or anointed one in Israel, would have been considered the ruling king in Jerusalem, a descendant of the line of David. In each of these sections in the books, that line is threatened. The first book of Kings opens with David near death. As the recipient of the promise of perpetual rule in Jerusalem for his dynasty (2 Sam. 7), the succession is crucial. The establishment of Solomon amid the brutality of the first three chapters demonstrates that God's promise is secure. Solomon's own apostasy ultimately leads to the division of the kingdom, a split that threatens the power of Solomon's successor, Rehoboam. Nevertheless, the line continues. Although Elijah's battle is with the northern kingdom's Ahab and Jezebel, the southern kingdom's ruler, Jehoram, married their daughter Athaliah. Both he and their son, Ahaziah, followed the worship practices of Ahab. Upon Ahaziah's death, Athaliah declared herself ruler and sought to execute the remainder of the royal family. The high priest protected one royal prince, Joash, by hiding him. Despite the attempt to destroy the line of the Messiah, God protects it in the person of young Joash, who becomes king after Athaliah's execution. The collapse of the northern kingdom and then of the southern kingdom, as described in detail at the end of Kings, raises the specter of no continuation of the line. Due to the people's sins, not even the righteousness of kings such as Hezekiah and Josiah can save the kingdom (2 Kings 20:16–19; 23:25–27). Yet, as with Solomon, Rehoboam, and Joash, there remains an heir to the line of David. The book concludes with Jehoiachin alive and well in exile in Babylon. Thus, both hope and God's anointed remain and can be found throughout the books of Kings. The promise of the Messiah is not lost.

Bibliography

Hess, R., and G. Wenham, eds. *Zion, City of Our God.* Eerdmans, 1999.

Knoppers, G. *The Reign of Jeroboam, the Fall of Israel, and the Reign of Josiah.* Vol. 2 of *Two Nations under God.* HSM 53. Scholars Press, 1994.

McConville, J. G. *Grace in the End.* Zondervan, 1993.

Noth, M. *The Deuteronomistic History.* JSOTSup 15. Sheffield Academic Press, 1981.

Provan, I. *1 and 2 Kings.* OTG. JSOT, 1997.

Rad, G. von. *Old Testament Theology.* 2 vols. Harper & Row, 1965.

Wiseman, D. *1 and 2 Kings.* TOTC. InterVarsity, 1993.

11

Chronicles

MARK A. THRONTVEIT

The two books of Chronicles were originally written as one by an anonymous author. Known as "The Book of the Events of the Days" in early rabbinic tradition, the translators of the Septuagint divided it in two and, assuming it was a supplement to the earlier history of Samuel and Kings, gave it the misleading title "The Things Omitted." Much of the earlier history is omitted (e.g., the history of the northern kingdom). Other parts are simply summarized (e.g., David's military victories in 1 Chron. 18–20; cf. 2 Sam. 8–23), or presented in significantly different ways (e.g., the account of Manasseh in 2 Chron. 33; cf. 2 Kings 21). The title "1–2 Chronicles" comes from Jerome, translator of the Latin Vulgate, who in the fourth century CE suggested that "a chronicle of all of sacred history" would better describe the contents of a work beginning with Adam and ending with Cyrus.

History of Interpretation

Chronicles has not received the attention it deserves in either Jewish or Christian theological circles for several reasons. In the first place, the LXX's misleading title ("Things Omitted") and its questionable placement among the historical books in subsequent Bibles have led some—who fail to recognize its inherently theological, if not homiletical, nature—to challenge its historical accuracy. Specifically, the question of the historical reliability of these books has dominated the discussion from earliest times. In the precritical period, though synagogue and church alike assumed Chronicles' reliability, its apparent supplementary character rendered it useful only in instances where Samuel–Kings was silent. This, more than any other reason, accounts for Chronicles being the least utilized portion of Scripture.

Second, only a few exemplars of Chronicles have appeared at Qumran. No ancient commentaries have survived the rabbinic neglect of these books that continued into the medieval period. This may be because both the Talmud and Mishnah regarded Chronicles as a book for the sages to ponder, rather than the laity. What pondering was done, however, saw Chronicles essentially as Ezra's midrash on the earlier histories of Samuel and Kings.

Third, the earlier, widespread assumption that any differences between Chronicles and Samuel–Kings were the result of tendentious alteration has been successfully challenged, especially since the critical work of Wilhelm de Wette in the nineteenth century. Text-critical investigation demonstrates the care with which the Chronicler used his sources. The sources were closer to the Lucianic version of the LXX and the parts of Samuel found among the Dead Sea Scrolls (4QSam[a]) than to the Masoretic text of Samuel, as previously thought. Understanding this fact accounts for many of the discrepancies and means that Chronicles must not simply be read as a theologically motivated rewriting of the earlier history.

Fourth, until recently it was supposed that Chronicles and Ezra-Nehemiah comprised two parts of a single composition, relating Israel's history from Adam to the postexilic community under Nehemiah. As a result, Chronicles was read through the theological lens of Ezra-Nehemiah. Today that assumption is questioned. While these books do display similarities of style, language, and general outlook, they differ on a number of key theological matters. These include the nature of "Israel," the Davidic covenant, the function of the Levites, the place and function of prophecy, retributive justice, the Sabbath, mixed marriages, and the significance of the exodus. Though still debated, an emerging consensus recognizes the separate authorship of Chronicles and Ezra-Nehemiah as well as the integral nature of the genealogies in 1 Chron. 1–9 to the work as a whole. This favors a date during the Persian period, somewhere in the fourth century BCE. Decisive here are the lists of David's descendants in 1 Chron. 3:17–24, extending to the late fourth century, and the inhabitants of Jerusalem in 9:2–34, extending to the early fourth century.

Finally, since interpretation depends upon prior decisions regarding setting, extent, and time of composition, the variety of opinion regarding the dating of Chronicles and its relationship to Ezra-Nehemiah has generated a corresponding variety in elucidation. For instance, a previous generation, following Noth, interpreted the Chronicler's work as a response to a rival Samaritan faction formed in the wake of the 332 BCE fall of the Persian Empire. Today, however, the schism is placed at the end of the second century, rendering the Chronicler's so-called anti-Samaritan polemic anachronistic. Among contemporary scholars, Welten, who continues to maintain the common authorship of Chronicles and Ezra-Nehemiah, has extensively investigated the Chronicler's battle reports and suggests that the early-third-century hostilities between the Ptolemies and the Seleucids are a more appropriate interpretative milieu for Chronicles. Those who reject common authorship are divided in their understanding of the Chronicler's context. Some find a likely backdrop in the early years of the return (529–515 BCE), influenced by the prophetic call of Haggai and Zechariah to rebuild the temple (e.g., Freedman; Newsome; Braun). Others suggest the need for faithfulness amid the tense repercussions of the Persian suppression of the Tennes revolt in 351–348 BCE (Williamson). Japhet, convinced that Ezra-Nehemiah precedes Chronicles, suggests the end of the fourth century, early in the Hellenistic period.

In sum, it is only in the modern period that Chronicles has been read for the very different historical and theological portrayal of Israel that it presents. From the ancient period through the middle of the twentieth century, Samuel–Kings provided the biblical version of that history, with Chronicles providing "supplementary" information. This, in turn, resulted in the substantial neglect of these books in rabbinic, patristic, medieval, and Reformation exegesis.

Context and Message

Comparisons between Chronicles and Samuel–Kings frequently fail to recognize the very different contexts of the two works. Samuel–Kings sought to answer the pressing questions of exiles who had experienced the fall of Jerusalem to Nebuchadnezzar II, the destruction of the temple, the end of Davidic rule, and deportation to Babylon in 587/6 BCE. Chronicles, however, addresses the postexilic community that, following the Persian defeat of the Babylonians under Cyrus in 539 BCE, had returned from Babylon to live under Persian rule and worship in the rebuilt Jerusalem temple. Instead of asking, "Why did this happen to us?" they sought their relationship with the past: "Who are we?" "Are we still the people of God?" and "What do God's promises to David and Solomon mean for us today?"

Chronicles addresses these questions by retelling the story of Israel and inviting the people to see themselves as living in situations of either "exile" or "restoration." Exilic situations result from unfaithfulness, serving other gods, or failing to seek the Lord. Even if literal exile does not occur, the loss of God's blessing inevitably results in devastating consequences. Blessing can be restored, however, through repentance (2 Chron. 7:14). Thus, Chronicles encourages the struggling postexilic community to seek and serve a loving and merciful God, who awaits their response and hears their prayers.

Contribution to the Canon

Modern versions of the Bible, the LXX, and the Vulgate group 1–2 Chronicles with the historical books, placing them between 2 Kings and Ezra-Nehemiah. In this arrangement, the prophet Malachi's announcement that Elijah will precede the arrival of the Lord immediately precedes the Gospels' portrayal of John the Baptist as the forerunner of the Messiah in the opening books of the NT. In the Hebrew canon, however, these books of Chronicles follow Ezra-Nehemiah in the Writings. This placement at the end of the Hebrew Bible is theologically significant in two ways. First, on the basis of chronology, Ezra-Nehemiah should close the Hebrew Bible. But their presentation of the return from exile soon deteriorates into the familiar problems of the postexilic community, issues only partially resolved in the reforms of Ezra and Nehemiah. The Chronicler's presentation of the return, though confined to a brief citation of the Cyrus Edict, ends with an invitation: "Whoever is among you of all his people, may the LORD his God be with him! Let him go up!" (2 Chron. 36:22–23 NRSV). This conclusion avoids the less-than-optimistic state of affairs found in Ezra-Nehemiah and lets the Hebrew canon end on a note of hope.

Second, the books of Chronicles function as a culminating summary and integration of all that has gone before. This is especially evident regarding worship. Disparate cultic considerations from the Psalter, the institution of Levitical functionaries, and the reorganization found in the Priestly Code are synthesized and brought together, thereby positing worship as the cohesive element lacking in the fragmented postexilic community. A Hebrew canon concluding with Chronicles also explains Luke 11:51, "From the blood of Abel to the blood of Zechariah," as a time frame extending from the murder of Abel (Gen. 4) to the murder of Zechariah (2 Chron. 24:20–22). No other OT book utilizes more biblical material than Chronicles, which draws extensively upon all three sections of the Hebrew canon. While the books of Samuel and Kings serve as the primary source, citations of or allusions to Genesis, Exodus, Leviticus, Numbers, Deuteronomy, Joshua, Judges, Ruth, Ezra, Nehemiah, several psalms, Isaiah, Jeremiah, Lamentations, Ezekiel, Zephaniah, and Zechariah all appear. In this way, Chronicles anticipates aspects of contemporary "inner-biblical exegesis."

Theological Significance

The explication of Chronicles' theological significance begins with recognition of its overall structure. A long genealogical introduction (1 Chron. 1–9) is followed by a presentation of the period of the united monarchy under David and Solomon (1 Chron. 10–2 Chron. 9). A third section discusses the period of the divided monarchy, concentrating upon the kings of Judah (2 Chron. 10–28). The work concludes with an interpretation of the period from Hezekiah to the Babylonian exile as a reunited monarchy (2 Chron. 29–36). Of these four, the long second section is fundamental for the Chronicler's theological position. The reigns of David and Solomon are presented as a unity. Within this unity, two divine promises establish the Chronicler's central theological principles. In the first of these, God promises David that his throne will be established forever, through his descendants (1 Chron. 17:3–14). In the second, God promises Solomon that all who humble themselves, pray, seek God's face, and repent will be forgiven (2 Chron. 7:12–22). The genealogies that precede this crucial section depict the people's original unity. By means of these twin principles of king and cult, the section that follows evaluates the kings of Judah, who ruled during the divided monarchy, following the reign of Solomon. The final section presents Hezekiah as a new David and Solomon, who restores that vision of all Israel, reunited under a Davidic king, and worshipping at the Jerusalem temple following the collapse of the north.

Within this narrative framework, three theological themes are especially important. First, the temple dominates these pages as the primary symbol of God's presence with Israel. The Chronicler's presentation of the reigns of David and Solomon consists, essentially, of David's preparations for and Solomon's construction of the temple. David's preparations for the temple include bringing the ark to Jerusalem (1 Chron. 13–16), military conflicts that consolidate the empire and amass the required wealth (18–20), the purchase of Ornan's threshing floor as the temple site (21:25), and the more-detailed preparations found in chapters 22–29, including numerous lists of temple personnel and God's placement of the blueprint for its construction into David's hands (28:19). Solomon is explicitly designated as the temple-builder (28:6, 10; cf. 28:5; 29:1), and the presentation of his reign has been drastically rewritten to emphasize this role (2 Chron. 1–9). Abijah's programmatic speech (ch. 13), often deemed a compendium of the Chronicler's theological interests, cites the northern tribes' abandonment of the temple and establishment of a rival priesthood as the primary form of their rebellion, in contrast to the faithful worship practiced in the south (13:8–12). Furthermore, every subsequent king is evaluated regarding the faithful preservation of proper worship in the temple. Finally, the Chronicler's concern for identity and continuity, first seen in the genealogies that linked the postexilic community with their roots (1 Chron. 1–9), is intimately tied to the temple. The central presence of the Levites within those genealogies suggests that worship, properly led by the Levites and carried out in the Jerusalem temple, provides the means by which the community connects with the traditions of the past.

"All Israel" is a second theological theme of the Chronicler. Earlier scholarship insisted that the Chronicler was uninterested in the northern kingdom after its fall to Assyria, and that his concept of "Israel" was narrowly exclusive and confined to the southern tribes of Judah and Benjamin, as in 2 Chron. 11:3; 12:1. The situation, however, is more complex than this. In 10:16; 11:13, "all Israel" clearly refers to the north, and in 9:30 both north and south are meant. Actually, the Chronicler's understanding of Israel is quite inclusive and seeks to revitalize the ancient ideal of the twelve tribes by regularly depicting the enthusiastic and unanimous participation of "all Israel" at major turning points in the narrative. These include the accessions of both David and Solomon to the throne (1 Chron. 11:1; 29:20–25), the capture of Jerusalem (11:1–4), the transfer of the ark (13:1–4, 5–6; 15:3; 16:3), and the construction and dedication of the temple (2 Chron. 1:2; 7:8). Consequently, the Chronicler sees the division of the kingdom into north and south as a tragic severing of God's people by Jeroboam's rebellion and Rehoboam's inability to deal with the insurrection (13:4–12). His hope is that "all Israel," north as well as south, will again be one. To that end, there are frequent calls for the people to return to common worship in Jerusalem, most notably, those of Abijah and Hezekiah that frame the period of the divided monarchy (13:4–12; 30:6–9).

A third theological theme is the Chronicler's so-called principle of immediate retribution, the view that obedience leads to blessing and disobedience leads to judgment. First Chronicles 28:9 first expresses this: "If you seek him, he will be found by you; but if you forsake him, he will abandon you forever" (NRSV). The blessing/judgment is immediate in that it occurs within the individual king's lifetime. Although many instances are regularly cited, a careful reading of Chronicles indicates that this characteristic principle of the Chronicler is neither as mechanical nor as simplistically applied as previously thought. In 2 Chron. 7:14 God promises Solomon, "If my people . . . humble themselves, pray, seek my face, and turn from their wicked ways, . . . I will forgive their sin and heal their land" (NRSV). When one remembers that judgment is typically preceded by prophetic warning (e.g., 16:7–9; 20:15–17; 36:15–16), and that judgment is withheld after a repentant response to prophetic warning (e.g., 12:5–8; 15:1–15), it is clear that the Chronicler is more concerned with repentance and restoration than retribution.

Bibliography

Allen, L. *The First and Second Books of Chronicles*. NIB. Abingdon, 1999.

Braun, R. *1 Chronicles*. WBC 14. Word, 1986.

Coggins, R. J. *Samaritans and Jews*. John Knox, 1975.

Freedman, D. N. "The Chronicler's Purpose." *CBQ* 23 (1961): 436–42.

Graham, M. P., et al., eds. *The Chronicler as Historian*. JSOTSup 238. Sheffield Academic Press, 1997.

Graham, M. P., and S. L. McKenzie, eds. *The Chronicler as Author*. JSOTSup 263. Sheffield Academic Press, 1999.

Japhet, S. *I and II Chronicles*. OTL. Westminster John Knox, 1993.

Kalimi, I. *Zur Geschichtsschreibung des Chronisten*. BZAW 226. De Gruyter, 1995.

Kelly, B. *Retribution and Eschatology in Chronicles*. JSOTSup 211. Sheffield Academic Press, 1996.

Klein, R. W. "Chronicles, Book of 1–2." *ABD* 1:992–1002.

Newsome, J. D. "Towards a New Understanding of the Chronicler and His Purposes." *JBL* 94 (1975): 201–17.

Noth, M. *The Chronicler's History*. JSOTSup 50. Sheffield Academic Press, 1987.

Selman, M. *1 Chronicles* and *2 Chronicles*. TOTC. InterVarsity, 1994.

Throntveit, M. "Linguistic Analysis and the Question of Authorship in Chronicles, Ezra and Nehemiah." *VT* 32 (1982): 201–16.

————. "The Relationship of Hezekiah to David and Solomon in the Books of Chronicles." In *The Chronicler as Theologian,* ed. M. P. Graham et al. JSOTSup 371. T&T Clark, 2003.

————. *When Kings Speak.* SBLDS 93. Scholars Press, 1987.

Welten, P. *Geschichte und Geschichtsdarstellung in den Chronikbüchern.* Neukirchener Verlag, 1973.

Williamson, H. G. M. *1 and 2 Chronicles.* NCB. Eerdmans, 1982.

————. *Israel in the Book of Chronicles.* Cambridge University Press, 1977.

12

Ezra

JOHN J. BIMSON

At first sight the book of Ezra is an uneven work that does not yield easily to theological interpretation. More than half of it concerns the first wave of returning exiles, from the decree of Cyrus in 538 to the completion of the temple in 516 BCE. Ezra does not appear until chapter 7, after a gap of almost sixty years. Events of the intervening decades are sketched out of chronological order in 4:6–23. Ezra's return to Judah with another group of repatriates is the substance of chapters 7–10, which cover the events of a single year (458/457). A particular barrier for Christian interpreters is the book's uncompromising Jewishness, expressed in its concern for genealogical purity and restored temple worship.

History of Interpretation

The book of Ezra was originally read as the first part of a longer work that included the book of Nehemiah (as is evident from the earliest listings of canonical books). The division into two books occurred in the early church, for reasons that are not clear, and is first attested in the third century. It is not found in Hebrew Bibles until 1448. The current arrangement should not be allowed to obscure the essential unity of Ezra-Nehemiah, and this article should be read in conjunction with that on the book of Nehemiah.

Precritical Christian interpreters either viewed the books of Ezra and Nehemiah typologically (e.g., the crises over mixed marriages point to the need to keep in mind at all times the distinction between the children of God and the children of this world) or held up the personal piety of the two men as examples to be emulated. Some commentators, taking a lead from Jerome's comment that Ezra means "the Helper" while Nehemiah means "the Consoler sent by the Lord," treated the two books as works of help and consolation in times of trouble. One bishop of the Church of England saw the combined work of Ezra and Nehemiah prefiguring and legitimizing the alliance of church and state, while another clergyman preferred to see the two as examples of the passive and active virtues of religion.

In sharp contrast to rabbinic tradition, which saw Ezra as the father of Judaism, Christian critical scholarship of the nineteenth and early twentieth centuries generally had a negative view of the man and of the book that bears his name. Postexilic Judaism was widely regarded as inferior to the earlier prophetic faith, and this naturally affected assessment of Ezra-Nehemiah. The view of Torrey, that Ezra was a fictional creation of the Chronicler, was an extreme expression of this tendency. Others merely played down Ezra's role or judged him a failure. Recent scholarship has moved toward a more positive assessment, though there are occasional attempts to revive the view that Ezra never existed.

According to the Babylonian Talmud (*B. Bat.* 15a), Ezra was the author of Ezra-Nehemiah and 1–2 Chronicles, and a few modern scholars have defended this view. The majority, however, have held that the anonymous author of Chronicles was responsible for putting Ezra-Nehemiah into more or less its final form (e.g., Clines; Blenkinsopp). This view has affected theological interpretation insofar as a uniform theological stance has been perceived throughout 1–2 Chronicles and Ezra-Nehemiah.

The two works certainly share many points of common interest (summarized by Blenkinsopp 53). However, since the 1970s a number of scholars have put more weight on the distinctive ideas and emphases of Ezra-Nehemiah and have strongly challenged the common authorship theory (notably Williamson, *Israel*, 5–70). The independent authorship of Ezra-Nehemiah has gained ground in recent years, but the issues are complex and by no means resolved.

The Message of Ezra

Because there is particularly clear evidence for diverse sources within Ezra-Nehemiah, interpretation of the work has tended to become bogged down in historical-critical issues (Childs 626–30). Notable exceptions are

Eskenazi's attempt to read Ezra-Nehemiah as a literary whole and Williamson's analysis ("Nehemiah") of the work's "overall theological shape" (see further in ch. 13, "Nehemiah"). Studies such as these, which focus on the message of the final literary product, facilitate theological interpretation. They show that it is important to read the book of Ezra not only as a literary whole but also as the first part of a larger work. The key theological issue that emerges is the continuity of God's purposes for Israel. Given that the return from exile fell far short of a return to preexilic status, was there any sense in which the earlier "Israel" could still be said to exist? Did its God-given identity and purpose remain intact?

The book of Ezra answers "yes" to these questions in a variety of ways. The opening verse establishes the continuity of God's purpose from before the exile. It is repeatedly emphasized that the temple was rebuilt on its original site (2:68; 3:3; 5:15; 6:7); it was thus to be seen as a reconstruction of, not a replacement for, Solomon's temple (cf. 6:3–4; 1 Kings 6:2, 36). The very same vessels that Nebuchadnezzar had looted from the temple were restored to it (1:7–11). Personnel were appointed according to "the Book of Moses" (6:18). Ezra himself was descended from the chief priests of the preexilic age (cf. 7:1; 1 Chron. 6:14). The genealogies of chapters 2 and 8 also serve to affirm continuity. The returned exiles represented all twelve tribes (6:17; 8:35) and could indeed be called "the people of Israel" (6:16, 21).

The continuation of God's purposes is also affirmed by means of typology (Williamson, *Ezra*, 84–86). The book of Ezra shares with Isa. 40–55 the view that the return from exile was a second exodus. Thus, 1:11b echoes the language of Exod. 3:17; 33:1; and so on, and may also recall a much earlier bringing-out from Babylonia (cf. Gen. 15:7). This exodus typology is not confined to the first wave of returnees. Ezra's own "journey up from Babylon" began on the first day of the first month (cf. 7:9 NRSV). But the party did not actually leave the River Ahava until the twelfth day of that month (8:31), a date that Ezra may have chosen because of its resonance with Exod. 12:2–6.

The use of typology indicates that the God who had created his people from unpromising beginnings and rescued them from slavery could be trusted to act in similar ways again.

Canonical Context

Because of its focus on continuity with the past, Ezra-Nehemiah may seem to stand at the end of a canonical trajectory, looking back rather than forward, and content with the Jewish community's status within the Persian Empire. References to the prophecies of Jeremiah (1:1), Haggai, and Zechariah (5:1; 6:14) might also seem to suggest that a point of fulfillment has been reached.

But this is to miss a powerful strand of discontent and a sense of only partial fulfillment. The attitude toward Persian kings is ambivalent. On the one hand they are God's agents for the reconstruction of the community; on the other, what the people experience under their rule is nothing less than bondage (9:8–9). In Ezra 6:22 the Persian king is called "the king of Assyria," and this is unlikely to be an error; it is probably an "indication that there is in the end little to choose between Empires" (McConville 38).

The restored Israel repeats the sins of earlier Israel (9:10–14), and the list of those who pledged to divorce their foreign wives in Ezra 10 provides no reassurance that the cycle of iniquity and shame is thereby ended. Indeed, the conclusion to Nehemiah provides yet more instances of backsliding after a time of renewed commitment to the covenant laws. These indications of a hope that is only partially fulfilled are reminders that the postexilic community was only one stage in the unfolding of God's purposes.

It is important to remember this when considering that community's exclusiveness. The racial purity established by genealogies, and safeguarded by the dissolution of mixed marriages, sounds like narrow nationalism and exclusive soteriology, but it must be set in both a historical and canonical context. Historically, the concern for continuity and legitimacy can be seen as a reaction to particular circumstances: the identity of the community was precarious and in need of safeguards. Canonically, the tenor of Ezra-Nehemiah is balanced by a more open attitude to Gentiles in other OT narratives (e.g., Gen. 41:50–52; Josh. 6:25; Ruth 4:13–17), and in numerous prophetic texts (e.g., Isa. 49:6; 56:3–8; Zech. 8:20–23). Thus, OT Israel lived within the tension of its election and its priestly role to the nations (encapsulated in Gen. 12:2–3; Exod. 19:5–6). Sometimes one aspect of the polarity is to the fore, sometimes the other.

Theology

Viewed historically, the restoration of Jerusalem and Judah was piecemeal, dogged by setbacks and reversals, and proceeding without any coherent plan. However, the theological perspective of Ezra-Nehemiah invites us to see the guiding hand of Israel's God in seemingly disconnected events. This explains the writer's disregard for chronological order and the fact that gaps of several years, and in one case decades, are passed over in silence (see further in ch. 13, "Nehemiah").

Related to this perspective is the writer's wish to trace the will of God in the affairs of state. A secular historian might explain the repatriation of Judean exiles and the rebuilding of the temple in terms of the Persian Empire's policy toward the religious life of its subject peoples. Ezra-Nehemiah acknowledges the important role of Persian kings (Ezra 1:1–4; 6:1–12), but wants us to know that it was Yahweh who stirred up the spirit of Cyrus and put a desire to beautify the temple into the heart of Artaxerxes (1:1; 7:27).

Ezra 6:14 is particularly telling. The writer informs us that the temple was completed by "command of the God of Israel and the decrees of Cyrus, Darius and Artaxerxes, kings of Persia." Artaxerxes actually reigned after the period mentioned in vv. 14–15, but he is included because all three Persian kings fulfilled the command of the God of Israel. The eye of faith does not sharply divide the acts of God from the actions of human rulers.

Bibliography

Blenkinsopp, J. *Ezra-Nehemiah*. OTL. SCM, 1989.

Childs, B. *Introduction to the Old Testament as Scripture*. SCM, 1979.

Clines, D. J. A. *Ezra, Nehemiah, Esther*. NCB. Eerdmans, 1984.

Douglas, M. "Responding to Ezra: The Priests and the Foreign Wives." *BibInt* 10 (2002): 1–23.

Eskenazi, T. *In an Age of Prose*. SBLMS 36. Scholars Press, 1988.

McConville, J. G. "Diversity and Obscurity in Old Testament Books: A Hermeneutical Exercise Based on Some Later Old Testament Books." *Anvil* 3 (1986): 33–47.

Torrey, C. *The Composition and Historical Value of Ezra-Nehemiah*. BZAW 2. Ricker, 1896.

Williamson, H. G. M. *Ezra and Nehemiah*. OTG. JSOT, 1987.

———. *Israel in the Books of Chronicles*. Cambridge University Press, 1977.

———. "Nehemiah: Theology of." *NIDOTTE* 4:977–82.

13

Nehemiah

JOHN J. BIMSON

The book of Nehemiah was originally a continuation of the book of Ezra, with which it is linked both thematically and narratively (see further in ch. 12, "Ezra"). There is little justification for separating the two books apart from the fact that Neh. 1:1 begins a first-person narrative by Nehemiah, who has not previously received mention (the Nehemiah of Ezra 2:2 is a different character). The twelve-year gap between the last events of Ezra 7–10 and Neh. 1:1 is not sufficient to warrant the break, since a much longer period separates Ezra 7–10 from Ezra 1–6. The separation into two books has done much to hinder a theological interpretation of the whole.

History of Interpretation

A good deal of precritical Christian interpretation focused on the personal qualities of Nehemiah: his humility, his devotion to God's suffering people in spite of his privileged position at the Persian court, and his ability to combine dependence on God with practical forethought. His success at rebuilding Jerusalem was sometimes seen as an example of how to revive the church while being prepared at all times for opposition.

More recently, theological interpretation has tended to be submerged beneath historical-critical issues. As Childs reports, many have approached Ezra-Nehemiah "with the assumption that its proper interpretation depends on establishing an accurate historical sequence of events" (630). To this end, a good deal of debate has centered on the chronological relationship between Nehemiah and Ezra. Many scholars have perceived difficulties with the traditional order of their arrival in Jerusalem and have amended and reordered the text accordingly. In fact, other approaches to the perceived problems are available, making such drastic solutions unnecessary (Kidner 146–58; Williamson, *Ezra*, 55–69).

Much scholarly contention has surrounded the identity of the law book whose legislation is enacted in Ezra-Nehemiah. Since Ezra was "a scribe skilled in the law of Moses" (Ezra 7:6 NRSV), it is logical to assume that the legislation he set out to teach was contained in "the Book of Moses" referred to in Ezra 6:18 and (with slight variations) in Neh. 8:1, 14; 10:29; and 13:1. The traditional view is that this book was the Pentateuch, but some source critics have doubted whether the complete Pentateuch could have existed as early as the fifth century BCE. Even if the antiquity of the Pentateuch is accepted, questions remain. Some of the legislation enacted in Ezra-Nehemiah seems to have no exact counterpart in the Pentateuch, and this has led Houtman to argue that it was based on a different work, which has not survived. This conclusion would have obvious implications for Ezra-Nehemiah's connection with other parts of the canon. However, it is possible to argue that the application of pentateuchal laws must have undergone development, to adapt them to changed circumstances (Williamson, *Ezra*, 90–98). If this is accepted, there is no good reason to doubt that the Pentateuch was the book that the postexilic community recognized as authoritative.

A refreshing attempt to read Ezra-Nehemiah as a literary whole is that of Eskenazi. She identifies a tripartite story structure: "potentiality" (Ezra 1:1–4, in which the objective is defined), "process of actualisation" (Ezra 1:5–Neh. 7:73), and "success" (Neh. 8:1–13:31, in which the objective is realized). The main theme is identified as "how the people of God build the house of God in accordance with authoritative documents." Eskenazi goes on to argue that the concept of the "house of God" expands to include the community (175–76)—a suggestive but contentious reading of the text.

A recent interdisciplinary reading of the book of Nehemiah (Tollefson and Williamson) has also contributed to an understanding of the book as a whole. The authors apply a model of cultural revitalization formulated by anthropologist A. F. C. Wallace in the 1950s, thereby finding that the sequence of events in the book of Nehemiah corresponds closely to the six phases described by the model. This explains better than most previous attempts how the various sections of the book cohere, and it removes the ground for suspicion that the present text has suffered serious dislocation. For example, the sequence of events in Neh. 8–10 corresponds well to the "Cultural Transformation Phase" of Wallace's model, and occurs exactly at the point predicted by the model. There thus is no reason to reposition these chapters, as many have suggested. On the other hand, the authors do not claim that the compiler of Ezra-Nehemiah recorded everything exactly as it happened. "Although the compiler may have altered the chronological order of certain specific events, his presentation may yet portray the social process taken as a whole more faithfully than any one of the sources at his disposal in isolation" (Tollefson and Williamson 65).

A recent study by Oded Lipschits, although focusing on Neh. 11, is also fruitful for theological interpretation of the book as a whole. Lipschits sees this chapter as a major climax, full of allusions to other parts of Ezra-Nehemiah, in which Jerusalem's past glory foreshadows a utopian future.

Canonical Context

The book of Nehemiah not only concludes the narrative begun in the book of Ezra; it also contains the latest events to be found in the historical books of the OT (assuming that Esther's King Ahasuerus = Xerxes and not Artaxerxes I). In the Jewish arrangement of the OT books, Ezra-Nehemiah is usually followed by Chronicles, which concludes the canon. This is surprising in view of the fact that thematically (leaving aside matters of authorship), Ezra-Nehemiah is the sequel to Chronicles. Chronicles may have been placed last because it effectively reviews the whole sweep of OT history, from Adam to the return from exile.

Nehemiah provides an ambivalent conclusion to the OT's historical narratives. On the one hand, Jerusalem has been furnished with a new wall, the population of the city has increased, and various reforms have been instituted to deal with religious and social problems. In view of these successes, the triumphant tone of chapters 8–12 seems entirely appropriate. On the other hand, the final chapter reminds us how easy it is for abuses and failures to recur, even after the most solemn act of dedication. Furthermore, the political context is viewed negatively: although God's people are back in the land God promised to their ancestors, they are "slaves" there.

The land's rich yield, instead of being theirs to enjoy, "goes to the kings whom you have set over us because of our sins; they have power also over our bodies and over our livestock at their pleasure, and we are in great distress" (9:36–37 NRSV; cf. Ezra 9:8–9).

In short, many elements that characterized the Babylonian exile (the people's sin, alienation from the land, and oppression by foreign rulers) are shown to be still continuing. This sense of ongoing "exile" also features in the intertestamental literature (e.g., Bar. 2:7–10; 2 Macc. 1:10–2:18), and many aspects of Jesus' message are best understood against this background (Wright 268–72; Evans). In this sense the book of Nehemiah points us forward, as surely as any prophetic book, to God's act of redemption in the NT.

Theology

To discern its theological message, it is important to read Nehemiah not merely as a literary whole but also as a continuation of the book of Ezra. To this end Williamson has helpfully discerned "the overall theological shape" of Ezra-Nehemiah (*Ezra*). He divides the work into five "chapters," of which the book of Nehemiah comprises the last three: Ezra 1–6 has as its focus the rebuilding of the temple in the face of opposition. Ezra 7–10 moves on to a second stage of the restoration project, the definition of the community in accordance with "the law of your God and the law of the king" (7:26). Nehemiah 1–7 echoes these earlier stages, beginning with God at work through another Persian king (cf. Ezra 1:1; 7:27) and moving on to the completion of Jerusalem's walls, again in the face of opposition. Then Neh. 8–12 brings us to what Williamson calls "the suspended climax" of the earlier achievements, culminating in a united celebration of the work of both Ezra and Nehemiah. However, Neh. 13, by illustrating subsequent setbacks, ends the work on a note of "now and not yet." Williamson concludes: "The narrative structure of the book as a whole thus points to past achievements as a model for future aspiration" ("Nehemiah," 981).

The theological perspective of Ezra-Nehemiah explains why chronological concerns take a backseat. This is evident in the compiler's preference for a thematic rather than a chronological ordering of material in Ezra 1–6, and the fact that he can leap almost six decades with the words "after these things" in Ezra 7:1. A twelve-year gap between the events of Ezra 10 and Nehemiah's receipt of news from Jerusalem (Neh. 1:1; 2:1) is passed over in silence. The events of Neh. 1–12 occur within less than a year, and nothing is said of the remaining eleven years of Nehemiah's first term as governor (13:6). Apart from a vague "after some time" (NRSV), no date is given for the events of his second term in 13:6–31. This is frustrating for the historian, but has its own significance for a theological reading. "Historically time-bound events are becoming detached from their chronological moorings in order to be viewed rather as divinely related steps in what may properly be regarded as a history of salvation" (Williamson, *Ezra*, 81).

Bibliography

Childs, B. *Introduction to the Old Testament as Scripture*. SCM, 1979.

Eskenazi, T. *In an Age of Prose*. SBLMS 36. Scholars Press, 1988.

Evans, C. A. "Jesus and the Continuing Exile of Israel." Pages 77–100 in *Jesus and the Restoration of Israel*, ed. C. Newman. InterVarsity, 1999.

Houtman, C. "Ezra and the Law." Pages 91–115 in *Remembering All the Way*, by B. Albrektson et al. Brill, 1981.

Kidner, D. *Ezra and Nehemiah*. TOTC. InterVarsity, 1979.

Lipschits, O. "Literary and Ideological Aspects of Nehemiah 11." *JBL* 121 (2002): 423–40.

Tollefson, K., and H. G. M. Williamson. "Nehemiah as Cultural Revitalization: An Anthropological Perspective." *JSOT* 56 (1992): 41–68.

Williamson, H. G. M. *Ezra and Nehemiah*. OTG. JSOT, 1987.

———. "Nehemiah: Theology of." *NIDOTTE* 4:977–82.

Wright, N. T. *The New Testament and the People of God*. SPCK, 1992.

14

Esther

PAUL L. REDDITT

The book of Esther is set in the reign of Ahasuerus (the biblical name for Xerxes, king of Persia 485–465 BCE), though the Septuagint version calls the king Artaxerxes, presumably Artaxerxes I Longimanus (464–424 BCE), but possibly Artaxerxes II Mnemon (404–359 BCE). The book narrates the life of a Jewish maiden who is orphaned, reared by her uncle, becomes queen of the Persian Empire, and saves the Jews living in the empire from the scheming of Haman, the Agagite. The Hebrew version cannot be earlier than the time of the events it relates (fifth century), and may be a product of the Greek period (i.e., after 332 BCE). The Septuagint version, which intersperses another 107 verses, probably took its shape in the second or first century BCE.

History of Interpretation

Early Jewish interpretation of Esther took the form of comments on individual verses, which were collected during the Middle Ages in the *Esther Rabbah*. The earliest, extant, complete Jewish commentary on the text was that of Rashi (1040–1105 CE). Generally speaking, Jewish opinion moved in two directions. On the one hand, Jews objected to its lack of specifically religious sentiments, and to its authorization of the Feast of Purim, which they think may well have originated as a pagan festival. On the other hand, because of its treatment of anti-Semitism, Jews through the centuries have often read it as their "story." Early Christian interpretation is relatively sparse, especially in Eastern churches that rejected it as canonical (see below). Nor did the Reformers Luther and Calvin devote much energy to it.

Modern interpretation of Esther has focused first on whether it is a work of historiography or fiction. Those favoring historiography point to places where what is known from other sources seems to corroborate the book of Esther. The dates given in the book fit appropriately in the reign of Xerxes, as do the extent of the Persian Empire from India to Ethiopia, the council of seven nobles, the efficient postal system, the keeping of official diaries, the use of impalement as a means of capital punishment, the practice of obeisance, and reclining on couches at meals. The book also uses Persian words and names (Clines, *Ezra*, 260–61). For example, the name "Marduka" appears in Babylonian sources, though it is not certain that name was equivalent to "Mordecai." The word "Purim" also derives from the Assyrian language (Hallo). The difficulty with that word is that in Esther it refers to one who "casts the lot" (singular) rather than "lots." Despite a variety of attempts to explain the plural term, it may be easiest to recognize that people "cast the lot" several times in the narrative—hence, the use of the plural form "lots."

On the other hand, several features seem historically improbable to scholars. Some find it unlikely that Xerxes orders thousands of Jewish subjects slaughtered for no good reason, then reverses himself and gives the Jews free rein to kill thousands of other Persian subjects. Others note that the elevation of a Jewess to the rank of queen contradicts Herodotus (Clines, *Ezra*, 257–60).

More recently, Craig has argued that the reversals occurring throughout the narrative indicate that the book is "carnivalesque." The dominant characteristic of carnivals is their use of reversals to ridicule the status quo. So in Esther, the Jewess heroine replaces the Persian queen; Mordecai replaces Haman. Parody takes the form of turning King Ahasuerus and Haman into fools, and the "nonreligious" festival of Purim subverts the status quo.

Clines employs a variety of methods of biblical study to find the primary "book" in 1:1–8:17, a book whose plot focuses on the threat to Jews (ch. 3) and its resolution in a decree counterbalancing the first (ch. 8). He takes 9:1–10:3 as a series of additions similar to those in the longer Greek versions of the book.

Feminist readings typically see Esther as forming a context for reflecting on the (in)visibility of women in history and historiography. The book of Esther teaches that danger to the community "can be averted . . . by mixing [physical] attractiveness, sense and faith" (Brenner 13). Nevertheless, this solution carries a price tag: assimilation into Persian culture.

The Message of Esther

First, the efforts of Mordecai and Esther show that Diaspora Jews can serve God through serving foreign leaders. Such service entails temptation to compromise their convictions. Nor is it without danger, as the books of Esther and Daniel both make clear. Governments, however, often influence people's lives so personally that a God-fearing public servant can do great good.

Second, Mordecai's urging Esther to become involved on behalf of her people (4:13–14) shows that holding positions of power carries with it the responsibility to use that power appropriately. Esther's ethnicity might well have enveloped her in the pogrom, too, so her action included the element of self-preservation. Even if it had not, however, she would have had the responsibility to act.

Esther and the Canon

Despite the fact that the book of Esther was composed relatively late, it makes few allusions to the rest of the OT. Yet the Joseph narratives in Genesis form an exception. Hebrew phrases are virtually identical in Esther 1:3 and Gen. 40:20; in 3:4 and Gen. 39:10; in 1:21 and Gen. 41:37; in 2:3 and Gen. 41:35; in 3:10//8:2 and Gen. 41:42; or similar in 4:16 and Gen. 43:14 (Moore, *Studies,* xliii, lxxix nn. 69–70). Another obvious connection is between Esther and 1 Sam. 15, which narrates the execution of Agag by Samuel. That event constitutes the background for Haman's hatred of the Jew Mordecai. The "additions" to Esther in the Greek translations, moreover, contain numerous allusions to other books in the Hebrew Bible.

Esther's place in the Jewish canon seems to have been secured by the second century CE, when it was listed among the books of the Hebrew Bible in the Talmud (*b. B. Bat.* 14b–15a). How much earlier it reached that status is a matter of discussion. No copy of it was found among the Dead Sea Scrolls. Further, Josephus spoke of a Hebrew canon of twenty-two books, rather than the generally recognized number of twenty-four, suggesting that he did not include Esther (or Ecclesiastes).

Probably the reason the rabbis accepted it was that it provided the warrant for the Feast of Purim, the origin of which the book describes. Reasons for debating its canonicity centered on the morality of the book in general and its glee over the slaughter of Persians in particular. Another problem is its failure to mention God even once! Consequently, the additions in the Septuagint mention God frequently, especially in prayers of Mordecai and Esther and in a speech by Mordecai.

The NT makes no allusions to Esther, and early Christians divided over its inclusion in the Bible. Generally speaking, Western churches accepted it, while churches farther to the East did not. As late as the Reformation, Luther could say that he wished the book did not exist at all, because it contained pagan impropriety.

Esther and Theology

One crucial issue in the book of Esther is that of vengeance. The book openly portrays God's people taking revenge on their enemies. Occasionally scholars have tried to mitigate that portrayal by translating the Hebrew verb *naqam* as meaning "to inflict just punishment" instead of "to take revenge." However, the verb appears in Gen. 4:24, where Lamech tells his two wives that he has avenged himself seventy-sevenfold by killing a man who wounded him.

Readers may sympathize with threatened Jews in the Persian Empire and understand their desire for revenge, but neither of those factors mandates that they approve of wholesale slaughter. Such readers do well to remember that the Bible depicts human beings as invariably sinful, so the mere fact that the book of Esther does not call this taking of revenge "sinful" does not mean that God approved the action. Furthermore, Wenham (109) advocates reading narratives like this one not by stressing the actions of the actors, but by stressing the outlook of the book itself. So, what was the theological outlook of the book of Esther?

Remarkably, the Hebrew book of Esther does not mention God explicitly even once, though it does include one possible circumlocution for God (Esther 4:14): "relief and deliverance will rise for the Jews from another place" (Meinhold). Wiebe (413) argues that the phrase actually is a rhetorical question: "If you [Esther] keep silent at this time, *will* relief and deliverance arise for the Jews from another place?" Either way, the omission of any reference to God gives the book what is often referred to as a "secular" tone. Hence, it is necessary to deal with this issue before saying anything about the book's theology. Clines (*Ezra*, 255) argues that so many pieces have to fall into place for the Jews to escape annihilation that an attentive reader will see the book as relating, not a series of remarkable coincidences, but the careful operation of a hidden God working behind the scenes. A survey of the book reveals the following examples: (1) the fall of Queen Vashti, which brings Esther to the attention of King Ahasuerus (1:10–12); (2) Mordecai's help when the king is in danger, followed by palace oversight in not rewarding him (2:21–23); (3) the king's sleeplessness, resulting in his discovery of Mordecai's unrewarded service, precisely while Haman is on duty in the palace and can be tapped to name and extend the reward to Mordecai (6:5); (4) Haman's jealousy of Mordecai, which results in his preparing a gallows for Mordecai—from which Haman himself is hung (5:14; 7:9–10); (5) when Esther discloses to the king the plot of Haman to destroy all Jews, herself among them, the king leaves the room in a rage, but returns just as Haman further compromises himself in the eyes of the king by flinging himself upon the queen to beg for mercy; and (6) the last-minute nature of rescinding the king's order to slay Jews and its replacement with an order to slay those who want to kill Jews (9:1–17). The king of Persia may think he is in control of matters, but the author of Esther knows better. Still, it takes the eyes of faith to see the hidden God, a worthwhile discovery for Jews in a foreign land.

The hidden God protects God's people in Persia, so God is universal, not limited to the land of Palestine. Moreover, God's victory on behalf of the Jews is to be celebrated in a festival. There is no mention of a temple, either in Jerusalem or Persia. (Ackroyd [34] reads Ezek. 11:16 as saying that God had made for the exiles a "temporary sanctuary" or a "sanctuary in small measure," but that translation is uncertain, with no other evidence that Jews built a temple in Mesopotamia or Persia.) The festival described in Esther is not one of the annual festivals mandated in the Torah as times to offer sacrifices to God. Possibly the author advocates a type of celebration of God that involves not sacrifice, but resting and exchanging food.

Also, the hidden God remains faithful to the people of Israel. This conclusion is justified even though there is no reference in the Hebrew version to the patriarchs and no appeal to God's covenant with them or with the people at Sinai because, paradoxically, the identity of the hidden God must be self-evident. In the Septuagint version, moreover, Mordecai prays to God as the "God of Abraham" (Add. Esth. 13:15; cf. Esther's allusion to the call of Abraham in 14:5), and reminds God of God's salvation of the people from Egypt (13:16). Even the pagan king Artaxerxes can recognize Jews as the "children of the living God" (16:16), probably but not necessarily a reference to the God of Israel.

Bibliography

Ackroyd, P. *Exile and Restoration*. OTL. Westminster, 1968.

Berg, S. *The Book of Esther*. SBLDS 44. Scholars Press, 1979.

Brenner, A. *A Feminist Companion to Esther, Judith, and Susanna*. FCB 7. Sheffield Academic Press, 1995.

Clines, D. J. A. *The Esther Scroll*. JSOTSup 30. JSOT, 1984.

———. *Ezra, Nehemiah, Esther*. NCB. Eerdmans/Marshall, Morgan & Scott, 1984.

Craig, K. *Reading Esther*. Literary Currents in Biblical Interpretation. Westminster John Knox, 1995.

Fox, M. *Character and Ideology in the Book of Esther*. University of South Carolina Press, 1991.

Gerleman, G. *Esther*. BKAT 21. Neukirchener Verlag, 1973.

Hallo, W. "The First Purim." *BA* 46 (1983): 19–26.

Levinson, J. *Esther*. OTL. Westminster John Knox, 1997.

Meinhold, A. "Zu Aufbau und Mitte des Estherbuches." *VT* 33 (1983): 435–45.

Moore, C. *Esther*. AB 7B. Doubleday, 1971.

———. *Studies in the Book of Esther*. Ktav, 1982.

Paton, L. *A Critical and Exegetical Commentary on Esther*. ICC. T&T Clark, 1908.

Wenham, G. *Story as Torah*. T&T Clark, 2000.

Wiebe, J. "Esther 4:14: 'Will Relief and Deliverance Arise for the Jews from Another Place?'" *CBQ* 53 (1991): 409–15.

15

Job

LINDSAY WILSON

Job presents both great opportunities and peculiar difficulties for those seeking to read it theologically. Why would God cause such disasters to happen to righteous Job? How do Job's protests and accusations against God fit with faith in the rest of Scripture? Are Job's laments still appropriate or permissible after the death and resurrection of Christ?

History of Interpretation

Two trends in early Christian interpretation can be seen in John Chrysostom (ca. 347–407) and Jerome (ca. 347–419). Chrysostom found in Job a model of self-denial for those struggling with the devil, and his perseverance under trial was therefore to be imitated. Yet, it is largely the Job of chapters 1–2 who is Chrysostom's model, not the protesting Job of the dialogue, nor the Job transformed by the Yahweh speeches (Glatzer 24–26). Instead of emphasizing the prologue, Jerome used texts such as 19:23–27 to establish the hope and reality of bodily resurrection as a key to a Christian reading. Thus, Job's trust in his Redeemer is the book's clear and distinctive contribution.

In *Moralia in Job*, Gregory the Great (ca. 540–604) argues for allegorical and moral readings. On the moral level, he seeks to explain away Job's bold words to God, and to portray him as the patient saint of the prologue. His preferred reading is an allegorical one so that, for example, the ostrich in 39:13–14 is the synagogue and her eggs are the apostles "born of the flesh of the synagogue." The book thus outlines the great doctrines of the Christian message, with Job himself being a type of Christ.

The variety of medieval views can be seen by contrasting Maimonides (1135–1204) and Aquinas (1225–74). Both saw that Job centered on the issue of God's providence, but Maimonides in *The Guide to the Perplexed* understands the story as a parable about a nonhistorical person who, though righteous, lacked some wisdom. He suggests that Job had wrong beliefs instigated by Satan, and it was Elihu's role to introduce the concept of the angel of correction and intercession, a kind of counterpart to Satan, who enables the "knowledgeless" Job to hear "the prophetic revelation" of the Yahweh speeches. Aquinas, however, in *The Literal Exposition of Job*, views Job as a real historical figure who, despite his advanced wisdom, was still sinful in his protests. He argued against "spiritual" readings of the story (allegorical, moral, anagogical) and opted for the "literal" or historical sense.

The Reformers strongly affirmed the literal sense rather than the allegorical. Luther (1483–1546), in his preface to the German translation of Job, argues that the theme of the book is whether the righteous can suffer misfortune. He thinks that Job, in his human weakness, spoke wrongly toward God, but was still more righteous than the friends. He does not explore how to read the book christologically. Calvin (1509–64) wrote 159 sermons on the book, but no commentary. He found in Job a resource for enduring suffering, although he often contrasts the more "humble" or submissive approach of the David of the psalms to the angry and impatient outbursts of Job, which cross the line of genuine piety (Schreiner). He found much truth in the words of the friends, but especially in Elihu's view of God's providence and the place of suffering. Despite his pride, Job came to see that God could be trusted to run his world justly.

In more recent times (nineteenth to mid-twentieth century; beyond in Germany), the historical-critical approach has dominated Joban studies, generally focusing on innocent suffering as the central theme of Job, and thus foregrounding the prologue and epilogue. This has led to some clarification of matters of language, date, authorship, and literary parallels in the ancient Near East, but has been accompanied by doubts about the authenticity of many segments in the book (e.g., ch. 28, Elihu, the Yahweh speeches, the epilogue). Such scholars usually assumed that the putative earlier versions of the book offer better clues for the meaning of the book than does its present form.

149

In the mid-twentieth century, the focus shifted to the dialogue and its discussion of the doctrine of retribution, often seen to be in tension with the prologue and epilogue. This also raised the issue of theodicy, or justifying God's moral governance of the universe. A third movement has been to concentrate on Yahweh's speeches and Job's reply, which makes the key issue the nature of God and how humans can respond to God. A fourth approach has been to explore the message of the book as protesting and unorthodox, calling into question such ideas as retribution or traditional understandings of God (Dell).

More recently, English-speaking scholars have tended to read the book as a literary and theological whole (e.g., Andersen; Habel; Hartley; Janzen; Newsom). Such final-form approaches have sought to give full weight to each section of the book, and they have regained a sensitivity to lament as a legitimate stance before God. Other contemporary interpretations include the liberationist approach of Gutiérrez, deconstructionist readings by Clines, a historicized reading by Wolfers (Job is the nation of Israel), and a variety of feminist, psychoanalytical, and philosophical perspectives.

This brief survey alerts us to several contentious issues. First, where do you look (if at all) for the teaching of the book as a whole? Is it in the prologue and epilogue, the dialogue between Job and his friends, or in the Yahweh speeches? Second, is the book about suffering, the nature of God and his activity in the world, or the appropriate stance for humans to take before God? Third, there is the difficulty with Job's strong laments and protests. Can Job be read in a way that reflects God's verdict in 42:7–8? Finally, how should the book be read as Christian Scripture? Can Job be seen as a person of faith apart from those passages in which he looks for a Redeemer? Does the book point to Christ, and if so, in what way? How is Job to be read as part of the canon? A theological reading of the book is committed to its coherence in its final form, even if there is some tension between the various parts. It will not excise parts that are problematic.

The Message of Job

The popular perception is that Job is a book about suffering, but in what sense? It does not explore why there is suffering, nor the quandary of innocent suffering, but rather the question of how a person can respond in the midst of suffering (Clines). However, this is really to assert that suffering is simply the setting in which the issue of the book is raised. The question of 1:9, "Does Job fear God for nothing?"—whether Job's faith is genuine or based on self-interest—is tested by the losses and suffering in the rest of the prologue. Suffering clarifies and isolates the central issue of faith. In a similar way, the Satan's role in the book is not to inform readers about Satan, who disappears after the prologue (though Fyall suggests that he reappears as Behemoth and Leviathan). The Satan functions simply to implement the testing of Job's faith.

Throughout the dialogue (chs. 3–31), Job's God-directed cries and complaints are best viewed as calls on the seemingly absent God to become present. Though he strongly accuses God (6:4; 13:21; 16:11–14), he longs to speak to God in person (13:15), in a relationship in which God would call and Job would answer (14:15). Job explores imaginative possibilities, including a figure variously described as an arbiter, witness, and Redeemer (9:32–35; 16:18–22; 19:23–27). His oath of clearance (ch. 31) climaxes in a cry that God might answer him (31:35). A legal metaphor is woven through the book (Habel), as Job desperately pleads for justice from God. Job persistently believes that only God can resolve his crisis (7:20–21; 10:1–2; 13:3, 15–19, 22–24; 19:25–27; 23:10–16).

A number of false trails suggest some unsatisfactory answers to Job's dilemma. The first is the advice of the friends. The final verdict of the book is that Eliphaz, Bildad, and Zophar have not spoken about God what is right, but that Job has (42:7–8). This has puzzled many readers since the dialogue is dominated by Job challenging, accusing, and complaining to God, while the friends attempt to defend God's justice and explain Job's suffering. Their trite formulas depict Job as a sinner suffering for his sins (4:17; 5:7, 17–27; 8:3–7; 11:6, 13–16). In the case of Job, their analysis and advice have missed the mark.

Another false trail is the suggestion that the wisdom poem of chapter 28 provides the answer, implying that Job needed to learn to fear God (28:28). However, the prologue has stated that Job already feared God (1:1, 8; 2:3). Furthermore, Job 28 is followed by chapters 29–31, in which Job repeats his complaints and calls for the presence of God. Chapter 28 has not provided the answer, and Job is still calling for a resolution. When God finally does appear, he does not mention fearing him as the way forward.

The final false trail is found in the Elihu speeches (chs. 32–37). While some misunderstand Elihu to be a fourth friend, his function is rather that of an adjudicator. Elihu narrows in on Job's words in the debate (34:3, 5–6, 9, 35–37; 35:16), rather than Job's conduct before the dialogue. His conclusion is that Job has not "spoken of God what is right," a verdict that is thus intentionally set up as a rival to the later words of God. He is thus a foil for the real answer (McCabe).

151

Job's situation is clarified when chapters 38–41 are seen to provide the answer. There is debate over whether these should be called the Yahweh speeches, drawing attention to what God said, or rather labeled a theophany, which highlights God's appearance. Some of Job's problems (e.g., God's apparent absence) are resolved simply by the arrival of Yahweh. Yet God's speeches also bring about a paradigm shift in the book, and God even needs to speak twice before Job finally understands. His survey of the natural world decisively shifts the issue from Job's question "Why am I not dealt with justly?" to the broader one of how God orders his creation. The dialogue is thus shown to have been telescopic, rather than panoramic. A delicate balance has to be maintained in these chapters, as Yahweh seeks to redirect Job's energies without crushing him. If Yahweh is too harsh, he would appear to endorse the views of the friends; if Yahweh is too soft, then Job will not hear what is needed. The playful irony of the Yahweh speeches preserves a right balance. Job's longings are met, but his broadened understanding has enabled him to persevere in faith.

This change of perspective is exactly what is found in Job's response (42:2–6). He concedes that he spoke of "things too wonderful for me, which I did not know" (v. 3 NRSV; hence the Yahweh speeches). Furthermore, before God's appearance, he had only heard of God "by the hearing of the ear, but now my eye sees you" (v. 5 NRSV; hence the theophany). His new direction is recorded in 42:6, which has often been misunderstood as Job repenting of his sin. This is most unlikely in view of God's endorsement of Job's words (42:7–8, including the honorific title "servant"), and Job's intercession for the friends, leading to their restoration (42:8–10). The Hebrew permits, and the context demands, a translation such as "therefore I reject and turn from the way of dust and ashes" (lamenting as a social outcast). Now that Job's horizons have been expanded and his thinking reconfigured, Job needs to change his perspective in life, which is precisely what he proceeds to do as he rejoins society (42:10–17). God's appearance and his speeches have enabled Job to move on. Since Job feared God for nothing, genuine human faith is possible.

Job as Part of the Bible

The intellectual or ideological setting of the book is more significant than its historical setting. Job is a part of the wisdom corpus and stands in counterpoint to Proverbs' insistence that the world is regular and ordered, due in part to the presence of wisdom at creation (Prov. 8:22–31; 3:19–20).

While Proverbs allows for temporary setbacks (24:15–16), it does proclaim that the righteous will be rewarded and the wicked punished (3:9–10; 10:27–32)—the doctrine of retribution.

The book of Job protests not against Proverbs, but against a fossilized misunderstanding of retribution that had misrepresented the mainstream wisdom tradition of Proverbs (Holmgren). Job's friends are examples of those who have ignored the flexibility of Proverbs (as seen in Prov. 26:4–5), and simply read off a person's spiritual state from their circumstances. The prologue to Job (chs. 1–2) reveals that Job's suffering is not a consequence of his sin, and God's failure to rebuke Job in chapters 38–41 clearly shows that his honest protests throughout the dialogue are seen as legitimate. The book of Job is not rejecting the doctrine of retribution, but simply insisting that retributive justice is not the only principle on which God runs his world.

Job's story is not reflected on at any length in the rest of the Bible, though Job is listed as a righteous person in Ezek. 14:14, 20. However, the issues grappled with in the book have strong echoes in the rest of the OT. The endorsement of Job's lamenting is understandable in the light of a significant OT theme that regards protest addressed to God as legitimate. This can be most clearly seen in the complaints of Lamentations, Jeremiah's laments, and the many lament psalms in the Psalter. These do not picture doubt and protest as illegitimate, but rather as needing to be directed to God, since he has the power to rectify any crisis.

The strong theology of creation in Job also integrates well with the rest of the OT. Genesis 1–11 reminds us that God is king over the whole world that he has created, and not just over Israel. Job is set outside Israel and before the giving of the law (Job 1:1), apparently to give a typically wisdom universal twist to the issues that the book explores. In the Yahweh speeches, Job is confronted with God's kingly rule as sustainer in everyday life, and this broadens his understanding of God's purposes. Until God spoke, he had understood too narrowly how God rules his creation, but now he sees that it is wider than the dispensing of justice. This fits well with the cameos of God's providential involvement in everyday life in books like Ruth and Esther.

The NT affirms many of these OT insights. The legitimacy of lament is reinforced by Christ's uttering the opening words of a lament psalm while hanging on the cross (Matt. 27:46, citing Ps. 22:1; cf. Heb. 5:7–8). Furthermore, God's purposes in Christ are clearly wider than human justice, for in his love and mercy Christ died for undeserving sinners. Yet, while the NT focuses less on the mighty Creator and Redeemer of the OT, and more on

God assuming humanity, some full-orbed descriptions of Jesus occur. He was in the beginning, and all things came into being through him (John 1:1–4). Colossians 1:15–23 describes Christ not only as Redeemer but also as the firstborn over all creation, and in him all things were created and hold together. Thus, while there is a focus in the NT on God's sovereignty in redeeming his people, there is certainly no denial of Christ's lordship over creation. All that Yahweh says in Job 38–41, Christ can say too. His mighty control of the created world surfaced in his nature miracles (Mark 4:35–41; cf. Job 38:8–11). Furthermore, the world to come will be a new creation (Rev. 21–22), in which the Lamb's majesty will be fully seen (Rev. 5:11–14; 21:22–23).

The connection between Christ as Lord of creation and the need for persevering faith is also manifest in the NT. At the climax of Col. 1:15–23, Paul's hearers are reminded to "continue securely established and steadfast in the faith" (NRSV). The supremacy of Christ as Creator and sustainer is meant to lead to persevering faith. In the miracle of stilling the storm Jesus asks the disciples, "Where is your faith?" expecting them to keep on trusting him. Significantly, the only time that the NT names Job, it singles out his steadfastness or perseverance (*hyponone*, James 5:11), and it invites us to understand Job's faith in light of his vindication in the end or outcome (*telos*) of his restored situation (1 Pet. 5:6–10).

Job and Theology

The book of Job testifies to a God who is sovereign over all creation. The God of the friends (despite the reference to 5:12–13 in 1 Cor. 3:19) seems to be a hollow and shrunken version of the one who appears and speaks in chapters 38–41. No human dogma, even that God must act with justice, can bind or restrict God (35:7 and 41:11, cited in Rom. 11:35). While God is undoubtedly just, his ordering of the world is broader than a reductionistic human concept of retributive justice in which he can do no more than reward righteousness and punish wickedness.

The picture that emerges in chapters 38–41 is one of God having been involved in his creation from its very beginning, both in the inanimate (38:1–38) and the animal realms (38:39–39:30). He has mastered the mythological forces of cosmic chaos, Behemoth and Leviathan (chs. 40–41), though these may be natural creatures described in hyperbolic terms. God is also sovereign ruler over the creation, so that the Satan must ask permission before afflicting Job (1:6–12; 2:1–6). God is also free to restore Job once the test is over (42:10–15), even though some object that this reestablishes the doctrine of retribution. The book never denies the flexible doctrine of retribution evident in Proverbs, but refuses to distort this into an ironclad dogma that shackles God.

The theology of creation is clearly pivotal in a comprehensive biblical theology. In Job, creation is mentioned in a couple of hymnic (9:5–10; 26:5–14) and other passages (10:3, 8–12, 18) in the dialogue, in chapter 28, and above all in the Yahweh speeches (introduced by Elihu in 36:27–37:24). Job urges his friends to learn from the natural world (12:7–10; 14:7–12, 18–19; 24:5, 19), and God certainly uses it as an object lesson in chapters 38–39. God's delight in his ordered creation is reflected in the leisurely nature of the guided tour, in his care for those bearing young (39:1), and in his evident pleasure in animals such as the warhorse (39:19–25). Yet, there are puzzling elements of God's ordering of creation such as the clumsy and neglectful ostrich (39:13–16) and those animals that devour others (38:39–40). Both order and apparent disorder are manifest.

Furthermore, the way in which God is ordering his creation makes it clear that his concerns are wider than humans alone. The clearest example of this is when he makes rainfall where there are no humans (38:26–27), while the series of impossible questions indicates that God's ordering of his cosmos is beyond human comprehension. These factors have significant implications for contemporary ecological debates, both in their assertion of God's ownership of creation as well as in the breadth of his concerns. The majestic picture of God as the Creator, distinct from his creation, yet involved in freely caring for it, is clearly different from process theology readings.

Job also contributes many insights for a better understanding of humanity. Job's successful passing of the test testifies that he does "fear God for nothing" (1:9), and thus it is humanly possible to have faith in God without ulterior motives. Incidentally, chapter 31 is a classic source of the OT picture of the personal ethics of a righteous person. What emerges from this oath of clearance is an "identikit" picture of unblemished righteousness and integrity. Cultic matters are not at the heart of this (only 31:26–28), nor is keeping the law, for Job's integrity extends to his thoughts and attitudes (31:1, 9, 24–25, 29) and not simply to his outward actions.

The nature of human piety is stretched to its extremities within the book. It is Job's strong, accusatory words of protest in the dialogue that seem to sit most awkwardly with his piety in the prologue. Yet, Job's laments and complaints are directed to God and assume God is in control and can alone right the situation. They are ultimately a call for a restored relationship with a seemingly absent God. In such trying circumstances as Job's, they are legitimated as a genuine part of faith. They deal with the hiddenness of God without giving up on the relationship or reducing God to less than God-sized proportions.

Room needs to be made in an understanding of prayer for such words, since God is big enough to take genuine hurt and bewilderment. Job's raw honesty in addressing God is part of a proper expression of faith, not an abandonment of it. His pain and confusion can be communicated openly to his God. Job's struggle is to break through the straitjacketed thinking of his friends to a restored relationship with God, and this only comes through his bold words addressed to the one who can help.

Bibliography

Andersen, F. *Job*. TOTC. InterVarsity, 1976.

Beuken, W. A. M., ed. *The Book of Job*. BETL. Leuven University Press, 1994.

Calvin, J. *Sermons from Job*, ed. and trans. by L. Nixon. Baker, 1952.

Clines, D. J. A. *Job 1–20*. WBC. Word, 1989.

Dell, K. J. *The Book of Job as Sceptical Literature*. BZAW. De Gruyter, 1991.

Fyall, R. S. *Now My Eyes Have Seen You*. NSBT. Apollos, 2002.

Glatzer, N. N., ed. *The Dimensions of Job*. Schocken, 1969.

Gutiérrez, G. *On Job*, trans. M. J. O'Connell. Orbis, 1988.

Habel, N. *The Book of Job*. OTL. SCM, 1985.

Hartley, J. *The Book of Job*. NICOT. Eerdmans, 1988.

Holmgren, F. "Barking Dogs Never Bite, Except Now and Then: Proverbs and Job." *AThR* 61 (1979): 341–53.

Janzen, J. G. *Job*. Interpretation. John Knox, 1985.

Lévêque, J. *Job et son Dieu*. 2 vols. J. Gabalda, 1970.

McCabe, R. V. "Elihu's Contribution to the Thought of the Book of Job." *DBSJ* 2 (1997): 47–80.

Newsom, C. "The Book of Job." *NIB* 4:317–637.

Schreiner, S. *Where Shall Wisdom Be Found?* University of Chicago Press, 1994.

Smith, G. V. "Is There a Place for Job's Wisdom in Old Testament Theology?" *TJ* 13 NS (1992): 3–20.

Wolfers, D. *Deep Things out of Darkness*. Eerdmans, 1995.

16

Psalms

J. CLINTON McCANN JR.

Contemporary resources on worship generally describe readings from the Psalms as *responses* to the OT lesson, suggesting at least implicitly that the book of Psalms is something other than Scripture itself. This perspective is sometimes reinforced by homileticians who resist preaching on the Psalms because, in their view, the Psalms originated as liturgical materials and should be used accordingly. To be sure, the book of Psalms may well have been "the hymnbook/prayerbook of the second temple" (or the first temple) but, in addition, "it became eventually something like an instruction manual for the theological study of the divine order of salvation" (Seybold 27). Or, as Martin Luther put it, the Psalms are "a little Bible" (Luther 254), a prime source for learning about God, God's will for the world, and life lived under God's claim.

History of Interpretation

In all probability, the early church continued to sing and pray the Psalms (see Eph. 5:19; Col. 3:16), but the extensive use of the Psalms in the NT indicates that they were also read as a source of illumination and instruction. In particular, the early church read the Psalms messianically, an interpretative practice that had already begun in postexilic Judaism. This makes sense, since David's name is associated with seventy-three psalms, and since the "anointed" (the Hebrew *mashiakh* or, more usually, *messiah* = the Greek *christos*) is featured in the book as early as Ps. 2:2 (see also Pss. 18; 20; 21; 45; 72; 89; 110; 132; 144, often categorized as royal). In any case, it is clear that the early church could not understand or proclaim its faith in Jesus Messiah/Christ without frequent use of the Psalms (see esp. Pss. 22; 32; 69).

Like all Scripture in the precritical era of interpretation, the Psalms were read on more than one level. But in every instance, the Psalms functioned as Scripture, a source for theological illumination and proclamation. Augustine's *Enarrations [Expositions] on the Psalms* are a prime example, as are both Luther's and Calvin's commentaries. In the preface to his commentary, for instance, Calvin maintains not only that the Psalms teach us how to pray and how to praise God, but also that they "principally teach and train us to bear the cross" (Calvin xxxix). In a sense, Calvin and others read the Psalms historically, although not in the modern sense—they found in the Psalms information about David's life and trials. But Calvin and others also read the Psalms prophetically—finding the life and trials of David, the "anointed," prefigured the experiences of Jesus, the "anointed." From this perspective, Jesus could be heard praying the Psalms.

Early critical interpretation of the Psalms has been called "the personal/historical method" (Bellinger 15). Attempts were made (and are still being made) to date individual psalms and to discern in them information about David and other persons, groups, or events. In the early twentieth century Hermann Gunkel, the pioneer of form criticism, took a decisive step beyond this personal/historical approach. Although he still maintained that the Psalms as we have them are products of pious individuals, he claimed that they are based on cultic prototypes. These prototypes can be described and classified; Gunkel suggested the following major types, along with several others: hymns (songs of praise), community laments, individual songs of thanksgiving, and individual laments (30–39). Gunkel's work still exerts a profound influence on contemporary Psalms scholarship. Sigmund Mowinckel took the next logical step, suggesting that the Psalms as we have them are the actual materials produced by and for use in the worship of Israel and Judah (with the exception of "The Learned Psalmography," or wisdom psalms). Like Gunkel, Mowinckel's cult-functional approach still influences contemporary scholarship, although his proposal that many psalms find their setting-in-life in a New Year festival no longer commands a consensus. More recent scholars have modified and extended the form-critical and cult-functional approaches, capitalizing especially upon advances made in the fields of sociology and cross-cultural anthropology. Erhard Gerstenberger, for instance, locates the life-setting of many psalms in small-group or familial settings rather than in large-group gatherings that would have taken place in the temple or later synagogues.

While the form-critical and cult-functional approaches continue to flourish, the most recent interpretation of the Psalms has partaken of the general movement in biblical studies toward more literary approaches. Rhetorical criticism attempts to explore and identify what is unique rather than typical; scholarship on the shaping of the Psalter investigates its possible meaningfulness, including how the placement of particular psalms may affect their message and the whole.

While any method may yield theological results, proponents of the literary approaches in recent years have shown the most interest in theological conclusions. For instance, in his commentary, James L. Mays refuses to provide the standard list of psalms by form-critical category, so as not to distract readers from matters of content and theology. In subsequent sections of this article, I shall rely heavily on insights derived from study of the Psalter's shaping.

Hearing the Message of Psalms

It is a nearly unanimous consensus that Ps. 1 was either written or very intentionally chosen to be the introduction to the Psalter, and many interpreters also conclude that Pss. 1–2 constitute a paired introduction. This conclusion is extremely important because it means that Pss. 1–2 provide an interpretative agenda for the entire book. More specifically, Ps. 1 invites attention to God's *torah*, "instruction" (twice in 1:2; NIV/NRSV "law"), claiming that genuine happiness derives from constant attentiveness to God and God's "instruction" (1:1–2). The traditional translation of *torah* as "law" has meant that Ps. 1 has often been understood to commend some form of legalism, but torah in the broadest sense connotes God's will. Not surprisingly, Ps. 1 features two Hebrew roots that constitute a concise summary of God's will—*shapat* and *tsadaq*, which underlie the words "justice" and "righteous(ness)." The interpretation of Ps. 1:5 is disputed, but it is possible to translate v. 5a as follows: "Therefore the wicked will not stand up for justice." In any case, the appearance of these two key roots, in a psalm that highlights God's "instruction" or will, serves to anticipate Pss.

93 and 95–99, which have aptly been described as "the theological 'heart'" of the Psalter (Wilson 92; see below).

These so-called enthronement psalms all address God as "King" (95:3; 98:6; 99:4) or explicitly assert "The LORD reigns" (93:1; 96:10; 97:1; 99:1) or "The LORD is king" (NRSV). In short, God's sovereignty is world-encompassing; what God wills for God's world is clear—"justice" (see the root *shapat* in 96:13 [2x]; 97:2; 98:9; 99:4 [2x]) and "righteousness" (see the root *tsadaq* in 96:13; 97:2, 6, 11, 12; 98:2 [NRSV: "vindication"], 9; 99:4). The two descriptions of God's "coming" (96:13; 98:9) are particularly revealing. God's presence in the world is marked by justice and righteousness: God "is coming to establish justice [on] earth . . . with righteousness" (96:13 AT; 98:9; NRSV: "is coming to judge the earth . . . with righteousness"). To be sure, God's intention to set things right in the world will mean opposition to those who oppose God's will. From this perspective, the root *shapat* means "judgment"; but the translation "justice" captures in a positive sense the harmony and order that God intends among "the nations" (96:10; 98:2; see also "families of the peoples" in 96:7) and among the entire creation (96:11–12; 98:7–8), which participate joyfully in the celebration of God's presence and the working out of God's will in the world. Given the focus on torah in Ps. 1, along with its anticipation of the enthronement psalms and their emphasis on God's will for justice and righteousness, it is not surprising that Ps. 2 features God's "anointed" (v. 2, *messiah*). God's "anointed" is the Judean king, entrusted with the earthly implementation of God's justice and righteousness toward the realization of God's will for world-encompassing *shalom*, "peace." This is especially evident in Ps. 72:1–7, which features the repetition of "justice/judge" and "righteousness" along with the repetition of *shalom*, which NRSV translates as "prosperity" in v. 3 and "peace" in v. 7. As Ps. 72:1–7, 12–14 make clear, the king's vocation of establishing justice and righteousness gives him a special responsibility for "the needy" (vv. 4, 12–13), "the poor" (vv. 2, 4, 12), and "the weak" (v. 13). The establishment of God's justice and righteousness takes the form of judgment only over against those who position themselves in relation to God and others as "the oppressor" (v. 4; cf. v. 14).

In any case, the king's administration is to have creation-encompassing effects (see 72:5–6, 8, 16). It is to benefit not only the king himself (vv. 8–11, 15–17), along with the weak and poor and needy (vv. 1–4, 12–14), but also ultimately everyone: "May all nations be blessed in him" (v. 17 NRSV). This world-encompassing extension of the king's vocation recalls Gen. 12:1–3, the beginning of Israel's story with Abraham and Sarah that is set in a context affirming God's sovereignty over the whole universe and all its people (Gen. 1–11). Not coincidentally, the king, whose administration of justice and righteousness will effect blessing for "all nations," is to be pronounced by them as "happy" (v. 17 NRSV). Thus, not only does the featuring of the king at the beginning of Ps. 72 recall Ps. 2, but also the conclusion of Ps. 72 recalls Ps. 1, especially 1:1–2. As Ps. 1 has already suggested, it is precisely the implementation of God's will—the concrete embodiment of justice, righteousness, and peace—that makes one "happy." The word "happy" also serves to link Pss. 1 and 2 with an envelope structure (see 1:1; 2:12). The occurrence of "happy" in 2:12 is explicitly associated with taking "refuge" in God. The necessity of taking refuge in God highlights another feature common to Pss. 1, 2, and 72—God, God's "anointed," and God's people are persistently opposed. These opponents are variously named—"the wicked" in 1:1, 5–6; "the nations," "the peoples," "the kings of the earth," and "the rulers" in 2:1–2; "the oppressor" in 72:4. As it turns out, these "foes" (3:1) or "enemies" (3:7) are a regular feature in the Psalter, especially in Pss. 3–72, which consist mostly of prayers generally known as psalms of lament or complaint.

In fact, the situation at the beginning of Ps. 3, the first prayer in the Psalter, is typical. The psalmist is surrounded by enemies, who say, "There is no help for you in God" (3:2 NRSV). This assertion, of course, is a direct contradiction of Ps. 2:12. The psalmists are sometimes tempted to join the wicked in their arrogant self-assertion and self-sufficiency (see Ps. 73:1–15, which includes a quotation of the wicked in v. 11; see also the speech of the wicked in 10:4, 6, 11, 13), but they always steadfastly resist this temptation. The conclusion of Ps. 3, again typically, demonstrates the commitment of the assailed psalmists to stand with God. Using the same Hebrew word that the foes had used in v. 2, the psalmist prays, "Help me, O my God!" (v. 7; "Deliver me . . . ," NRSV). Then the psalmist affirms, "Help comes from the LORD" (v. 8; "Deliverance belongs to the LORD," NRSV). This confidence that God stands with the persecuted psalmist, and this commitment to continue standing with God, is what the Psalms mean by taking refuge in God. Given the predominance of prayers in Books I–II (Pss. 1–72), it is not surprising that "refuge" is a major theme (Creach; Pss. 7:1; 11:1; 14:6; 16:1; 17:7; 18:2, 30; 31:1–2, 19; 34:8, 22; etc.).

The fact that the prayers are typically composed of complaint (3:1–2; 13:1–2), petition (3:7; 13:3–4), and expressions of trust and/or praise (3:8; 13:5–6) is extremely important. In each prayer the effect is to juxtapose the realities of hurt and hope, pain and praise, suffering and glory. Of course, it is possible to conclude that pain and praise represent separate moments or movements in a psalm. For instance, some scholars conclude that the praise/trust sections of the prayers were spoken or written later than the complaint sections, after the threat had been removed or after conditions had improved. Others conclude that the psalmist moves through the pain and comes out safely, as it were, at the praise end of the psalm, perhaps with the assistance of some sort of cultic intervention that the psalm leaves unmentioned. But it is more likely that the pain and praise are meant to be understood as *simultaneous* realities. In other words, the psalmists complain and celebrate at the same time; the theological import is profound. As Mays concludes ("Psalm 13," 282), the prayers thus teach us about what it means to live as people of God: "The agony and the ecstasy belong together as the secret of our identity." In any case, as Mays again concludes, Ps. 3 and the other prayers in the Psalter demonstrate that prayer is "the ultimate act of faith in the face of the assault on the soul" (*Psalms,* 53). Prayer, in essence, represents the renunciation of self-sufficiency and self-help as one fully entrusts life and future to God (see Ps. 31:5, 14–15). To be sure, one could conclude that praise too is an act of faith. The Hebrew title of the Psalter is *Tehillim,* "Praises," and there are a significant number of psalms in which praise stands alone without the expression of pain. Even so, it is clear that the songs of praise should be heard in the context of the prayers, so as to avoid the temptation for praise to become merely a celebration of the status quo. Of course, the content of the songs of praise should be sufficient to avoid this temptation. As the central verse of Ps. 100 makes clear, praise is a matter of knowing "that the Lord is God . . . and not we ourselves" (v. 3, NRSV margin). Not coincidentally, Ps. 100 follows the aforementioned enthronement collection (Pss. 93, 95–99) that explicitly asserts God's universal sovereignty and celebrates God's will for world-encompassing justice and righteousness. In essence, then, praise is both the liturgy and the lifestyle of those who, denying self-sufficiency and self-assertion, entrust themselves to God and commit themselves to God's ways in the world. Praise is "lyrical self-abandonment" (Brueggemann 67) expressed in constant gratitude to God (see "thanksgiving/thanks" in the title of Ps. 100 and twice in v. 4) and constant commitment to the justice, righteousness, and *shalom* that God wills for individual lives and the life of the whole creation. Quite appropriately, the final verse of the Psalter envisions a world-encompassing community of praise: "Let everything that breathes praise the Lord!" (150:6 NRSV).

As we have seen, however, the Psalter is not naively optimistic about the existence of such a universal community of praise and obedience. From its very beginning in Pss. 1–2, the Psalter is well aware of the persistent opposition to God, God's will, and the community that God has gathered to represent God's purposes in the world. This persistent opposition serves to explain another prominent feature of the Psalter evident already in Pss. 1–3—namely, the request for God to destroy the wicked, or the confidence expressed that God does or will destroy the wicked (see Pss. 1:6; 2:8–12; 3:7; 5:10; 7:12–16; 9:5–6; 11:6; 12:3–4; passim). Indeed, the theme of retribution or vengeance is so prominent in some psalms that they have traditionally been known as imprecatory psalms, or more simply, as psalms of vengeance (Zenger; see Pss. 12, 44, 58, 83, 109, 137, 139).

This aspect of the Psalms often proves to be particularly problematic for Christian readers, who are genuinely and rightly troubled by the violent imagery and the portrayal of God as fiercely wrathful. Indeed, the psalms of vengeance are often effectively ignored in Christian circles; or sometimes, they are edited for use in Christian worship by removing the "objectionable" portions (e.g., Ps. 137:8–9). But a careful reading of the Psalter reveals that God simply does *not* act unilaterally to wipe out God's enemies. If God did so, the enemies of God and God's will would not be such a pervasive feature of the Psalms (or of contemporary life!). What message, then, is to be derived from the expressions of vengeance in the Psalms?

In the first place, these expressions function to communicate the pervasiveness of the opposition to God and God's will, as well as the hurtful consequences of injustice and unrighteousness. Pastorally and ethically speaking, victimization needs to be acknowledged, articulated, and opposed. The worst possible response to evil would be divine and human silence. The psalms of vengeance thus voice both the human and divine objection to the injustice and unrighteousness that creates victimization. The vengeance psalms are the outcries of victims, the theological thrust of which is to affirm that God stands with the victimized. Or, as the conclusion to Ps. 109 puts it: "For he [God] stands at the right hand of the needy" (v. 31; also 9:8; 12:5; 40:17; 140:12).

From this perspective, the psalms of vengeance, as well as the pleas for vengeance throughout the Psalter, can be seen as essentially prayers for justice, righteousness, and *shalom*. In Christian terms, they amount to praying the prayer that Jesus taught his disciples, "Your will be done on earth as it is in heaven" (Matt. 6:10), a petition immediately following the request that also echoes the Psalter's affirmation of God's universal sovereignty, "Your kingdom come" (6:10). That the psalmists regularly pray for God to set things right in the world is entirely in keeping with the Psalter's initial focus on the centrality of God and God's will for the experience of human happiness (see above on Ps. 1:1–2). It is theologically revealing that at a key point the Psalter includes the end of Book III, a psalm that articulates God's wrath against God's "anointed" (Ps. 89, esp. vv. 38–51, noting the repetition of "anointed" in vv. 38, 51). In short, Ps. 89 indicates that God shows no partiality, except to stand with the victimized (see Pss. 72, 82). When God's own "anointed" one fails to be a servant of God's justice and righteousness, as he was supposed to be (Ps. 72), then the "anointed" one is as much a target of God's wrath as anyone else is when they oppose God.

Historically and canonically speaking, the appearance of Ps. 89 at the end of Book III probably reflects the rupture represented by the Babylonian exile. In any case, it is almost certainly not coincidental that Book IV (Pss. 90–106) begins with the only psalm attributed to Moses, who presided over the people of God before they had a land, a temple, or a monarch. Not coincidentally too, Book IV goes on to feature the theological perspective first articulated explicitly by Moses and the people at the conclusion of the Song of the Sea: "The LORD will reign for ever and ever" (Exod. 15:18). This is precisely the message of Pss. 93, 95–99, the enthronement psalms. Because they follow and seem to respond to the crisis articulated in the pivotal Ps. 89, they constitute "the theological 'heart'" of the Psalter (see above).

The remainder of the Psalter seems also to have been shaped to address the theological crisis of exile and its aftermath. For instance, Book V gives a prominent, pivotal place to the massive Ps. 119, as if to represent that matters pertaining to both exodus (Pss. 113–118, the Egyptian Hallel used at Passover) and Zion (Pss. 120–134, the Psalms of Ascents that focus attention on Jerusalem) find their focal point in relation to *torah* (the key word in Ps. 119, occurring twenty-five times). This is but one more way that the Psalter continues to indicate the pervasive significance of *torah* (see Ps. 1:1–2)—that is, God's will, which directs human life toward the happiness (Ps. 1:1) or peace God desires for humankind and the creation.

Given the prominence of the "anointed" one as early as Ps. 2, plus at key points elsewhere in the Psalter (Ps. 72, at the end of Book II, and Ps. 89, at the end of Book III), it is also quite revealing that Ps. 149 recalls Ps. 2. After the exile, the monarchy never reappeared, thus raising the question of which earthly agency was to be responsible for the concrete enactment of God's will in the world. Psalm 149 offers a response to this question, for here it is God's "faithful" (vv. 5, 9) who, recognizing God as their "King" (v. 2), are entrusted with the vocation formerly assigned to the monarchy and articulated as such in Ps. 2 (cf. Ps. 149:7–9 and Ps. 2:8–9). To be sure, the imagery in both cases is shockingly violent; but as Ps. 149:9 makes clear, the issue is essentially *mishpat*, "justice" ("judgment," NRSV). Particularly when heard in relationship to Ps. 89, with its reminder that God's chosen agents are also subject to God's wrath (see above), Ps. 149 is a crucial affirmation that God entrusts God's "faithful" with the enactment and embodiment of God's will in the world—in a word, with God's "justice." Thus, Ps. 149 maintains the Psalter's ubiquitous focus on God's *torah*— God's will for justice, righteousness, and *shalom*—that was introduced in Pss. 1–2 and celebrated at the Psalter's theological heart (Pss. 93, 95–99). Along the way, of course, the prayers protest the absence of God's justice and righteousness, articulate the hurtful effects of disobedience, and plead that God's will be done. The songs of praise invite all peoples and nations to submit themselves to the sovereign God, who wills their well-being and, indeed, nothing short of peace on a cosmic scale.

The Psalms and the Canon

Given Luther's description of the Psalms as "a little Bible," it is not surprising that the messages of the Psalms resonate throughout both the OT and NT. Indeed, Psalms is the OT book most quoted in the NT.

The affirmation at the heart of the Psalter—that God reigns, and wills justice, righteousness, and peace on a universe-encompassing scale—might itself be considered a sort of summary of the Bible's fundamental message. As suggested above, Israel understood the exodus from Egypt to be decisive evidence of God's eternal reign. But, as Terence Fretheim points out, the exodus event aims at the fulfillment of God's creational purposes. To affirm God as Creator of the universe (Gen. 1–11) already affirms God's sovereign claim, including all peoples and nations. When the story appears to narrow from all humankind to Abraham and Sarah and their descendants, the intent of God is still to effect a blessing for "all the families of the earth" (Gen. 12:3 NRSV). This creation-wide perspective is especially evident in the songs of praise, including not only in the enthronement psalms (Pss. 93, 95–99) that explicitly assert God's sovereignty, but also in other songs of praise that regularly invite "all the earth" (66:1; 100:1), "all you nations" and "all you peoples" (117:1), and ultimately "everything that breathes" (150:6) to praise God. The apostle Paul apparently understood the practical theological implications of this expansive view of God's claim on the world. As part of his warrant for including the Gentiles (nations) in the church, Paul cites Ps. 117:1 (Rom. 15:11).

Of course, the Psalter's representation of God's will for justice, righteousness, and peace, along with its featuring of the "anointed" and his responsibility for enacting God's will (see esp. Pss. 2, 72, 89), puts the Psalms in conversation with major portions of the OT, including key texts like 1 Sam. 8 (Israel's request for a king and God's granting of this request) and 2 Sam. 7 (God's promise to David and his descendants; cf. Ps. 89). When the kings failed to do what God had entrusted to them, it fell upon prophets to call king and nation back to God's will. The prophets often articulated this call in terms of justice and righteousness (e.g., Isa. 1:21, 27; 5:7; 9:7; 32:1, 16–17; Jer. 22:13–17; Amos 5:24). Not surprisingly, a psalm like Ps. 82 sounds as if a prophet could have written it. As for postexilic prophecy, there are major connections between the enthronement psalms (Pss. 93, 95–99) and the material in Isa. 40–55, including the affirmation that God reigns (Isa. 52:7; Pss. 96:10; 97:1; 99:1) and the invitation to sing "a new song" (Isa. 42:10; Pss. 96:1; 98:1). Then too, the book of Isaiah as a whole portrays God in the same way as the Psalms—a God whose sovereign claim upon the whole creation means that God wills nothing short of universal peace on earth (Isa. 2:2–4; 42:1–9; 49:1–6).

This same complex of theological affirmations—God's sovereignty, God's will, and the agency of God's "anointed" in enacting it—plays a major role in the NT as well, especially in the Synoptic Gospels and their presentation of Jesus Christ (the Greek *Christos* is the translation of Hebrew *Messiah*, "anointed"). The titles for Jesus at the beginning of the Gospel of Mark, "Christ" and "Son of God," are the same ones found in Ps. 2 ("anointed" in v. 2 and "son" in v. 7). When Jesus is baptized (Mark 1:11), the heavenly voice recalls Ps. 2:7, "You are my son." Jesus' fundamental proclamation of "the kingdom of God" (Mark 1:15//Matt. 4:17) echoes the message that lies at the Psalter's theological heart; according to the Gospel of Matthew, Jesus' teaching begins with the same word that begins the Psalter: "Happy" or "Blessed" (Matt. 5:3). In fact, the Beatitudes of Jesus in Matt. 5:3–11 pronounce "happy" or "blessed" precisely the same kind of people who regularly appear as the pray-ers of the Psalms—the poor, the meek (cf. Matt. 5:5 with Ps. 37:11), the persecuted. In a real sense, the Beatitudes reinforce the affirmation of the Psalms that God stands with the dispossessed, the suffering, and the victimized, an affirmation further illustrated by the whole thrust of Jesus' ministry among the poor, weak, and needy. This whole direction, according to Matt. 5:17, serves to fulfill the Torah and the Prophets; it is the fullest expression of the will of God, the greater "righteousness" that "exceeds that of the scribes and Pharisees" (Matt. 5:20 NRSV). As suggested above, the Psalter also begins with a focus on *torah* (Ps. 1:2), commending constant orientation to God's will, which is subsequently described as righteousness and justice (see esp. Pss. 96–99).

Not surprisingly, therefore, the Gospel writers cannot tell the story of Jesus, especially Jesus' passion, without using the Psalms as a major source. Jesus' entry into Jerusalem recalls Ps. 118, thus suggesting that Jesus' upcoming death and resurrection continue God's salvific activity in the exodus and other OT deliverances (Mark 11:9 cites parts of Ps. 118:25–26). And the passion narratives in all four Gospels echo Pss. 22 and 69. In Matthew and Mark, Jesus' words from the cross are drawn from Ps. 22:1 (Matt. 27:46//Mark 15:34). Luke's account differs, but it is another psalm that supplies Jesus' words from the cross (Luke 23:46; see Ps. 31:5).

Not coincidentally, Pss. 22, 31, and 69 are the three longest and most intense prayers in the Psalter. The canonical effect is to portray Jesus' passion as the fullest expression of one whose suffering communicates not divine punishment, but rather oneness with God. Indeed, as is the case with the psalmist in Ps. 69, it is clear that Jesus suffers precisely *because* he is faithful to God and God's purposes. The profound theological significance of this reality will be considered further below.

While Pss. 22, 31, and 69 are more clearly related to the story of Jesus' suffering and death, their hopeful and praise-filled conclusions may also have helped the Gospel writers appreciate the meaning of Jesus' ministry and even his resurrection. Psalm 22, for instance, portrays the psalmist gathering around himself a community of grateful praise, beginning with the afflicted (v. 24) and the poor (v. 26), but eventually extending to "all the families of the nations" (v. 27) and including the dead (v. 29) and "people yet unborn" (v. 31). While Ps. 22 should not be understood as a prediction of Jesus' ministry among the outcast or the reality of his resurrection, it certainly anticipates Jesus' expansive ministry to all people, as well as his proclamation and embodiment of a communion with God that even death itself cannot destroy (Davis).

Theology in the Psalms

The preceding sections have already begun to discuss theological dimensions, but it is appropriate in this concluding section to consider more explicitly the Psalter's portrayal of God and some of its implications. Of paramount importance is the Psalter's affirmation of God's universal sovereignty and its simultaneous recognition that God has enemies (Ps. 2). This situation, of course, virtually forces the reader to explore the nature of God's sovereignty or power. If God's power is simply force, then God should have no enemies, at least not for long. But God always does, as do the people committed to God's justice, righteousness, and peace in the world. Thus, God's power must be understood not as sheer force, but rather as something like sheer love.

As contemporary Reformed theologians are pointing out, the Bible portrays a loving God who wills authentic relationship with humankind. Because love cannot be coerced, human beings must genuinely be able to choose to obey or disobey God (Hall 71–72; Placher). The Psalter's portrayal of God conforms to this understanding. Because God loves the world and wills to be in relationship with it (note that justice, righteousness, and peace are all relational terms), God simply will not coerce obedience. This explains why opposition to God is possible, and indeed, why the Psalms are full of such opposition (even from God's own people; see Pss. 32, 51, 130).

All this does not mean that God is powerless, however. The good news that God stands with the poor and needy (see Pss. 22:24; 31:21–22; 34:18; 109:31; 140:12) serves to energize and empower them to resist oppression, and to pursue for themselves and others the life that God wills. Such resistance and pursuit are powerful, and it is *God's* power. But this is the power of incarnational love, not coercion or enforcement. God loves the world into obedience.

This portrayal of God certainly has profound implications for understanding the human situation, including suffering. Most dramatically, perhaps, suffering cannot simply be understood as divine punishment. Although the psalmists themselves sometimes seem to view their suffering as punishment (Pss. 6:1; 38:1), they actually undercut this view by claiming God's presence with themselves and with other sufferers. Like the book of Job, the Psalter finally obliterates any comprehensive doctrine of retribution. The psalmists suffer, not because God wills or causes it; rather, they suffer because they themselves or their enemies have chosen not to enact and embody the justice, righteousness, and peace that God wills. Injustice and unrighteousness always have bad consequences; they hurt people, and they anger God. If the negative consequences of injustice and unrighteousness are considered divine "punishment," then one must at least stipulate that such "punishment" does not necessarily correspond to what one might deserve, and that its occurrence is actually an indication that God's will is *not* being accomplished.

To put it slightly differently, only when the doctrine of retribution has been obliterated is there any logical space for grace, which by definition means that the guilty do *not* get what they deserve. Thus, the Psalms finally participate with the rest of the canon in portraying God as essentially "merciful and gracious, slow to anger, and abounding in steadfast love and faithfulness" (Exod. 34:6 NRSV). Given this portrayal of God, it is entirely understandable not only that certain psalms echo Exod. 34:6 (86:15; 103:8; and less directly, 25:10; 36:5; 40:10–11; 57:3; 61:7; 85:10; 89:14; 115:1; 138:2), but also that God's *khesed*, "steadfast love," is regularly celebrated in the songs of praise (as in 33:5; 100:5; 103:11, 17; 106:1; 107:1, 8, 15, 21, 31, 43; 117:2; 118:1–4, 29; 136:1–26), appealed to in the prayers for help (6:4; 17:7; 25:7; 26:3; 31:16; 51:1), and cited as ground for trust in psalmic professions of faith (5:7; 13:5; 23:6 NRSV, "mercy"; 33:18; 63:3).

From the Christian perspective, the portrayal of a gracious God, whose love makes God vulnerable to the disobedience of humankind, reaches its culmination in the incarnation, life, death, and resurrection of Jesus. As suggested above, the Gospel writers could not tell the story of Jesus without the Psalms. The Psalter's regular juxtaposition of pain and praise, hurt and hope, suffering and glory anticipates the death and resurrection of Jesus, who then and now calls people to experience the glory of life by taking up a cross to follow him (see Mark 8:34–35). As Calvin discerned, the Psalms do finally "teach and train us to bear the cross."

Bibliography

Bellinger, W., Jr. *Psalms*. Hendrickson, 1990.

Brown, W. *Seeing the Psalms*. Westminster John Knox, 2002.

Brueggemann, W. "Bounded by Praise and Obedience: The Psalms as Canon." *JSOT* 50 (1991): 63–92.

Calvin, J. *Commentary on the Book of Psalms*. Vol. 1. Calvin Translation Society, 1845.

Creach, J. *Yahweh as Refuge and the Editing of the Hebrew Psalter*. JSOTSup 217. Sheffield Academic Press, 1996.

Davis, E. "Exploding the Limits: Form and Function in Psalm 22." *JSOT* 53 (1992): 93–105.

Fretheim, T. *Exodus*. Interpretation. John Knox, 1991.

Gerstenberger, E. *Psalms, Part 1, with an Introduction to Cultic Poetry*. FOTL 14. Eerdmans, 1988.

———. *Psalms, Part 2, and Lamentations*. FOTL 15. Eerdmans, 2001.

Gunkel, H. *The Psalms*. Fortress, 1967.

Hall, D. J. *God and Human Suffering*. Augsburg, 1986.

Limburg, J. *Psalms*. Westminster Bible Companion. Westminster John Knox, 2000.

Luther, M. *LWorks*. Vol. 35. Fortress, 1960.

Mays, J. L. *The Lord Reigns*. Westminster John Knox, 1994.

————. "Psalm 13." *Int* 34 (1980): 279–83.

————. *Psalms*. Interpretation. John Knox, 1994.

McCann, J. C., Jr. "The Book of Psalms: Introduction, Commentary, and Reflections." *NIB* 4:641–1280.

————. *A Theological Introduction to the Book of Psalms*. Abingdon, 1993.

Mowinckel, S. *The Psalms in Israel's Worship*. Vols. 1–2. Abingdon, 1962.

Placher, W. *Narratives of a Vulnerable God*. Westminster John Knox, 1994.

Seybold, K. *Introducing the Psalms*. T&T Clark, 1990.

Tate, M. *Psalms 51–100*. WBC. Word, 1990.

Wilson, G. H. "The Use of the Royal Psalms at the 'Seams' of the Hebrew Psalter." *JSOT* 35 (1986): 85–94.

Zenger, E. *A God of Vengeance?* Westminster John Knox, 1996.

17

Proverbs

RAYMOND C. VAN LEEUWEN

Proverbs is the foundational wisdom book of the Bible, teaching the ABCs of wisdom and introducing more complex issues that are further elaborated in Ecclesiastes, Job, and the wisdom teaching of the NT, such as the Sermon on the Mount. In an extraordinary way, Proverbs raises the theological question of the relation of ordinary life in the cosmos to God the Creator. Moreover, the complexity of interpreting Proverbs has implications for biblical hermeneutics as a whole.

History of Interpretation

A history of reading Proverbs remains to be written, partly because the use of short sayings in Jewish and Christian literature is widely scattered, and systematic exposition of the book in Christian circles was rare until Melanchthon's translation and three commentaries in the sixteenth century (Sick). With rare exceptions, the Eastern and Western exegetical traditions suffered from a lack of Hebrew learning. In contrast, Jewish midrashim regularly interpreted the Torah by juxtaposing texts from Proverbs (e.g., Prov. 8:22, 30 and Gen. 1:1 in *Gen. Rab.* 1.1). Medieval Jewish commentaries richly mined the Hebrew text (cf. Fox 12–13). The twelfth-century

Christian *Glossa ordinaria*, with its compilation of observations going back to the fathers, served as a commentary on Proverbs well into the Reformation period (cf. Froehlich).

Proverbs was often exploited for its pithy wisdom by writers ranging from Augustine and Chaucer to Erasmus and Shakespeare (*Henry IV*, 1.2.98–100), while its use in theological debate was sporadic if spectacular. Of particular note was Lady Wisdom's utterance in Prov. 8:22 ("Yahweh *begot* [*qanah*] me as the first of his way") as used in the Arian controversy of the fourth century. Both parties interpreted Wisdom as Christ: the Arians took the Hebrew term *qanah* to mean "created" (so LXX), so that Christ could not properly be God; the Orthodox took it as "possessed" (so other Greek versions and Vulgate; see Clifford 96, 98–99; Pelikan 191–200). Such a direct reading of female Wisdom as Christ was allegorical. In similar fashion, premodern Jewish tradition interpreted wisdom in Prov. 8 as Torah (cf. Sir. 24:23).

Generally, allegorical reading of Proverbs (apart from the short sayings in chs. 10–29) dominated its use by the church and synagogue until the Reformation, when the great shift to exclusively "literal" reading began to take place (Wolters, *Song*). With the Enlightenment's focus on science and universally true principles, interest especially in the short sayings of Proverbs waned, partly because they seemed internally contradictory (a fact already noted in the Talmud concerning 26:4–5; *b. Šabb.* 30b) and not universally borne out by experience (e.g., the righteous sometimes do hunger, in spite of 10:3; cf. Van Leeuwen, "Wealth").

The 1923 publication of the Egyptian Teaching of Amenemope (with parallels to Prov. 22:17–23:14) gave rise to a resurgence of scholarly interest in Proverbs, focused on the international character of wisdom (Whybray 6–18). Yet ancient Near Eastern wisdom, especially as it appears in Mesopotamian nonwisdom genres, remains a largely ignored gold mine. In spite of gains from ancient Near Eastern studies, the most profound discussion of the theological and human significance of Proverbs remains G. von Rad's *Wisdom in Israel*, which focuses on the text of Proverbs within the biblical canon (unfortunately, the ET is often unreliable).

The Message of the Text

Discerning the "message" of Proverbs is complex because the book is a collection of collections (cf. 10:1; 22:17–20; 24:23; 25:1; 30:1; 31:1) that grew over time (cf. LXX). The book also contains a variety of genres: "lectures" and "speeches" (chs. 1–9), short "sayings" and "admonitions" (chs. 10–29), brief poems (including a prayer, ch. 30), maternal instruction and a "Hymn to a Valiant Woman" (ch. 31). Yet the book forms an edited whole, with an introduction (1:1–7) and a hermeneutical prologue (chs. 1–9), which provide the worldview within which the smaller genres that follow are to be understood. In addition, Prov. 10–15 teaches the elementary patterns of acts and consequences, while chapters 16–29 develop the exceptions to the rules (Van Leeuwen, "Proverbs"). But the complexity of the book's interpretation, especially of the short sayings whose contextual relations are not always clear, has important implications for reading Scripture as a whole, since the Bible itself is a collection of books composed over time. Consequently, not every word of the Lord is valid for every time and place (contrast the fate of Jerusalem according to Isaiah and Jeremiah!). Wise interpretation is always needed.

It is generally acknowledged that 1:7 and 9:10 ("the fear of the LORD is the beginning of knowledge/wisdom") form the thematic inclusio of chapters 1–9 and the motto for the entire book (cf. 31:30, an inclusio with 1:7 for the whole book). For Israel, knowledge (of the world and human affairs) and wisdom are inextricably related to God (von Rad, *Wisdom*, 53–73). The point is fundamental, for wisdom concerns the relation of creation to God, in every aspect of creation, and the implications of this relation for human piety and conduct in the ordinary affairs of life, whether high (8:15–16; 16:1–15; 31:1–9) or low (25:11; 27:8, 14). This is an essential point of the "Hymn to a Valiant Woman" (31:10–31), whose fear of the Lord (her "religion") is demonstrated precisely in her wise conduct in the areas of life considered by many moderns to be merely "secular" (Wolters, "Nature"; Wolters, *Song*).

The purpose of the whole book is stated in 1:2–7. It is to help the young become wise and the mature wiser, to help them interpret wise sayings, using them to think and act in real-life circumstances, and for general discipline and instruction (*musar* means both, as the Greek translation *paideia* suggests) in "righteousness, justice, and equity," especially in socioeconomic and judicial relations (1:3 NRSV; cf. 11:1; 14:31, 34; 16:11–13; 25:18; 28:5, 8–9; 29:4, 7, 12, 14; and the general opposition of "righteous" and "wicked" in chs. 10–15).

In addition to the general concern for justice and righteousness in all areas of life, the art of understanding "a proverb and a figure, the words of the wise and their riddles" (1:6 NRSV) suggests that the book itself is aware of the hermeneutical task (cf. 8:9; 26:7). The wise use of sayings requires interpretation of people and situations as well as of texts. In the modern period, proverbial wisdom has fallen into disrepute (except among advertisers) partly because of its contradictory, local, and "unscientific" character (cf. Toulmin). Moreover, its apparent generalizations do not always appear true to specific cases. But this fact is an essential character-istic of sayings and makes them hermeneutically significant. Vernacular proverbs of all cultures present patterns of reality that are frequently ob-served, but which have exceptions. One son is advised to "Look before you leap"; another is told, "He who hesitates is lost." "Birds of a feather flock together," but also, "Opposites attract." Consequently, "He who knows one, knows none." Proverbs is a repository of many observations, some of which are true in the majority of cases, others only in a minority or even exceptionally. The wise person knows which saying or admonition is "fitting" or proper for the right person at the right time, in the right circumstances, and in the right way.

In a certain sense, it takes wisdom to use wisdom. A few examples from Proverbs will illustrate. Proverbs 17:17–18 say contradictory things about "friends." The contradiction is obscured in most translations because the word for "friend" (re'a) in v. 17 is translated as "neighbor" in v. 18. Read instead, "A *friend* loves at all times, and a brother is born for adversity. A man who lacks sense strikes a deal, becoming a guarantor for his *friend*" (AT). The contradiction concerns the ambiguity of those we designate as "friends," and how we relate to them, wisely or unwisely. It is not wise to cosign a loan for every "friend." But other "friends" will lay down their life for you, and perhaps you for them, as Jesus showed in word and deed. The ambiguity of friendship is captured in English by other proverbial say-ings: "He's a fair-weather friend" (who will not stick with you in adversity) and "A friend in need is a friend indeed." Similarly, 17:27–28 explores the contradictory and ambiguous character of silence.

The most famous contradiction in Proverbs is 26:4–5, which contains contradictory admonitions about whether to speak or be silent when deal-ing with a fool. The Talmud already wrestled with the problem, arguing whether Proverbs, containing such a contradiction, belonged among the sacred books. The medieval *Glossa ordinaria* solved the problem correctly by explaining that the verses apply to different matters. Most wisdom utter-ances are situational: they need to be applied fittingly to the contradictory and complex circumstances of life. One may compare the contradictory sayings of Jesus (Matt. 5:16; 6:1; 7:1, 6; Ridderbos) and Paul (Gal. 6:2, 5; Hays). Like many utterances of Scripture, the full truth of a saying like 11:4 will only be resolved eschatologically. This means that the promises of Proverbs (e.g., righteousness leads to prosperity and well-being) are not always realized in this life. The wicked sometimes do prosper, while the godly suffer unjustly (cf. Van Leeuwen, "Wealth").

The range of topics covered in Proverbs, especially in the short genres of chapters 10–30, reminds us that wisdom and folly involve all of life. Every human endeavor from farming (12:10–11; 28:19) and metallurgy (17:3) to politics (16:10–15; chs. 25, 28–29), economics (11:1; 16:11), and psychology (12:25; 14:10, 13) is fair game. What is more, these sayings have a metaphorical applicability far beyond their literal concerns.

Proverbs 1–9 is designed to provide the underlying worldview and theology for understanding the diverse sayings of chapters 10–29. Here we find "lectures" addressed by a parent to a "son" ("child" in NRSV is misleading), who is on the verge of adult responsibilities, including marriage. There are also speeches by cosmic Wisdom herself, personified as a woman (1:20–33; 8:1–9:6). Rather than focusing on the complexities of life (as esp. chs. 16–29 do), these chapters show life as lived in a structured world of boundaries. This world has a fundamental opposition of good and bad, represented primarily by the opposition of two ways, and the two (types of) women and houses at the end of the ways, one a doorway to Sheol, the other to life. The opposition of wisdom and folly in 1–9 finds its correlate in the opposition of righteous/ness and wicked/ness in 10–15. One can be morally righteous without being wise, but one cannot be wise without being righteous, for sin is a fundamental breach of the cosmic order. The contrary ways, women, and houses are both literal and symbolic. The young man can be seduced by the "strange" (*zarah*) or "other" (*nokriah*) woman ("loose woman," RSV; "adventuress/adulteress," RSV/NRSV). But the literal wife (5:15–19; cf. 31:10–31) also symbolizes Lady Wisdom (cf. 8:35; 18:22), while the other woman represents the attractive seductions of Lady Folly (9:13–18). Especially significant are the passages where the imagery of ways, women, and houses come together. This happens usually with reference to folly and death (2:16–19; 5:3–6, 8; 7:24–27; 9:1–18), but also with reference to life (5:15–19, where cistern and well imply house, and water implies life; 9:1–6).

These passages, however, teach more than the contrast of deadly versus life-enhancing sexuality. The imagery of woman, ways, and houses implicitly teaches about the nature of the cosmic "house" that God created with wisdom (3:19–20; 8:22–31; 9:1–6; Van Leeuwen, "Book"), in which we humans live. The "ways" convey the communal and traditional character of life: humans follow good and bad paths laid down by previous generations, whether in the language they speak or the ethics they live. Moreover, life is ultimately a journey toward, and determined by, the object of our desire: godly wisdom or deadly folly. The desirable "women" that entice the young man on the way to their respective houses are metaphors for *all* created goods that humans desire, whether properly and within created bounds, or wrongly and out-of-bounds—like my neighbor's property or good name.

Proverbs 1–9 presents our world as one of boundaries and limits, shown most powerfully by the division of sea and dry land (8:29; cf. Job 38:8–10; Ps. 104:9; Jer. 5:22). The waves of the sea may play within that limit, but when they flood dry land, death and destruction result. This cosmic principle has its cultural aspect as well, symbolized in the sexual teaching of 1–9. The "waters" of sexuality are good within the limits of marriage, but destructive outside of it (5:15–20). The worldview of Prov. 1–9 insists on freedom within form, life within law, and love within limits. Practically, this means that wise persons are constantly aware of the boundaries and limits that separate wise from foolish behavior and excess from enough. They are also aware that behaviors need to be appropriate to the specifics of situations, and to the nature and kinds of persons and things we relate to (Van Leeuwen, "Liminality"). In this world, the acts, habits, and eventually character that are a human "way" have consequences that lead ultimately to life or death (von Rad, *Wisdom,* 124–37).

Proverbs and the Canon

Modern scholarship has exaggerated the differences between Proverbs and the rest of Scripture. For example, the lack of salvation history in Proverbs is a function of its genre and purpose, rather than of differences in worldview and theology. And the affinities of Proverbs with other ancient Near Eastern literatures are by no means unique to this book (cf. Roberts). Proverbs thus forces us to think about the reality of "common grace" and the general human condition that is common to Christians and non-Christians alike. Wisdom "speaks" to all humans in the cosmos (ch. 8), even those who do not have special revelation, so that all human cultures respond with varying degrees of *relative* wisdom, much of which finds counterparts in biblical Proverbs. The attempt to deny the significance of the Wisdom literature for Christian theology (Preuss 186–90) has more to do with a fear of "natural theology" and a focus on salvation history narrowly conceived than it does with a proper understanding of Proverbs and its role in the canon. This view is belied by the NT's frequent quotation of Proverbs and its use of Lady Wisdom to articulate Christ's role in creation (cf. John 1:1–18; Rom. 1:18–20; 2:14–15; Col. 1:15–20). Similarly, Christ's insistence that he is "the way" cannot be understood except against the background of Proverbs. An adequate treatment of the NT's use of Proverbs remains to be written.

Theology and Significance for the Church

Proverbs provides the church with a spirituality of the ordinary, not unlike Paul's insistence that Christians "glorify God in your body" (1 Cor. 6:20 NRSV). Here, life's daily actions take place in the presence of the Creator. Moreover, the creation is humanity's partner, the correlate of our humanity. Israel did not separate reason and revelation, religion and knowledge. "Experiences of the world were for [Israel] always experiences of God as well, and experiences of God were for her experiences of the world"—without confusing God and world. Again, "Humans are always entirely in the world, yet are always entirely involved with Yahweh" (von Rad, *Wisdom,* 62, 95; my translation of *Weisheit,* 87, 129). Scholarly attempts, on form-critical grounds, to separate the cosmology of Prov. 1–9 from the anthropological focus of chapters 10–29 (Doll; Westermann) underestimate the wisdom of the book's final redaction, which establishes the nature of the world as stage and criterion for human actions before dealing further with human conduct. Likewise, Gen. 1–3 does this for the Bible as a whole, and Rev. 21–22 for the world to come. Proverbs guides the church in serving God wisely and righteously in all its doings and interactions with creatures (12:10) and fellow humans alike (14:31).

Bibliography

Clifford, R. *Proverbs.* OTL. Westminster John Knox, 1999.

Doll, P. *Menschenschöpfung und Weltschöpfung in der alttestamentlichen Weisheit.* SBS. Verlag Katholisches Bibelwerk, 1985.

Fox, M. *Proverbs 1–9.* AB 18A. Doubleday, 2000.

Froehlich, K. "Glossa ordinaria." Pages 449–50 in *Dictionary of Biblical Interpretation,* ed. J. Hayes. Abingdon, 1999.

Hays, R. "The Letter to the Galatians." *NIB* 11:183–348.

Pelikan, J. *The Emergence of the Catholic Tradition (100–600).* Vol. 1 of *The Christian Tradition.* University of Chicago Press, 1971.

Preuss, H. *Einführung in die alttestamentliche Weisheitsliteratur.* Kohlhammer, 1987.

Rad, G. von. *Wisdom in Israel,* trans. James D. Martin. Abingdon, 1972.

Ridderbos, H. "The Significance of the Sermon on the Mount." Pages 26–43 in *When the Time Had Fully Come.* Eerdmans, 1957.

Roberts, J. *The Bible and the Ancient Near East.* Eisenbrauns, 2002.

Sick, H. *Melanchthon als Ausleger des Alten Testament.* Mohr/Siebeck, 1959.

Toulmin, S. *Cosmopolis.* Macmillan, 1990.

Van Leeuwen, R. "The Book of Proverbs." *NIB* 5:17–264.

———. "Liminality and Worldview in Proverbs 1–9." *Semeia* 50 (1990): 111–44.

———. "Proverbs." Pages 256–67 in *The Complete Literary Guide to the Bible,* ed. L. Ryken and T. Longman III. Zondervan, 1993.

———. "Wealth and Poverty: System and Contradiction in Proverbs." *HS* 33 (1992): 25–26.

Westermann, C. *Roots of Wisdom.* Westminster John Knox, 1995.

Whybray, R. *The Book of Proverbs.* Brill, 1995.

Wolters, A. "Nature and Grace in the Interpretation of Proverbs 31:10–31." *CTJ* 19 (1984): 153–66.

———. *The Song of the Valiant Woman.* Paternoster, 2001.

18

Ecclesiastes

CRAIG G. BARTHOLOMEW

Ecclesiastes is particularly challenging for theological interpretation. The vigorous debate among Jewish schools in the first century as to whether or not Ecclesiastes "defiled the hands" continues to this day. Now the discussion is about the extent to which Ecclesiastes is good news. A minority of scholars argues that Ecclesiastes affirms joy, while the majority finds it to be pessimistic, even hopeless.

History of Interpretation

By the fourth century CE, allegorical reading of Ecclesiastes was dominant among Jews and Christians, with "eating and drinking" being taken as referring to the Torah or the Eucharist, and the vanity element as a warning against excessive attachment to this world compared to "eternal" life. An allegorical reading of Ecclesiastes remained the dominant mode until the Reformation. It took the revival of literal interpretation by the Reformers to recover, for example, the possibility that "eating and drinking" refers to legitimate enjoyment of the God-given creation. Whether interpreted allegorically or literally, Ecclesiastes, prior to the rise of modern criticism, was read as Scripture, with the epilogue regarded as *the* key to the book.

Siegfried pioneered the source-critical approach to Ecclesiastes, identifying nine different sources in the book. Within English-speaking circles, McNeile and Barton developed more moderate source-critical approaches to Ecclesiastes. As the twentieth century progressed, a radical source-critical approach to Ecclesiastes became rare, and the book has come to be seen more and more as a unity, with the exception of the epilogue, which is almost universally seen as a later addition. The prime legacy of source criticism in the interpretation of Ecclesiastes is the tendency to read the book without the epilogue.

Hermann Gunkel initiated form-critical analysis of Wisdom literature, and the assessment of the forms used in Ecclesiastes has continued to play a fundamental role in the interpretation of the book. However, on the macrolevel of the form of Ecclesiastes, no consensus has been reached with regard to genre and structure. The tradition history of Ecclesiastes has been a matter of concern throughout the twentieth century. Within the OT wisdom tradition, Ecclesiastes has regularly been seen as a negative, skeptical reaction to mainline wisdom as represented by Proverbs. Gese identified Ecclesiastes with a crisis of wisdom in Israel, but scholars remain divided over the existence and extent of this "crisis."

A limited consensus has emerged out of historical-critical interpretation of Ecclesiastes. Few scholars nowadays defend Solomonic authorship; most regard Ecclesiastes as having been written by an unknown Jew around the latter part of the third century BCE. Most regard the book as a basic unity apart from the epilogue. However, there is no agreement regarding Ecclesiastes' structure, message, and relationship to OT traditions and to international wisdom. Historical-critical scholarship differs from precritical readings in its general rejection of the need to harmonize Ecclesiastes with theological orthodoxy. However, this loss of theological constraint has not produced agreement about the message of Ecclesiastes, as, for example, the variety of proposals for translating *hebel* indicates.

In recent decades a variety of new reading strategies have been applied to Ecclesiastes.

Childs's canonical reading has led him to reappropriate the epilogue as the key to the canonical function of Ecclesiastes. Childs reads Ecclesiastes as a corrective within the broader wisdom tradition, comparable to James's relationship to Romans in the NT.

The literary turn in biblical studies in the 1970s resulted in a spate of fresh literary readings of Ecclesiastes. Wright ("Riddle of the Sphinx") has analyzed the structure of Ecclesiastes by means of a close reading along the lines of "New Criticism." The theme of Ecclesiastes is understood to be the impossibility of understanding what God has done. The only advice that Qoheleth (the "preacher" or "teacher" of Ecclesiastes) gives is to enjoy life while one can. Loader (*Polar*) performs a modified structuralist reading of Ecclesiastes, whereby he discerns polar opposites as the heart of its structure. These polar opposites reflect the tension between Ecclesiastes' view and that of general wisdom. However, for Loader, Ecclesiastes finally is negative; he rescues it theologically as a negative witness to the gospel.

Perry approaches Ecclesiastes as the transcript of a debate between Koheleth (K) and the Presenter (P). Perry argues that Ecclesiastes elaborates on the paradigmatic contradiction in Hebrew Scripture that is introduced in the creation story of Genesis. It has to do with the way religious consciousness distinguishes itself from empirical or experiential modes of viewing life. Fox ("Frame") proposes reading Ecclesiastes as a narrative-wisdom text, with openness to distinguishing between narrator, implied author, and Qoheleth. Longman, Christianson, and others have pursued Fox's narrative proposal in a variety of ways. There are also examples of poststructuralist, feminist, and psychoanalytic (Zimmerman) readings of Ecclesiastes.

Hearing the Message of Ecclesiastes

There is something wonderfully ironic about a book on the enigma of life being terribly difficult to grasp, so that Ecclesiastes enacts its own message. Yet the following hermeneutical steps enable us to discern that message.

First, it is important to read Ecclesiastes and not just "Qoheleth." The legacy of historical criticism is to try to get behind the text to the "real Qoheleth." However, the case for reading the book as a literary whole is compelling; one is always on highly speculative ground when trying to get to the "real Qoheleth." The way forward is to focus on the different voices in Ecclesiastes, inquiring after the perspective of the implied author. Perry, Fox, Longman, and Christianson have done important work in this direction.

Second, reading the text as a literary whole must involve taking the epilogue seriously as part of that whole. An urgent issue in Ecclesiastes scholarship is to reopen the debate about how the epilogue relates to the main body of the text.

Third, Ecclesiastes must be read in the context of the canon of Scripture and especially of the OT Wisdom literature. Fox (*Time*) has done seminal work on the epistemology of Qoheleth in comparison with Proverbs and

181

rightly argues that Qoheleth's epistemology is empiricist, whereas that of Proverbs is not. However, Fox does not note the significance of this for the canonical interpretation of Ecclesiastes. Although Qoheleth goes out of his way to stress that he embarked on his quest by *khokmah* (1:13; 2:3), the key elements of his epistemology are reason and experience alone, and these always lead him down to the *hebel hebalim* ("vanity of vanities") conclusion (1:2; 12:8). Read against Proverbs, in which "the fear of the LORD is the beginning [foundation and starting point] of wisdom" (9:10), it becomes apparent how ironic Qoheleth's description of his epistemology is. In this sense Ecclesiastes is an ironic exposure of an empiricist epistemology as always leading one to a *hebel* conclusion. Further work needs to be done on irony and epistemology in Ecclesiastes.

Fourth, considerable attention needs to be given to the poetics of Ecclesiastes. Only comparatively recently have scholars come to recognize that the Wisdom books are literary compositions in their own right. Repetition, for example, is a significant characteristic of Ecclesiastes. Most significant are the repetitions of the *hebel* (vanity) conclusion and the joy/carpe diem passages. From one angle the history of the interpretation of Ecclesiastes is a sustained attempt to level the book to one or the other of these two poles. Either the joy passages are made subsidiary to the negative *hebel* conclusion, or the *hebel* passages are made subsidiary to the joy conclusion. The crucial question is how the *hebel* passages relate to the joy passages.

My suggestion is that in Ecclesiastes the *hebel* conclusions, arrived at via Qoheleth's empiricism applied to the area he examines, are juxtaposed with the joy passages, which express the positive perspective on life that Qoheleth received from his Jewish upbringing. These perspectives are set in contradictory juxtaposition so that, in the reading, gaps are opened up that have to be filled as the reader moves forward. The book thereby raises for readers the question of how these perspectives are to be related. Especially in the postexilic context in which Ecclesiastes was probably written, it would have been tempting for Israelites to use reason and experience to conclude that life is *hebel hebalim*.

A crucial question is whether or not Ecclesiastes itself gives us clues as to how to bridge the gaps between these perspectives. Understanding the irony of Qoheleth's epistemology is one major clue, telling us that if one starts with reason and experience alone in difficult situations, one will always end up with *hebel*. The other major clues to bridging the gaps come toward the end of the book. Normally in Ecclesiastes, a *hebel* conclusion is reached and then juxtaposed with a joy passage. Toward the end of the book this order is reversed (11:8–10), and particularly important is the exhortation prefacing the final section before the epilogue: "Remember your creator" followed by a threefold "before . . ." (12:1–8). This exhortation to remember is the equivalent of starting with the fear of the Lord. It means developing a perspective integrally shaped by a view of this world as being the Lord's.

Ecclesiastes and the Canon

Read positively, Ecclesiastes complements rather than contradicts Proverbs and Job. Proverbs is already well aware of retributive paradox (Gladson), especially in its latter chapters; Job and Ecclesiastes explore such paradox in detail, Job through a story of terrible suffering, and Ecclesiastes through an intellectual struggle for meaning. Also, Ecclesiastes, with its affirmation of creation and its understanding of work as toil and life as *hebel*, has strong links with Gen. 1–3.

Ecclesiastes never is quoted in the NT, although Rom. 8:20 perhaps alludes to it, as *mataiotēs* (frustration, futility) is the usual Septuagint word for *hebel*. Ecclesiastes, like Proverbs, hopes for justice, although it manifests no doctrine of the new creation, as do some of the prophets and the whole NT. Like Proverbs, Ecclesiastes contains reflections upon diverse topics such as wealth, pleasure, work, time, injustice, wisdom and folly, and government. Considerable work remains to be done in exploring these themes in relation to the rest of the Bible.

Ecclesiastes and Theology

The theological relevance of Ecclesiastes depends upon one's reading of it. Read as negative and hopeless, Ecclesiastes' only contribution will be as a negative witness to the gospel. However, a positive reading of Ecclesiastes indicates that it has an important positive contribution to make theologically.

Qoheleth's affirmation of joy is an expression of the doctrine of creation. In line with the goodness of creation, Qoheleth celebrates life under the motifs of eating and drinking, working, and enjoying marriage. This is not hedonism in the context of despair, but an affirmation of life as God has made it.

In a fallen world there is much that raises the most serious questions about the goodness of life. The empirical strength of those questions comes into focus in the *hebel* passages and conclusions. In terms of pastoral theology, Ecclesiastes is most important in its juxtaposition of *hebel* and joy in the experience of Qoheleth as he wrestles with the value of life under the sun. Ecclesiastes explores the struggle that believers go through as they endeavor to affirm life amid suffering, injustice, and disillusionment.

Qoheleth's struggle is more intellectual than that of Job. His quest is summed up in a rhetorical question: "What do people gain from all the toil at which they toil under the sun?" (1:3 NRSV). Central to Qoheleth's quest is the issue of how we know in such a way that we can trust the results—epistemology. In my view, Ecclesiastes is an ironic exposure of a way of knowing that depends upon reason and experience alone, as opposed to an approach that starts with remembering one's Creator, with faith and obedience. Ecclesiastes explores these issues in a narrative fashion, telling the story of Qoheleth's quest. It is not a philosophical book. Nevertheless, it does have implications for the theology of epistemology. In line with Proverbs and Job, Ecclesiastes affirms the importance of a theological starting point comparable to "faith seeking understanding." Ecclesiastes' exposure of empiricism and its logical consequences are of great contemporary relevance in the face of the nihilism so common in postmodernism.

Bibliography

Barton, G. A. *A Critical and Exegetical Commentary on the Book of Ecclesiastes.* ICC. T&T Clark, 1912.

Childs, B. *Introduction to the Old Testament as Scripture.* Fortress, 1979.

Christianson, E. S. *A Time to Tell.* Sheffield Academic Press, 1998.

Fox, M. "Frame Narrative and Composition in the Book of Qoheleth." *HUCA* 48 (1977): 83–106.

———. *A Time to Tear Down and a Time to Build Up.* Eerdmans, 1999.

Gese, H. "The Crisis of Wisdom in Koheleth." Pages 141–53 in *Theodicy in the Old Testament,* ed. J. Crenshaw. Fortress, 1983.

Gladson, J. A. *Retributive Paradoxes in Proverbs 10–29.* University Microfilms International, 1979.

Loader, J. A. *Ecclesiastes.* Eerdmans, 1986.

———. *Polar Structures in the Book of Qohelet.* De Gruyter, 1979.

Longman, T. *The Book of Ecclesiastes.* NICOT. Eerdmans, 1998.

McNeile, A. H. *An Introduction to Ecclesiastes: With Notes and Appendices.* Cambridge University Press, 1904.

Perry, T. A. *Dialogues with Koheleth.* Pennsylvania State University Press, 1993.

Siegfried, C. *Prediger und Hoheslied.* HAT. Vandenhoeck & Ruprecht, 1898.

Wright, A. G. "The Riddle of the Sphinx: The Structure of the Book of Qoheleth." *CBQ* 30 (1968): 313–34.

———. "The Riddle of the Sphinx Revisited: Numerical Patterns in the Book of Qoheleth." *CBQ* 42 (1980): 38–51.

Zimmerman, F. *The Inner World of Qoheleth*. Ktav, 1973.

19

Song of Songs

Tremper Longman III

From beginning to end, the Song of Songs contains poetic speeches of the most sensuous kind. An unnamed woman and an unnamed man speak lovingly to each other and also occasionally describe their love to an anonymous group of women, often referred to as the chorus. The topics of the poems are love and intimacy between a man and a woman, with no reference at all to God, the covenant, the history of Israel, or anything that has explicitly theological significance. What then does theological interpretation mean when it comes to the Song of Songs?

History of Interpretation

The history of the interpretation of the Song of Songs begins around 100 CE with the earliest preserved comments on the book. The voice that breaks the silence is that of Rabbi Aqiba, who famously stated: "Whoever sings the Song of Songs with a tremulous voice in a banquet hall and (so) treats it as a sort of ditty has no share in the world to come" (quoted from Murphy 13). Though brief, this statement says much about the early understanding of the book. First, those who were singing it with a tremulous voice obviously treated the Song's sensual imagery literally, while Aqiba,

186

certainly representative of institutional sentiments, sought to repress such readings.

Aqiba himself treated the Song in a manner similar to that which dominated synagogue and church until relatively recently, as an allegory. Approaching the Song as an allegory is a way of understanding its message as different from its surface meaning. The most commonly held form of allegorical interpretation of the Song in the synagogue understood the man to represent God and the woman to represent Israel. The story of the relationship of the man and the woman in the Song was actually a veiled way to present the history of God's redemption of Israel.

The targum to the Song (ca. 700–900 CE) is a case in point. The targum paraphrases the first unit of the Song (1:2–4), in which the woman, understood as Israel, begs the man, God, to take her into his chamber; it interprets this request as Israel's desire that God bring it into the promised land. In other words, the Song begins with the exodus from Egypt. From this point, the targum's allegorical interpretation follows Israel through its history.

Christian interpretation followed this strategy, only making necessary adjustments for its distinctive religious beliefs. Interpreters such as Hippolytus, Origen, Jerome, and Bernard of Clairvaux read the Song as an allegorical expression of the love between Jesus (the man) and the church or individual Christian (the woman). Often the details of the text were pressed into the service of a theological reading. This is illustrated by Cyril of Alexandria's comment on 1:13, that the woman's two breasts represented the OT and NT, and the sachet of myrrh that lodges between them stood for Jesus Christ, who spanned the two parts of the Bible.

Historical allegory was the interpretative method of choice from the earliest witnesses down to the mid-nineteenth century, but it was not the only type of allegorical interpretation. Also popular, particularly among some Jewish interpreters, was a mystical or philosophical allegorical understanding of the book. From the medieval period we have the example of the interpretation of Levi ben Gershom (thirteenth century), an Aristotelian, who distinguished between the material intellect, the acquired intellect, and the Active Intellect (Kellner). The last stood for God, and the first was the capacity for God's creatures to learn. The acquired intellect was knowledge accumulated through life. Levi read the Song as an allegory on two levels. The man represents the Active Intellect and the woman the material intellect; the Song shows them in dialogue, and their union is "a human being's highest perfection and greatest felicity" (Kellner xxi).

187

One further twist on the allegorical approach to the Song is provided by Don Isaac Abravanel, a rabbi from the sixteenth century (Pope 110–11). In his reading, the man is Solomon, and the woman stands for wisdom. Thus, their union represents Solomon.

No matter what the particular brand, the evidence is overwhelming that the dominant interpretative approach to the Song up to the mid-nineteenth century was allegorical. On the rare occasion that a theologian objected to the traditional interpretation and concluded that the Song was really about the intimate love of a man and a woman, this conclusion was typically accompanied by the argument that the book was not worthy of the canon. Theodore of Mopsuestia (350–428 CE) was such a theologian, and his interpretation was judged "not fitting the mouth of a crazy woman" by his own student Theodoret (Davidson 3).

Though allegorical interpretation of the Song held almost exclusive sway over the synagogue and church for many centuries, the nineteenth century saw a dramatic swing toward the position that the Song concerned human, rather than divine, love. Three factors led to this shift.

In the first place, allegory lost force as an interpretative strategy. To be sure, ancient and modern literature has allegories. Perhaps the best-known allegory, particularly to Christian audiences, is *Pilgrim's Progress*, by John Bunyan. As this book illustrates, however, true allegories do not hide their "deeper meaning." After all, the main character is a man named Christian, who is journeying toward the Celestial City, encountering obstacles like the Slough of Despond. On the other hand, the Song of Songs never hints at another level of meaning. Why take the two breasts of 1:13 as a reference to the OT and NT? For that matter, are there any indications within the text that the man represents God and the woman represents Israel? The answer is obviously negative. The allegorical interpretation was kept alive by the force of tradition, and in the post-Enlightenment period, this was not adequate to sustain it.

In the second place, the nineteenth century witnessed the rediscovery of ancient Near Eastern cultures, as the architecture and literature of Sumer, Babylon, Assyria, and Egypt, among others, were excavated and interpreted. Among that literature were a number of love poems that shared many of the themes, poetic devices, and metaphors of the Song of Songs. These texts were nonreligious, and this fact led many to conclude that the Song of Songs was also human love poetry (Watson; White; Fox; Westenholz; Cooper).

Finally, the nineteenth century was also a time of increased Western political involvement in the Middle East. In new ways biblical scholars became aware of Arab customs, and often connections were made. As relates to interpretation of the Song, there is a famous interchange between a German consul to Damascus named J. G. Wetzstein and the well-known Lutheran commentator Franz Delitzsch. Wetzstein attended weddings of local Arab leaders and noted in amazement that the songs they sang at their celebrations sounded similar to the Song. Delitzsch cites Wetzstein's correspondence in his commentary.

During this period the conclusion of most scholars was that the Song had been fundamentally misunderstood in the preceding centuries. It was read as an allegory when in reality it was love poetry. In retrospect, it appears that the synagogue and the church imbibed a form of Neoplatonic philosophy that created a contrast between spirituality and sexuality (so Davidson). The body and its desires were something to be repressed as inimical to one's relationship with God. If this is true, how could there be a book as sensual as the Song in the canon? To resolve the tension, an allegorical strategy of interpretation was adopted to shift the meaning of the text from what it seemed to say to what it "really" said (Phipps). The Song of Songs is an unfortunate example of the tendency to use theology/ philosophy to skew the interpretation of a text.

For the past century and a half, interpretation of the Song has moved away from allegory, but what has replaced it? Further, and more central to the purpose of this essay, if the Song is not about the relationship between God and his people, then what is the theological contribution of this book?

As the allegorical approach began to fade, most scholars adopted what has been called the dramatic approach to the Song. Delitzsch himself argued that the poetry of the Song told a story about Solomon and a woman named the Shulammite (6:13). He believes that the Shulammite is an actual historical figure. But, unlike many before and after him, he does not think she is the Egyptian princess or any prominent woman. Instead, he sees her as "a country maiden of humble rank, who, by her beauty and by the purity of her soul, filled Solomon with a love for her which drew him away from the wantonness of polygamy, and made for him the primitive idea of marriage, as it is described in Gen. ii 23ff., a self-experienced reality" (Delitzsch 3). He treats the story as a drama consisting of six acts, each with two scenes.

While Delitzsch represents the so-called two-character dramatic approach, the more recent commentary by Provan argues in favor of another popular interpretation that sees three characters. The Song is not a story about the love between a man and a woman, pure and simple, but rather concerns a love triangle. In Provan's own version of the story, the Shulammite has already entered Solomon's harem, but she has preserved her love for the young shepherd boy back home. The moral of the story is that true love overcomes coerced legal love.

Scholars have suggested other approaches to the book. The cultic interpretation of Pope (anticipated by Meek), the political interpretation of Stadelmann, and the psychological interpretation of Landy have not won many adherents. The main competitor to the dramatic approach today is the anthological interpretation of the Song. Since this view represents my own opinion (see Longman), I will describe it in the next section, though that discussion should be seen as completing our survey of the history of interpretation.

Hearing the Message of the Song of Songs

The problem with the dramatic approach is highlighted by its inability to settle on a single story. There are as many permutations of the drama, even to the point of disagreement over whether there are two or three main characters, as there are scholarly advocates. Every story has gaps that the reader must fill in, but the gaps in the Song are too large to be filled in with confidence. It appears that scholars are not reading a story from the text, but rather creating a story.

The Song of Songs is, thus, what its title implies: a single song constructed from a number of different songs. It is an anthology of love poems, bound together by a unity of purpose, consistency of character, and a few repeated refrains. The goal of the interpreter is not to describe the story, but rather to unpack the rich metaphors and explore the strong emotions expressed by the poet.

To be sure, those who recognize the anthological nature of the Song disagree about the number of individual poems. My own conclusion that there are twenty-three poems is closer to Falk than to Goulder, who believes there are only fourteen songs, or Landsberger, who does not give us a full study but gives us the impression that virtually every verse is a separate song. But in reality it does not really matter how many poems there are since the number does not affect interpretation.

Whether there are fourteen or a hundred poems, the Song's primary significance relates to love and sexuality, an important aspect of our humanity. The Song affirms human love, intimate relationship, sensuality, and sexuality. According to the Song, love is mutual, exclusive, total, and beautiful (Hubbard 260–63). The Song not only celebrates love; it also warns its readers not to hurry love (2:7; 3:5; 8:4) because sometimes the desire for intimacy brings pain (5:2–6:3; so Schwab).

Song of Songs and the Canon

The Song is one of only a handful of OT books whose canonicity was questioned (Beckwith 1–2, 275–76, 279, 282–84, 308–22). Those questioning its authority did so because they doubted that a book of such sensuality could be sacred. The fact that God's name is not found in the book (the supposed occurrence in 8:6 is unlikely) added to the skepticism. Their doubts, as we have suggested above, rested on a problematic contrast between spirituality and sexuality. Even those early witnesses that demonstrate the Song was widely accepted as canonical (2 Esdras, Josephus, Aquila, Melito, Tertullian) did so based on a faulty understanding of the book's interpretation. Unfortunately, the book's immediate reception is lost in obscurity.

In any case, once the false dichotomy between body and spirit is rejected, it becomes clear why such a book might be found in the canon. God loves his human creatures as whole people, not just as temporarily embodied spirits. Love is a powerful emotion and sexuality a large part of the human experience, bringing great joy and pain. The book's affirmations and warnings about love express God's concern for his people. As the last section explains, the book also makes a powerful contribution to biblical theology.

Song of Songs and Theology

Contrary to preconceptions, the Song of Songs fits into the rest of the canon as an integral part of a biblical theology of love and sexuality. As Trible has pointed out, the story begins in the Garden. Adam and Eve are there, naked, and feeling no shame. The implication is that, before sin, the two are completely open with one another, not only sexually, but also psychologically and spiritually. Genesis 3, however, narrates the fall, at which time the alienation between God and his human creatures has repercussions in the relationship between Adam and Eve. They cover themselves from the gaze of the other, and God removes them from the Garden. Reading the Song of Songs, in which many poems present the man and the woman in the Garden, enjoying one another's nakedness, makes one think of Eden and understand that the Song is about the redemption of sexuality. However, it is an already–not yet redemption because of the continuing problems acknowledged by some of the poems (5:2–6:3).

Furthermore, when understood within the context of the canon as a whole, the Song makes yet another important theological contribution. To be sure, God is not named or even alluded to within the book. Nonetheless, by celebrating the intimacy of the male-female relationship, it reminds us of the pervasive use of the marriage metaphor to throw light on God's relationship with his people. In the OT, that metaphor is used negatively, in that Israel's apostasy is often likened to adultery (Ezek. 16, 23; Hos. 1–3), but behind this negative use stands the positive statement that God's relationship with his people is like a marriage (see Jer. 2:1). Accordingly, the more we understand the depth of desire and the power of marital intimacy, the more we will understand our relationship with God. The exclusivity of the marriage relationship, as opposed to other human relationships, also makes it an appropriate vehicle to give insight into the divine-human relationship. Of course, in the NT the Christian's relationship with Jesus is compared to the relationship of a husband and wife (Eph. 5:21–33), and our ultimate union with our Lord at the end of days is described as a wedding (Rev. 19:6–8).

Bibliography

Beckwith, R. *The Old Testament Canon of the New Testament Church*. SPCK, 1985.

Cooper, J. S. "New Cuneiform Parallels to the Song of Songs." *JBL* 90 (1971): 157–62.

Davidson, R. "Theology of Sexuality in the Song of Songs: Return to Eden." *AUSS* 27 (1989): 1–19.

Delitzsch, F. *Proverbs, Ecclesiastes, Song of Solomon*. German, 1885, trans. M. Easton. Eerdmans, 1975.

Falk, M. *Love Lyrics in the Bible*. Almond, 1982.

Fox, M. "Love, Passion, and Perception in Israelite and Egyptian Love Poetry." *JBL* 102 (1983): 1–14.

———. *The Song of Songs and the Ancient Egyptian Love Poetry*. University of Wisconsin Press, 1985.

Goulder, M. *The Song of Fourteen Songs*. JSOTSup 36. JSOT, 1986.

Hubbard, D. *Ecclesiastes, Song of Solomon*. Communicator's Commentary. Word, 1991.

Kellner, M. *Commentary on the Song of Songs: Levi ben Gershom (Gersonides)*. Yale University Press, 1998.

Landsberger, B. "Poetic Units within the Song of Songs." *JBL* 73 (1954): 513–28.

Landy, F. *Paradoxes of Paradise*. Almond, 1983.

Longman, T., III. *The Song of Songs*. NICOT. Eerdmans, 2001.

Meek, T. "Babylonian Parallels to the Song of Songs." *JBL* 43 (1924): 245–52.

———. "Canticles and the Tammuz Cult." *AJSL* 39 (1922–23): 219–28.

Murphy, R. *The Song of Songs*. Hermeneia. Fortress, 1990.

Phipps, W. "The Plight of the Song of Songs." *JAAR* 42 (1974): 82–100.

Pope, M. *Song of Songs*. AB 7C. Doubleday, 1977.

Provan, I. *Ecclesiastes and Song of Songs*. NIVAC. Zondervan, 2001.

Schwab, G. *The Song of Songs' Cautionary Message concerning Human Love*. P. Lang, 2002.

Stadelmann, L. *Love and Politics*. Paulist, 1990.

Trible, P. *God and the Rhetoric of Sexuality*. Fortress, 1978.

Watson, W. G. E. "Some Ancient Near Eastern Parallels to the Song of Songs." Pages 253–71 in *Words Remembered, Texts Renewed*, ed. J. Davies et al. Sheffield Academic Press, 1995.

Westenholz, J. "Love Lyrics from the Ancient Near East." Pages 2471–84 in *Civilizations of the Ancient Near East,* ed. J. Sasson. Vol. 4. Charles Scribner's Sons, 1995.

Wetzstein, J. "Die syrische Dreschtafel." *Zeitschrift für Ethnologie 5* (1873): 270–301.

White, J. *A Study of the Language of Love in the Song of Songs and Ancient Egyptian Love Poetry*. Scholars Press, 1975.

20

Isaiah

RICHARD L. SCHULTZ

The book of Isaiah has had a profound effect on Judaism and the Christian church. The prophet Isaiah is often viewed as the most significant of ancient Israel's prophets. Furthermore, due to its well-known messianic prophecies, Isaiah has been known as the "Fifth Gospel" since early in the Christian era (Sawyer 1). Nevertheless, for more than a century, its theological legacy has been obscured by historical-critical claims that, in addition to the eighth-century prophet, two or more major authors or prophetic circles as well as numerous editors and glossators over a period of nearly half a millennium contributed to the book. They supposedly produced a diverse and diffuse anthology with a prophetic voice that, theologically, makes "an uncertain sound." In recent decades, however, a renewed focus on the book's unity has led to a greater appreciation of its major themes and literary motifs.

History of Interpretation

Isaiah's significance was immediately recognized, becoming the prophetic book most frequently quoted in the NT and cited in the Mishnah, as well as the most copied prophetic book among the Dead Sea Scrolls. Sirach 48:17–25 recounts the events of Hezekiah's reign, just as Isa. 36–39 does. Sirach describes the prophet Isaiah as "great and faithful in vision" (v. 22 AT) and as the one who "by the spirit of might . . . saw the last things and comforted those who mourned in Zion" (vv. 23–24 AT; likely referring to Isa. 61:2–3). The existence of the first-century CE pseudepigraphical book *The Martyrdom and Ascension of Isaiah* also attests to Isaiah's import. The Talmudic tractate *Baba Batra* (15a) claims, "Hezekiah and his colleagues wrote Isaiah."

The LXX translator(s) tended to "personalize" the text, turning third-person references into first- and second-person statements, and to create a "preached text" by turning statements into commands. Jewish nationalism was asserted, contrary to the Hebrew text's "generosity toward the nations" (Baer 278–79). The targum affirmed the messianic understanding of Isa. 9; 11; and 52:13–53:12 (as well as 10:27; 16:1, 5; 28:5; 43:10), but not of 7:14. The targum describes the Messiah not simply as an eschatological figure but as "something of an eternal figure," for there is a "tendency to move from anticipation to actuality in respect of God's action" with regard to Messiah. Israel's "saving response to God is seen as already under way" (Chilton xviii–xix).

Origen (185–254) authored the first known commentary on Isaiah, but it remained incomplete. Early full commentaries were written by Eusebius of Caesarea, Jerome, and Cyril of Alexandria. The importance of the book for the fathers was due primarily to its messianic prophecies, and their interpretation basically followed that of the NT. Patristic commentators emphasized Israel's rejection of the Messiah and consequent judgment, although a remnant would be saved, as well as God's blessing on the nations. They used Israel's legalistic blindness as a warning to Christians to beware of idolatry (McKinion xxi). According to Jerome, Isaiah "should be called an evangelist rather than a prophet, because he describes all the mysteries of Christ and the church so clearly that one would think he is composing a history of what already happened rather than prophesying what is to come" (McKinion 3). A sampling of patristic interpretation illustrates their christological and ecclesiological emphases: Isaiah 2:1–6 refers to the law being first given to the apostles and then delivered to all peoples by them (Theodoret of Cyr). The seven women of 4:1 are the seven churches (Victorinus of Petovium). The branch of 4:2–4 is Jesus (Bede). The angelic cry "holy, holy, holy" displays the Trinity (Jerome). The desolation of the land announced in 6:11 refers to that carried out by the Romans (Eusebius of Caesarea). The animal harmony described in 11:6 depicts the makeup of the church (Chrysostom). And 35:6 refers to the healing ministry of Jesus.

Nine complete commentaries remain from the medieval period. Two medieval interpreters, in particular, helped pave the way for later modernist approaches. Andrew of St. Victor gave exceptional attention to historical concerns, writing a prologue to Isaiah in which he described the prophet's life and character. Unlike his contemporaries, he interacted with both Jerome and the rabbis, citing without refutation the rabbinic interpretation of 7:14 as referring to Isaiah's son, even though affirming the messianic interpretation. In the case of 53:3, however, he accepted the Jewish interpretation that this refers to the Jews in the Babylonian captivity or to the prophet (Smalley 162–65). Another medieval interpreter, Abraham Ibn Ezra, is credited with being the first extant commentator (in 1155) to attribute the second part of the book to an anonymous prophet in Babylon on the eve of the Persian conquest. In this claim, Ibn Ezra by more than six centuries anticipated the similar conclusion of two German scholars, Döderlein and Eichhorn.

Various scholars built on the insights of late-eighteenth-century German scholars. Isaiah 40–66 was viewed as distinctive in three major respects: (1) It addresses a different audience than 1–39, exiles in Babylon anticipating an imminent return to Zion, even naming the Persian ruler Cyrus. (2) It contains different theological emphases, focusing on God as Creator of Israel and sovereign over the nations and on God's servant as the bringer of salvation, rather than on God's exaltation through judgment and through the reign of the messianic king. (3) It has a more flowing and lofty poetic style, making extensive use of repetition and rhetorical questions. This culminated in Bernhard Duhm's influential commentary of 1892, distinguishing three primary authors: one preexilic, associated with chapters 1–39; one late exilic, associated with 40–55; and one postexilic, associated with 56–66. These authors eventually became known as First Isaiah, Second Isaiah, and Third Isaiah. However, these three major sections were hardly to be viewed as unified compositions. According to Duhm, for example, chapters 13–23 were edited in the second half of the second century BCE, 24–27 were composed around 128 BCE, 34–35 stemmed from the Maccabean period, 36–39 were added from 1–2 Kings, and four "Servant Songs" that neither Second nor Third Isaiah had authored were inserted into chapters 40–55. From Duhm onward, more than half a dozen authorial and editorial hands were seen as involved in the production of the final canonical book, with only a few hundred verses being ascribed to the eighth-century prophet.

This "search for the historical Isaiah" essentially eliminated any possibility of a unified theological reading. For nearly a century, those rejecting authorial unity ceased to write on the entire book, commenting instead on critically distinguished subsections thereof. Nor did they give much attention to developing plausible explanations for how all of the diverse writings ultimately came to be included in one prophetic scroll. The focus rather was on discerning those texts that, for various reasons, could *not* have originated with the eighth-century prophet. The prophet ceased to be viewed as a divine spokesperson who received a revelation of God's plan for his covenantal people, both present and future, which he, in turn, communicated to them with passion, persuasion, and poetry with the words "thus says the LORD."

In the late 1970s a new phase of Isaianic studies began, as scholars began to investigate various unifying elements. For the most part they focused on phenomena within the text that generations of conservative scholars had pointed out in support of Isaianic authorship. These scholars variously attributed the observed unity (Schmitt 117–27) to a connecting hinge (Ackroyd), canonical relationships (Childs), thematic patterns (Clements), cultic prophetic activity (Eaton), symbolic structures (Lack), prophetic schools (Mowinckel), unitary editing (Rendtorff and Steck), or editorial insertions and stylistic imitation (Williamson). In addition, a number of "assured results" of Isaianic studies since Duhm have been questioned, including the late dating of much of 13–23, the apocalyptic label for 24–27, the Deuteronomistic origin of 36–39, the distinctiveness of the Servant Songs, and the existence of Third Isaiah (Schultz, "How Many 'Isaiahs,'" 154). The application of newer rhetorical-literary approaches (such as those of Conrad, Gitay, Melugin, Muilenburg, Polan, and Quinn-Miscall) has also contributed to more holistic readings. Conrad focuses on "repetition in vocabulary, motif, theme, narrative sequence, and rhetorical devices" that creates cohesion (30), while Quinn-Miscall reads Isaiah "as a single work, a vision expressed in poetic language," emphasizing imagery, "the picture displayed by Isaiah" (169). As a result, the dominant focus has once again shifted to the unity of Isaiah rather than on its many authors and editors. However, now the emphasis is not on the one *prophet* Isaiah, as was the predominant view up until the nineteenth century, but on the one *book* Isaiah.

Hearing the Message of Isaiah

The current focus on the common themes, motifs, and verbal parallels throughout Isaiah, leading to a new focus on the unity of the book, allows

197

one to once again hear the message that has been largely drowned out by more than a century of historical-critical debate. Such a unified reading is not dependent on one's ability to identify the particular "prophetic voice" that is speaking in a given passage (contra Goldingay 2–5); rather, one must trace the development of prophetic thought in the course of the book. One such approach is to follow a macrostructural model for understanding the message. William J. Dumbrell (107) divides the book into eight sections that alternate between *history* and *eschatology*, with the first and final sections containing both elements. W. H. Brownlee, C. A. Evans, and A. Gileadi view the book as following a symmetrical, or "bifid," structure (Evans), dividing Isa. 1–33 and 34–66 into seven corresponding sections. David Dorsey expounds the book following an ABCDC′B′A′ chiastic structure (234). Although each of these proposals reflects recurrent thematic emphases, it is difficult to distinguish clearly between history and eschatology within blocks of prophetic texts or to assume that a competent reader can discern and adequately evaluate elaborate structural patterns. *Therefore, in unfolding the message, it is preferable to proceed through the book sequentially,* synthesizing section-by-section how major themes are developed through the repetition of key words, images, and motifs, intertextual links, and narrative analogies.

Barry Webb notes four indicators of formal and thematic unity within the book ("Zion," 67–72): the title in 1:1, the emphasis on the heavens and the earth at the beginning and end of the book, the role of the Hezekiah narrative in 36–39 within the overall structure, and the focus on Zion/Jerusalem throughout. Each of these indicators will be discussed in our journey. Isaiah 1:1 claims all that follows not simply *includes* but *is* "the vision concerning Judah and Jerusalem that Isaiah son of Amoz saw during the reigns of Uzziah, Jotham, Ahaz and Hezekiah, kings of Judah," a prophetic ministry spanning more than half a century. The reference to a succession of Davidic kings fully roots the book in the events that unfolded in eighth-century Israel, while the use of the term "vision" (*khazon*) indicates that the prophecy results from divine revelation rather than from human insight. The visionary role of the eighth-century prophet is noted in 1:1; 2:1; and 13:1; no new prophetic figure is explicitly introduced in Isa. 40 or 56 to give legitimacy to the presence of a Second or Third Isaiah.

Chapter 1 offers an introductory indictment of Judah and Jerusalem, announcing both the ongoing beating of God's rebellious child and the future purging of the morally polluted city.

However, a second title introduces a vision not of contemporary Jerusalem but of Jerusalem's future exalted temple mount to which all nations will stream (2:1–4), indicating that the scope of Isaiah's vision extends from the prophet's day to the "last days." The prophet implores the house of Jacob to "walk in the light of the LORD" now, just as all nations will do then. Numerous parallels between the initial chapters (1:1–2:4) and the final chapters (63–66, see Tomasino) form an inclusio (bookends) around the main body: the (present or new) "heavens and earth," the future glorification of Zion, and the reference to God's people as rebels (*pasha'*, 1:2; 66:24). The central section of chapters 1–5 (within an apparent ABCB′A′ structure) describes God's judgment against all "the proud and lofty" men and women, humbling them so that the LORD alone will be exalted (2:6–4:1; cf. 2:11–12, 17). The coming devastation is contrasted with the future glory of Mt. Zion (4:2–6//2:1–5), before the section ends with a second indictment against Judah and Jerusalem (5:1–30//1:2–31), this time portrayed not as a rebellious child or harlot but as an unfruitful vineyard.

In Isa. 6, against the backdrop of the end of the half-century reign of Uzziah, Isaiah encounters the LORD of Hosts as the exalted King who sends him to his estranged people, although the prophetic proclamation will result in hardening and judgment rather than repentance and salvation. Isaiah 7–8 presents the first of three tests within the first half of the book.

King	Object of Trust	Outcome	Text
Test 1: Ahaz	Assyria	Failure	Isa. 7–11
Test 2: Unnamed	Egypt	Unclear	Isa. 28–33
Test 3: Hezekiah	God	Success	Isa. 36–39

In each test, the Davidic king is tempted to trust in foreign alliances rather than in Yahweh's covenantal election of Zion. (The second and third passages are tied to the first by numerous intertextual and thematic links, cf. 7:9 + 28:16; 8:7–8 + 28:17–29; 8:14 + 28:16; 8:15 + 28:13; also 37:1; 7:3 + 36:2; 7:4 + 37:6; 7:11, 14 + 37:30; 38:7, 22.) The prophet's trust (8:17) is in sharp contrast to Ahaz's doubt (7:11–13). In the face of the present Davidic king's failure, Isa. 9–11 announces God's future intervention in history (note the inclusio formed by 5:3 and 8:22, bracketing Isa. 6–8). This is to happen both in judging Assyria (10:24–27) and in the coming of a future Davidic ruler who will not falter (Isa. 9; 11). A hymn caps all this off, celebrating the future victory (Isa. 12, a partial reprise of the Song of the Sea in Exod. 15).

The so-called oracles concerning the foreign nations section (Isa. 13–23) affirms God's sovereignty over both the neighboring states (14:28–17:14) and the great powers (chs. 18–21). Accordingly, God's people are neither to fear them nor to trust them. Although these chapters frequently have been ascribed to a much later date, Hayes and Irvine offer a convincing interpretation of them against the backdrop of eighth-century political developments (17–33). In the introductory subsection, Babylon is addressed (13:1–14:23) and is already a major player in Isaiah's day (see 39:1, 5–7). Serving as "a fitting symbol of that arrogant pomp and power of the world," the fall of the king of Babylon is described in hyperbolic poetic terms, anticipating "the eventual fall of the whole world system which stands in opposition to God" (Webb, *Message*, 81). But Zion is equally prominent: the next two subsections begin by affirming Zion's security (14:32; 18:7) and conclude by describing an assault on Zion (17:12–14; 22:1–14; Jenkins 239).

Isaiah 24–27 usually is labeled as "late apocalyptic" and therefore often ignored in tracing Isaiah's message. However, most of its major motifs and emphases can be found in nonapocalyptic prophetic texts, and key apocalyptic elements are lacking in these chapters (e.g., symbolic visions, schematization of history, angelic interpreter). Furthermore, this section displays thematic continuity with Isa. 13–23 in its depiction of a world judgment expressing divine wrath against human pride and national presumption (Isa. 24). Expressions of praise are also prominent: 24:14–16a; 25:1–5, 9–12; 26:1–19. Intertextual links with earlier chapters are striking (25:4 → 4:6; 26:1 → 12:2; 26:15 → 9:3; 27:2–5 → 5:1–7). This section also develops major themes from the preceding chapters: the humbling of the proud and lofty (25:10–12; 26:5–6), rebellion (24:20), faith (26:2–4), and Zion's future (24:23; 25:6–8; 27:13). The focus is on two unidentified cities: the ruined city (*qiryat-tohu*, 24:10) that opposes God, and the strong city (*'ir 'az*, 26:1) that trusts him (cf. 24:10, 12; 25:2 [2x], 3; 26:1, 5; 27:10), thus evoking divine visitation (*paqad*: 24:21–22; 26:14, 16, 21; 27:1, 3). Isaiah 24–27 lacks datable historical allusions, portraying more generally than chapters 13–23 how the fate of the nations ultimately will be determined when God triumphs over his enemies (chs. 24–25) on behalf of his people (chs. 26–27). At the heart of this section is a banquet for all peoples on Mt. Zion, culminating in the cessation of death (25:6–8; on the latter, see also 26:19–27:1).

Isaiah 28–33 is parallel in structure to Isa. 7–11, and contains a series of woe oracles (28:1; 29:1–15; 30:1; 31:1; 33:1) in which the rulers of Judah are once again challenged to trust Yahweh (i.e., Test #2 //chs. 7–8). In the course of these chapters, the specific situation becomes clearer. Rather than trusting in the assurances linked to the divine election of Zion (28:16), they are "obstinate children . . . who go down to Egypt without consulting me; who look for help to Pharaoh's protection, to Egypt's shade for refuge"

(30:1–2) against "Assyria[, who] will fall by a sword that is not of man" (31:8). Just as in Isa. 7–8, the description of failed human leadership in Zion is juxtaposed with the announcement of a coming ruler who will reign in righteousness and justice (chs. 32–33//9–11; esp. 32:1 and 33:17, but also 33:22, which recalls 6:5). The quietness and trust that was lacking in Isaiah's day will then be experienced forever (cf. 30:15 and 32:17), and the dulled senses will be sharpened (29:9–10, 18; 32:3–4).

Isaiah 34–35 has been variously described as a little apocalypse (Duhm), as poems dislocated from Second Isaiah (McKenzie), as postexilic additions forming a redactional bridge between First and Second Isaiah (Steck), and as the original conclusion of First Isaiah (Clements). However, proceeding from the previously mentioned suggestion that Isaiah has a two-part structure—perhaps supported by the DSS manuscript 1QIsaᵃ, which leaves three blank lines between Isa. 1–33 and 34–66—these chapters are best viewed as introducing the great reversal within the book: the theological transition from judgment to salvation. Seitz (*Isaiah 1–39*, 242) understands Isa. 34–35 as portraying the promise of the ultimate victory of Zion along with the defeat of the representative opponent of God (Edom in ch. 34, similar to the role of Babylon within 13–23 and Moab [25:10–11] within 24–27). The following chapters, 36–38, then offer a concrete historical example of this victory, with Assyria as the foe. Within the structure of Isaiah, these chapters function analogically in announcing eschatological promise and praise: 1–11 + 12; 13–23 + 24–27; 28–33 + 34–35. Chapters 34–35 are in stark thematic contrast. In 34 the garden becomes a desert; in 35 the desert becomes a garden (see the verbal parallels: vengeance, 34:8 + 35:4; streams, 34:9 + 35:6; haunts of jackals, 34:13 + 35:7; abode [*khatsir*], 34:13 + 35:7; will not pass through/journey on it [*'abar*], 34:10 + 35:8). In its introductory function, Isa. 34 anticipates the day of divine vengeance (v. 8), which will be described more fully in the final section (59:17; 61:2; 63:4). More significantly, Isa. 35 introduces numerous images and motifs of salvation and restoration that are prominent in Isa. 40–55 (according to one calculation, nearly 90 percent of the words in the chapter recur in the latter).

Since Duhm, it has been commonplace to assume that Isa. 36–39 has been inserted into the book from 2 Kings when Second Isaiah was added to First Isaiah. However, Seitz has argued that these chapters are more at home within the Isaianic tradition (*Zion's Destiny*, 193–94), especially in its development of God's sovereign control over history (37:26), the giving of a sign to the Davidic king (37:30), and the promise of a remnant from Zion (37:32). Taken together, these chapters serve two functions: (1) They present the third historical test, which King Hezekiah passes. (2) They facilitate the historical transition from Assyrian to Babylonian domination as insolent Sennacherib's doom is both predicted and described (37:21–38) and the prophet makes the first announcement of the Babylonian conquest of Jerusalem (39:5–7). Chapters 38 and 39 are nonchronological in order, both taking place *during* the Assyrian siege of Jerusalem, which is probably the event underlying the initial description of "the Daughter of Zion, . . . left like a shelter in a vineyard, like a hut in a field of melons, like a city under siege" (1:8). Chapter 38 describes Hezekiah's exemplary trust in God in a time of personal crisis, being rewarded with personal and national deliverance (38:5–6). Then chapter 39 describes his prideful failure in a time of personal recognition, being rebuked by the prophet who announces Jerusalem's coming destruction. These chapters form the climax toward which the entire first half of the book has been heading: the ultimate showdown between Yahweh and Assyria as Yahweh intervenes on behalf of Zion.

However, as a result of the announcement of Jerusalem's ultimate destruction, the question of Zion's future is necessarily raised. Following the transitional sections of Isa. 34–35 and 36–39, the remainder consists of three sections of nine chapters each. The first two end in a refrain-like warning: "There is no peace . . . for the wicked" (48:22; 57:21); the third ends with a graphic description of the ultimate end of the rebels (66:24). The book describes Zion's future restoration in three movements: (1) God's people will first be restored to the land through his anointed political deliverer, Cyrus (chs. 40–48). (2) Israel will be restored to God through the spiritual deliverer, the Suffering Servant (Isa. 49–57). (3) Then once again Zion will be glorified by Yahweh and the nations (Isa. 58–66).

Isaiah 40–48 begins with words of comfort to God's people. Following Sennacherib's western campaign ending in 701, the people of the northern kingdom (Israel) and many of the southern kingdom (Judah) were already in exile. (According to Sennacherib's Annals, he conquered 46 strong cities and countless small villages, leading 200,150 people into captivity.) Thus, reassuring words regarding restoration would have been in order already in Isaiah's day. Isaiah 40 offers the thematic introduction: your incomparable God returns! Paralleling Isa. 6, the prophet receives a fresh commission to announce the new thing about to happen: the coming "salvation." All but one of the major themes are addressed in Isa. 40: the powerful prophetic word, which transforms everything; the unrivaled sovereignty of the Creator God; the futility of idols and the gods they represent; the divine preparation and execution of the return (second exodus); and Jerusalem's comfort. The LORD's servant, the final theme, is developed in the following chapters. In Isa. 41, Yahweh's sovereignty is demonstrated in the calling of Cyrus (still unnamed) from the east, subduing kings before him (41:2). In Isa. 42 the true Servant of God is introduced and is contrasted by juxtaposition with Cyrus, whose violent ways (41:2, 25) he will not follow (42:2–3). Both Cyrus and God's Servant are called in righteousness (41:2; 42:6), called by name (45:4; 49:1), grasped by the hand (45:1; 42:6), and will accomplish Yahweh's will (44:28; 53:10, both using *khepets*). This servant is also contrasted with the chosen nation, which is blind and unresponsive (42:18–20), in need of redemption (chs. 43–44; cf. 43:1, 14; 44:6, 22–24). In 44:24–45:25, Cyrus is explicitly named and his work is described: he will bring about the destruction of Babylon (chs. 46–47). However, the focus remains on Yahweh rather than on Cyrus: he is the God who has carried and will continue to carry his people—in sharp contrast to the Babylonian gods, which must be carried in carts (46:1–4, each verse using some form of *nasa'*). The anticipatory call for the exiles to "leave Babylon" can already be sounded, for "the LORD has redeemed his servant Jacob" (48:20).

In Isa. 49–57, the coming spiritual deliverance through God's Servant is announced. Three passages describing the Servant's election, opposition, and vicarious suffering and exaltation (49:1–13; 50:4–11; 52:13–53:12) alternate with three extended passages describing Zion's current condition, coming comfort, and glorious future (49:14–50:3; 51:1–52:12; ch. 54). The servant has a twofold mission: to restore Israel, being made a "covenant for the people" (the means of reestablishing their relationship with God); and to "bring my salvation to the ends of the earth" as a "light for the Gentiles" (49:6, 8–9; cf. 42:6–7). The events of Isa. 53 bring about a remarkable shift. In Isa. 54–66, the word "servant" (*'ebed*) occurs only in the plural (11x): "The work of the individual suffering servant restores the national servant so that individuals within Israel once again can serve God" (Schultz, "Servant, Slave," 1195). The section concludes by offering the free gift of salvation to "all you who are thirsty" (55:1), while also setting forth its demands (chs. 56–57; cf. 55:6–8). However, the new exodus in its fullness will be postponed due to the "failure of Jacob-Israel to fulfil its role" (R. Watts, *New Exodus*, 58–59).

The final section of the book is framed by an indictment of the rebels among the people (*pasha'*, 58:1; 66:24)—not all of them will choose to become God's servants. However, the primary focus is on the glorification of God and Zion (*kabod*, 58:8; 59:19; 60:1–2, 13; 61:6; 62:2; 66:11–12, 18–19, a word that does not occur once in Isa. 49–57; cf. also "splendor," *pa'ar*, 60:7, 9, 13, 19, 21; 61:3, 10; 62:3). In response to God's accusations, the people confess their rebellion (59:12–13; cf. v. 20), and the Divine Warrior, in turn, zealously avenges them (59:15b–19; 63:1–6). His actions frame the description of the resultant blessings: foreigners will help to rebuild and glorify Zion (ch. 60), the mourners will be comforted and made participants in an eternal covenant (61:1–3, 8–9), and God's estranged bride will be restored (62:4–5). The climactic summary announces: "They will be called The Holy People, The Redeemed of the LORD; and you will be called Sought After, The City No Longer Deserted" (62:12). The praise and petition of the prophet (63:7–64:12) evoke the divine promise of judgment against the obstinate people and the creation of a new heaven and new earth, in which a restored Jerusalem rejoices in unmitigated material blessing and peace and an intimate relationship with God (65:17–25). People from all nations will come and see God's glory and worship him (66:18–23), but the rebels will be subjected to unending punishment (66:24).

A close analysis of Isaiah as a whole reveals a carefully edited composition. Each section has its own distinctive structure and emphases; numerous intertextual links serve to connect various sections. Repeated words and images indicate the centrality of Zion and faith, and of judgment followed by salvation. The book develops along a redemptive-historical trajectory, beginning with a portrait of Zion in Isaiah's day as it weathers several political-military crises. Then it moves ahead through the Babylonian exile and restoration under Cyrus to the renewal and glorification of Zion in the context of the new heavens and the new earth.

Isaiah and the Canon

As do most Israelite prophetic books, Isaiah draws frequently on historical traditions: creation (40:26; 42:5; 45:7, 12, 18; 57:16), the flood (24:18; 54:9), Sodom and Gomorrah (1:9–10; 3:9; 13:19), Abraham (29:22; 41:8; 51:1–2; 63:16), the exodus and wilderness rebellions (11:16; 43:14–21; 48:20–21; 51:9–10; 52:11–12; 55:12–13; 63:9–13), Joshua and the judges (1:26; specifically Gideon: 9:4 and 10:26; 28:21), David (28:21; 29:1; 37:35; 38:5; 55:3), and the post-Solomonic split into two kingdoms (7:17). More important are the covenantal foundations of Isaiah's portrayals of rupture and transformation:

1. Creation/Noahic: 24:5–6; 51:3; 54:9–10
2. Patriarchal: 10:22; 41:8–10; 48:19; 49:18–21; 54:1–3; 61:7, 9; 65:9
3. Sinai: 2:3; 4:2–6; 5:18–30; 42:24–25; 56:1–8

4. Davidic: 9:6–7; 11:1–5, 10; 16:5; 32:1; 55:3
5. New: 32:15–20; 33:24; 51:4–7; 61:8

The book's central passage, Isa. 36–39, appears in nearly identical form in 2 Kings 18:13–20:19 (although Hezekiah's written prayer following his illness is without parallel; Isa. 38:9–20). Second Chronicles 32:1–26, 31 summarizes these events much more briefly, offering an intriguing inter- pretation involving a divine test of "all that was in [Hezekiah's] heart" (v. 31). His heart reflected initial pride and ingratitude, which provoked divine wrath, as well as self-humbling, delaying the consequences of divine wrath (vv. 25–26). There are also similarities between 2 Kings 16:5 and Isa. 7:1. Second Chronicles 26:22 and 32:32 claim that Isaiah wrote accounts of Uzziah's and Hezekiah's reigns.

The verbal and thematic parallels between Isaiah and other prophets, such as with Micah (esp. Mic. 4:1–3//Isa. 2:2–4) or Jeremiah, have often been recognized (Schultz, *Search for Quotation*, 34–42, 290–329), indicating that Isaiah both influenced and was influenced by his prophetic colleagues.

More profound and pervasive, however, is Isaiah's influence on NT writ- ers. According to J. Watts (111; see Sawyer 26–28), 194 NT passages contain allusions to verses from 54 of Isaiah's 66 chapters. Citations are especially frequent in Matthew, Luke/Acts, Romans, Hebrews, and Revelation, with Isa. 6:9–10; 40:3; and 56:7 being quoted three times each. If one analyzes the explicit NT quotations of Isaiah, one can identify four main categories: (1) messianic prophecies, distinguishing (a) texts fulfilled by Jesus (apolo- getically useful examples of fulfilled prophecy: 9:1–2; 11:10; 42:1–3, 4; 49:6; 53:1, 4, 7–8, 9; 61:1–2) and (b) texts applied (or transferred) to Jesus (54:13; 55:3; 56:7; 62:11); (2) eschatological texts (referring to salvation history and the "last things": 25:8; 27:9; 45:23; 49:8, 18; 59:20–21; 65:1–2); (3) texts applied to the Christian life or used to teach doctrine (22:13; 40:6–8, 13; 45:21; 52:7, 11, 15; 53:12; 59:7–8; 64:4; 66:1–2); and (4) texts pointing to parallels between events or Israel's conduct in the OT and in the NT (1:9; 6:9; 7:14; 8:14, 17; 10:22–23; 28:11–12, 16; 29:10, 13, 14; 40:3–4; 43:20–21; 52:5; 54:1). Going beyond individual citations, scholars have identified the foundational use of Isaiah in various biblical books. R. Watts dem- onstrates that a "dual perspective of salvation and judgment—both within the context of the INE [the Isaianic new exodus]—seems to provide the fundamental literary and theological structure of Mark's Gospel," and that the "Markan Jesus apparently understood his death in terms of the Isaianic 'servant'" (*New Exodus*, 4, 384). Similarly, "the entire Isaianic New Exodus program provides the structural framework for the narrative of Acts as well as the various emphases developed with this framework" (Pao 250). According to Hays, Paul quotes Isaiah thirty-one times, since, as is especially evident in Romans, Paul "reads in Isaiah the story of God's eschatological redemption of the world" (223). After examining fifty allusions to Isaiah in Revelation, Fekkes claims that his "interpretation of Isaiah in particular was clearly one of the more important pre-visionary influences which provided the substance and inspiration for the vision experience and for its final redaction" (290). In sum, one must conclude that Isaiah has influenced the NT more than any other OT book.

Isaiah and Theology

Isaiah's potentially rich contribution to systematic and practical theology has been more piecemeal than profound for a number of reasons. For more than a century, historical-critical scholars have divided up the book among various authorial and editorial hands. They thus claim that it is impossible to find—and even inappropriate to seek—a unified theology in the book (Roberts 130–31). Typical of this approach is Hans Wildberger, whose massive German-language commentary on Isa. 1–39 concludes with (fifty pages of) summaries of the theology of both the Isaianic and the non-Isaianic portions, even excluding Isa. 40–66 from consideration. Furthermore, even when synthesizing Isaiah's theology, interpreters commonly turn instinctively to systematic categories such as Yahweh—LORD of the nations, Israel—the people of God, Christology, and eschatology.

Accordingly, theologians typically have mined Isaiah's theological riches in search of raw materials for constructing various doctrines. Two examples offer illuminating illustrations. Following early Christian interpreters, such as Origen, Tertullian, and Gregory the Great, some systematic theologians (such as Henry Thiessen) find in Isa. 14 (especially vv. 12–15) a characterization and description of the fall of Satan, which is linked to Ezek. 28 as well as Luke 10:7–19 and Rev. 12:7–9. Others reject such use of Isa. 14 as "double-meaning" exegesis. However, the former approach ignores the context of the description at the head of Isaiah's Oracles concerning Foreign Nations (Isa. 13–23). The latter approach disregards the function of Babylon within canonical Scripture as the prototypical foe of God and his purposes in the world, perhaps accounting for its placement as the first of the oracles.

A more significant example is the use of messianic texts drawn from Isaiah to construct an OT Christology or as reading selections for the church year. On the one hand, such approaches often focus primarily on the triad Isa. 7, 9, and 11 as advent texts and on Isa. 53 as a passion text. On the other hand, historical-critical scholars often view the former and the latter as presenting distinctive or even contradictory messianic portraits stemming from different authors and eras. More commonly, historical-critical scholars view the former as too theologically advanced to come from the eighth-century prophet or as simply reflecting idealized poetic portraits of leadership that focused on Hezekiah or Josiah or some other future king of Judah. However, such approaches overlook the placement and intertextual relationship between these texts. As argued above, the Davidic-king texts within Isa. 1–39 and the servant texts within Isa. 40–66 are integral to the progression of thought in their respective contexts (the terms "king" and "servant" therein being uniquely suited as messianic designations). Isaiah 32 and 33 also should be included in christological reflections, since they also mention the future king, functioning similarly to Isa. 9 and 11. Furthermore, in portraying the servant's act of vicarious atonement, Isa. 53 must be viewed as "part of a grander and more comprehensive vision of purification" within the book (Groves 87).

Moreover, these two messianic figures legitimately can be identified (see Schultz, "The King," 157–59). Both possess the Spirit (11:2; 42:1) and are linked to the Davidic covenantal promises (9:7; 11:1; cf. 55:3, with the servant serving as a covenant for the people: 42:6; 49:8). And both are royal figures who establish justice (11:5; 42:3–4), the latter being honored by kings (49:7; 53:12). In fact, Isa. 61:1–3 may be taken as a final "servant" text, especially in light of its use in Luke 4:16–22. However, the Immanuel text of Isa. 7:14, despite its use in Matt. 1, functions within the first historical test of faith as a confession of trust in the divine presence in the midst of a national crisis, rather than as a messianic prediction. Reading this text within its canonical context requires that we see Matthew's fourfold use of "fulfillment" language in Matt. 1–2 (1:20–23 → Isa. 7:14; 2:13–15 → Hos. 11:1; 2:16–18 → Jer. 31:15; 2:19–23 → Isa. 11:1).

In employing this term, the evangelist apparently is identifying events within the personal biography of Jesus the Messiah that echo events in Israel's corporate history and *fill* these earlier prophetic utterances *full* of meaning. It is therefore legitimate to affirm that "the gospel of earthly Jesus and risen Lord is found in Isaiah, *in nuce*. . . . In its temporal, literary, and theological organization, the Book of Isaiah is a *type of Christian Scripture*, Old and New Testaments" (Seitz, *Figured Out*, 104).

To be sure, Isaiah is neither a dogmatics textbook nor merely an anthology of ancient religious texts; rather, it is a prophetic witness to the divine word addressing the fears and hopes of God's people within the context of their historical situation. Accordingly, a theological synthesis of Isaiah will recognize the centrality of Jerusalem (48x)//Zion (46x) as God's chosen dwelling place, climaxing in its divine deliverance from Sennacherib's siege (Isa. 37:33–37; cf. 36:14–20), an event that may well have been the catalyst for the composition of the present book. Isaiah is thus clearly theocentric in focus. The Holy One of Israel (28x) is variously portrayed metaphorically as a disappointed father (1:2), a vinedresser (5:4–6; 27:3), a king (6:5; 33:22; 43:15; 44:6), a barber (7:20), a sanctuary and stumbling stone and snare (8:14), a banquet host (25:6), a warrior-hero (27:1; 28:21; 30:32; 42:13; 51:9; 59:17), a builder (28:16–17; 34:11), a shepherd (40:11), a pregnant woman (42:14), a husband (54:5), and a potter (64:8). He is Immanuel, the God who is with us (7:14; 8:8–9), standing behind every act of judgment or salvation, regardless of who his immediate agent may be.

In stark contrast to God's holiness is the people's guilt ('awon, 24x, as in 1:4), incurred through both idolatry and social injustice. A central sin of Israel as well as of the nations is pride (at least 17x), presenting two options— self-humbling or divine humbling (at least 15x), so that God alone will be exalted (esp. 2:11–12, 17; 5:15–16). God's sovereignty over the nations and over history is demonstrated as expressing his plan ('etsah, 5:19; 46:10–11). The nations play a central role in that divine plan (see Seitz, *Zion's Destiny*, 152–57), both as divine agents (10:5, 12) and as those who ultimately will worship and serve the one true God (2:1–4). Sometimes the movement is centripetal (45:5–6, 22–23) and sometimes it is centrifugal (49:6–7; 66:19–21), but throughout it is clear that God's covenantal blessings and salvation are not reserved for Israel alone. Isaiah is about mission. Through his mighty word God asserts his superiority over the gods (10:10–11; 44:9–10, 15, 17) and announces his acts of deliverance through his King, through his Servant, and through his own deeds as Divine Warrior (42:13; 51:9; 63:1–6). Thereby, he brings about the eschatological glorification of Zion on behalf of the remnant (10:20–22; 11:11, 16), so that there is a radical contrast between Zion's immediate and eschatological future (1:27; 2:3; 24:23; 46:13). In terms of the book's central images, the divinely prepared highway will lead the people back to their God (11:16; 19:23; 35:8; 40:3; 42:16; 43:19; 49:11; 57:14; 58:11; 62:10). Then their dulled and limited (spiritual and physical) senses will once again be fully operational (6:9; 29:9–10, 18; 30:10–11; 32:3–4; 33:23; 35:5–6; 42:7, 18–20; 43:8; 44:18; 59:10), and light ('or, 27x) will permanently dispel the darkness (*khoshek*, 13x, as in 9:2; 42:16).

These theological claims and assurances call for behavioral changes from God's people: salvation has its demands (55:6–8; chs. 56–58), and confession of sin is in order (59:9–15; 63:15–64:12). Isaiah's vivid portrayal of Israel's ungodly behavior parallels contemporary societal woes (5:8–25; 10:1–4). As modern readers, we are drawn into the "we-words" of Isaiah (Conrad 83–116; esp. 25:9; 26:1, 8, 12–13, 17–18; 33:2; 53:1–6). We, like the leaders of ancient Judah, are challenged to place our faith and trust in God alone (*'aman*, 7:9; 28:16; 43:10; 53:1; *batakh*, 17x, esp. 26:3–4). It is God alone whom we should fear, rather than fearing people or our circumstances (7:4; 8:12–13; 10:24; 11:2–3; 12:2; 19:16; 33:6; 35:4; 37:6; 40:9; 41:10, 13–14; 43:1, 5; 44:2, 8; 50:10; 51:7, 12; 54:4, 14; 57:11; 59:19), for God is ever with us. This is the abiding message of Isaiah.

Bibliography

Baer, D. *When We All Go Home*. JSOTSup 318. Sheffield Academic Press, 2001.

Chilton, B. *The Isaiah Targum*. The Aramaic Bible 11. M. Glazier, 1987.

Conrad, E. *Reading Isaiah*. OBT. Fortress, 1991.

Dorsey, D. *The Literary Structure of the Old Testament: A Commentary on Genesis–Malachi*. Baker, 1999.

Duhm, B. *Das Buch Jesaia*. HAT. Vandenhoeck & Ruprecht, 1892.

Dumbrell, W. *The Faith of Israel*. Apollos/InterVarsity, 1988.

Evans, C. A. "On the Unity and Parallel Structure of Isaiah." *VT* 38 (1988): 129–47.

Fekkes, J. *Isaiah and Prophetic Traditions in the Book of Revelation*. JSNTSup 93. JSOT, 1994.

Goldingay, J. *Isaiah*. NIBCOT. Hendrickson, 2001.

Groves, J. A. "Atonement in Isaiah 53." Pages 61–89 in *The Glory of the Atonement*, ed. C. Hill and F. James III. InterVarsity, 2004.

Hays, R. "'Who Has Believed Our Message?' Paul's Reading of Isaiah." Pages 205–25 in *SBLSP: Part One*. Scholars Press, 1998.

Jenkins, A. "The Development of the Isaiah Tradition in Isaiah 13–23." Pages 237–51 in *The Book of Isaiah*, ed. J. Vermeylen. Leuven University Press, 1989.

McKinion, S., ed. *Isaiah 1–39*. ACCSOT 10. InterVarsity, 2004.

Pao, D. *Acts and the Isaianic New Exodus*. WUNT. Mohr/Siebeck, 2000.

Quinn-Miscall, P. *Reading Isaiah*. Westminster John Knox, 2001.

Sawyer, J. F. S. *The Fifth Gospel*. Cambridge University Press, 1996.

Schmitt, J. *Isaiah and His Interpreters*. Paulist, 1986.

Schultz, R. "How Many 'Isaiahs' Were There and What Does It Matter? Prophetic Inspiration in Recent Evangelical Scholarship." Pages 150–70 in *Evangelicals and Scripture*, ed. D. Okholm et al. InterVarsity, 2004.

———. "The King in the Book of Isaiah." Pages 141–65 in *The Lord's Anointed*, ed. P. Satterthwaite et al. Baker/Paternoster, 1995.

————. *The Search for Quotation*. JSOTSup 180. Sheffield Academic Press, 1999.

————. "Servant, Slave." *NIDOTTE* 4:1183–98.

Seitz, C. *Figured Out*. Westminster John Knox, 2001.

————. *Isaiah 1–39*. Interpretation. Westminster John Knox, 1993.

————. *Zion's Final Destiny*. Fortress, 1991.

Smalley, B. *The Study of the Bible in the Middle Ages*. University of Notre Dame Press, 1964.

Tomasino, A. "Isaiah 1.1–2.4 and 63–66, and the Composition of the Isaianic Corpus." *JSOT* 57 (1993): 81–98.

Watts, J. D. W. *Isaiah*. Word Biblical Themes. Word, 1989.

Watts, R. "Consolation or Confrontation? Isaiah 40–55 and the Delay of the New Exodus." *TynBul* 41 (1990): 31–59.

————. *Isaiah's New Exodus and Mark*. WUNT. Mohr/Siebeck, 1994.

Webb, B. *The Message of Isaiah*. InterVarsity, 1996.

————. "Zion in Transformation." Pages 65–84 in *The Bible in Three Dimensions*, ed. D. J. A. Clines. JSOT, 1990.

21

Jeremiah

J. G. McConville

Jeremiah, one of the longest OT books, has given us the most memorable portrayal of a biblical prophet, and is also the source of the idea of the "new covenant."

History of Interpretation

Interpretation of Jeremiah has often focused on the prophet himself. The first great phase of modern study of the book, initiated by Duhm, distinguished between its prose and poetry. In isolating the poetry, Duhm was searching for the authentic words of the prophet, and therefore for the true prophetic experience. In this sense, his critical questions were inseparable from a religious interest. Duhm's work gave rise to further studies that pursued strictly historical questions, such as Mowinckel's classic division of the book's material into three strands: A (poetic oracles), B (prose sermons), and C (prose narratives about Jeremiah); others manifested religious interest. A supreme example is Skinner's treatment, in which the prophet is regarded as a model of prayer and of the individual's experience of God.

As a fruit of this phase in the critical study of the book, Jeremiah became the initiator and parade example of religious individualism, by contrast with the older type of religion in Israel, which was characterized as corporate and ritualistic. Jeremiah's qualification as an example of personal piety lay particularly in his prayers. A group of these prayers came to be known (inappropriately) as his "confessions" (viz., 11:18–23; 12:1–6; 15:10–14, 15–21; 17:14–18; 18:18–23; 20:7–12, 14–18). These prayers keenly express his pain and protest that arise directly from his call to be a prophet. Their honesty and boldness seemed new and important to the older critical scholars.

In this phase of interpretation, the new covenant (31:31–34) was regarded as a high point in individualistic religion, because of the idea of a transition from written code to knowledge of God that was "written on the heart."

A second important phase in modern interpretation focused, not on the prophet himself, but on the meaning of the book in its final redaction. Hyatt inaugurated the tendency to see the book as "Deuteronomistic" (or "Deuteronomic"). One theological advantage of this development was that it reinstated the prose sections of the book, which had been devalued in the first phase (and which often still suffer from that legacy). The Deuteronomistic interpretation allowed the accent to fall on the experience of the community in exile, and the capacity for prophecy to be reappropriated in new circumstances. The Deuteronomistic interpretation branched into a variety of models. Nicholson, for example, saw the prose sermons as the preaching of Jeremiah's message in exile, with developments and innovations. Carroll and McKane think, in contrast, that the book grew rather haphazardly over a protracted period.

In this phase the central theological issue was how the promises of Yahweh might be valid in the wake of the exile, which seemed to have changed everything. The new covenant could now be seen as the key to a new way of thinking about God's activity in Israel. For example, Unterman perceived a theological shift from a theology of repentance (in which Israel could avoid judgment by repenting) to one of "redemption," in which Yahweh took a quite new initiative in Israel's salvation, by *enabling* the people to be faithful (32:39–40). (How far the new covenant was really "new," however, was a matter of debate; Carroll.)

A final phase may be identified as that in which the book is regarded as a literary text. An example is Polk, for whom the "persona" of the prophet is a figment of the religious community's imagination, and who embodies aspects of their experience. One focus in this context is the parallel between the depicted life of the prophet and the life of Israel. Jeremiah's restoration after suffering becomes an earnest of the community's own restoration (cf. 15:19; 31:18).

In a modern reading of Jeremiah with theological questions, historical, literary, and canonical factors all play a part. In seeking to apply the message to church and individuals, we need to be aware first of its challenge to a Jewish people exiled in Babylon. We should, second, attend to its shape as a whole. In this way its "gospel," in the shape of new covenant and restoration, can be heard along with Jeremiah's analysis of the ills that brought judgment in the first place. The new covenant itself can be heard, not only as foreshadowing salvation in Christ, but also as a challenge to understand the radical nature of covenantal commitment, and of "worship in spirit and in truth." Finally, the ministry of Jeremiah is a model of courage, faithfulness, and true leadership, without becoming a pretext for an unbiblical "individualism."

The Message of Jeremiah

The message of Jeremiah can be traced initially by an account of the book's progression. Following the prophet's call (1:1–19) is a series of poetic oracles of judgment, together with exhortations to repent (2:1–6:30). The people's falseness in worship and faith is characterized, along with Jeremiah's grief over this (7:1–20:18). The failure of Judah's kings is lamented, and we are given initial visions of a wholly new order, including a messianic promise and judgment on Babylon (21:1–25:38). The stubbornness of the people is a major theme in 26:1–36:32, but at the heart of this section, paradoxically, is the Book of Consolation (BC; 30:1–33:26), which in turn is constructed around the new covenant. The fall of Judah and subsequent events are narrated (37:1–45:5). The last main section consists of Oracles against the Nations (OAN) and a further account of the fall of Judah (46:1–52:34).

Such an account is inevitably overly schematic. For example, the division offered above is that of the MT, while the LXX differs, being much shorter, but also having the OAN in the middle of the book rather than at the end. These two redactional types of Jeremiah have adopted different strategies to highlight the OAN, which play an important part in demonstrating a reversal of fortunes by God's grace. The account given is overly schematic in another way, for in drawing attention to the centrality (literally and theologically) of the new covenant, it passes over the fact that from an early stage salvation-notes are interspersed among passages of judgment (e.g., 3:14–18).

However, this overview does highlight key movements and themes. The first half of the book, up to chapter 25, gives an analysis of the problem with Judah in God's eyes. They have abandoned him for other gods (ch. 2), mistaken a trust in institutions for true religion (7:1–15), and become deeply corrupt as a society, so that no truth or trust is known or practiced (8:22–9:9). For this, God will act against them. His action can be seen as a dismantling of the elements of the covenant: temple, Davidic king, historic land (Stulman). Up to this point the organization of the book shows how such hope as Jeremiah might have originally had for a renewal in Judah closed down as the stubbornness of the people became evident (McConville). Such closure is symbolized by the prohibition placed on Jeremiah's intercessory prayer (7:16; 11:14; cf. 15:1).

In tandem with this systematic undermining of Judah's false trust is a strong theme of God's own empathy with the people, manifested through the portrayal of the prophet. Jeremiah stands on both sides of the issue, feeling the grief of the people that will surely come with the judgment (4:19–22), and also the anger of God because of their perversity (11:11–20). The unity of Jeremiah and God in grief and alienation from sinful Judah is clearly expressed in 8:22–9:3, which grounds Jeremiah's reputation as "the weeping prophet," yet where the true grievance turns out to be God's. On the other hand, the symbolic and representative character of Jeremiah's life is illustrated, for example, by the embargo on marriage placed upon him, as a witness to the tragic brevity of the life now held out to the people (16:2–4).

The emotional burden of this dual role on Jeremiah is extreme and leads to a lament in which he curses his birth (20:14–18). The death he thus seeks corresponds to the "death" that Judah itself must endure; and the continuation of prophet and message into the second half of the book is a token of life beyond that death for the people (Clines and Gunn).

The book is constructed so as to affirm that God's judgment is not the final word. The perspective of salvation beyond judgment occurs sporadically in the first half (3:14–18; 16:14–15), but it is stronger in the second half. Important turning points are the Davidic messianic promise (23:5–6), following hard on the condemnation of the historic kings (ch. 22), God's first promise that he will enable faith among the returned exiles (24:7), and the seventy-year term put on the exile, after which Babylon will be judged in turn (25:12–14). From chapter 24, the challenge to faith becomes the acceptance that God will first act in judgment. The insistence on this, which informs Jeremiah's confrontation with the false prophet Hananiah, for example (ch. 28), is also an insistence that God in the end will vindicate himself and his faithful people, as exemplified by Jeremiah.

A key phrase that expresses God's intention to save after judging is "I will restore your fortunes" (NRSV; "I will . . . bring you back from captivity," NIV), which comes first in 29:14, then seven times in Jer. 30–33 (BC). The core of this idea is God's "turning" (*shub*). Indeed, there is extensive play on this word in Jeremiah, since it can mean repenting and returning (on Israel's part) and a turning (of fortunes) brought about by God. In Jer. 30–33 the dramatic turn from judgment to salvation is vividly depicted. One device is the non sequitur, exemplified in 30:12–17 (picture of sin and judgment, vv. 12–15, followed "illogically" by a declaration of salvation, vv. 16–17). Another is the story of Jeremiah's purchase of a field in the midst of siege (ch. 32), an apparently nonsensical act that signifies a future for Judah against all likelihood.

God's turning Judah's fortunes is depicted as a new miraculous act. Jeremiah declares to God, "Nothing is too hard for you!" (32:17, cf. v. 27), and his intention to save hard-hearted Judah after the Babylonian devastation is put on a par with his primary acts in both creation and deliverance of Israel from Egypt (32:17, 21–22).

In the middle of the BC is the famous promise of the new covenant (31:31–34). This covenant has several elements: It will be made "with the house of Israel and with the house of Judah." It will be unlike the former covenant, in that its requirements (the *torah*) will be written "on their hearts." They consequently will need no teacher. And God will forgive their past sins. The agency of God himself in bringing about the renewed faithfulness of the people is prominent in this, and is repeated later in the BC (32:39–40). This becomes an important explanation of how there can be a future for Judah in covenant with God, given that they have so persistently flouted it in the past. The continuity with historic, geographical Judah should also be noted, since the new covenant promise is followed almost immediately by an assurance that the devastated city of Jerusalem will be rebuilt (31:38–40).

After this theological high point, the narrative returns to the account of the fall of Jerusalem and Judah, together with its causes. This account is not strictly chronological, since it embraces both Zedekiah, the last king (597–587 BCE; chs. 34, 37–39), and the earlier king Jehoiakim (609–598 BCE, chs. 35–36). Right to the end, Jeremiah continues to declare God's purpose to punish Judah by means of Babylon, and he is beaten and imprisoned for what is perceived as treason (37:13–16). Following the fall of the city, Jeremiah himself is spared the exile by the Babylonian authorities, but then is taken to Egypt by a party that sought its salvation in that quarter, despite Jeremiah's consistent warnings against this (24:8–10; 42:18–22).

Even so, the word of God still comes through Jeremiah to the people in Egypt, implying the possibility of grace even after this new act of disobedience (ch. 43).

In the last main section of the book are the OAN (chs. 46–51). These confirm the commission at Jeremiah's call that he would be a "prophet to the nations" (1:5). Unexpected is the application of the formula "Afterward, I will restore [their] fortunes" (48:47; 49:6, 39) to Moab, Ammon, and Elam. This shows how far the theology of the BC affects the structure of the whole book of Jeremiah. The oracles also confirm, however, God's intention to save Judah in the end. The demise of Babylon, accordingly, occupies most space here (chs. 50–51). In saving Judah, God is called their "Redeemer" (50:34).

Jeremiah and the Canon

The canonical importance of Jeremiah is evident not only from its length and its prominent position, but also from its influence on later books. Chronicles, Ezra, and Daniel cite Jeremiah's "seventy years" in their respective assimilations of the idea of a purposeful "exile" followed by salvation (2 Chron. 36:21; Ezra 1:1; Dan. 9:2). The Daniel text in particular shows how the principle established by Jeremiah goes well beyond the immediate historical circumstances for which it was conceived.

Jeremiah also develops themes already present in Hosea: God's faithfulness, the covenant people's unfaithfulness, the prophet's deep involvement in his message, signifying God's personal engagement with his people, and salvation after judgment (note Hos. 14). These then may be seen to have a broad grounding in the prophetic message. In fact, the judgment-salvation pattern, so clearly exemplified in Jeremiah, is embedded deeply in the whole prophetic corpus. While only Jeremiah gives the name of "new covenant" to the decision of God to save out of and in spite of sin, the theme is present in other prophetic books. Ezekiel, for example, also knows of the divine agency in replacing "the heart of stone" with "a heart of flesh" (Ezek. 11:19). (Dumbrell has shown how "new covenant," properly understood, is a feature of the prophets in general.) Moreover, Jeremiah's embodiment of the suffering of God is an important OT witness to the incarnation, and it has affinities with the Suffering Servant of the book of Isaiah. The primacy of God in the achievement of Israel's ultimate salvation, therefore, is not a matter of doctrine only, but entails his personal, costly commitment to his purpose.

The pattern of judgment-salvation in Jeremiah is also present in Deuteronomy. That book too knows of a judgment inevitably consequent upon Israel's stubbornness (Deut. 9:4–6; 30:1), and converts an exhortation to "circumcise your hearts" (Deut. 10:16; cf. the metaphor in Jer. 4:4) into a declaration that God himself will undertake to do this (30:6). While critical scholarship does not always recognize the historical priority of Deuteronomy over Jeremiah, the agreement of the two books on the pattern of salvation prohibits any simplistic antithesis between Law and Prophets in canonical terms. Therefore, in any explanation of the new covenant, the contrast between the law "written on stones" and "written on hearts" should not be absolutized into a categorical repudiation of Moses. A rhetorical aspect of the contrast should be recognized. The Law and the Prophets share an analysis of the human problem (persistence in sin), call for thoroughgoing moral and spiritual reconstruction (from the "heart"), and point to the grace of God, ultimately, as the source of reformation.

Jeremiah should also be placed in relation to the books of Kings. This is partly because there is material overlap between the two corpora (esp. in 2 Kings 25 and Jer. 52), reflecting the fact that both account for the same cataclysmic events in the history of Israel and Judah. In canonical terms, they tell the story of the covenant that is set up in Exodus–Deuteronomy, showing how the covenantal curses, threatened in Lev. 26 and Deut. 28, finally fall (Jer. 11:3–4; 2 Kings 17:19–20). While Kings knows that the exile of Judah will not be the end of the covenant between Israel and God (1 Kings 8:46–53), Jeremiah is more explicit on an actual restoration to its full blessings, especially in terms of return to the promised land. In this respect, Jeremiah echoes Deuteronomy more fully than Kings does (Deut. 30:3–5).

Finally, new covenant finds fulfillment in the NT. The Gospels attest to Jesus as fulfilling the "covenant" in his own blood (Mark 14:22–24; Matt. 26:26–28; cf. John 6:54). The sacrificial terminology in the context of a Passover meal comprehends Jesus' covenant-fulfillment in relation to the Mosaic covenant. Some ancient texts insert the word "new" in the Synoptic accounts here, testifying to an understanding in the church that the covenant inaugurated by Jesus was in fact the new covenant. This understanding is found expressly in 1 Cor. 11:25 (cf. 10:16; Rom. 11:27) and Heb. 8:8–13; 9:15; 10:16–17; 12:24.

The fundamental NT witness, therefore, is that Jesus fulfills the covenant with Israel. The adoption of the language of new covenant, especially in Hebrews, draws attention to the promise in Jeremiah (and behind it Deuteronomy) that God himself would act decisively to bring about the salvation that had always eluded his people because of their hardness of heart. The coming of Jesus is thus presented as the culmination of that "incarnational" trend, already visible in Hosea and Jeremiah, in which God commits himself, at cost, to the salvation of his people. Since Jeremiah's new-covenant language should not be used to evacuate the Mosaic covenant of force or meaning, as if it were a failed experiment, so its adoption in Hebrews, being part of that book's strong pattern of new replacing old, has a certain rhetorical aspect. "Fulfillment" and "abolition" are both tropes that, if pressed logically, can hardly be reconciled. Rather than postulating an "old" covenant abolished, it is better to think of a combined canonical witness to God's resolve ultimately to make his covenant with humanity effective.

Jeremiah's Theological Significance

Jeremiah tells a story that promises renewed salvation after judgment and names this as a new covenant, which, canonically, leads to fulfillment in God's act of salvation through Christ. However, as a word to the church, it functions not merely as a story with a happy ending. While the story line in Jeremiah depicts the prophet's call to repent as something in the past that went unheeded, a reading of the book paradoxically continues to witness to the perennial need to return to God. The memorable "return [repent], faithless children" (3:14)—where "faithless" is *shobabim*, a play on *shub*, "return/repent"—ironically depicts the moral condition of those who are ever under God's call to obedience, while displaying a tendency at heart to strain in the opposite direction (here Jeremiah is not far from Paul in Rom. 7:14–25). The structure of judgment-salvation, then, can be heard, not only as a once-for-all story leading to the triumph of Christ, but also as a portrayal of an ever-present possibility in God's dealings with people.

The book of Jeremiah helped its first readers to face an unmitigated calamity and come to terms with new acts of God. Its demolition of false objects of trust still speaks to those who have an unhealthy attachment to any particular form of "church," tradition, or any way of being religious that has become entrenched and comfortable. Judah's road to idolatry (Jer. 2) was strewn with the good intentions of much worship of Yahweh in his temple (7:1–15). Modern idolatries too may seem to cohabit easily with the form of religion.

Correspondingly, exile and restoration can call us to readiness for new ways of being in relationship with God. When false attachments are exposed for what they are, the way of faith can seem unsettlingly to lack familiar markers. Change can seem synonymous with chaos. In Jeremiah, salvation is both restoration of the old and exploration of the radically new. The return to land would be no mere recovery of the *status quo ante*; yet it was properly a restoration. The ambivalence is in the idea of "renewal" itself. Whatever shape the new might take, the same God leads and finds us there. With this reassurance we can sit lightly to religion as a familiar set of symbols, and find it again as the worship of God in spirit and truth.

Jeremiah uses "heart" metaphors to speak about this true religion (4:4; 31:33). The specific metaphors (involving circumcision, torah) are based, trenchantly, on elements in the religious tradition. With such language Jeremiah appeals for a loyalty and devotion of will and energies that run through the whole being. This prompts, finally, considerations about individual and community.

As we noticed, the appeal to the "heart" is not a mark of a turn to "individualistic" religion. Rather, in Jeremiah as in Deuteronomy (6:5), it calls for the thorough reformation and renewal of a whole community. There is thus no sanction here for the false polarities of individual versus community, or institutional versus spontaneous (notwithstanding the point about false attachments to institutional forms). Rather, Jeremiah calls the community of faith to be constantly renewed, in its breadth and depth.

What then of Jeremiah as the OT's greatest witness to an individual in communion with God? This individualism is precisely "prophetic." That is, Jeremiah demonstrates by his calling, ministry, and life how an individual can bear the responsibility for the burden of memory and obligation that belongs properly to the whole community. Jeremiah did not willingly choose the lonely path; it was laid on him by the people's abandonment of God, his own attachment to the "ancient paths" (Jer. 6:16), and God's call to him to be a prophet. He is thus not a model of individual piety as such. Rather, as a faithful Israelite, he proved equal to the challenge of standing against the powerful tide of his contemporary "modernity." That is his perennial challenge to believers, whatever form the temptation to compromise and apostasy might take in their time and place.

Bibliography

Carroll, R. P. *Jeremiah*. OTL. SCM, 1986.

Clines, D., and D. Gunn. "Form, Occasion and Redaction in Jeremiah 20." *ZAW* 88 (1976): 390–409.

Duhm, B. *Das Buch Jeremia*. Mohr, 1901.

Dumbrell, W. *Covenant and Creation*. Paternoster, 1984.

Hyatt, J. "The Deuteronomic Edition of Jeremiah." *Vanderbilt Studies in the Humanities* 1 (1951): 71–95.

McConville, J. G. *Judgment and Promise*. Eisenbrauns, 1993.

McKane, W. *Jeremiah*. Vol. 1, *1–25*. Vol. 2, *26–52*. ICC. T&T Clark, 1986–96.

Mowinckel, S. *Zur Komposition des Buches Jeremia*. Jacob Dybwad, 1914.

Nicholson, E. *Preaching to the Exiles*. Blackwell, 1970.

Polk, T. *The Prophetic Persona*. JSOTSup 32. JSOT, 1984.

Skinner, J. *Prophecy and Religion*. Cambridge University Press, 1922.

Stulman, L. *Order amid Chaos*. The Biblical Seminar 57. Sheffield Academic Press, 1998.

Unterman, J. *From Repentance to Redemption*. JSOTSup 54. JSOT, 1987.

22

Lamentations

CHRISTIAN M. M. BRADY

The book of Lamentations is one of the smallest works in the Bible and yet one of the most powerful and enigmatic. Written in the aftermath of the destruction of Jerusalem and its temple by the Babylonians, Lamentations expresses the grief and disbelief of those who lived through the horror and yet still looked to their God for their hope and deliverance.

Canon, Date, and Authorship

The book of Lamentations is found in the Jewish canon as one of the Megillot, the Five Scrolls. The LXX placed Lamentations after Jeremiah and Baruch, assuming the prophet to be the author, thus leading to its current place in the Christian canon. Wherever its location, its existence within the canon has never been challenged, within either Jewish or Christian tradition.

Almost all scholars agree that the book of Lamentations was written in the years immediately following the destruction of Jerusalem. Certainly these five poems express the kind of shock and despair that we might expect from an eyewitness, yet their form and style demonstrate that they were created as an act of reflection on their tragedy and as a memorial of it. Lamentations does not contain any glimpse of the restoration of Jerusalem and the temple that occurred after Cyrus the Great and the Persians defeated the Babylonians. They allowed the Jews to return and rebuild their holy city in 538 BCE. Thus, the time of composition is set within the years immediately following 586 BCE and before Jerusalem's restoration. Moreover, it is likely that the poet was one of the many who were not exiled to Babylon but remained in Judah and endured the daily reminders of the Babylonian conquest (Dobbs-Allsopp 4).

Jeremiah has traditionally been ascribed as the author of Lamentations, largely based upon the reference in 2 Chron. 35:25 to Jeremiah's having composed laments for the death of Josiah, but also due to the similarities in message and vocabulary between portions of the books of Jeremiah and Lamentations. The text of Lamentations itself is, in fact, anonymous, and most scholars today agree it is unlikely that it is the work of Jeremiah. In many ways it is the anonymity of the work that provides it with such great power, especially for today's reader. It is not a work by a named and distant prophet; rather, it is a work by "anyone/everyone" who has gone through such tragedy, and the reader is invited to identify with the author's perspective (e.g., Lam. 3, "I am the man . . .").

Form and Genre

The form and genre of Lamentations are unique within the biblical canon and as such deserve some comment. Lamentations is a collection of five poems, each intimately related by both structure and content. The first four are acrostics: the first letter of each stanza is a sequential letter of the Hebrew alphabet. Thus, the first stanza begins with *aleph*, the second with *beth*, and so on. There is variation within this form: chapter 4 has only two couplets per stanza, and chapter 3 has one couplet per stanza and repeats each letter three times (so the first three lines each begin with *aleph*, etc.). The final chapter does not have an alphabetic acrostic but echoes the acrostic form, with twenty-two lines paralleling the twenty-two letters in the Hebrew alphabet. The acrostic form is found in other ancient Near Eastern texts and may be merely intended as an aid to memory; however, it is more likely intended to demonstrate the completeness of Judah's grief, which is "from A to Z" (Gottwald).

Another key feature of Lamentations is the rhythm. In biblical Hebrew poetry the fundamental unit is two lines (or units) on each line of text, usually of similar length. In Lamentations and in other lament poems in the Bible, many lines are of unequal length, the first being longer than the second. This "limping" pattern is referred to as *qinah* meter and provides a solemn and mournful rhythm to the recitation of the poem. (For a brief discussion of the poetry of Lamentations and its literary context, see Berlin 2–30.)

The lament genre dominates Lamentations and has particularly strong parallels to the city-lament genre widely attested in Mesopotamian literature (e.g., see Kramer). Some key features of the city-lament genre that have been incorporated into Lamentations include the structure and form, the assigning of responsibility, the abandonment of the city by its patron deity, weeping of the female figure (in this case, Lady Zion), lamentation, and the restoration of the city (see Dobbs-Allsopp 9). As Dobbs-Allsopp has pointed out, however, Lamentations "is no simple Mesopotamian city lament." The author has transformed and adapted the forms and styles available to him, including those well-known from Hebrew poetry, to compose a unique Judean lament of the destruction of Jerusalem.

The most significant departure from the city-lament genre in terms of theological consideration is that the destruction of Jerusalem is *not* attributed to the action of a capricious god. While God is always the primary agent in that he allowed Jerusalem's destruction ("The Lord has destroyed without mercy all the dwellings of Jacob" [2:2 NRSV]), the author of Lamentations makes it abundantly clear this has only come about because of Judah's sin. "Jerusalem sinned grievously, therefore she became filthy" (1:8 RSV; see also 2:14, 17; 3:25–33).

Liturgical Use

The earliest recorded use of these poems is within the Tishah-b'Ab liturgy commemorating the destruction of Jerusalem (see Zech. 7:3–5). They were used and perhaps written as monuments of memorial and continue in such use within Jewish tradition. The early church saw reference to Jesus' messiahship in passages such as Lam. 4:20 ("The LORD's anointed") and his suffering on the cross in 1:12. Portions of the text continue to be used in Christian liturgy such as in the Tenebrae service during Holy Week (1:15).

Interpretation

In seeking a theology of Lamentations, many scholars have failed to take adequate notice of the emotive elements, and instead have focused upon the moments of confession and contrition that employ covenantal language. The language of confession is certainly present within Lamentations and clearly reflects Deuteronomic theology; hence, it fits within the larger canonical context of the Torah and Jeremiah. But Lamentations was written as an expression of grief rather than a systematic theological reflection. These poems are raw and poignant replies to the atrocities that the poet had just survived. Where the book of Job addresses suffering on the personal level, Lamentations addresses it on the national scale. By entering into the text with the author, as *both* the individual (ch. 3) and the nation/church, we may find solace in the deepest despair, even if that solace is long in coming.

Perhaps the most theologically challenging aspect of Lamentations is the presence of God. Where was God during this tragedy? Where is he now, as we seek to make sense of our own tragedies? The book of Lamentations brings this question home with dramatic power. Although the poet repeatedly appeals to God, God never responds; his voice is not heard. "Look, O LORD!" is a repeated refrain (as in 1:11). Yet, even as the personified Zion begs God to see her plight, she has already been ravaged. Zion's cry for God's help and mercy echoes hollowly, and there is no reply. The divine silence is awful. Yet in that silence the poet confronts Israel's responsibility and confesses that "the LORD is in the right, for I have transgressed his word" (1:18 AT).

Even in this confession of responsibility, the poet also asserts throughout Lamentations that God is the active agent. It is the Lord who sent fire from on high that "went deep into my bones" (1:13 NRSV). The Lord "destroyed without mercy all the dwellings of Jacob" (2:2 NRSV). The poet speaks directly to God, declaring, "You have wrapped yourself with anger and pursued us, killing without pity" (3:43 NRSV). Such a direct accusation against God may sound offensive to us, yet it contains within it a powerful statement of faith. In spite of all the famine, torture, and killing, the poet continues to believe that his God, "the LORD" alone, is ruler of the universe and is thus capable of bringing about such utter destruction of his people.

Yet God is silent. This is where life becomes interpretation. Lamentations contains the complaints, prayers, and petitions that any of us might address to God in our grief. God's response is not found in the text, but in history. While the poet recognizes the sin of Israel and declares God just in punishing them, the book ends with a question: "Or have you utterly rejected us and are angry with us beyond measure?" (5:22 AT). God responded to the complaints of Lamentations by fulfilling his word given through Jeremiah (29:10): he restored his people to Judah by the act of Cyrus.

Bibliography

Berlin, A. *Lamentations*. Westminster John Knox, 2002.

Dobbs-Allsopp, F. W. *Lamentations*. Interpretation. Westminster John Knox, 2003.

Gottwald, N. *Studies in the Book of Lamentations*. SCM, 1954.

Kramer, S., trans. "Lamentation over the Destruction of Ur." *ANET* (1950): 455–63.

23

Ezekiel

Thomas Renz

The book of Ezekiel is most famous for its visions, especially of the dry bones (ch. 37) and the new temple (chs. 40–48). More recently, the sexually charged language of chapters 16 and 23 has provoked comment. The book is addressed to an audience in the Babylonian exile. It speaks to those who have lost everything and yet have everything to gain, if only they acknowledge their guilt and put their trust in the God of the covenant. Its main concern is the true identity of the people of God, which is not to be found in history or genealogy but in the purposes of God. The theocentric message of the book is reinforced by frequent use of the recognition formula ("then they/you will know that I am Yahweh").

The Argument of the Book

While the book of Ezekiel is the only prophetic book largely written in the first person, the prophet is portrayed not so much as a preacher as someone addressed by the word of God. The prophet is a model for how to receive the word of God, which is contrasted with his audience's lack of receptiveness (2:8–3:11). In fact, the resistance of Ezekiel's exilic audience to the prophetic word is a major theme in the book, and 37:1–14 appears to comment on the fact that the prophetic word will accomplish its task only the second time round, in its written form (Renz, *Function*, 204–9). This task is the reconstitution of the people of Israel, which requires a change of allegiance on the part of the exiles. They must dissociate themselves from their sinful past and identify with the restored Israel that God is about to create—a new people as far as attitudes are concerned, although a branch from the same ethnic stock. The task of dissociation is undertaken primarily in the first part of the book, while the new orientation is offered particularly in chapters 34–48.

There are several subcollections in the first part of the book. They are marked by a narrative portion that includes either a date (1:1–3), a notice about elders approaching the prophet (14:1), or both (8:1; 20:1). In four cycles, which all end on a strong note of finality, the destruction of Jerusalem is justified as deserved punishment for its rebellion, but the argument is developed in specific ways in each cycle. The first cycle, chapters 1–7, presents the basic case: Judah's and Jerusalem's sin will lead to its end. The second cycle, 8–13, strengthens the plausibility of this case by answering possible objections, such as the idea that God could not possibly abandon his people (8–11) or the idea that judgment is for the distant future, not for the present time (12:21–13:23). The third cycle, chapters 14–19, outlines more precisely what the exiles' response should be to this disaster and includes explicit calls to repentance (14:1–12; 18:1–32). Repentance cannot avert the disaster that will befall Jerusalem, but it offers life for the exilic community, which without repentance is as doomed as Jerusalem. The last section (in the book's first part), chapters 20–24, summarizes the first three cycles and brings the narrative to the point when Jerusalem is laid under siege. Ezekiel's response to his wife's death is a model for how the exilic community should respond to Jerusalem's fall. Public mourning would signal sympathy, which in the case of Jerusalem's deserved judgment, is inappropriate. Instead, the exiles are to accept the judgment and groan over their own sins (24:15–27).

In the compilation of prophecies concerning nations other than Judah in chapters 25–32, three collections can be identified: prophecies against Judah's nearest neighbors (25), prophecies against Tyre (26–28), and prophecies against Egypt (29–32). The following points are made: (1) The fact that the Babylonian king is Yahweh's instrument can be seen not only in the events surrounding the fall of Jerusalem but also throughout Nebuchadnezzar's western campaign. (2) Yahweh does not tolerate malice and self-righteousness, and thus, by implication, he himself does not act out of malice or self-righteousness. (3) No other nation will be allowed to take possession of the land—indeed, seven nations are dealt with before Israel reenters the land (cf. Deut. 7:1). (4) The oracles against Tyre and Egypt affirm that Yahweh deals with rebellious, self-sufficient pride and shows up its futility wherever he encounters it. (5) Egypt will never again be attractive as a substitute for trusting Yahweh. And (6) the frequency of the recognition formula reminds us that in all this God is revealing himself, making each of these events in international affairs "a moment of self-disclosure for Yahweh" (Block 2:12).

The reuse of the watchman motif in chapter 33 forms a closing bracket, paired with its first occurrence in chapter 3, and signals the function of the intervening chapters: to warn of impending danger. The prophet did not return to his homeland to warn Jerusalem, the community most obviously under threat. His ministry was to the exilic community, for whom the warning was not yet too late. Chapter 33 picks up motifs from chapter 18 to remind readers that the proper response to the warning is repentance. The arrival of a refugee from Jerusalem informing the exiles that the city has been destroyed (33:21) changes the rhetorical situation but not the message. Ezekiel reaffirms that physical descent from Abraham is insufficient for reestablishment in the land. At the same time, the chapter gives a discouraging picture of Ezekiel's post-586 audience; only "when this comes—and come it will!—then they shall know that a prophet has been among them" (33:33). The first part of the book has already indicated that "this" includes judgment as well as restoration (20:32–44), and glimpses of judgment are found throughout chapters 34–48.

This last major part of the book is arranged in a palistrophic pattern (ABCDCBA), with the vision of the dry bones in the center (37:1–14), and at the outer ends an affirmation of Yahweh's kingship as the beginning and end of Israel's restoration (chs. 34, 40–48). The first inner ring is formed by two-panel prophecies claiming the land for Israel against other nations (35:1–36:15; chs. 38–39). The second is formed by anthologies summarizing the work of transformation and the blessings resulting from it, with 36:16–38 focusing on the spiritual, and 37:15–28 on the political. The two are aspects of the one transformation brought about by acknowledging Yahweh as king. Yahweh's kingship is affirmed vis-à-vis self-serving human rulers (ch. 34) and in the way space is organized in chapters 40–48, with the temple forming the new center of the nation independent of the palace, confirming Yahweh as absolute power holder (43:7). The messiah plays no part in the nation's restoration, but a new David will guarantee the nation's unity (37:15–28). He will exercise rather than challenge the rule of Yahweh (34:23–24). There is a certain shift from responsibility to passivity in the oracles of salvation. Yahweh will not only bring repentant exiles back to the land but also will himself bring about the repentance. He does this work of transformation through the prophetic word, as the central vision makes plain.

Ezekiel within the Canon

God's sovereignty and glory are central to the book of Ezekiel, but his anguished passion is stressed as well. This combination, together with a focus on the fate of Jerusalem, is also found in the book of Isaiah, but developed in Ezekiel with a greater focus on the Babylonian destruction of the city. There are close parallels to the book of Jeremiah. It is possible that Ezekiel heard Jeremiah and that later material from Jeremiah came to Babylon via people who were in contact with Jeremiah (Vieweger). Ezekiel is characteristically more expansive (cf., e.g., Jer. 23:1–8 with Ezek. 34). Both stress that the future lies with the exiles, even though they deserve no better than the inhabitants of Jerusalem. In the language of Ezekiel, Israel's future lies in God's concern for his name, not in any virtue on the part of the exiles. While the book of Jeremiah has many links with Deuteronomy, Ezekiel borrows priestly language and categories. Common to both traditions is the adultery motif for depicting disloyalty to God. Characteristic for priestly thinking is an emphasis on the polluting effect of sin. By polluting land and sanctuary, sin jeopardizes God's presence among his people and the people's presence in the land. The effect is such that the prophet at one point wonders whether there will be a future for Israel (9:8). The punishment is not so much deportation from the land but death: in the city, in flight, and in exile. It is appropriate that a priestly prophet should draw this stark distinction between life and death, since Israel's cultic system is based on this fundamental contrast. Rebellion against God leads to death, but "I have no pleasure in the death of anyone, declares the Lord Yahweh; so turn, and live" (18:32 AT). Thus, the book of Ezekiel can be read as an illustration of Rom. 6:23: "For the wages of sin is death, but the free gift of God is eternal life in Christ Jesus our Lord" (NRSV).

A vital theme of biblical theology, covenant, is also important in the book of Ezekiel. Ezekiel fulfills a role similar to Moses, renewing the covenant at a time of breakdown of the relationship. In the biblical narrative, Ezekiel is the only person other than Moses to communicate divine laws to Israel (chs. 43–48). The covenant motif stresses the need for loyalty and the catastrophic effect of disloyalty. Zedekiah's disloyalty to Nebuchadnezzar reflects his disloyalty to God (17), and Jerusalem's disloyalty to God is portrayed as a wife's disloyalty to her caring husband (16). The covenant metaphor rests on the concept of an ordered relationship. The heart of the problem is the people's rejection of God's governance. This also explains why the leaders of Judah are often singled out for condemnation: they have usurped God's sovereignty. But God's sovereignty is not founded in the covenant relationship itself, which is why any creature's appropriation of glory rightly belonging to the Creator leads to destruction. Ezekiel demonstrates that judgment begins with the household of God (cf. 1 Pet. 4:17), but also that it does not end there. The Oracles against the Nations in chapters 25–32 focus more narrowly on one set of historical events than those found in Jeremiah and Isaiah. Nevertheless, they presume that divine standards are the same for everyone, and they offer a particularly vivid condemnation of human pretensions to power and self-sufficiency (cf. Rom. 1:18–23).

The definition of God's people as those who submit to God's rule stresses that descent from Abraham does not guarantee inheritance of Abraham's promises (33:23–29); this definition resonates with a similar emphasis in the NT (cf. John 8:39; Rom. 9:8–16; Gal. 3:29; 4:24–31). In both Ezekiel and the NT, submission to God's rule finds expression in how one relates to a specific act of God's judgment. Jerusalem's destruction is for the exiles, who deserve the same judgment, chance, and challenge to repent. Similarly, the cross is an exercise of God's sovereignty and judgment over human pride and rebellion, an exercise that allows others to go free. Yet only Christ's death deals with sin. Ezekiel's concern for accepting Jerusalem's destruction as God's just judgment is consequently transformed in the gospel concern to accept Christ's death as the judgment that makes peace (e.g., Col. 1:20).

Perspectives from the History of Interpretation

The impact of the book of Ezekiel on the postexilic community is visible in the book of Zechariah, though it is less obvious in other postexilic writings. Ezekiel was an inspiration also for the Qumran community (Cothenet). Philo and Josephus paid little attention to Ezekiel, but rabbinic interest in the book was strong in spite of difficulties in making it agree with the Mosaic Torah. Especially after the fall of Jerusalem in 70 CE, Ezekiel's vision of the throne-chariot gained prominence as an attempt to integrate the transcendence and immanence of God without the tangible reality of a temple (*merkabah* mysticism). Maybe to stress the need for communal guidance in reading Ezekiel, parts of the book were apparently declared off limits for Jews under thirty years old, as Jerome noted.

The use of motifs from Ezekiel in the Johannine literature, and especially in the book of Revelation, is well known (see, e.g., Moyise). More recently, Newman traced Ezekiel's influence on the apostle Paul's understanding of divine glory. The early church remained fascinated by the book, and especially the concluding vision as a picture of heaven or the church. The four faces of the creatures bearing the throne-chariot in the opening vision became symbols of the four Gospel writers, and the king of Tyre was identified with the antichrist (both already in Hippolytus). Such luminaries as Origen, Ephraim the Syrian, Jerome, Theodoret of Cyrus, and Gregory the Great expounded Ezekiel. It was also used outside exegetical and homiletical literature. Along with the chapters stressing repentance (14; 18), other passages (3:17–21; 33:1–9; 34:1–24) were used frequently, especially in expressing a theology of church offices and in dealing with questions such as whether bishops who fled from persecution should be reinstalled. Ezekiel 37 is often cited as a prediction of the eschatological resurrection of the body, most forcefully by Tertullian.

Central to the church's reading of the book is recognition of Christ in Ezekiel. The early church was reluctant to offer a detailed christological interpretation of the figure in the opening vision. Thus, Jerome insisted that the figure primarily represents God the Father, then the Son as image of the invisible God. Nevertheless, after the Council of Chalcedon, the combination of metal and fire in the appearance of the figure in Ezekiel's opening vision (1:26–27) served for defending the doctrine of Christ's two natures (Theodoret, Gregory). It was also popular to find the protective sign of the cross in 9:4, and the shut gate in 44:1–3 was often applied to the Virgin Mary. These are cases where the doctrine rather than the biblical text must bear all the weight of the interpretation. Ezekiel's prophecies of a new David stress divine sovereignty and the unity of God's people, saying little about the new David himself. Most promising is the lead given by commentators such as Origen and Isidore of Seville, who saw Ezekiel himself as a sign of Christ. It is noteworthy that in the *Targum of Ezekiel* "son of man" is rendered as "son of Adam," suggesting that in this early interpretation Ezekiel was seen as the first member of the new creation.

The book of Ezekiel retained its popularity in the Middle Ages among Jewish interpreters (e.g., Rashi, Eliezer of Beaugency, David Kimhi), but the church's interest appears to have waned over time. Indeed, Anselm of Laon used the widespread neglect of the book to justify his lecture series on Ezekiel in 1121–23. Where there was interest, it was often focused on the visions, whether they be understood allegorically (e.g., Rupert of Deuz) or literally (Andrew of St. Victor), an interest also reflected in illustrations and paintings related to Ezekiel, which often combined the throne vision of Ezek. 1 with Isa. 6. With the Reformation, the allegorical reading was more and more sidelined, although it remained popular in the Puritan tradition (Greenhill). John Calvin devoted his last written efforts to Ezekiel, producing a historical and theological exposition of the first twenty chapters.

Early modern scholarly interpretation focused on philological matters and poetic style, while the book gained prominence in African-American spirituals ("Dem Bones") and preaching as a message of hope to exiles. The historical-critical method left the book's literary unity and integrity of authorship intact for a long time. Indeed, the book was in favor by some critics for its supposed teaching of individualism, a view based on a misunderstanding of Ezekiel's use of individualistic legal language to affirm generational responsibility (see, e.g., Joyce). But a publication by Hölscher in 1924 opened up an era of wide disagreement about all aspects of the origin and content of the book, with dates suggested from the time of Manasseh to the Maccabean period (for a brief summary, see Childs 357–60).

While the variety of positions held is still striking, three main approaches can be distinguished today. The majority of interpreters identify different levels of growth in the book, with later layers interpreting earlier layers. The material from the Ezekiel "school" is often thought to have been added in exilic and early postexilic times (Zimmerli), but many commentators argue that the book was completed in exile (e.g., Hals; Allen). This is also the view of a number of "holistic" interpreters, who focus on reading the book as a literary whole addressed to the Babylonian exiles (e.g., Greenberg; Block). Theological interpretation is not greatly affected by the disagreements between these first two approaches. A third group of scholars claims to identify up to more than a dozen redactional layers in the book (e.g., Pohlmann). In their view the book of Ezekiel originated over a period of more than 250 years and provides little or no reliable evidence for the existence of a prophet Ezekiel.

Theological interpretation undertaken in this context would look different, but the methodology used appears misguided and unreliable, and its advocates have not yet offered a theological interpretation of the book based on their analyses. Feminist interpretation has raised important issues (Patton) that have entered mainstream study of the book, unlike the attempt at a psychoanalytical interpretation offered by Halperin. More popular interest has focused on the eschatological visions (Lindsey), and the book is sometimes used as evidence for premillennialism (Rooker). Throughout this history, arguably the most successful interpretations have been those that paid attention to the rhetorical force of the book. Thereby readers discover what behavior God punishes and what kind of community he re-creates. They also reflect on the prophetic office and word as a means of establishing the new community.

Ezekiel and the Church Today

Each generation needs to explore afresh how Ezekiel reveals behavior that leads to death. The condemnation of idolatry and false prophecy was transformed in the early church to warnings against heresy and pagan lifestyle. This can still serve us today, if we remember that these judgment passages apply to God's people first of all. The stark alternatives of allegiance to God or rebellion against him, and thus consequences of life or death, must be presented to everyone. Nevertheless, the book's particular thrust is to remind us that we have all been on the way to death and that receiving life in Christ is no cause for self-congratulation. Similarly, the fall of the king of Tyre from a divinely given position of privilege may be seen as illustrative of the fall of the antichrist or Satan, but this should not distract from its application to individual and collective human pride and arrogance. Being a member of God's people presumes proper acknowledgment of the cause of death and the source of life. The original function of the book for the Babylonian exiles, and its use in spirituals, remind us that socioeconomic aspects do not define the people of God. At the same time, finding one's identity in God's purposes ought to influence all aspects of life, including the socioeconomic. Communal life and, by implication, personal life need to be ordered in such a way that nothing compromises God's sovereignty. Given the harsh critique of human pretensions to power and the careful limitation of human power in the concluding vision, any use of Ezekiel to bolster one's own power (e.g., husbands over wives, priests over laity) is an abuse of the book.

Because it is in Christ that the people of God experience death and resurrection, Ezek. 37 is ultimately fulfilled in Christ's death and resurrection. As a second Adam and Moses, the prophet is a type of Christ, who is the ultimate second Adam and Moses, the beginning of a new creation. The central role of the prophetic word in bringing about this new creation prefigures the transformation of God's people through the incarnated Word. Now as then, the word gives life by bringing forth faith in the purposes of God. Like those who saw the return from exile, the church today experiences fulfillment of God's purposes, while awaiting the time when everything will be ordered in a manner that acknowledges God's lordship. The way spiritual and political restoration are intertwined in Ezek. 34–48 and the flexible use of motifs from Ezekiel in the book of Revelation (e.g., Magog changed from person to nation) counsel against identifying a sequence of eschatological events in the latter part of the book, let alone any sequence that separates spiritual from political restoration.

In our contemporary cultures, which often link identity with consumption and marginalize the church, Ezekiel offers the promise of new life in the wilderness for a community that finds its identity in God and his purposes.

Bibliography

Block, D. *The Book of Ezekiel.* Vol. 1, *Chapters 1–24.* Vol. 2, *Chapters 25–48.* NICOT. Eerdmans, 1997–98.

Calvin, J. *Ezekiel 1 (Chapters 1–12),* trans. D. Foxgrover and D. Martin. Calvin's Old Testament Commentaries 18. Paternoster, 1996.

Childs, B. *Introduction to the Old Testament as Scripture.* Fortress, 1979.

Cothenet, E. "Influence d'Ézéchiel sur la spiritualité de Qumran." *RevQ* 13 (1988): 431–39.

Dassmann, E. "Hesekiel." *RAC* 14 (1988): cols. 1132–91.

Duguid, I. *Ezekiel and the Leaders of Israel.* VTSup 56. Brill, 1994.

Galambush, J. *Jerusalem in the Book of Ezekiel.* SBLDS 130. Scholars Press, 1992.

Greenhill, W. *An Exposition of Ezekiel.* London: Henry G. Bohn, 1846. Reprint, Banner of Truth Trust, 1995.

Halperin, D. J. *Seeking Ezekiel.* Pennsylvania State University Press, 1993.

Hölscher, G. *Hesekiel.* BZAW 39. De Gruyter, 1924.

Jerome. *Commentariorum in Hiezechielem libri XIV,* ed. F. Glorie. S. Hieronymi presbyteri Opera 1/4. CCSL 75. Brepols, 1984.

Joyce, P. *Divine Initiative and Human Response in Ezekiel.* JSOTSup 51. JSOT, 1989.

Levey, S. H. *The Targum of Ezekiel.* The Aramaic Bible 13. T&T Clark, 1987.

Lindsey, H. *The Late Great Planet Earth.* Zondervan, 1970.

Matties, G. *Ezekiel 18 and the Rhetoric of Moral Discourse.* SBLDS 126. Scholars Press, 1990.

Mein, A. *Ezekiel and the Ethics of Exile.* Oxford University Press, 2001.

Milgrom, J. "Leviticus 26 and Ezekiel." Pages 57–63 in *The Quest for Context and Meaning*, ed. C. A. Evans. Biblical Interpretation 28. Brill, 1997.

Moyise, S. *The Old Testament in the Book of Revelation*. JSNTSup 115. Sheffield Academic Press, 1995.

Newman, C. *Paul's Glory Christology*. NovTSup 69. Brill, 1992.

Patton, C. L. "'Should Our Sister Be Treated Like a Whore?' A Response to Feminist Critiques of Ezekiel 23." Pages 221–38 in *The Book of Ezekiel*, ed. M. S. Odell and J. T. Strong. SBL Symposium Series 9. SBL, 2000.

Renz, T. "Proclaiming the Future: History and Theology in Prophecies against Tyre." *TynBul* 51 (2000): 17–58.

———. *The Rhetorical Function of the Book of Ezekiel*. VTSup 76. Brill, 1999.

Rooker, M. F. "Evidence from Ezekiel." Pages 119–34 in *A Case for Premillennialism*, ed. D. Campbell and J. Townsend. Moody, 1992.

Stevenson, K. R. *The Vision of Transformation*. SBLDS 154. Scholars Press, 1996.

Vieweger, D. *Die literarischen Beziehungen zwischen den Büchern Jeremia und Ezechiel*. BEATAJ 26. Lang, 1993.

24

Daniel

ERNEST C. LUCAS

History of Interpretation

Qumran

The eight manuscripts of Daniel found at Qumran indicate its importance for that community. *Florilegium* (4Q174) 2:3 cites Dan. 11:32 and 12:10, using the same citation-formula as for other biblical prophetic books. The *Community Rule* (1QS) echoes Dan. 11:33–34 in calling a teaching official a *maskil*, and the members of the community the *rabbim*. Although in column 1 it alludes to Dan. 11–12, the *War Scroll* (1QM) does not mention resurrection (Dan. 12:1–3).

Jewish Apocalyptic

In the *Similitudes (Parables) of Enoch* (ca. 50 CE) the figure called "that/ the Son of Man" originates from Dan. 7:13. He casts down kings from their thrones, taking his seat on the throne of glory as a judge—probably based on Dan. 7:9–10. He is equated with the messiah in *1 En.* 48:10; 52:4. *First Enoch* 70:1 distinguishes Enoch from the Son of Man, while in 71:14 the two seem to be identified. Some argue that 71:14 is simply comparing Enoch to the Son of Man, others that *1 En.* 71 is a later addition and development of the tradition.

In 2 Esd. 13 (late first century CE) a wind stirs up the sea, out of which comes "the figure of a man" who "flew with the clouds of heaven" (cf. Dan. 7:1, 13). The man takes his stand on a great mountain that was "carved out without hands" (cf. Dan. 2:34). The preceding vision of an eagle that rises out of the sea (2 Esd. 11–12) refers to Dan. 7. The interpreting angel says that the eagle is the fourth kingdom of Daniel's vision, but indicates that identifying it as Rome is an innovation (12:12).

Later Jewish Interpretation

Josephus (*A.J.* 10.10–11) counts the fourth kingdom in Dan. 2 as Rome, but refuses to comment on the stone, probably to avoid offending Roman readers by speaking of Rome's downfall. This may explain why he ignores Dan. 7. Josephus identifies the little horn of Dan. 8 with Antiochus Epiphanes. Also in *Lev. Rab.* 13:5, Rome is the fourth kingdom. Later commentators modify the interpretation to make Islam the fourth empire. The seventy weeks of Dan. 9:20–27 are usually interpreted as the period between the destruction of the first and second temples. The Talmud (*b. Sanh.* 97b) records a curse on those who try to calculate the date of the End. Nevertheless, various Jewish scholars attempted to do that by using the numbers in Daniel (see Silver).

Christian Interpretation

For Hippolytus (early third century) Christ is the stone in Dan. 2 and the fourth figure in the furnace in Dan. 3. The little horn of Dan. 8 is Antiochus, but the fourth kingdom in Dan. 7 is Rome and the little horn the antichrist. The birth of Christ comes after sixty-nine weeks of Dan. 9:20–27, with the last week referring to the distant future. Most other patristic commentators saw the seventy weeks fulfilled either in the life and death of Christ or in the destruction of Jerusalem. Jerome took the latter view. He defended the historicity and christological interpretation of Daniel against Porphyry. He opposed allegorization of the stories by Alexandrian exegetes such as Origen. Antiochus is the little horn in Dan. 8, and a type of the antichrist, who is the little horn of Dan. 7 and the subject of Dan. 11:24–45. Identification of references to the antichrist in Daniel continued into the Middle Ages. Dissident Catholics, such as Franciscans in the early fourteenth century and Jan Hus (d. 1415), identified the pope with the antichrist (see McGinn).

In Luther's preface to his translation of Daniel, the fourth empire is Rome, living on in the German Empire. Although threatened by the Turks

(Muhammad is the little horn in Dan. 7), it would last until the coming of God's kingdom. He saw dual reference to Antiochus and the antichrist in Dan. 8 and 11. The antichrist is the sole subject of 11:36–45, where Luther saw references to the papacy. Luther wrote a more detailed exposition of Dan. 8 in terms of the antichrist/the pope.

John Calvin held that Daniel's visions extended only to the time of Nero. The fourth beast is the Roman Empire. The giving of the kingdom to the holy ones refers to the spread of the gospel. The little horn of Dan. 8 is Antiochus. The seventy weeks of Dan. 9 end with the coming of Jesus and the Romans' destruction of Jerusalem. Daniel 11:36–45 refers to the Roman Empire.

Late medieval apocalyptic millennialism drew inspiration from Daniel. Thomas Müntzer (ca. 1489/90–1525) defended the German Peasants' Revolt as the coming of the "fifth kingdom," the stone of Dan. 2. The "fifth monarchy men" in mid-seventeenth-century England saw themselves in similar terms. Another kind of apocalypticism is William Miller's (1782–1849) calculation, based on Dan. 8:14, that the world would end in 1843. The dispensational movement based on J. N. Darby's (1800–1882) teaching sees Daniel's prophecies culminating either in the coming of Jesus or in the "end times" yet to come (e.g., the whole or last half of the seventieth week).

A few seventeenth-century scholars, such as Hugo Grotius (1583–1645), argued that the fourth beast was Greece and that Daniel's prophecies refer only to the events of the Antiochene period. In the nineteenth century this was strongly advocated, with a second-century BCE date for the book, in commentaries by Bertholdt (1806), von Lengerke (1835), Hitzig (1850), Ewald (1868), and others. There was a strong response from conservative scholars such as Hengstenberg (1831), Pusey (1864), and Keil (1867). Commentaries by F. W. Farrar (1895) and S. R. Driver (1900) popularized the German critical consensus among English readers. By the turn of the century this was the majority view, though the conservative position continued to be defended down through the twentieth century.

This survey shows that Daniel has often been a center of controversy, particularly over interpretation with regard to eschatology, but also regarding authorship and date. In the midst of this debate, the book's theological message has often been neglected; three approaches combine to help in discerning it. The growth of literary approaches to the OT is helpful, with emphasis on recognizing how different genres convey meaning. The study of intertextuality is particularly useful in Dan. 7–12; recognition of allusions to, or the reuse of, material from elsewhere in the OT provides important indicators of the underlying theology. Third, Childs's canonical approach rightly stresses the importance of understanding an OT text first in its own context, and then also in the context of the revelation of God in Christ in the NT.

The Message of Daniel

Daniel 1:1–2 introduces the theme of human and divine sovereignty. The Babylonian king's capture of Jerusalem and removal of some temple vessels to the treasury of his gods might evidence the superiority of Babylon's gods. Daniel 1:2 counters this. The Lord, the God of Israel, "gave" the king of Judah and the temple vessels into Nebuchadnezzar's power—for reasons not specified. The Lord is the ultimate sovereign, who "sets up kings and deposes them" (2:21a) and has a goal for history, the establishing of "a kingdom that will never be destroyed" (2:44). Nebuchadnezzar confesses that "he does what he wills with the host of heaven and the inhabitants of the earth" (4:34–35 NRSV) and, importantly, that "all his works are truth, and his ways are justice" (4:37 NRSV). God's rule is morally determined. The Ancient One judges the world powers, taking sovereignty from the bestial, subhuman powers and giving it to "one like a human being" (7:9–14 NRSV; NIV: "son of man"). In God's kingdom humanity reaches its full potential. Salvation history culminates in the achievement of God's purpose in creation—a world in which sovereignty is given to human beings (Gen. 1:26–28). However, God's people will experience suffering before receiving the kingdom (Dan. 7:21–22). The cry "How long?" (8:13) reinforces this point. Why does God's purpose sometimes seem to be frustrated? Daniel 9–11 provides a partial answer, countering any idea that God's sovereignty makes humans merely puppets. Daniel's prayer explains why the Lord gave Judah into the power of Babylon. This was a moral act, arising from Judah's persistent unfaithfulness to God. The prayer assumes that God responds to human behavior. Daniel 11 balances allusions to God's sovereignty (vv. 27, 29, 36, 45) with statements that, within limits, a human sovereign can "do as he pleases" (vv. 3, 16, 36).

Daniel 1 introduces a second major theme: human and divine faithfulness. Kings are prone to hubris, believing they can exercise a godlike sovereignty. As a result, those committed to God are challenged to a lifestyle of faithfulness. In Dan. 1 the issue is personal integrity. Daniel's stand is made privately and diplomatically. The Jews in Dan. 3 have to oppose idolatry publicly. The plot in Dan. 6, motivated by jealousy, is targeted at Daniel's religious practice because that seems the best way to succeed. Daniel could still pray to God secretly, but since his piety was well known, that would have been to compromise. In each case God is faithful to the faithful Jews. The stories emphasize the Jews' preservation *in* the furnace or lions' den and not just their being saved *from* it. They are preserved because an angel mediates God's presence to them. In the context of the whole book, these stories are not simplistic promises of divine deliverance, but prepare the way for the intimations of suffering, persecution, and martyrdom of the faithful in chapters 7–12. They assert that God is faithful to his people and that his purposes will triumph.

In Dan. 1 God rewards Daniel's faithfulness by giving him exceptional wisdom. The stories emphasize the superiority of Daniel's wisdom over that of the Chaldeans. But God does not reveal things to satisfy curiosity. Nebuchadnezzar's dream about the tree is a warning against hubris and an opportunity to repent. The writing on the wall is a judicial sentence on Belshazzar's idolatrous blasphemy. The visions of Dan. 7–12 encourage the faithful to remain firm until the triumph of God's purpose. Those given wisdom are to use it to instruct others and to "lead many to righteousness" (11:33; 12:3).

Talk of angels enables talk about God's involvement in the world while preserving God's transcendence. Daniel 10:13 and 10:20–11:1 describe a struggle between heavenly beings, called the "princes" or "leaders" of Persia, Greece, and Israel. The main theological points expressed here are that history has a transcendent dimension, and that there is a synergy between events in heaven and events on earth. What happens in heaven does not totally determine what happens on earth, and vice versa.

Daniel and the Canon

Given the different Hebrew and Greek forms of Daniel, canonical interpretation raises the question: Which canon? Childs argues for the primacy of the Hebrew canon, on the ground that only this corpus is common to both Jews and Christians, and so provides the theological bridge between the peoples of the two covenants. In practice, Daniel's inclusion in "the Writings" rather than "the Latter Prophets" in the Hebrew Bible is of little theological significance, since Jews usually treat Daniel as a prophetic book alongside those in the Latter Prophets.

Daniel and the OT

Daniel 4 echoes tree imagery in Ezek. 17, 19 (vine), and 31. Daniel 10 has verbal links with the theophanies in Ezek. 1–3 and 9–10. Daniel 9 contains parallels in thought and vocabulary with Lev. 26:27–45, a passage about sabbatical years and divine wrath. Daniel 9:2 refers explicitly to Jeremiah. Second Chronicles 36:20–21 understands Jeremiah's seventy years symbolically, as ten sabbatical cycles. This suggests that Dan. 9:24–27 is a symbolic, not a chronological, schema. The theological basis of the symbolism is the jubilee cycle (forty-nine years, seven sabbatical cycles, Lev. 25:8–12) as the prelude to release from slavery. In Daniel's schema one jubilee cycle leads to release from Babylon. This foreshadows the ultimate release after ten jubilee cycles (for more detail, see Lucas). Daniel 11:40–45 has verbal links with the prophecies about Assyria in Isa. 8, 14, 28, 37, and others in Ezekiel and Zechariah. Maybe it is not a detailed prediction about Antiochus's end, but a promise that that end will come, using the language of earlier prophets about the downfall of Assyria.

Daniel and the NT

Luke 20:18 concludes the parable of the Wicked Tenants with, "Everyone who falls on that stone will be broken to pieces; and it will crush anyone on whom it falls" (NRSV), alluding to Isa. 8:14–15 and Dan. 2:34–35. Jesus is identified with the stone that crushed the statue, and thus with the kingdom of God.

Scholars disagree about the background of the phrase "Son of Man" as used by Jesus, and how far the Synoptics reflect Jesus' own usage or develop it. The Synoptic sayings fall into three groups: (1) those about the future "coming" of the Son of Man with clouds and/or angels; (2) those about his suffering, death, and resurrection; (3) a small number about the present authority of the Son of Man. There is wide agreement that Dan. 7:13 lies behind the first group. These identify Jesus with the figure in Daniel who finally receives the kingdom, the coming of which was a central theme of Jesus' preaching. The idea of the Son of Man suffering may arise from his association with the suffering "people of" (7:27) "the holy ones of the Most High" (7:18, 22, 27 NRSV). Those who suffer martyrdom are promised resurrection and vindication (12:1–3). The third group may reflect the "dominion" given to the "one like a son of man" in 7:13.

Revelation's major antichrist figure is "the beast" that rises out of the sea and is a hybrid of Daniel's four beasts (Rev. 13:1–4). It shares features with the little horn in Dan. 7 and 8. The time for which it exercises authority (Rev. 13:5) seems based on Dan. 8:14. This is a reapplication of the theological significance of the little horn without any attempt to treat what Daniel says of it as detailed predictions about the antichrist.

Daniel and Theology

Daniel presents a salvation-history metanarrative that integrates and interprets the smaller narratives within history. Postmodernists are averse to metanarratives, claiming that they are "oppressive." However, Daniel's metanarrative empowers the oppressed by challenging the metanarrative of the oppressor, who in his hubris seeks to shape history according to his will.

Although Daniel exposes the hubris of human rulers and the divine judgment it attracts, it also states that God gives rule and dominion to humans. Daniel 4:10–12 paints a picture of the good that can be achieved by human rulers. When humans *image* God, they have the right to rule in his name. When they try to *be* God, they forfeit that right and may become "bestial." Those who recognize God's rule *over* them are in a position to allow God to rule *through* them.

Because God allows rulers enough freedom to become bestial, the faithful sometimes suffer. Daniel's stories encourage the faithful to become involved in a pagan world, with the hope of some measure of success and effective witness, even if there are risks. In the visions this seems impossible. God's sovereignty means that the faithful cannot take his response to their situation for granted. Belshazzar's blasphemous conduct meets with swift retribution; that of the little horn is allowed much longer before being ended. The faithful may be delivered *from* death in a fiery furnace (ch. 3) or *through* death in the fires of persecution (ch. 12).

The references to "the wise" and the "many" whom they influence (Dan. 11:33; 12:3) may allude to the Suffering Servant of Isa. 52:13–53:12. If so, this emphasizes that the way to glory is faithful service, even through the suffering that this may bring. The response to the cry "How long?" is a call to endurance, trusting in the faithfulness of God and holding to hope of resurrection. Jesus, the Son of Man, exemplified this.

Bibliography

Archer, G. *Jerome's Commentary on Daniel*. Baker, 1958.

Beale, G. *The Use of Daniel in Jewish Apocalyptic Literature and in the Revelation of St. John*. University Press of America, 1984.

Calvin, J. *A Commentary on Daniel*. Calvin Translation Society, 1852–53. Reprint, Banner of Truth Trust, 1986.

Childs, B. *Introduction to the Old Testament as Scripture*. SCM, 1979.

Collins, A. Y. "The Influence of Daniel on the New Testament." Pages 90–112 in *Daniel*, J. Collins. Hermeneia. Fortress, 1993.

Collins, J. *Daniel*. Hermeneia. Fortress, 1993.

Collins, J., and P. Flint, eds. *The Book of Daniel*. 2 vols. Brill, 2001.

Dunn, J. D. G. "The Danielic Son of Man in the New Testament." Pages 528–49 in *The Book of Daniel*, ed. J. Collins and P. Flint. Vol. 2. Brill, 2001.

Fewell, D. *Circle of Sovereignty*. Abingdon, 1991.

Goldingay, J. *Daniel*. WBC. Word, 1989.

Knowles, L. "The Interpretation of the Seventy Weeks of Daniel in the Early Fathers." *WTJ* 7 (1944): 136–60.

Lucas, E. *Daniel*. Apollos OT Commentary. Apollos/InterVarsity, 2002.

McGinn, B. *Visions of the End*. Columbia, 1979.

Russell, D. S. *Daniel*. Saint Andrew Press, 1989.

Silver, H. *A History of Messianic Speculation in Israel*. Macmillan, 1927.

25

Hosea

MARY J. EVANS

History of Interpretation

In earlier times comment on Hosea tended to concentrate on the book's imagery rather than its place in the history of Israel. Special attention was paid to the varied pictures of God's love and judgment, and it was often related in typological fashion to the work of Christ. In recent years Hosea has not been the focus of as much scholarly interest as some of the other OT prophets. Often literary-critical or historical issues have been of most interest. Questions concerning Hosea's family have occupied a lot of attention: the identity of his wife, Gomer; the nature of her adultery; whether or not she and the wife of chapter 3 are the same person; whether any or all of her children are fathered by Hosea and what the precise significance of their names might be; and whether indeed these are real people or merely literary constructs. Most scholarly articles have concentrated on chapters 1–3. Those who have considered the later chapters have focused on the interpretation of the many and varied images and metaphors used by Hosea to describe Israel's unfaithfulness and God's attitude toward his people. The familiarity with the imagery of bread-making (in ch. 7) and of farming and shepherding has led some to draw conclusions about Hosea's own background.

The question as to the relation of the more positive approach of chapter 14 with the strong judgmental emphasis of chapters 4–13 has occupied the attention of some. So also have other questions relating to the unity and integrity of the book, sometimes relating to the many textual difficulties or to the various canonical links mentioned below. In more recent years feminist scholars have looked again at chapters 1 and 3 and questioned whether Hosea is in fact here portrayed as an obsessive, possessive, power-hungry, and abusive husband—with Gomer in reality the heroine rather than the villain of the piece. Others, in response, have argued that it is not valid to read such a modern agenda into the text.

The Message of Hosea

Hosea speaks directly into the situation of Israel within the eighth century BCE, and it is not really possible to understand what is going on in Hosea without some awareness of that situation. On the one hand, Israel as a whole was economically prosperous and stable during and after Jeroboam's long reign. They were at peace, with the southern kingdom of Judah equally flourishing under their longtime king Uzziah. They benefited economically from their situation on the major trade route between Assyria and Egypt. Assyria had removed surrounding threats but as yet had not really troubled Israel itself. But the prosperity of the nation was not shared by all. Many of the previous generation of small farmers had lost their land after repeated Syrian incursions and several years of drought. A huge, almost unbridgeable gap had developed between rich and poor, with justice almost inevitably the prerogative of the rich.

Religiously speaking, things were going well. Worship of Yahweh was popular; all the required sacrifices and feasts were kept with rigorous attention to detail, great ceremony, and no regard for expense. However, alongside this religiosity, idolatry was rampant, respect for the law was nonexistent, and the people were in effect treating Yahweh as an idol or a baal who could be pacified by presents and bribed into acting on Israel's behalf.

Within this context Hosea takes the imagery used by surrounding nature cults, with a strong emphasis on fertility, and completely transforms it. Chapters 1 and 3 speak of his own fairly disastrous family life. Sandwiched between is a poetic description of the unfaithfulness and adultery of God's people Israel, dramatically pictured here as God's wife, and of the consequences of that unfaithfulness, which puts their identity as the

245

people of God at severe risk. Chapters 4–13 present a series of sermons or oracles using a whole range of methods, pictures, images, and metaphors to set out the reality of Israel's attitudes and actions, the reaction of God to these, and the consequences that had been set in motion. Interspersed within this are insights into the nature of God, his deep love, the hurt he feels at Israel's behavior, his desire for them to return to be his people in reality, but also God's justice and the inevitability of their punishment and destruction if there is no repentance.

Hosea's main aim seems to have been to show Israel that their religious confidence was spurious, their behavior was unacceptable, their understanding of God was quite deficient, and their future was at risk. Hosea 1:1 makes it clear that the book was completed after Hosea's ministry was ended, and 14:9 indicates awareness of future readers. However, in between, certain editorial comments have been incorporated within the messages that Hosea delivered to his contemporaries. The whole is clearly seen as having ongoing relevance, reflecting Hosea's own conviction that history repeats itself. Those from different generations and different situations can certainly be challenged by Hosea's message.

Hosea and the Canon

Hosea's closest links are with Amos, who also spoke out in the northern kingdom during the reign of Jeroboam II. Amos brings to the foreground and extends the picture of Israel's economic and social corruption that is reflected in Hosea, while Hosea extends and develops Amos's portrayal of the idolatry and syncretism that was rife throughout the land. There are also many connections with Isaiah and Micah, the other eighth-century prophets working in the south. The understanding of the covenant presented especially in Deuteronomy and Exodus has a strong influence on Hosea's reflections. In turn, Hosea's exploration of what is involved in being God's people stands as a background to the more event-based account of the period in 2 Kings and to the teaching of the later prophets.

There are few direct references to Hosea in the NT. Yet, Matthew (9:13; 12:7) records Jesus twice quoting from Hosea's clear statement in 6:6 that God desires "mercy, not sacrifice." And Paul uses Hos. 1:9–10 and 2:23 in Rom. 8:14 and 9:25–26 as part of his discussion on who exactly it is that is eligible to be called "my people." It is debatable whether the Israelites' conviction that "on the third day he will raise us up" (Hos. 6:2 NRSV), almost certainly spoken in the context of a spurious repentance, lies behind the references to Jesus' resurrection on the third day in, for example, Matt. 16:21; 17:23; and Luke 9:22.

Hosea and Theology

Hosea's understanding of God, Israel, and the world is founded on the concept of covenant, specifically the covenant between God and Israel. Israel's very existence was bound up with the people's identity as those in covenant relationship with God, whose calling was to represent God before the world. They were Yahweh's people, and he was their God. If the covenant collapsed, then Israel would, in effect, no longer exist. Any kind of relationship is costly. It makes demands in both emotional and behavioral terms. Hosea portrays the covenant requirements incumbent on God's people and the cost that is involved for Yahweh himself. The marriage metaphor, where Israel is pictured as God's wife, was avoided by many of the prophets due to the danger of misunderstanding arising from the widespread use of sexual imagery in the surrounding fertility cults. As in all the prophetic literature, this book totally rejects everything that Baalism stands for and, in particular, the use of sex in magical and cultic fertility rites. However, Hosea's transformation of the image becomes quite appropriate. God had committed himself to Israel as a husband to a wife, and Israel had also committed itself to the covenant. The corollary of this is that both sides must remain faithful. Hosea's point is that just as physical adultery shatters a marriage relationship and in the process causes great pain, so Israel's spiritual adultery will shatter their relationship with God. On the other hand, with evidenced forgiveness and mercy on the one hand and evidenced repentance on the other, even a shattered marriage can be repaired.

God's Love for Israel

The "marriage" between Yahweh and Israel was based on his love for them. Even when they deserted him and served other gods—committed spiritual adultery—he still loved them and longed to have them back. Hosea's own experience helped him to understand God's position, and he therefore strongly attacks Israel's idolatry but also pleads desperately with them to repent and return to God, who in that circumstance will gladly forgive and restore them. The constancy of God's love is a theme that runs through the book. In the past he has blessed and cared for them (2:15; 11:1; 13:4–5). In the present he longs to restore them (7:1; 11:8–9).

247

The future is still in question, depending on their response. God takes them seriously as people and allows them the dignity of taking responsibility for their own actions even when that results in negative consequences. The way they exercise their responsibility will influence their own future. Those who argue that God is portrayed here as abusive and controlling miss this point altogether. He cannot be in relationship with those who are not his people and, if they persist in their refusal to act as his people, then they are inevitably signing their own death warrant (4:6–9; 9:7–9; 13:9–16). However, because of God's ongoing and gracious love, there is still hope for salvation (11:10–12; 14:4–9). This is Yahweh's ongoing and deep desire.

The marriage metaphor is profound, but it is not big enough to tell the whole story. Hosea also portrays God, among other things, as a caring parent (11:1–4), a doctor (7:1; 11:3; 14:4), and a shepherd (11:4; 13:5). The implication is that God is able to supply all their needs.

The Requirements of Relationship

Because of God's nature as "the Holy One" (11:9, 12), relationship with him can only exist on his terms. If Israel is to be his people, they must be a holy people; their commitment to him must be exclusive, and their behavior must reflect his nature. Wholehearted devotion and faithfulness to God are vital, but right behavior toward other people as well as toward God himself is an essential part of being God's people. Hosea does not major on social responsibility in the way that Amos does, but he is very well aware of the importance of justice, righteousness, and compassion as characteristics of God's people (2:19; 6:6; 12:6). Relationship also requires knowledge, and Hosea stresses the importance of Israel studying God's word in order to know what he has revealed about himself. The priests who had been given the responsibility for ensuring the people's knowledge of God therefore come under particular condemnation (4:6–9). God's terms for a restored relationship include their repentance and turning back to him (3:5; 5:4; 11:5, 10–11). Hosea wants Israel to grasp the seriousness of sin (1:2; 2:1–5; 3:1–5). The imagery he uses to describe the faithfulness and betrayal of Israel is almost as varied as what is used to describe the love of God. Israel needs to see itself not just as an adulterous wife or an unresponsive child, but also as a stubborn heifer, a half-baked and half-raw cake, a sick person or a foolish bird (4:16; 5:13; 7:8–12; 9:11; 11:1–3). In Israel there is "only cursing, lying and murder, stealing and adultery" (4:2), prostitution, idolatry, immorality, arrogance, and hypocrisy (2:7–8; 4:10–13; 5:7; 8:2–6; 12:7–8). Like adultery in marriage, Israel's sin is not something that can simply be ignored; it needs to be acknowledged and dealt with. But repentance must be real. Sacrifices without major lifestyle changes are completely unacceptable. Renewed commitment is evidenced not by a renewed demonstration of religious fervor but by transformed lives (6:1–6).

Hosea was apparently not very hopeful that Israel in general would respond to God's pleading with them, but he was convinced that in the end God's love would triumph (11:8–11; 14:4–9). In this way he points forward to the later revelation of God's love revealed in Jesus. The people cannot defeat sin by ignoring or avoiding it, but a way nevertheless does exist to deal with its otherwise inevitable consequences.

Beeby's theological commentary on Hosea brings out strongly the link demonstrated between the love of God and the knowledge of God, providing an illustration of the way in which others have used Hosea to discuss a range of epistemological questions. Several of the essays edited by Vanhoozer helpfully use Hosea to illustrate their understanding of the love of God in today's world. Stuhlmueller, in the book cowritten with Senior, shows how Hosea can provide stimulation for modern mission. Hosea's critique of attitudes toward economics found among his wealthier contemporaries certainly speaks into today's consumer cultures. Hosea has much to say to all who accept the challenge of reflecting theologically on today's world.

Bibliography

Achtemeier, E. *Minor Prophets 1*. Hendrickson, 1996.

Bal, M. *Lethal Love*. Indiana University Press, 1987.

Beeby, H. D. *Grace Abounding*. Eerdmans, 1989.

Birch, B. C. *Hosea, Joel, and Amos*. Westminster John Knox, 1997.

Goldingay, J. "Hosea 1–3, Genesis 1–4 and Masculist Interpretation." *HBT* 17 (1995): 37–44.

Kidner, D. *Love to the Loveless*. InterVarsity, 1981.

Mays, J. L. *Hosea: A Commentary*. OTL. SCM, 1968.

Senior, D., and C. Stuhlmueller. *The Biblical Foundations for Mission*. SCM, 1983.

Stuart, D. *Hosea–Jonah*. WBC. Word, 1987.

Vanhoozer, K., ed. *Nothing Greater, Nothing Better*. Eerdmans, 2001.

Ward, J. M. *Hosea*. Harper & Row, 1966.

————. *Thus Says the Lord*. Abingdon, 1991.

Williamson, H. G. M. "Hope under Judgment: The Prophets of the Eighth Century BCE." *EvQ* 72 (2000): 291–306.

Wolff, H. W. *Hosea*. Hermeneia. Fortress, 1977.

Yee, G. A. "Hosea: Commentary and Reflection." *NIB* 7:195–297.

26

Joel

WILLEM VANGEMEREN

The book of Joel is the second book in the Minor Prophets (the Twelve, MT). The superscription (1:1) connects the prophecy with Joel the son of Pethuel. The name Joel is fairly common, and the father's name is otherwise unknown. The book lacks data that suggest a specific historical context. No chronological setting is provided, and nothing else is known of Joel.

Date

Interpreters vary greatly in dating the book (from the ninth to the second century BCE). The cumulative evidence is suggestive of a date as early as the late sixth or fifth century (Crenshaw, *Joel*), or as late as the late fifth to mid fourth century (Wolff). Calvin's assessment that the theological message of Joel is unaffected by the issue of the date is still relevant.

The Locust Plague

The thematic variation between images of the locusts and the drought (1:4, 5–7, 8–10, 11–12; 2:3–8, 16–20) and warriors (1:6; 2:2–11, 20) has raised the issue of the reality of the locusts. Some rabbinic, patristic, and medieval interpreters understood the locust plague as an image of an enemy attack, such as the Assyrians or Babylonians. Rashi, Calvin, and Luther interpreted the plague as a realistic portrayal of an agricultural disaster that may have evoked memories of foreign invaders ("the northern army," 2:20, 25). Most recent interpreters agree with this conclusion, but Stuart has returned to the metaphorical interpretation and links the prophecy with an invasion by Assyrians (701 BCE) or Babylonians (598 or 588 BCE).

Joel among the Twelve

The placement of Joel in the LXX after Micah varies from the MT. The LXX is more chronological throughout, and this is also true for the Twelve: Hosea, Amos, Micah, Joel, Obadiah, Jonah, Nahum, Habakkuk, Zephaniah, Haggai, Zechariah, and Malachi (Crenshaw, *Joel*). The arrangers of the MT paid more attention to literary links between the books of Joel and Amos, such as Yahweh's roaring from Zion (Joel 3:16 [4:16 MT]; Amos 1:2) and the mention of nations (Philistia in Joel 3:4 [4:4 MT] and Amos 1:7; Tyre and Sidon in Joel 3:4 [4:4 MT] and Amos 1:9–10; Edom in Joel 3:19 [4:19 MT] and Amos 1:11). Further, the Zion focus in Joel provides a balance to the Israelite orientation of Hosea and Amos. Each part of the Book of the Twelve makes a contribution to the thematic network of the Minor Prophets and particularly to the theme of the Day of the Lord.

Theological and Literary Unity

Rabbinical, patristic, medieval, and Reformation interpreters viewed the book as unified. The critical analysis of the nineteenth century questioned the book's literary and theological unity (Duhm). The unity of the book has found general acceptance in recent literature except for isolated passages, such as 2:3b; 2:29 (3:2 MT); and 3:4–8 (4:4–8 MT) (Wolff; Crenshaw, *Joel*). The various proposed structures support the unity of the book, but there is little unanimity on the structure.

The Message of Joel

The literary reading of Joel as a unit engages several gaps that open the theological dimensions of the book. First, the text connects the locust plague *in history* with the *eschatological* day of the Lord (1:15–18; 2:2–11). Joel links the real world of human phenomena (1:1–14) with the expectation of the eschatological day of the Lord (2:1–11). The superhuman strength of the locusts dramatically heightens the catastrophe. The images of darkness (2:2), fire (1:19–20; 2:3), and earthquake (2:10) suggest a theophany. God himself is behind the image of the locusts, as he comes to bring devastation on the land and to judge his people (2:10). His coming is near (2:1), cosmic (2:10), and awe-inspiring (2:11). The experience of the locust plague in history is a mirror image of the coming day of the Lord in the future (eschatology).

Second, the language and images of the oracle of salvation (2:18–27) combine what can be conceived in history with what is not readily conceivable (eschatology). The prophecy anticipates that Yahweh's renewal will embrace all aspects of their suffering. The Lord will send rain (2:23), so the crops will provide food and drink (2:19, 21–23, 24, 26). He will protect his people from the disgrace they have suffered from the "northerner" (2:20, 25–27).

The imagery of the renewal is so radical that the oracle conjures up a world unlike the world known to humans: the radical elimination of evil and the absolute presence of God's goodness, resulting in the beneficent joy of his people. The Lord assures them that they will never again suffer (2:19, 26–27). The abundant provisions and the protection offered by the Lord mark the age of a new creation. The whole of creation (humans, fields, animals) shares in the benefits of this renewal (2:21–22). The sound of crying and lament is exchanged for the sound of joy (v. 23) and of praise in Zion (v. 26).

Third, the promise of restoration links up with the coming of the Spirit. But what is the connection between the two? The key to the interpretation lies in the first words of 2:28 (3:1 MT): "And afterward." Is the Spirit's coming subsequent to the era of restoration, or are the two events more closely related? Many take "afterward" to be subsequent to God's act of restoration from the agricultural disaster. The promise of the Spirit (2:28–32 [3:1–5 MT]) confirms God's reversal of fortunes, his goodness, and his presence (2:18–27). The phenomena of God's goodness are not an end in themselves. They evidence God's presence among his people (2:27). The self-declaration, "You will know that I am in Israel" (v. 27), and the recognition formula, "I am the LORD your God," attest to the beneficent presence of Yahweh and to his commitment to bring about all that he has promised. Yahweh alone is God, and he will remove suffering from his people (2:26–27; cf. v. 19; 3:17 [4:17 MT]). The benefits of God's assurance take place in history and extend to the time of the renewal of all things (the new creation).

Fourth, the Spirit comes on the "whole" community ("all flesh," 2:28 [3:1 MT]). The long-expected Spirit (cf. Num. 11:25–29) will come and manifest Yahweh's presence in the new community. Each member in the new community shares in the gift of the Spirit. The democratization by the Holy Spirit transforms the community from a hierocratic (ruled by priests) to a theocratic community. The totality of God's people, nevertheless, is marvelously diverse: male and female, young and old, free and servants. The new community consists of those who "rend [their] heart" rather than their garments (2:13). They are further defined by their "call" (vv. 28, 32 [3:1, 5 MT]). On the one hand, they are "all who call on the name of the LORD" (v. 32 AT). The prophet has already prepared the reader for the importance of this call, because he, too, has called on the Lord (1:19). On the other hand, this group is defined as the remnant "whom the LORD calls" (2:32).

Fifth, Yahweh is sovereign over the nations *in history* (3:1–16 [4:1–16 MT]). This section gives hope to the new community as they still face the real world, with adversaries and enmity. Yahweh promises that he will hold the nations accountable for what they have done to his people and to the land (3:2–4 [4:2–3 MT]). As *time* (the day of the Lord) was the focus in the previous chapters, *space* ("the Valley of Jehoshaphat" = "the Valley where Yahweh judges") is the focus of this section (3:1–2, 14 [4:2, 14 MT]). The principle of judgment is the law of retribution (*lex talionis*; 3:4–8 [4:4–8 MT]). The Lord responds by bringing the nations into judgment ("the Valley of Jehoshaphat," v. 12 [4:12 MT]). The combination of agricultural and war images powerfully presents the bloody nature of the eschatological battle (vv. 10, 13 [4:10–13 MT]), as do the cosmic signs of the day of the Lord (3:15 [4:15 MT]; cf. 2:10, 31 [3:4 MT]). The day of the Lord is terrifying for the wicked nations, but he is the refuge for his people (3:16 [4:16 MT]).

Sixth, the center of Yahweh's promise is his presence in Zion, from which oppressive and evil people are removed (3:17 [4:17 MT]; cf. 2:26–27). Zion is the transcendent reality of Yahweh's dwelling with the new community (3:21 [4:21 MT]). Yahweh's beneficence is expressed in images of the new creation (wine, milk, water, 3:18 [4:18 MT]). The image of water flowing from the temple further reinforces the image of the new creation (3:18 [4:18 MT]; cf. Ezek. 47:1–12; Zech. 13:1; 14:3–9). This oracle, too, comforts God's people in any age, giving hope of a world that far surpasses the present reality. The language of imagination in Joel, as in all the prophets, projects transcendence in images of space and time. The combination of a world in and out of time is characteristic of prophetic speech. The images are best taken as representative of the benefits God's people enjoy throughout redemptive history, as tokens of the renewal of creation. Salvation, the new community, and the new creation are already a present reality, but they also await a greater fulfillment.

Joel and the NT

The book of Joel suggests three major intertextual connections with the NT. First, the day of the Lord imagery is prevalent in the Gospels and in the book of Revelation. The day of the Lord is a general designation for the judgment-to-come (Matt. 24:21, 42; cf. 1 Thess. 5:1–11). The apostles cite or allude to aspects associated with the day of the Lord: the locusts (1:6; 2:2, 4–5; cf. Rev. 9:7–9), the cosmic phenomena (2:10, 31; 3:15 [4:15 MT]; cf. Matt. 24:29 et par.; Rev. 6:12–13; 8:12), the sounding of the trumpet (2:1; cf. Rev. 8:6), and the sickle (3:13; cf. Mark 4:29; Rev. 14:15; cf. 19:15). The question "Who can endure/stand?" in Joel 2:11 occurs in Rev. 6:17. The eschatological day of the Lord is the time of the judgment inaugurated by the coming of Jesus Christ, but it is experienced in the history of the church as well, such as in the fall of Jerusalem in 70 CE.

Second, the coming of the eschatological Spirit (2:28–32 [3:1–5 MT]; cf. Acts 2:17–21), including calling on the name of the Lord and being called by the Lord (2:32 [3:5 MT]; cf. Acts 2:39; 22:16; Rom. 10:13), shapes the book of Acts and the apostolic mission of Paul. The Spirit as the mark of the new community defines the church as the body of Christ and individual believers as members of his body. He constitutes the new community that awaits the coming of Jesus Christ. The coming of the Spirit on Gentile believers evidences the inclusion of Gentiles as copartners with Israel. All who call on the name of the Lord are not only saved (Rom. 10:12–15), but also receive his Spirit (ch. 8; 15:16). The new community of Joel's days is continued in the church, but Israel too will share in this promise (11:28; cf. Acts 2:38–39).

Third, John adopts the image of the fountain flowing (Joel 3:18 [4:18 MT]) from God's throne to describe the new creation (22:1).

Bibliography

Achtemeier, E. *Minor Prophets*. Vol. 1, *Hosea–Micah*. NIBCOT. Hendrickson, 1996.

Allen, L. *The Books of Joel, Amos, Obadiah, Jonah, and Micah*. NICOT. Eerdmans, 1976.

Barton, J. *Joel and Obadiah*. OTL. Westminster John Knox, 2001.

Crenshaw, J. "Freeing the Imagination: The Conclusion to the Book of Joel." Pages 120–47 in *Prophecy and Prophets*, ed. Y. Gitay. Scholars Press, 1997.

———. *Joel*. AB 24C. Doubleday, 1995.

———. "Joel's Silence and Interpreters' Readiness to Indict the Innocent." Pages 255–59 in *Lasset uns Brücken bauen*, ed. K. D. Schunck and M. Augustin.

Dillard, R. "Joel." In *An Exegetical and Expository Commentary: Hosea, Joel, and Amos*, ed. T. E. McComiskey. Baker, 1992.

Duhm, B. *The Twelve Prophets*, trans. A. Duff. Black, 1912.

———. "Who Knows What YHWH Will Do? The Character of God in the Book of Joel." Pages 185–96 in *Fortunate the Eyes That See*, ed. A. Beck and A. H. Bartelt. Eerdmans, 1995.

Garrett, D., and P. Ferris. *Hosea, Joel*. NAC. Broadman & Holman, 1997.

Kapelrud, A. S. *Joel Studies*. Almqvist & Wiksells/Harrassowitz, 1948.

Marcus, D. "Nonrecurring Doublets in the Book of Joel." *CBQ* 56 (1994): 56–67.

Meinhold, A. "Zur Rolle des Tag-JHWHs-Gedichts Joel 2,1–11 im XII-Propheten-Buch." Pages 207–23 in *Verbindungslinien: Festschrift für Werner H. Schmidt zum 65. Geburtstag*, ed. A. Graupner et al. Neukirchener Verlag, 2000.

Prinsloo, W. S. *The Theology of the Book of Joel*. BZAW 163. De Gruyter, 1985.

Stuart, D. *Hosea–Jonah*. WBC. Word, 1987.

Sweeney, M. "The Place and Function of Joel in the Book of the Twelve." *SBLSP* 38 (1999): 570–99.

Sweeney, M., et al., eds. *Hosea, Joel, Amos, Obadiah, Jonah*. Berit Olam 1, ed. D. W. Cotter. Liturgical Press, 2000.

VanGemeren, W. "The Spirit of Restoration." *WTJ* 50 (1988): 81–102.

Watts, J. D. W. *The Books of Joel, Obadiah, Jonah, Nahum, Habakkuk and Zephaniah*. CBC. Cambridge, 1975.

Wendland, E. R. *The Discourse Analysis of Hebrew Prophetic Literature*. Mellen Biblical Press, 1995.

Wolff, H. W. *Joel and Amos*, trans. W. Janzen et al. Hermeneia. Fortress, 1977.

27

Amos

KARL MÖLLER

The book of Amos is widely regarded as the earliest legacy of the "writing prophets" and as a paradigm of the prophetic genre. Amos's main theological contributions are the uncompromising censure of the social injustice prevalent in Israelite society in the eighth century BCE, together with the concomitant threat of a severe divine punishment.

History of Interpretation

"Precritical" Readings

The members of the Qumran community were particularly interested in passages that illuminated their own beliefs and practices. These include Amos's reference to David's "fallen tent" (9:11), which was reinterpreted in line with their own missionary expectations (4QFlor 1.11–13), and the threat of Israel being exiled beyond Damascus (5:26–27), which was seen to justify the community's own existence "in the land of Damascus" (CD 7.14–21).

In the Talmud, a range of passages from the book of Amos is used for a variety of ceremonial, ethical, paraenetic, and apologetic purposes (see *y. 'Abod. Zar.* 39a, 40 on Amos 4:4; *b. Nid.* 65 on 4:6; *b. Mo'ed Qat.* 25b, 28b on 8:9; and *b. Ḥul.* 59b–60a on 3:8).

With Origen's commentary (see Eusebius, *Hist. eccl.*, 6.36.2) having been lost, Jerome's work of ca. 406 CE is the earliest and most important commentary of the patristic period. Jerome offers primarily historical exegesis, paired with a christological understanding of the prophet's message. Theodore of Mopsuestia and Theodore of Cyrrhus, exponents of the Antioch school, while aware of the text's metaphorical and salvation-historical dimensions, similarly favored literal readings. Even Cyril of Alexandria, who was strongly indebted to Jerome, sought to avoid the excesses of mystical-allegorical interpretation associated with the school of Alexandria (Dassmann 340–44).

In the patristic writings, quotations from Amos were often restricted to the same dozen verses. For instance, 4:13 played an important role in dogmatic discussions about the creatureliness of the Holy Spirit (advocated by the Pneumatomachs), and 8:9 was frequently understood to refer to the darkness that came over the land at Jesus' death. Amos 5:18–20 was interpreted as referring to the horrors of the final judgment, 9:6 and 9:11–12 were understood christologically, and 8:11 was used by preachers to instill in their audiences a hunger and thirst for God's word (Dassmann 344–50).

Amos in Modern Perspectives

Modern research on Amos shows the same trends as the scholarly investigation of the OT prophets generally. From the 1880s to the 1920s, scholars focused on the innovative impetus of the prophet, understood as an "ethical monotheist," whose task it was to announce the divine ethical imperative (Wellhausen; Duhm). This stress often went hand in glove with a search for Amos's *ipsissima verba*, the very words of the prophetic genius.

From the 1920s onward, form and tradition critics reversed this trend. They focused on the social and institutional settings (such as the Israelite cult or certain wisdom circles) of the speech forms used by Amos and understood the prophet largely as a transmitter of traditional theological convictions (Reventlow).

While these approaches were most concerned with the oral stages of the prophet's words, redaction criticism, which originated in the 1960s, attends to the book's literary prehistory and attempts to trace its stages of growth (Wolff). Contrary to their predecessors, redaction critics affirm the value of redactional contributions, rejecting pejorative labels such as "secondary" or "inauthentic" (Jeremias).

Simultaneously with the redaction-critical quest, other scholars have begun to focus on the text's final form, investigating the structure, poetics, or rhetorical nature of the book (Carroll R., *Contexts*; Möller, *Prophet*). Yet another recent trend is to concentrate on the contribution made by the reader in the generation of meaning.

The Message of Amos

As with every text, our appreciation of Amos's message depends on a variety of hermeneutical decisions. One of these is well illustrated by Brevard Childs's comment, made vis-à-vis redaction criticism's interests in the text's literary prehistory, that historical interpretation of the redactional layers of Amos often runs counter to the perspective demanded by the literature itself (408). Thus, while redaction critics might regard some material as later additions to the prophet's message, the book's canonical form invites a reading that treats the text as what it purports to be: the words of the eighth-century prophet Amos (1:1).

We should also recognize that the book is addressed to subsequent Judean readers, who would have seen Amos's struggle—and ultimate failure—to convince his Israelite audience of the imminent divine punishment in the light of the catastrophic events of 722 BCE. Read from this "past-fulfillment perspective," the book thus becomes a powerful warning, admonishing its readers not to repeat the stubborn attitude of their northern brothers and sisters, lest they too face the divine judgment.

An Outline of Amos's Message

Following the superscription (1:1) and motto (1:2), a series of oracles threatens Israel's neighbors with a divine punishment for their atrocious war crimes (1:3–2:5). Yet, the series eventually culminates in a judgment speech against Israel (2:6–16). Amos thus singles out God's people as the prime target of punishment, which is presented as the divine response to Israel's oppression of the weak and marginalized.

The book then gives the ensuing debate between Amos and his complacent audience (5:14; 6:1–3; 9:10; Möller, *Prophet*), who reject his message of judgment, relying instead on their cherished theological traditions. Amos's reinterpretation and subversion of concepts like the exodus (2:9–10; 3:1–2; 9:7) and the day of Yahweh (5:18–20), his "hymns" extolling God's destructive powers (4:13; 5:8–9; 9:5–6), and the acerbic criticism of Israel's religious activities (4:4–5; 5:21–23)—these are all best understood from the polemical perspective demanded by this dialogical context.

Amos 3–6 contains five judgment speeches (chs. 3 and 4; 5:1–17, 18–27; ch. 6) introduced by "hear this word" or "woe to you who . . ." They reiterate the threat of a divine punishment, arguing that its annunciation was unavoidable (3:3–8). They also corroborate God's verdict (3:9–11; 4:6–12; 5:10–13) and underline the absurdity of the social injustice prevalent in Israelite society (6:12).

The visions in Amos 7:1–8:3—together with the embedded narrative report of Amos's clash with the priest Amaziah, which confirms the hostile attitude of Amos's audience (7:10–17)—underline that the punishment, while not desired by Amos, will not be averted (7:8; 8:2). Another judgment speech (8:4–14), introduced by "Hear this," repeats some of Amos's charges before giving way to various announcements of judgment.

In the final vision (9:1–4), this judgment is depicted as actually occurring, while 9:8–10, in line with the book's implied distinction between culprits and victims, identifies the "sinful kingdom" and "all the sinners among my people" as the prime targets of the divine punishment. An image of future restoration, agricultural abundance, and security in the land concludes the book (9:11–15).

Amos and the Canon

Amos and the Twelve

Recent scholarship has stressed the unity of the Book of the Twelve. On this view, echoes such as that of Joel 3:16a (4:16a MT) in Amos 1:2 are understood as indicating a deliberate linkage and juxtaposition of the two writings. Yet from a canonical perspective Amos's message of judgment might just as fruitfully be compared with a passage like Hab. 1:12–17. While Amos readily depicts the divine judgment as an enemy invasion, Habakkuk, in raising the question of theodicy, offers an intriguing canonical counterperspective.

Amos and the OT

Regardless of the historical relationship between the prophets and the Torah, in canonical perspective Amos is presented as presupposing some of Torah's stipulations (cf. 2:8 with Exod. 22:26; 3:12 with Exod. 22:13).

As Douglas Stuart has shown (xxxi–xlii), Amos also frequently employs the language of the pentateuchal blessings and curses.

Amos in the NT

The NT quotes Amos twice. In Acts 7:41–43, Amos 5:25–27 is understood as referring to the Israelites' idolatry during the wilderness period. In Acts 15:13–18, James applies the rebuilding of David's fallen tent (Amos 9:11–12) to God forming a new people for himself from among the Gentiles.

Some statements in the letter of James about the rich and their treatment of the poor (James 2:6–7; 5:1–6) also show a connection with Amos's message or, more likely, that of the OT prophets generally.

Amos and Theology

There has been a tendency to regard Amos as the harbinger of an inescapable and all-encompassing divine judgment. Others have rejected this construal of the prophet as the messenger of a nation-murdering God, arguing that the prophetic proclamation is instead aimed at repentance. A possible way out of this impasse is suggested by sociolinguistic approaches like rhetorical criticism and speech-act theory, which can help to demonstrate that the possibilities of inescapable doom and of mercy invoked by repentance both inhere in the use of prophetic judgment oracles (Möller, "Words").

Yet our construal of Amos's theology is also affected by judgments about the authenticity of passages such as the salvation oracle in 9:11–15, which is frequently understood to contradict the prophet's uncompromising message of judgment. From a canonical perspective, the oracle does represent an important contribution to the book's theology. Since recent sociolinguistic approaches refute historical criticism's literalistic fixation on the supposed discrepancies of the surface text, they actually invite us to regard this salvation oracle as an integral part of the prophet's original message.

A "full" theological reading thus entails an appreciation not only of Amos's denunciation of the social injustice prevalent in Israelite society and the concomitant threat of an impending divine punishment; it also includes the prophet's vision of a restored people, who once again will fully enjoy life in the land. The oracles against foreign nations (Amos 1–2), furthermore, point to God's sovereign control of this world and his determination to hold the nations responsible for their oppressive and inhumane treatment of the weak and powerless.

In current theological discussion, Amos has been inspirational particularly for Latin American theologies of liberation. They have appropriated its message in an attempt to change existing political and economic structures and create a society marked by solidarity with the poor and "sacrificial service in the struggle to eradicate oppression" (Carroll R., *Contexts*, 19).

Bibliography

Carroll R., M. D. *Amos*. Westminster John Knox, 2002.

———. *Contexts for Amos*. JSOT, 1992.

Childs, B. *Introduction to the Old Testament as Scripture*. Fortress, 1979.

Dassmann, E. "Amos." *RACSup* 1 (2001): 334–50.

Duhm, B. *Die Theologie der Propheten*. Marcus, 1875.

Jeremias, J. *The Book of Amos*. Westminster John Knox, 1998.

Möller, K. *A Prophet in Debate*. Sheffield Academic Press, 2003.

———. "Words of (In-) Evitable Certitude?" Pages 352–86 in *After Pentecost,* ed. C. Bartholomew et al. SHS. Zondervan/Paternoster, 2001.

Reventlow, H. G. *Das Amt des Propheten bei Amos*. Vandenhoeck & Ruprecht, 1962.

Stuart, D. *Hosea–Jonah*. Word, 1987.

Wellhausen, J. *Die kleinen Propheten*. 4th ed. De Gruyter, 1963.

Wolff, H. W. *Joel and Amos*, trans. W. Janzen et al. Hermeneia. Fortress, 1977.

28

Obadiah

PAUL R. HOUSE

The history of Obadiah research mirrors OT studies in miniature. Early
Christian interpreters used Edom's fall as a type of the fall of Jerusalem.
They also stressed the day of the Lord and final judgment, and treated Mt.
Zion and Mt. Edom as types of the church (Ferreiro). Late-nineteenth- and
early-twentieth-century historical-critical scholars tended to discuss the
book's authorship and date along lines established in analyses of the Pentateuch. Thus, scholars debated how the book was shaped over time, since
they did not think it probable that one writer included threats against Edom
and hope for Israel's future in the same book (Wellhausen; Bewer). In the
first three-quarters of the twentieth century, form-critical experts focused
particularly on the book's setting and literary form. Most concluded that
the book was a prophetic denunciation from shortly after the fall of Jerusalem in 587/6 BCE, though this opinion was by no means universally
accepted (Wolff; Watts). Like historical critics, form critics struggled with
the presence of threats and promise in the same short book. In the late
twentieth century scholars debated whether Obadiah should be read as a
unified construction (Raabe), as part of the Book of the Twelve as a whole
(Nogalski), or as a redacted prophetic book (Ben Zvi). Such discussions
reflected the trend toward treating the canonical text and reactions to

this strategy. By the end of the twentieth century, Obadiah had been the subject of lengthy analyses, but it was still not analyzed as often as longer prophecies.

Even some of the excellent longer studies of Obadiah do not highlight the book's theology. Though understandable, this situation is somewhat regrettable, since a study of the final form of Obadiah provides examples of several of the OT's most significant canonical-theological issues (Barton). These include visionary prophecy as divine revelation, human pride and hatred of one's neighbor as great ethical problems, the day of the Lord, and the significance of Zion.

Visionary Prophecy and Divine Revelation (v. 1)

Of all the prophetic books, only Isaiah's and Obadiah's superscriptions identify the words that follow as "a vision." Isaiah conveys messages related primarily to the present and future of Judah and Jerusalem. In Obadiah's case, messages concerning Edom's current sins and future judgment unfold. The designation of these books as "vision" underscores their divine origins, for this term establishes the belief that Yahweh has given these words to the prophets. Further, having established the term "vision" in verse 1, Obadiah then uses quotation formulas in verses 1, 4, 8, and 18, and utilizes first-person recorded speech in most of 2–18.

Thus, despite the visual implications of "vision," Obadiah consists of words that express what has been seen. These words provide a permanent record of this prophet's personal experiences in a way that benefits the community of faith and calls the sinful into account. This movement from vision to speech (and possibly) to written word given to and accepted by faithful persons mirrors the canonical process of other OT books. Furthermore, Obadiah was considered part of the Book of the Twelve in the Hebrew tradition. As such, it is part of twelve connected prophecies that together express in written word prophecy's great themes: covenant, sin, judgment, renewal, and consummation.

Human Pride (vv. 2–10)

Like Isaiah, Obadiah considers pride the root of other sins. The Edomites' pride is based on their status among the nations (v. 1), their seemingly impregnable capital (vv. 3–4), their famous wise men (v. 8), and their valiant warriors (v. 9). These attainments have led to the self-deception that they are beyond the reach of any higher power (v. 3). Thus, they believe they can act as they wish against Israel (v. 10). In other words, Obadiah depicts Edom in a manner similar to Isaiah's description of Assyria (Isa. 10:1–19). If so, it is ironic that small nations have the same delusions of self-sufficient grandeur as larger ones.

Hatred of Neighbor (vv. 11–14)

Edom's mistreatment of Israel is the reason Obadiah gives for their coming judgment. The Edomites have stood by when invaders ransacked Israel and took captives (vv. 11–12). Worse yet, they rejoiced in Israel's downfall and cut down those trying to flee (vv. 13–14). They did this despite the fact that they were Israel's "brother" (v. 12), a reference to the fact that Jacob and Esau, the patriarchs of Israel and Edom respectively, were brothers. Amos adds the fact that Edom was famous for slave trade (1:9) and for fierce wrath in battle (1:11–12). They have made money from hating their neighbor, and their status and security make them think they can do so forever.

The Day of the Lord and Zion Theology (vv. 15–21)

As in the rest of the prophetic corpus, Obadiah asserts that all nations will be judged on "the day of the LORD" (v. 15). This term signifies a certain, specific event at an unspecified time in the future. It also indicates the Lord's sovereignty over the whole of creation, not just the covenant nation, Israel. The belief that one God rules all nations is indicative of the OT's emphasis on monotheism, and as such it varies greatly from the ancient henotheistic and polytheistic attitudes of most, if not all, of Israel's neighbors. The day of the Lord will remove Edom's proud populace from their secure mountain home and exalt Judah's humble survivors. Edom will experience Yahweh's justice by having their deeds turned against them (v. 15). They will learn the fundamental fact made clear in Joel 3:16–19 and Amos 1:3–2:3 that Yahweh's justice is universal (v. 15).

Further, on the day of the Lord Edom will discover that Zion is special to Yahweh (v. 17), a point underscored in Isa. 4:2–6; Isa. 62; Jer. 30–33; and Ezek. 40–48. There will be deliverance on Mt. Zion, but none on Mt. Seir. There will be deliverance for the house of Jacob, but there will be none for his brother Esau's house (v. 18). Israel's captivity will end (v. 20), and

Zion's deliverers will rule Edom (v. 21). Yahweh's rule in Zion on behalf of Israel's survivors constitutes the kingdom of God on earth (v. 21; cf. Isa. 25:6–8). Yahweh is sovereign, and Yahweh fights for Israel, which fulfills the promise made to Abraham to defeat his descendant's enemies (Gen. 12:1–3). Thus, in this last section of Obadiah it is clear that Zion is not simply Jerusalem. Nor is Edom simply a neighboring nation. Rather, Zion is the place where Yahweh lives with his faithful people in the absence of sin and danger. Similarly, Edom represents all nations that threaten Yahweh's redeemed ones. This long-term foe of Israel provides a pattern for what it means to have a determined, harsh enemy.

Like other prophets, Obadiah based his eschatological expectations on concrete historical events. Edom's real acts in history provided a paradigm for how sinful Gentiles behave, and Edom's eventual defeat served as a basis for belief in ultimate redemption for those who please Yahweh. Survival in historical circumstances became the impetus for theological reflection on the future. Therefore, Obadiah provides patterns for theological understanding, not just predictions about the future.

Conclusion

Obadiah's theological significance is at least twofold. First, its significance lies in its ability to present a vision in words that relate common historical events to the larger pattern of eschatology. Concrete events that take place repeatedly at an unspecified point in time prove typical enough to provide a paradigm for the future. Second, its significance lies in its ability to connect with significant OT themes and to adjoining books. One could not reproduce the entirety of prophetic theology from these verses, but one could make a good start. This brief prophecy should therefore be seen for what it is: a tightly packed, theologically rich essay on Yahweh's sovereignty over Israel and Israel's neighbors. When viewed this way, Obadiah highlights the transbiblical belief that Yahweh deserves and demands exclusive worship and service. There are no other gods, so there is no salvation outside of a relationship with Israel's God, who is the Creator and Judge of everyone. Those who deny this exclusive sovereignty place themselves in Edom's precarious position.

Bibliography

Barton, J. *Joel and Obadiah*. OTL. Westminster John Knox, 2001.

Ben Zvi, E. *A Historical-Critical Study of the Book of Obadiah*. BZAW 242. De Gruyter, 1996.

Bewer, J. *A Critical and Exegetical Commentary on Obadiah and Joel*. ICC. T&T Clark, 1911.

Ferreiro, A., ed. *The Twelve Prophets*. ACCSOT 14. InterVarsity, 2003.

Nogalski, J. *Literary Precursors to the Book of the Twelve*. BZAW 217. De Gruyter, 1993.

———. *Redactional Processes in the Book of the Twelve*. BZAW 218. De Gruyter, 1993.

Raabe, P. *Obadiah*. AB 24D. Doubleday, 1996.

Watts, J. *Obadiah*. Eerdmans, 1969.

Wellhausen, J. *Die Kleinen Propheten übersetzt und erklart*. 3rd ed. G. Reimer, 1898.

Wolff, H. W. *Obadiah and Jonah*, trans. M. Kohl. Augsburg, 1986.

29

Jonah

JOHN H. WALTON

Highlights in the History of Interpretation

Sherwood has thoroughly documented the history of interpretation of
this popular book that has served as a "cultural hologram" of religious
and theological sentiments and trends (71). Early Christian interpretation found its interpretative key in Matt. 12:40 and focused on Jonah
and Jesus as "typological twins" (Sherwood 11–21). Jerome and others
constructed a web of parallels between the book and the events of Jesus'
ministry. Augustine accepted this approach, but alongside it he adopted
the idea of the prophet as an embodiment of carnal Israel, inaugurating
the second phase of interpretation: Jonah as negative stereotype of Jews.
Even into the Reformation, this is evident in Luther's assessment of the
book as showing the superiority of Christianity to Judaism. Thus, the
book became a lightning rod for anti-Semitic and supersessionistic sentiment and theology (Sherwood 32). The period of the Reformation also
saw a shift to a third category, evident in Calvin's treatment of the book
as warning against fleeing from God or chiding that people are more
important than plants.

Post-Enlightenment exposition focused on the phenomena of the
book, whether from a vantage point of skepticism or reacting against it

apologetically. Thus, the details of the book came under close scrutiny. Even as the Age of Criticism was dawning and "adolescing," the older modes of interpretation were transmogrified rather than discarded. The eighteenth-century interpreters sermonized about Jewish envy of Gentiles, while the nineteenth century adopted Jonah as the poster child for anti-Semitic sentiment (Sherwood 25–27). As critical study reached the apex of modernism and began the transition to postmodern interpretation, attention turned to deeper discussion of genre, even as more traditional communities continued to argue for the historicity of the book's events.

Contemporary literary analysis is prone to resort to rhetorical labels such as satire (Ackerman 227), parody (Orth), or irony (Simon) to describe the book. Such suggestions are often rejected by evangelical interpreters who view these as modern categories and consider them threatening to biblical authority. On the first count, parody at least has now been identified in ancient literature (Michalowski 84–86), and on the second, it can be observed that satire and parody do not imply fictionalization. The real issue can be framed in the question, "Should the book be categorized as a 'truth-telling' genre or as 'nonrealistic' writing?" Complexity increases if we consider options such as "nonrealistic" writing based on a kernel of historical information, or "truth-telling" tailored so that certain stereotypes surface. While consensus on these questions may exist within particular interpretative communities, a universal consensus has not yet been reached.

The above survey categorizes ways that the book of Jonah has been exploited over the years, commandeered for social, theological, or methodological agendas. Alternatively, the interpretations of the book can be sorted out with relation to its message rather than its use. Alexander identified four approaches to the interpretation of the text: that the book was about repentance, about unfulfilled prophecy, about Jewish attitudes toward Gentiles, or about theodicy (Alexander et al. 81–91). Simon uses a similar list to represent the history of Jewish interpretation (vii–xiii), all still reflected in interpretative communities today.

Deciding about the theological message of the book concerns what equations it sets up: Israel = Nineveh? Jonah = Israel? Jonah = Jesus? The purpose and message are going to derive from whichever equation is adopted. The challenge interpreters face is arriving at a cohesive reading that would have been recognizable to the author—to arrive confidently at an understanding of what could be called the "face value" of the book.

Literary Structure

The book of Jonah is characterized by a highly artistic literary structure. Chapter 1 parallels chapter 3 as each highlights a non-Israelite audience threateningly confronted by Yahweh. In both cases the response is exemplary, contrasting favorably to the prophet's questionable behavior. God is seen as initiator, non-Israelites as responders, and prophet as foil. Both chapters conclude with God's merciful deliverance. Chapters 2 and 4 are likewise parallel as Yahweh interacts in each with his prophet. These chapters conclude recognizing God's character.

Overview of the Message

The above literary structure highlights many of the major elements that bind the book together. Yet despite parallels, chapter 4 has often been seen as incompatible with the unity of the book. If the persuasiveness of a particular understanding is found in its ability to integrate every aspect into the whole, then the object lesson and the abrupt ending of chapter 4 must be addressed. As the conclusion, it is the key to the book's purpose and message, which in the end is not about Nineveh, Jonah, or Israel, but about God.

The object lesson gives the reader the operative equation by which the book operates: Jonah becomes a surrogate Nineveh. The initial indicator of this is signaled by the variations in the divine name. Through most of the book, Jonah interacts with Yahweh, while the non-Israelites predictably use the term *'elohim* (except 1:14–16, after the sailors have been introduced to Yahweh). Consequently, in 4:6 the sudden use of the compound divine name, Yahweh-Elohim, catches the attention of the reader and signals a temporary and meaningful switch. The object lesson then uses Elohim through its conclusion in 4:9. This suggests that Jonah has been relocated among the non-Israelites in the object lesson.

The second indicator is the repetition of the Hebrew root *ra'ah* in 3:10 and 4:6. For Nineveh, this describes the impending "destruction," from which they are spared. For Jonah, it is the impending "discomfort," from which he is initially spared, but eventually experiences in full. Again, Jonah is thus equated with Nineveh. This opens up the full parallelism incorporated in the object lesson (from Walton 49):

1. Both Nineveh and Jonah have an impending calamity from which they desire to protect themselves (their *ra'ah*), respectively the prophesied destruction and discomfort of the weather.

2. Both Nineveh (by repentance) and Jonah (by his hut) embark on a course of action to prevent the *ra'ah*.

3. Both attempts are supplemented and actualized by an act of divine grace: God grants Nineveh a reprieve and provides Jonah a protective plant.

4. At this point there is a change. Rather than allowing his gracious act to continue to protect Jonah, God's protection is removed. A parasite devours the plant, and Jonah is exposed to the full force of the calamity, left only with the protection of his own provision, the hut, which does him no good.

Thus, the object lesson draws out the message of the book. The lesson puts Jonah and Nineveh on the same side, with God on the other side, and establishes its significance relative to God, regardless of the results for Nineveh/Jonah.

What did the incident teach Nineveh? Some consider Jonah as the story of a remarkable conversion of pagan Nineveh to true faith in God, and they focus on what Nineveh learned. Nevertheless, evidence for a conversion to true Yahwism is difficult to find in the text. Unquestionably, they repent of "their evil ways." But there is no mention of turning to Yahweh, being instructed about the covenant, or discarding their other gods. The description of their belief indicates only that they believed what God had said through Jonah about their impending doom (Walton 53–54). It is their action that is commended in 3:10, not their faith.

In addition, once the nature of the object lesson is understood, it becomes clear that Nineveh's response is important for its inadequacy. It is paralleled by Jonah's hut, unable to shelter him from the calamity. In short, then, the Ninevites learned little. But even in their ignorance and paganism, they recognized the need to respond to the word of Deity. They thus offer an important model both to the Israelite audience and to future audiences (Matt. 12:41).

What did the incident teach Jonah? Jonah's function in the narrative is to be the foil—static and recalcitrant. The only "change" in him came simply in response to the inevitable. Once he learned that he had no choice but to go to Nineveh, he did so. He was consistent in self-righteously seeing himself as justified in all his actions and attitudes. We could conclude, then, that he did not learn anything, other than that sometimes God will not take "no" for an answer. The book does not depend on his making progress.

What did the book teach Israel? The purpose of the book, we suggest, focuses on the changes accompanying the period of classical prophecy.

The example of Nineveh serves to educate Israel and its prophets regarding the "ground rules" of this era. Through the eighth-century prophets, a new age had dawned in which Israel and Judah were warned of coming judgment in the form of prophetic pronouncement—usually deemed irrevocable. The book of Jonah illustrates that repentance was a proper and acceptable response, and could even turn back the judgment. It worked even for naive, wicked, pagan Nineveh. When Israel faced such warnings, this model for response suggests that even in the shadow of pronounced doom, repentance can bring mercy. It therefore becomes important to recognize the Ninevites' response as shallow and uninformed. The book is counting on that contrast to drive home the point that the response of Israel, God's covenant people, would surely be able to elicit similar compassion from God.

In choosing this interpretation, we reject the popular reading that the book was written to scold Jewish exclusivism in the postexilic period. That view assumes that Jonah was asked to preach repentance and did so. We find no conclusive evidence for such an assumption.

What does the book teach about God? In the interpretation offered here, this is the key, as it should be when we consider Scripture as God's self-revelation. The book ends with God and makes a clear point about his compassion. Jonah is angry that God's grace is stimulated by his compassion rather than requiring a minimal level of theological sophistication or faith. Instead, God's compassion is stimulated by responsiveness. This proclaims a God of second chances, who delights in even small steps in the right direction. Even though Jonah is theologically offended by such grace benefiting Nineveh, he is glad enough of it when his own comfort is at stake, as Israel would be when the classical prophets proclaim their doom-laden oracles. The God of threatening oracles of judgment is a compassionate God, prone to be gracious at the slightest hint of response.

What does the book teach us? We are not receiving messages of doom from prophets, but the judgment of God still threatens the unrighteous. It is most important for us to use the message of the book to deepen our understanding of God. It is not unusual for people to feel that something they have done has put them beyond the reach of God's mercy, disqualified for his grace or compassion. The book of Jonah has encouraging words to offer: God's compassion is boundless. Should anyone feel that their straying has left no way back to God, the encouragement of the book is that God is inclined to respond to even the smallest steps in the right direction. The jump from prodigal to sainthood need not be made in a single leap. We need only to climb the fence out of the pigsty and take a step toward home. A compassionate God waits with open arms and is ready to meet us on our journey.

The Book's Contribution to the Canon as a Whole

If the book offers a model response to classical prophecy, it can be seen as canonically integrated with the prophetic corpus. It also offers some nuancing of Deut. 18:22 concerning a prophet's authentication. Jonah qualifies that principle with the allowance for God's grace to postpone judgment if there should be a positive response.

Jonah appears in the Book of the Twelve as a transition between the juxtaposed books of Hosea–Obadiah and the chronologically arranged books, Micah–Malachi. If Jonah serves as conclusion or synthesis of the initial juxtapositions, one can explore them to discover Jonah's role.

Hosea proclaims the impending judgment that grain, new wine, and oil will be taken away (2:9). Joel shows a repentant response to a prophet in whose time this same sort of threat is realized in a locust plague. As a result of the positive response, God restored those commodities (2:19). The juxtaposition of these two books shows the positive result of response by God's errant people. In contrast, Amos pronounces coming judgment on the nations. Edom is not only included in the initial list (1:11–12), but is targeted at the end (9:12). It is logical, then, that Obadiah should follow Amos, illustrating the result of nonresponse found in the destruction of Edom. Joel and Obadiah then serve as postexilic illustrations of the ongoing relevance of preexilic prophetic messages. In the process they exemplify the deliverance that comes when people do respond and the judgment that comes when they do not.

With these two examples juxtaposed for the audience, the book of Jonah provides a synthesis. Even the most pagan of cities, Nineveh, showing even the most uninformed response, experienced mercy at the hands of God. The appropriate response to the prophetic oracles of indictment and judgment is to begin taking steps in the right direction. As Jonah synthesizes the fruits of the juxtaposition of the two previous pairings of books, it also then provides transition to the chronological sequence of prophetic collections. This sequence is concluded and synthesized by Malachi, who summarizes the call and response for the postexilic audience.

The NT connections concern the "sign of Jonah" (Matt. 12:39–41; 16:4; Luke 11:29–32). The Pharisees request a "sign," presumably to authenticate Christ's message, and are told they will receive no sign but the sign of Jonah. In Matt. 12 Christ proceeds with the analogy that as Jonah was three days in the belly of the fish, so the Son of man will be three days in the earth. In both Matt. 12 and Luke 11, Christ comments that the Ninevites will stand up at judgment and condemn the Pharisees for their unbelief. Neither the three-day analogy, nor the future act of the Ninevites, is textually identified as the "sign of Jonah." Luke 11:30 gives the only positive clue: "For just as Jonah became a sign to the people of Nineveh, so the Son of man will be to this generation" (NRSV). We must ask, then, how Jonah "was a sign to the Ninevites." The only indication that the book offers for Jonah to be a sign to the Ninevites (not just to the Pharisees or us) is that he proclaimed a message of judgment. This served as a sign preceding the impending judgment of God.

Bibliography

Ackerman, J. "Satire and Symbolism in the Song of Jonah." Pages 213–46 in *Traditions in Transformation*, ed. B. Halpern and J. Levenson. Eisenbrauns, 1981.

Alexander, D., D. Baker, and B. Waltke. *Obadiah, Jonah, Micah*. InterVarsity, 1988.

Allen, L. *The Books of Joel, Obadiah, Jonah, and Micah*. Eerdmans, 1976.

Clements, R. "The Purpose of the Book of Jonah." *VTSup* 28 (1974): 16–28.

Cook, S., and S. C. Winter. *On the Way to Nineveh*. Scholars Press, 1999.

Craig, K. "Jonah in Recent Research." *CurBS* 7 (1999): 97–118.

Fretheim, T. "Jonah and Theodicy." *ZAW* 90 (1978): 227–37.

———. *Message of Jonah*. Augsburg, 1977.

Holbert, J. C. "Deliverance Belongs to Yahweh! Satire in the Book of Jonah." *JSOT* 21 (1981): 59–81.

Landes, G. "Jonah: A *Mas[h]al?*" Pages 137–58 in *Israelite Wisdom*, ed. J. Gammie, W. Brueggemann, et al. Scholars Press for Union Theological Seminary, 1978.

———. "The Kerygma of the Book of Jonah." *Interpretation* 21 (1967): 3–31.

———. "Matthew 12:40 as an Interpretation of 'the Sign of Jonah' against Its Biblical Background." Pages 665–84 in *The Word of the Lord Shall Go Forth*, ed. C. Meyers and M. O'Connor. Eisenbrauns, 1983.

Michalowski, P. "Commemoration, Writing, and Genre in Ancient Mesopotamia." Pages 69–89 in *The Limits of Historiography*. Brill, 1999.

Orth, M. "Genre in Jonah: The Effects of Parody in the Book of Jonah." Pages 257–82 in *The Bible in the Light of Cuneiform Literature*, ed. W. W. Hallo, B. W. Jones, and G. L. Mattingly. E. Mellen, 1990.

Sasson, J. *Jonah*. Doubleday, 1990.

Sherwood, Y. *A Biblical Text and Its Afterlives*. Cambridge University Press, 2000.

Simon, U. *Jonah*. JPS, 1999.

Stuart, D. *Hosea–Jonah*. Word, 1987.

Trible, P. *Rhetorical Criticism*. Fortress, 1994.

Walton, J. "The Object Lesson of Jonah 4:5–7 and the Purpose of the Book of Jonah." *BBR* 2 (1992): 47–57.

Wiseman, D. J. "Jonah's Nineveh." *TynBul* 30 (1979): 29–51.

30

Micah

MIGNON R. JACOBS

Overview

The book of Micah is evidence that the size of a book does not determine its significance to scholars, the quantity of studies focused on its interpretation, or its place in theological discourse. Its content constitutes interpretative challenges to the extent that the various macrounits appear to have different historical contexts, different conceptual foci, and different types of elements signaling the interrelationship of these units.

Sequentially, Micah is sixth in the Book of the Twelve, sandwiched between Jonah and Nahum. Like others (e.g., Amos, Hosea), it opens with a superscription (1:1), a redactional element that relates the prophetic activity to a particular historical context by mentioning rulers of that period. Micah is designated as eighth-century-BCE activity, though some of its content presupposes other historical settings, such as the mention of Babylon (4:10; seventh century BCE). It consists of two macrounits and their microunits: I. 1:1–5:15 (A. 1:2–16; B. 2:1–5:15); and II. 6:1–7:20 (A. 6:1–8; B. 6:9–7:20). Within its seven chapters, it moves from announcement of judgment on Samaria (1:6–7) to declaration of a promise of preservation, of forgiveness for a remnant (2:12–13; 7:18–20).

History of Interpretation

Like much of the OT, Micah has been the focus of various methodological approaches that yielded various interpretative conclusions. Some of the earliest studies centered on questions of authenticity—a question as reflective of the historical context of the interpreters as of the apparent conceptual tensions within the book. As exemplified by Stade, in the nineteenth century, apparent inconsistencies in the extant form of the book (style, historical context, conceptual unity) became the basis for questioning its authenticity. Stade concluded that there are at least three distinct historical contexts—Mic. 1–3 (eighth century); 4–5 and 7:7–20 (sixth century); and 6:1–7:6 (seventh century).

While twentieth- and twenty-first-century scholarship acknowledges the inconsistencies within the book, the concern is not so much about authenticity as about the coherence of the whole. Among the first to look at redactional order of the constitutive units, Haupt observed that the extant order contributes to the incoherence of the book, and that restoration of an original order may restore coherence. Others, including Wolff, Lescow, and Wagenaar, later attempted to discern the composition history of the book through identification of the various redactional accretions, their historical contexts, and the redactional intent.

Mays addressed theological unity in his investigation of the historical context and redactional intention of the book's extant form. Willis and Hagstrom also voiced concerns about coherence and tried to define it by using literary and conceptual elements such as the alternation between judgment (chs. 1–3) and hope (chs. 4–5), and the recurrent concepts within the discernible macrounits (e.g., sin in chs. 1–3; 6–7). Jacobs notes these recurrent concepts in light of their semantic indicators (e.g., *khatta'ah*, "sin"; *pesha'*, "crime/transgression"), genres (e.g., judgment speeches), inquiries about their interrelationship within the book, and also the conceptual framework of the OT.

Multicritical approaches are also part of the methodological orientation toward the book. These methods employ and acknowledge various critical resources in their analysis. Ben Zvi (*Micah*) addressed concerns about the form of the book, identifying the infractions of those against whom judgment is pronounced ("Wrongdoers"). He is also concerned about issues of "readership" as a decisive interpretative element. In this way, he exemplifies others who use the book of Micah to address issues of reader orientation, oppression, and class struggles. In delineating the composition history of chapters 2–5, Wagenaar identified the methodological parameters of her approach: form and redaction criticism. As a part of their historical-critical analysis, Andersen and Freedman employed text criticism in addition to redaction criticism, resulting in a comparative analysis of the LXX and MT editions.

Within all of these approaches, one cannot miss the book's focus on judgment and hope. These are connected with the challenge to correct injustices and to know that God requires one's religious practices to be in line with godly social practices.

Content and Theological Concerns

The message of the book demands that Israel go beyond the external forms of worship and penitence to implement justice, but it does not promise to avert punishment. Rather, it promises to restore Jerusalem after the judgment. To further accentuate the severity of the sins, the priests' abuse of their role resulted in compromises in teaching Torah (cf. Mal. 1:1–9).

Sin and Forgiveness

The pervasive sin is presented through the repeated use of the terminology and depiction of practices: *pesha'* ("crime/transgression," 1:5; cf. 6:7), *khatta'ah* ("sin," 1:5; cf. 3:8; 6:7), *'awen* ("wickedness") and *ra'* ("evil," 2:1–2; cf. 3:1–2), and *'awon* ("iniquity" of the remnant, 7:18). The leaders and other accused are characterized as abusing their power (e.g., 3:1, 5–6) and seizing people's lands and possessions, thus reducing them to poverty (2:1–5). The judgment is extended to the whole nation: *mishpakhah* ("family," 2:3 NRSV). The Deity forgives all types of sins—the terminology may reflect the gamut of forgiveness—taking away iniquity (7:18), overlooking transgression (7:18), trampling upon iniquity (7:19), casting sin into the depth (7:19). Even so, forgiveness is particular to the remnant (*she'erith*—7:18–20), indicating God's selectivity in whom and when to forgive (cf. Jer. 31:34; 36:3; 1 John 1:9).

God's Requirement

One of the challenges encountered by the people is their understanding of God's requirement. First, they assume that God's presence in their midst exempts them from adversity (3:10–11). Second, they believe that God's total requirement is giving sacrifices, and they view this requirement as burdensome (cf. Amos 5:21–25; Isa. 1:11). They thus give sacrifices and expect them to be sufficient to appease if not to please God, rather than seeing that God may be wearied by their sins and sacrifices (6:6–8; cf. 1 Sam. 15:22; Isa. 1:17; 43:22–24; Hos. 6:6; Mal. 1:13). Micah 6 clarifies that God requires doing justice, loving solidarity, and being circumspect in relationship with God (6:8). God does not reject religious rituals; but neither is God pleased simply by the external performances devoid of obedience manifested in repentance and justice (Isa. 1:17; 43:24; Jer. 6:20; Amos 5:21–24; cf. 2 Tim. 3:1–5).

Remnant and Hope

Unlike the book of Amos, which held out the possibility of changing God's resolve to bring judgment, in the book of Micah judgment is inevitable. The identity of *she'erith* (the "remnant") is as much a concern as its relationship to the judgment. First, God promises to restore Jerusalem and inaugurate a new age in the latter days (4:6–7; cf. Isa. 2:2–4). To that end, God promises to restore a remnant identified as those whom God has subjected to adversity (4:6–7). Second, the remnant will be formed without any concern to distinguish between the innocent and the guilty (cf. Isa. 10:20–22; 11:11). Third, the remnant will be forgiven of its sins and will be used to form the new nation in and through which Yahweh will rule. Fourth, the remnant is also identified as the *she'erith ya'aqob* ("remnant of Jacob," 5:7–8 [vv. 6–7 MT]), referring to those who survive from Judah, the southern kingdom (cf. Isa. 37:31–32). It appears that 2:12–13; 4:6–8; 5:9 (v. 8 MT); and 7:18–20 may also refer to this group rather than the northern kingdom. Fifth, the remnant is characterized as both a temporary and a destructive presence in the midst of other nations (5:7–9 [vv. 6–8 MT]), but not every remnant of Judah will be used in God's plan (cf. Jer. 44:12–14).

Through the concept of remnant, the issue of hope is raised. First, the hope is that through the experience of devastation the nation will be made aware of God's involvement in all phases of its existence (4:1–5:15 [v. 14 MT]). Second, in the eschatological perspective of actualizing the restoration, those to whom the promise is articulated may not live to experience it (cf. Jer. 24; 25:9–14). As with patriarchs waiting for the actualization of the promise, Israel's test of faith is to persist when the present circumstances bear no resemblance to the envisioned future.

Hermeneutical Challenges

Retribution

God punishes people. To some, this sounds like a manifestation of God's justice against the unjust; however, this concerns the nature of judgment, of a God who uses judgment to address sin, and judgment as a prerequisite for actualizing hope. Part of the challenge is that God not only punishes people (e.g., 3:4, 7) but also includes the innocent in the punishment (e.g., 2:3–5; 3:12; Hos. 13:16 [14:1 MT]; cf. Jer. 18:19–23). Consequently, those ravaged by the injustices committed against them are further ravaged by the manifestation of judgment. Additionally, while punishing a nation for its sins, God uses nations to punish each other—such as Babylon versus Judah (Mic. 4:10–11; Jer. 39), and Assyria versus the remnant of Judah (Mic. 5:8–9 [vv. 7–8 MT]). This may be viewed as a manifestation of God's sovereignty in its prophetic literary context. Yet, it is problematic within the modern framework for several reasons, at least when it involves (1) discerning God's desires, plans, and involvement in any act that demolishes a nation (cf. Isa. 10:12–14; ch. 13; 43:14; Jer. 50); and (2) distinguishing God's acts and plans from human plans and motives to do harm. There is an inherent danger in unequivocally claiming God's approval for one's own violence.

God's Selectivity

While one may rejoice that in the book judgment is not the final word concerning Jerusalem's existence, one is also haunted by the representation of the remnant—the survivors. God will preserve a group of survivors and forgive its sins, without distinguishing between the innocent and the guilty in forming the remnant (7:18–20; cf. 2:12–13; 4:6–8). On the other hand, Jeremiah reflects God's selectivity in distinguishing between those who will be used to restore Jerusalem (good figs, 24:2–7) and those who will be perpetually rejected (bad figs, 24:8; 29:17; 44:12–14). This divine prerogative to choose or reject persons and nations is fundamental to the election and the covenantal relationship (Gen. 12; 15:2–4; Mal. 1:2–5). Yet God further distinguishes among those who constitute the covenant community: not all of them are to be part of God's chosen (cf. Ezek. 18; Rom. 9:6–9, 11–14). It epitomizes the tension among Christians—the nominal as compared to the committed Christian.

Second, God's selectivity is the timing of the judgment brought against nations, as perceived in the gap between the devastation on Samaria (eighth century BCE) compared to Jerusalem (sixth century BCE). God seems to be more patient and tolerant toward some while readily punishing others. The third aspect of God's selectivity is the choice of nations to be used as instruments and subjects of devastation and the selection criteria—hence, the implications of belief in and pleasing such a Deity.

God's Requirements

The message of Micah confronts any community that extols the virtues of religion while fostering various forms of injustice. The people of Micah's day were accused of oppressing simply because they had the power to do so, and the injustices broke down trust in all arenas of the community. The family bonds are not enough to counter the mistrust in the community (Mic. 7:1–7). As in the Pentateuch, the concern is to protect those who are vulnerable within the community—the widow, orphan, poor (Exod. 22:21–24; Lev. 23:22; Deut. 15; Isa. 9:1–7; 11:1–9; Jer. 7:5–7; 22:3; Ezek. 22:7; Mal. 3:5). The justice accomplished is that those who abuse their power will be deprived of that power, but the modern settings including the church seem to tolerate abuse of power. It becomes difficult to discern God's voice in the midst of misteachings that have become the sanctioned beliefs among Christians and that allow persistent injustices (2 Tim. 4:3).

Bibliography

Andersen, F., and D. N. Freedman. *Micah*. AB 24E. Doubleday, 2000.

Ben Zvi, E. *Micah*. FOTL 21B. Eerdmans, 2000.

———. "Wrongdoers, Wrongdoing and Righting Wrongs in Micah 2." *BibInt* 7 (1999): 87–100.

Hagstrom, D. *The Coherence of the Book of Micah*. SBLDS 89. Scholars Press, 1988.

Haupt, P. "Critical Notes on Micah." *AJSL* 26, (1910): 201–52.

Jacobs, M. *Conceptual Coherence of the Book of Micah*. JSOTSup 322. Sheffield Academic Press, 2001.

Lescow, T. "Redaktionsgeschicht Analyse von Micha 1–5." *ZAW* 84 (1972): 46–85.

Mays, J. L. *Micah*. OTL. Westminster, 1976.

Stade, B. "Bemerkungen über das Buch Micha." *ZAW* 1 (1881): 161–72.

Wagenaar, J. A. *Judgement and Salvation*. VTSup 85. Brill, 2001.

Waltke, B. "Micah." Pages 591–764 in *The Minor Prophets,* ed. T. E. McComiskey. Vol. 2. Baker, 1993.

Willis, J. T. "The Structure, Setting, and Interrelationships of the Pericopes in the Book of Micah." PhD diss., Vanderbilt University, 1966.

Wolff, H. W. *Micah,* trans. G. Stansell. Augsburg, 1990.

31

Nahum

THOMAS RENZ

The book of Nahum is a "prophecy concerning Nineveh, the document of a revelation to Nahum the Elkoshite" (1:1 AT). The revelation concerns the downfall of Nineveh in 612 BCE. The prophetic exposition puts this downfall into a theological framework, focusing on the nature of God, especially his jealous anger and vengeance. Nahum depicts God as powerful and passionate but in a protective rather than possessive way.

The Argument of the Book

Following the superscription (1:1), a hymn describes Yahweh's character and the different fates of two groups, depending on how they relate to Yahweh (1:2–8); to this is added a prophetic challenge (1:9–10) and a statement of the situation that gave rise to the prophecy (1:11). A divine declaration promising liberation from oppression and defeat of the enemy (1:12–14) forms a bridge to images of the fall of Nineveh (2:1–10), which are introduced by a picture of the announcement of victory (1:15). Appended to these images is a rhetorical question stressing defeat (2:11–12) and a prophecy of complete destruction (2:13). In chapter 3 an announcement of doom for a murderous city (3:1–4) precedes a prophecy of complete humiliation (3:5–7). The exposition denounces the city's complacency (3:8–12) before depicting the uselessness of the city's defenses (3:13–17) and the helplessness of the city's ruler (3:18–19). Attempts to separate the message of restoration (for Judah) from the message of destruction (for Nineveh) go against the thrust of the book, which has them closely intertwined. Vengeance executed against the oppressor means liberation for the oppressed.

Addressee and reference of the text are frequently left undetermined (the ambiguity is removed in some translations by insertion of "Judah" and "Nineveh" in 1:7–2:1), suggesting that God's "zealous ardour for the maintenance and promotion of his own legal claims" (Peels 203–4) applies without partiality. The real opposition is not between two nations, but between those who put their trust in a God who loathes injustice and those who are his enemies. The opening hymn ensures that Nineveh is seen as an illustration of God's judgment against all human evil and injustice, an anticipation of God's final triumph against his adversaries.

Nahum within the Canon

The condemnation of imperialism and injustice finds parallels elsewhere in Scripture, as in the judgment on Assyria in Isa. 10:5–15, on Edom in Isa. 34, on Babylon in Jer. 50–51, and on Tyre and Egypt in Ezek. 26–32. The theme is further developed in Rev. 17–18. Nahum makes the fullest link to God's character. It has been argued that the allusion to Exod. 34:6–7 in Nah. 1 is part of a redaction of the Book of the Twelve (Nogalski; cf. Van Leeuwen). This may underestimate the number of links to the creedal language of Exod. 34:6–7 elsewhere in the OT, as well as the close relationship between Nahum and Isaiah, but it is helpful to reflect on the use of Exod. 34:6–7 in the Book of the Twelve. Appeal to God's character functions in Joel 2:13–14 as a motivation for repentance. In Jon. 3:9–4:4, God's compassion is the basis for a change of course regarding Nineveh, just as God is praised in Mic. 7:18 for his grace, which enables his people to be forgiven.

The book of Jonah—with its movement from divine anger to mercy, described with the root to which the name Nahum is related (*nakham*, "relent"; Jon. 3:9–10; 4:2)—is often considered to have been written in response to Nahum, its message being interpreted as "an outright contradiction of Nahum's prophecy" (Weigl 105). In traditional interpretation, it is commonly assumed that the repentance of the Ninevites was either superficial or short-lived. In any case, both within the Book of the Twelve and as far as the depiction of Nineveh's history is concerned, Nahum speaks the final word on Nineveh. The book of Jonah is more about Israel's vocation than the fate of Nineveh, especially so if the book was written after the demise of the Neo-Assyrian Empire. It reminds us that the judgment on Nineveh should not be reduced to the benefits it brings to Judah. The rhetorical question on which Nahum ends affirms God's concern for other nations as much as the one that concludes Jonah.

The good news of victory of which Nahum speaks (1:15) is of course not limited to the downfall of the Assyrian Empire. Isaiah 52:7 indicates that the return from exile was another instance of God asserting his reign over evil. Supremely, God's victory over evil was won on the cross so that Nah. 1:15 is again fulfilled in the proclamation of the gospel (cf. Rom. 10:15; Eph. 6:15).

Perspectives from the History of Interpretation

The section 1:14–2:1 was particularly popular in Christian interpretation. The traditional fourfold interpretation of the book is neatly summarized in an exposition (wrongly) attributed to Julian of Toledo: "The prophet Nahum is set in the kingdom of the Assyrians. According to the historical sense, he speaks of the destruction of Nineveh, its capital; in the allegorical sense, of the world's being laid waste; in the mystical sense, of the restoration of the human race through Christ; in the moral sense, of the restoring of his first dignified state, or to yet greater glory, of the sinner fallen into wickedness" (from Ball 212).

Modern historical-critical research has been concerned with distinguishing the words of the prophet from those of later editors, and with establishing the setting of the prophet. Particularly, denying Nahum's authorship of the opening hymn would make the prophet's message appear in a quite different light from that of the book. The view that Nahum was one of the false prophets condemned by Jeremiah (J. M. P. Smith) and the view that he was a cult prophet who wrote a liturgy for the celebration of the fall of Nineveh after the event (Humbert; Sellin) are no longer upheld in contemporary scholarship (see Childs; Weigl). Recently, Baumann has read the text as condoning sexual violence against women who are unduly self-confident. But Nineveh is not depicted as an ordinary prostitute making a living, let alone as a sexually liberated and self-confident woman. Rather, she is a source of ensnarement and thinks nothing of selling peoples for her pleasure. The picture of her paying out rather than receiving money (cf. Ezek. 16) distances the metaphor from "ordinary" prostitution and suggests that the text is not intended to be read as saying something about women.

Nahum and the Church Today

Nahum invites a celebration of divine sovereignty and justice, affirming that God's retributive anger is good news. Traditional interpretation is certainly correct to claim that Nahum prefigures the final judgment that will end the cycle of violence: "Everything said to Nineveh is going to happen in the judgment on the devil and his associates" (Haimo of Auxerre, as quoted in Ball 214). This judgment is anticipated in historical events such as the demise of empires and the deconstruction of injustice, not least in the proclamation of the gospel, through which enemies of God become his children. Nahum at the same time expresses a challenge to trust and submit to God, and not to be counted among his adversaries.

Bibliography

Ball, E. "'When the Towers Fall': Interpreting Nahum as Christian Scripture." Pages 211–30 in *In Search of True Wisdom*, ed. E. Ball. JSOTSup 300. Sheffield Academic Press, 1999.

Baumann, G. "Das Buch Nahum: Der gerechte Gott als sexueller Gewalttäter." Pages 347–53 in *Kompendium feministische Bibelauslegung*, ed. L. Schottroff and M. Wacker. Kaiser, 1998.

Becking, B. "Passion, Power and Protection: Interpreting the God of Nahum." Pages 1–20 in *On Reading Prophetic Texts*, ed. B. Becking and M. Dijkstra. Biblical Interpretation Series 18. Brill, 1996.

Childs, B. *Introduction to the Old Testament as Scripture*. Fortress, 1979.

Nogalski, J. *Redactional Processes in the Book of the Twelve*. BZAW 218. De Gruyter, 1993.

Peels, H. *Vengeance of God*. Brill, 1995.

Van Leeuwen, R. "Scribal Wisdom and Theodicy in the Book of the Twelve." Pages 31–49 in *In Search of Wisdom*, ed. L. Perdue et al. Westminster John Knox, 1993.

Weigl, M. "Current Research on the Book of Nahum: Exegetical Methodologies in Turmoil?" *CurBS* 9 (2001): 81–130.

32

Habakkuk

Thomas Renz

The book of Habakkuk deals with the question of whether and how the cycle of injustice and violence can be broken. Its most famous assertion is that "the righteous shall live by . . . faith" (2:4b RSV). Across the ages, the interpretation of this phrase has concerned readers. Similar attention has been given to exploring the nature and role of chapter 3, the prayer suggesting that the answer to the problem of suffering and injustice cannot be found apart from the language of worship.

The Argument of the Book

The book is set during the twilight of the Assyrian Empire. It opens with the prophet's complaint (1:2–4) about the prevalence of injustice; 1:5–11 is generally considered to reflect God's response, although others view it as the revelation that caused the complaint (e.g., Floyd). The complaint is intensified in 1:12–17, which suggests that 1:5–11 was not considered an adequate response. If injustice is punished by violence, that only leads to further injustice—where shall it end? In any case, 2:1 marks a break between Habakkuk's argument in chapter 1 and the report of God's reply in 2:2–20, which consists of a statement of principle (2:2–5), followed by its application to the specific situations about which Habakkuk is concerned (2:6–20). The prayer in chapter 3 opens with the confession that the prophet is "alarmed" at what he has heard, combined with a plea for renewal of God's work, which includes mercy in the midst of turmoil (v. 2). The fear is not lost through the prayer (cf. 3:16), but Habakkuk nevertheless concludes with a note of exultation, expressing confidence in God's salvation (3:17–19). The main part recalls the manifestation of God's presence in the exodus event (although without referring to the exodus itself or even to the people of Israel) in 3:3–7, before verses 8–15 address God directly as a fully armed chariot-riding warrior. It concludes with the affirmation that God's "going out" is for the deliverance of his people (vv. 13–15). With 3:16 the prayer moves back to the specific situation addressed in the book.

Chapter 3 is sometimes considered to be the vision of which 2:2–3 speaks (e.g., Andersen), but more likely the vision is set out in verses 4–5 and exposited in the rest of chapter 2. Faith and faithfulness (both seem implied by the Hebrew) are the antithesis to presumptuous desire. The former is the way to life. The latter brings destruction upon the greedy because "wine" (standing in for a number of things being desired; 2:5) is a traitor—too much of it will lead to downfall. Verses 6–20 allow application of this principle beyond greed for conquest. The revelation is guaranteed by the fact that this is how God has organized the universe (cf. 2:13): just as greed will destroy the greedy, violence will fall back on the aggressor (2:17). The end of greed and violence arrives when the whole world submits to Yahweh (v. 20, cf. v. 14) in the way that Habakkuk and the people of God do in praying chapter 3.

Habakkuk within the Canon

Habakkuk follows Nahum canonically and logically. The situation of injustice mentioned at the beginning of the book may well have been caused in part by Assyrian domination, whose end is celebrated in Nahum. The rise of the Babylonian Empire is the solution to the problem of Assyrian domination as well as Judean wrongdoing (1:5–11), but only at the price of further injustice (1:12–17). The hymn with which Nahum opens promises that God will make an end to all ungodly power; until this promise is fulfilled, the hymn with which Habakkuk closes remains pertinent. The righteous live by faith in the faithfulness of this revelation.

A theological reading of the book will take into account not only the immediate canonical context but also the fact that a critical stage in the fulfillment has been reached with the revelation of God's righteousness in the cross and resurrection of Jesus Christ. The object of faith is now defined more precisely (Rom. 1:17; Gal. 2:16; 3:11–12). In Pauline polemic, the emphasis shifts from the righteous "living by faith" to living through "becoming righteous by faith" rather than works of the law. If so, this aligns with Habakkuk's contrast between faith and arrogance in the context of torah's inability to restrain wickedness (1:4) and the revelation of God's wrath in a new deed. The alternative is formulated in John 3:36, "Whoever believes in the Son has eternal life; whoever disobeys the Son will not see life, but must endure the wrath of God" (NRSV; cf. 1 John 5:10–12). Similarly, Paul's address to the synagogue community of Antioch in Acts 13 presumes that the climactic continuation of salvation history in the cross and resurrection of Christ constitutes another divine intervention. It brings such surprise that it separates listeners into those who believe and those who scoff (using the Old Greek translation of Hab. 1:5 in v. 41).

In Hebrews (10:38), Hab. 2:4b is used as an introduction to its famous passage on the nature of faith, emphasizing the need for perseverance in the assurance that the hope for things not yet seen will not be disappointed. The eschatological thrust is thus preserved. The issue of delay introduced in Hab. 2:3 is explained in 2 Pet. 3:9 as due to God's patience. The discussion in 2 Thess. 2:3–12 can be understood in the light of Jewish reflection on what causes final redemption to be delayed, which took its starting point from Hab. 2:3 (see below).

Links between the books of Habakkuk and Isaiah have often been observed (cf., e.g., Hab. 2:1 and Isa. 21:6) but maybe of greater theological significance is the use of the exodus and theophany tradition in chapter 3 (cf. Exod. 15; Deut. 33; Judg. 5; Pss. 68; 77; et al.). The exodus is the archetype of God's deliverance, and the NT use of the exodus tradition in understanding Christ's coming prepared the way for applying Hab. 3 to Christ's coming.

Perspectives from the History of Interpretation

An eschatological understanding of the book of Habakkuk is reflected in the standard Old Greek text and the Barberini manuscript, a translation of chapter 3. Also, within the Qumran community Habakkuk served the sectarian self-understanding as an embattled eschatological community. Especially following the destruction of the temple by the Romans, the interpretation of 2:3 was hotly disputed in apocalyptic writings and rabbinical discussion; the key issue was whether the time of the final redemption was fixed or dependent on human factors (see Strobel). In Christian reception of the verse, as in *1 Clem.* 23:5, the certainty of final redemption is often focused upon; yet there is also discussion of what it is that delays the final redemption (e.g., Hippolytus of Rome and Tertullian). Alongside historical interpretation, a spiritual interpretation is often given, identifying Christ as the righteous one, and Satan or the antichrist as the wicked (e.g., Jerome, Cyril of Alexandria). Augustine belongs to the few who apply the verse to the first rather than the second coming of Christ (*Civ.* 18.31). *Didache* 16.5 still makes a link between this eschatological perspective and the reception of Hab. 2:4, but from then on the two verses (3 and 4) are dealt with independently from each other.

Habakkuk 3 appears to have found its way into Jewish liturgy fairly early, probably in pre-Christian times. Its first use in Christian worship appears to have been in connection with the Easter liturgy, from which it found its way into some weekly liturgies. This may explain that the christological interpretation of this chapter was firmly established, even with commentators who preferred a historical interpretation for the first two chapters (e.g., Theodoret of Cyrus). In the Syrian liturgy, chapters 1–2 were also read during passion week.

Habakkuk and the Church Today

Throughout history it has been obvious to readers of the book that what is said about the Babylonians in Habakkuk also applies to (contemporary) powers from the Roman Empire onward. The claim that God uses military powers to respond to wrongdoing is not unique to Habakkuk, but maybe nowhere else is the problematic side of this arrangement highlighted as much. There is no answer to this problem except for the revelation that violence will not prevail, because the greed that motivates it is self-destructive, and faith in God makes the righteous live. Faithfulness to God is enacted in worship and sustained by the memory of divine deliverance. The implicit claim is that divine use of violence is not unlimited. The NT message adds to this that the defeat of injustice and ungodliness does not occur in demonstration of superior military power but through God allowing violence done to himself. This is surely the most astounding use of injustice for the deliverance of God's people. In keeping with Habakkuk's vision, the supreme expression of human injustice is the beginning of the end of all injustice.

Bibliography

Andersen, F. *Habakkuk*. AB 25. Doubleday, 2001.

Floyd, M. *Minor Prophets, Part 2*. FOTL 22. Eerdmans, 2000.

Strobel, A. "Habakkuk." *RAC* 13 (1986): cols. 203–26.

Thompson, M. E. W. "Prayer, Oracle and Theophany: The Book of Habakkuk." *TynBul* 44 (1993): 33–53.

Watts, R. "'For I Am Not Ashamed of the Gospel': Romans 1:16–17 and Habakkuk 2:4." Pages 3–25 in *Romans and the People of God*, ed. S. K. Soderlund and N. T. Wright. Eerdmans, 1999.

33

Zephaniah

THOMAS RENZ

The concept of the day of Yahweh as a day of decisive punishment permeates the book of Zephaniah, which nevertheless ends on a note of joy for those who have come through the judgment. From the sweeping declaration at the beginning onward, Zephaniah is characterized by its use of comprehensive language for the scope of this judgment (see esp. 1:2–3, 18; 2:11; 3:8). This scope is reflected in twenty-three occurrences of the phrase "all/the whole." Key issues in the interpretation of the book are the identification of the "people humble and lowly" (3:12 NRSV; cf. 2:3) and the historical setting with regard to Josiah's reforms in the seventh century.

The Argument of the Book

Zephaniah is often thought to follow a tripartite pattern, as also presumed for other prophetic books: punishment of Jerusalem and Judah (1:1–2:3), followed by punishment of other nations (2:4–3:8), and finally the promise of redemption for Jerusalem and the whole world (3:9–20). This pattern is understood to outline an eschatological sequence of events and is usually considered to be the product of a postexilic redaction. Yet the pattern does not do justice to the arrangement of Zephaniah (cf. Sweeney; Weigl). The book opens with an announcement of a comprehensive punitive action, which is subsequently focused on particular groups in Jerusalem (1:2–18). The call to Judah's humbled population in 2:1–3, to escape the judgment through submission to Yahweh, is supported by the observation that the Philistine cities will certainly be devastated (2:4; cf. 3:6–7). The words of doom over other nations are in two parts. The first is shot through with promises for the remnant (!) of Judah (2:5–11); the second is addressed against Assyria's claim to be the force that matters (2:12–15). The Assyrian defeat of the Cushite dynasty that governed Egypt until 663 BCE was in fact Yahweh's doing (2:12), and thus the word against Assyria (2:13–15) underlines the point that not Assyria but Yahweh is the force next to which there is no other.

Chapter 3 juxtaposes condemnation of Jerusalem's leadership with Yahweh's punitive intervention in other nations (3:1–7). Yet Jerusalem's punishment is only alluded to; it appears to be a consequence of Yahweh's universal decree to have the whole world experience his anger and be transformed to true worship (3:8–13). In isolation, the concluding section (3:14–20) could be read as a summons to rejoice after an oppressive enemy has been defeated. Yet in the context of the book, the victory is won not only against taunting Moabites and domineering Assyrians, but also against the oppressive regime of unbelief in Jerusalem itself. There is ambiguity within the book as to whom Judah regards as its king (cf. 1:5). The day of Yahweh is the day when Yahweh executes his decision and establishes himself as king (cf. 3:15).

Zephaniah within the Canon

There are numerous links between Zephaniah and other parts of the Bible, with literary influence going both ways (cf. Berlin 13–17, 117–24). The judgment in chapter 1 is reminiscent of the flood, survived by only a remnant. The claim on foreign land made in chapter 2 may be based on Gen. 10 and Deuteronomy as well as the contemporary political situation (cf. Berlin 117–24). The promise in 3:9 of unity and pure speech for the peoples may be considered a reversal of Gen. 11 (Berlin 14). What at first sight looks like complete annihilation is seen in the light of these links as a purifying judgment, which restores the original design. Zephaniah's hope for the emergence of a spiritually humble remnant among those of a materially, or at least politically, humble background found an application among those left behind by the Babylonians (cf. 2 Kings 24:14; 25:12; Jer. 39:10; 40:7). It is part of the common biblical motif of God's election of the disregarded. The restoration of Israel through a humble remnant was again enacted in Christ who, unlike Zephaniah's poor, ensures this by taking the judgment upon himself. This enables the reversal of Babel's confusion at Pentecost and extends Yahweh worship beyond the confines of ethnic Israel; yet it affirms the division of humanity into the humble, who inherit the world, and the proud, upon whom the judgment remains. This judgment constitutes "the day of the LORD"—a time when God executes his decision about the fate of a community. Such a day is described in many other places as a cosmic upheaval, even when applied to specific historical events. Zephaniah's universalistic language prepares the way for an understanding of "the day of the LORD" (1:14) as an eschatological event, the day when God's purposes for all peoples are executed.

Regarding the trappings of wealth and power, Zephaniah's message is reflected in Jesus' warning that it is hard for the rich to enter God's kingdom (Mark 10:23 et par.). As elsewhere in Scripture, poverty is neither an ideal to aspire to nor a guarantee for favor with God, but wealth may well be a hindrance (cf. James 1:9–11; 2:5–6; 5:1–6).

Perspectives from the History of Interpretation

Luther thought that among the Minor Prophets, Zephaniah "makes the clearest prophecies about the kingdom of Christ" (319). He saw in the prophet someone who, like himself, proclaimed a divine message unacknowledged as such by the authorities. For Luther, Zephaniah ruthlessly rejects human righteousness and religion, preparing the kingdom of Christ. The gathering of kingdoms and nations he sees fulfilled through the spread of the gospel (355), which is a message declaring the outpouring of God's wrath and calling for repentance (356). Zephaniah agrees with all of Scripture in its battle against "the powerful, the wise, and the holy" (326), and in addressing the promise to the "humble, oppressed, . . . those who lack honor and wealth," like Christ and Mary in the NT (339).

Key issues discussed in modern research are Zephaniah's relationship to Josiah's reforms and the literary history of the book, which often affects the understanding of the "poor"—with the socioeconomic interpretation favored for an early date, a religious interpretation with a postexilic date. Along with the presumed tripartite structure (see above), talk of a remnant and return from exile are often thought to reflect a postexilic setting, but

293

this need not be the case. The remnant motif is an integral aspect of the concept of inevitable disaster, and return from exile has been an issue ever since the deportation of northern Israelites by Assyria. Christensen's attempt to link 2:4–15 specifically to Josiah's policies has problems, but it is clear that Zephaniah's message fits with the aims of Josiah's reforms. Yet, with different emphases, it remains relevant for the postexilic community and beyond.

Zephaniah and the Church Today

The history of interpretation reminds us of the need to find our place within the drama that unfolds in Zephaniah, as well as the fact that the same message looks somewhat different from within different contexts, whether or not the book was reshaped after the exile. The church in the Western world is warned that being implicated in a syncretistic and oppressive regime makes it hard to escape the judgment of God, and that God may again choose to continue his history with those who are despised and rejected. The oppressed church is encouraged to trust God's ability to act on a large scale for those who belong to him who became poor so that we might become rich (2 Cor. 8:9). Together we are challenged to seek first God and his righteousness (2:3; cf. Matt. 6:33) and to order all our doings accordingly.

Bibliography

Berlin, A. *Zephaniah*. AB 25A. Doubleday, 1994.

Christensen, D. "Zephaniah 2:4–15: A Theological Basis for Josiah's Program of Political Expansion." *CBQ* 46 (1984): 669–82.

Dietrich, W. "Die Kontexte des Zefanjabuches." Pages 19–37 in *Der Tag wird kommen,* ed. W. Dietrich and M. Schwantes. SBS 170. Katholisches Bibelwerk, 1996.

Floyd, M. *Minor Prophets, Part 2*. FOTL 22. Eerdmans, 2000.

Luther, M. "Lectures on Zephaniah." *LWorks* 18:317–64.

Sweeney, M. "A Form-Critical Reassessment of the Book of Zephaniah." *CBQ* 53 (1991): 388–408.

Veijola, T. "Zefanja und Joschija." Pages 9–18 in *Der Tag wird kommen,* ed. W. Dietrich and M. Schwantes. SBS 170. Katholisches Bibelwerk, 1996.

Weigl, M. *Zefanja und das "Israel der Armen."* ÖBS 13. Österreichisches Katholisches Bibelwerk, 1994.

34

Haggai

PAUL R. HOUSE

As is true of most of the OT's shorter books, Haggai research has generally followed in the wake of how larger books have been treated. Early
Christian interpreters of Haggai offered several symbolic readings of the
book's contents. These included treating Zerubbabel as a type of Christ,
the restored temple as a prophecy of the new covenant, and Zerubbabel's
signet ring as a symbol of Jesus' kingly power (Ferreiro). Early-twentieth-
century historical-critical scholars highlighted Haggai's historical references and the light they shed on the postexilic period. They tended to
accept the accuracy of the book's statements and noted the book's links to
Zech. 1–8. They also discussed the probability that an editor or chronicler
wrote down the prophet's utterances and added them to a brief history
of Haggai's activities. Thus, the book was treated as a basically accurate
historical treatment of the prophet Haggai's work among the postexilic
Israelite community (Mitchell).

In the 1960s and 1970s form and redaction critics tended to accept these
findings and sought to further define the book's setting and the levels of
the book's editing (Beuken; Wolff). By the 1980s, however, a few historical
critics had begun to question the old consensuses and started to posit ways
that the book could be read as a unified construction by a single author

(Verhoef; Meyers and Meyers), or at least as a substantially unified edited work (Petersen). Of course, some experts tended to agree with earlier historical critics (Redditt). Finally, literary and canonical critics looked for ways to analyze the book in its final form (Childs; House).

A treatment of the book's final form in its overall canonical context indicates that the book's role in the OT is significant. The Law and Prophets emphasize Israel's loss of land due to sin and Yahweh's ultimate restoration of some segment of Israel to the land (Lev. 26; Deut. 27–28; 30; Isa. 4:2–6; Jer. 30–33; Ezek. 36–37; Hos. 11:1–9; etc.). This restoration is sometimes described in very ideal terms (Ezek. 40–48). Haggai, Zechariah, and Malachi ministered during the tumultuous era in which Israel had begun to return to the land, and each addresses what needs to happen for full national renewal to occur. In particular, Haggai focuses on fulfilled prophecy, on the people's obedience to the prophetic word, on the temple's importance in a renewed community, and on the Davidic covenant's role in Yahweh's continued blessing of Israel.

Fulfilled Prophecy (1:1)

Haggai and Zechariah were near contemporaries. Haggai's messages may be dated ca. 520 BCE, while Zechariah's were delivered during 520–518 BCE. Thus, both prophets work after Persia displaced Babylon as the greatest world power in 539 BCE. This event was itself a fulfillment of promises made in such passages as Isa. 13:1–14:23, Jer. 50–51, and Hab. 2:1–20. Both prophets also ministered in the wake of Cyrus's decree and after the initial return. His edict allowed Jews to return to their homeland, as promised in a variety of texts (Isa. 35; 44:28–45:1; Jer. 29:1–14) and happening in 538–535 BCE (Ezra 1–2). These momentous events could be rightly considered evidence that Israel's seventy years of exile (Jer. 29:1–14) had given way to a new era in which Israel might once again live in the promised land, renew the covenant, and enjoy Yahweh's blessings (Deut. 28:1–14). Prophecy was coming true in Haggai's lifetime, and the question was what that fulfillment would look like in lived experience.

Obedience to the Prophetic Word and Divine Blessing (1:2–15)

Haggai's people may well have expected great blessings because of the pronouncements of earlier prophets (1:9), yet they experienced Yahweh's judgment instead (1:6). Haggai declares that this situation is due to the fact that they have not finished the temple and thus do not honor the God who brought them to the land (1:2–11). Since Yahweh receives no honor, they do not receive the benefits of the land (1:8). They remain a punished people, though in their own land. Haggai's solution is for them to rise and build.

To their credit, the Israelites respond positively. Therefore, Yahweh is with them, renewing, stirring, motivating, and empowering their spirits and bodies (1:13–14). Their response separates this generation from the countless unheeding audiences endured by earlier prophets (2 Kings 17). They recognize that the God who restored them to the land (1:1) and who controls nature (1:2–11) merits the honor a temple symbolizes. They also recognize the inextricable link between obedience and the full presence of Yahweh.

In calling for temple renewal, Haggai concurs with the emphasis on a central sanctuary found in Exodus, Leviticus, Deuteronomy, 1–2 Kings, Isaiah, and Psalms. The temple signifies God's presence in Israel (1:12–14; Exod. 32–34; 1 Kings 8) and demonstrates Israel's commitment and obedience (1:2–6; Exod. 35–40; 1 Kings 5–7). Haggai also agrees with the view of the future displayed in Deut. 28:64–68 and 30:1–10; Isa. 60–62; Jer. 30–33; and Ezek. 40–48. Haggai expects a better future because Yahweh has begun to intervene in history, and he connects temple building to that better future. Thus, Haggai definitely anchors his belief in the events of 520 BCE, yet he also anticipates Yahweh's great future work.

The Temple and the Renewed Community (2:1–19)

As the people build they can easily see that their temple hardly attains to the beauty of, for instance, Ezekiel's envisioned temple (Ezek. 40–48). Thus, the prophet encourages the people with three basic promises. First, Yahweh promises to be with this people the way he was with Israel in the exodus (2:4–5). Yahweh has not forgotten the Sinai covenant or the Sinai covenant partner. Second, Yahweh's Spirit will be among them, thereby removing any need for fear (2:5). Third, the God who fills the earth will fill the temple with the treasures of the nations of the earth (2:6–8). Divine presence and universal sovereignty will make the latter glory of the temple greater than its former glory (2:9). Through the temple, then, Yahweh's glory and Israel's prominence will be evident among all peoples.

But such glory cannot come unless Israel becomes a cleansed people. Before the temple building began, everything Israel did was unclean due to their disobedience (2:10–14). Now, however, Yahweh will bless them as a holy people. All their needs will be met (2:15–19), which reflects a return to the blessing mentioned in Lev. 26:3–13 and Deut. 28:1–14. Yahweh will honor their repentance.

The Davidic Covenant and Renewed Blessing (2:20–23)

With the people, temple, and presence of Yahweh all addressed, it is hardly strange for the prophet to conclude with a message on the importance of the Davidic covenant. After all, the appearance of the perfect Davidic ruler is part of many renewal passages (Isa. 9:2–7; 11:1–9; Jer. 23:1–8; Ezek. 34:20–24; etc.). Haggai claims that Zerubbabel, a Davidic descendant and current leader of Israel, is "like [a] signet ring" on Yahweh's hand (2:23). Haggai does not say Zerubbabel is the coming king. Nonetheless, he is a symbol that the Lord has not abandoned the Davidic covenant (2 Sam. 7). David's line has not been extinguished, so Israel has long-term hope. This text works like 2 Kings 25:27–30, where Jehoiachin, the exiled Davidic descendant, is honored. Jehoiachin is not the promised Davidic ruler, but his existence keeps the Davidic promise alive.

Conclusion

Haggai's theological vision balances the past, present, and future. It is anchored in both the covenant promises and the eschatological vision of previous biblical writers. It thereby links covenant promise and covenant obedience to current trouble and future blessing. It claims that what is to come begins now with obedient servants of Yahweh. In many ways, then, Haggai stresses the "now" and "not yet" aspects of life, promise, and the *eschaton* that mark the whole of Scripture. Thus, there is little difference between the OT and the NT's approach to prophetic promises. Both are more subtle than a simple one-for-one prediction-fulfillment scheme.

Bibliography

Beuken, W. *Haggai–Sacharja 1–8: Studien zur Überlieferungs der frühnachexilischen Prophetie.* SSN 10. Van Gorcum, 1967.
Childs, B. *Introduction to the Old Testament as Scripture.* Fortress, 1980.
Ferreiro, A., ed. *The Twelve Prophets.* ACCSOT 14. InterVarsity, 2003.

House, P. *The Unity of the Twelve*. JSOTSup 97/BLS 16. Sheffield Academic Press, 1990.

Meyers, C., and E. Meyers. *Haggai, Zechariah*. AB 25B. Doubleday, 1987.

Mitchell, H. G., et al. *Haggai, Zechariah, Malachi and Jonah*. ICC. T&T Clark/ Scribner's Sons, 1912.

Petersen, D. L. *Haggai and Zechariah 1–8*. OTL. Westminster, 1984.

Redditt, P. *Haggai, Zechariah, Malachi*. NCB. Eerdmans, 1995.

Verhoef, P. *The Books of Haggai and Malachi*. NICOT. Eerdmans, 1987.

Wolff, H. W. *Haggai*. Augsburg, 1988.

35

Zechariah

ALBERT WOLTERS

The book of Zechariah has often been called one of the most difficult books of the Bible. With the exception of the middle section (chs. 7–8), which consists of a series of relatively straightforward ethical and religious exhortations, the book is obscure for a variety of reasons. The first section (chs. 1–6) is obscure because it consists largely of dreamlike visions accompanied by apparently unconnected oracles, and the third section (chs. 9–14) because it is composed almost entirely of a kaleidoscope of divine threats and promises regarding the future of Jerusalem, the nations, and the cosmos, but often having no clearly identifiable historical referents. On the other hand, the book has many messianic predictions, which in the light of the NT clearly find their fulfillment in Jesus Christ.

History of Interpretation

Much of patristic exegesis (e.g., the recently rediscovered commentary by Didymus the Blind) was characterized by an uninhibited allegorical interpretation. The great exception is Theodore of Mopsuestia, who espoused a more literal and historical reading. He and a number of Syriac commentators (notably Ephraim Syrus) interpreted the predictions of chapters

9–14 as referring primarily to the history of Israel before the coming of Christ, especially the time of the Maccabees. Jerome wrote an influential commentary on two levels: one "literal," in which he drew on the Hebrew text and Jewish sources, and one "spiritual," which was heavily dependent on Didymus's allegorical commentary.

Jerome's commentary overshadowed the interpretation of Zechariah in the Latin West until the time of the Reformation. Early modern interpretation is dominated by Protestant exegetes, and by a turn away from allegory toward a philological and historical understanding of the Hebrew text. Nevertheless, it was still characterized by great diversity, especially regarding the historical referents of chapters 9–14. Zechariah 14, for example, was taken to refer to the fortunes of God's people at the time of the Maccabees (Hugo Grotius), in the church age (Luther), in the period between the exile and Christ (Calvin), or in the end times and preceding the last judgment (Oecolampadius). Until the late eighteenth century, there nevertheless was broad agreement (also among those who, on the basis of Matt. 27:9, assigned part or all of Zech. 9–14 to Jeremiah) that the canonical book of Zechariah was a divinely inspired part of Holy Scripture, spoke the truth about future events, and portrayed the coming Messiah in terms that were fulfilled in Jesus Christ.

All of this changed with the rise of historical criticism, which began to exclude such confessional commitments from biblical scholarship, and to focus on questions of multiple authorship and dating. Zechariah 9–14, for example, was attributed to as many as four different authors, and assigned to dates ranging from the eighth to the second century BCE. The constituent parts of Zechariah were read with a view not to hearing the voice of God, but to hearing a diversity of human voices, which each reflected its own milieu and agenda. Among confessional interpreters of Scripture in the nineteenth and twentieth centuries, the chief innovations have been the detailed defense of traditional positions (e.g., unity of authorship) against the results of mainline historical criticism, and the rise of a dispensationalist hermeneutic. The latter stressed literal fulfillment of Zechariah's prophecies and thus saw many of these as fulfilled, not in the church, but in a future separate group of converted Jews (Unger). Of significance in recent decades have been discussions of the category "apocalyptic" (variously said to apply to all, part, or none of Zechariah), the analysis of literary structure (leading to widely divergent results), and the softening of the classical dispensationalist hermeneutic (Merrill). A remarkable development in the tradition of historical criticism is the recent trend in dating chapters 9–14 ("Deutero-Zechariah"). After a time (most of the nineteenth century) when these chapters were almost unanimously assigned a preexilic date, there had followed a time (from about 1880 to 1960) when almost all critical scholars assigned them to the Hellenistic period. Since then, a growing consensus has emerged that "Deutero-Zechariah" should be dated to the early postexilic period (Hanson; Meyers and Meyers; Petersen; Sweeney). Thus, there is currently widespread agreement that the entire book of Zechariah could have been written during the lifetime of the sixth-century prophet whose name it bears.

The Message of the Text

In coming to a theologically responsible reading of the message of Zechariah, we must take seriously its literary and canonical unity, its embeddedness in an authoritative canon that culminates in the Christ of the NT evangelists and apostles, and the historic Christian claim that Scripture in all its parts communicates the word of God to every generation of believers in their own situation.

Despite the obscurity and apparently jumbled character of much of Zechariah, there are broad themes that come through clearly. Among such themes we find the centrality of Jerusalem ("Jerusalem" and "Zion" occur a total of forty-seven times, quite evenly distributed throughout the book). It is to Jerusalem that Yahweh returns in mercy (1:16); it is Jerusalem that he chooses again (2:12), where his temple is to be rebuilt (1:16), and where he himself will take up residence (2:10). It is to Jerusalem that the remaining exiles are exhorted to return (9:12), and it is to Jerusalem that all nations will eventually come to serve Yahweh (14:16). Other themes are the future inclusion of all nations in Yahweh's covenant (2:11 [v. 15 MT]; 8:20–23) and the continuity with earlier prophecy (passim). As in so many of the prophets, overshadowing all these themes is the emphasis on the sovereignty of God in both judgment and grace. Terrible judgment is threatened both against the nations (1:21; 2:9; 6:7–8; 9:1–7; 12:3–4, 9; 14:3, 12) and against God's own disobedient people (11:3, 6; 13:8–9; 14:1–2). Particularly chilling is the passage where God promises to send two shepherds to rule over his people, both of whom will eventually abandon and ruin them (11:4–16). But inexplicable grace is the dominant note. It is not only manifested in the present, as God returns in mercy to his people after the scourge of the exile (1:16–17), but also promised for the future (8:1–5, 12–13; 9:8, 16–17; 10:6). Especially prominent among these promises of grace are the predictions concerning a coming messianic figure called the Branch (3:8; 6:12–13), a figure later described in four remarkable passages (9:9–12; 12:1–2; 12:10–13:1; 13:7–9). These texts appear to echo and amplify Isaiah's accounts of the Suffering Servant (Lamarche 125–47).

Zechariah and the Canon

Zechariah was one of the last OT prophets, and he wrote at a time when the OT canon was near completion. As a result, his prophecies are laced with allusions (sometimes direct quotations, as in 9:10b, citing Ps. 72:8) to the canonical writings that preceded him, especially the books of Isaiah, Jeremiah, and Ezekiel. He clearly sees himself as standing in the tradition of what he calls "the former prophets" (NRSV: 1:4; 7:7, 12). At the same time he points forward to the NT fulfillment of the messianic prophecies that he has delivered, and to the ultimate restoration of all things. The NT often quotes Zechariah, especially with reference to the passion of Christ (Matt. 21:5; 26:31; 27:9–10; Mark 14:27; John 12:15; 19:37).

Theological Significance

In light of the foregoing, it is clear that the book of Zechariah is both deeply rooted in the preceding history of revelation and is itself revelatory of the messianic and cosmic future. In it God promises to reclaim Jerusalem as the center of his empire and to rebuild the temple as his royal dwelling. Meanwhile, he reassures his people that, through a long history marked by judgment and grace, the coming future Messiah will expand the significance of both Jerusalem and the temple into unprecedented and unimagined dimensions. In a word, Zechariah is all about the world-historical and indeed cosmic coming of the kingdom of God (Webb).

Bibliography

Baldwin, J. G. *Haggai, Zechariah, Malachi.* TOTC. InterVarsity, 1972.
Hanson, P. D. *The Dawn of Apocalyptic.* Rev. ed. Fortress, 1979.
Lamarche, P. *Zacharie IX–XIV.* Lecoffre, 1961.
Merrill, E. *Haggai, Zechariah, Malachi.* Moody, 1994.
Meyers, C. L., and E. M. Meyers. *Zechariah 9–14.* AB 25C. Doubleday, 1993.
Petersen, D. L. *Zechariah 9–14 and Malachi.* OTL. Westminster John Knox, 1995.

Sweeney, M. A., ed. *Micah, Nahum, Habakkuk, Zephaniah, Haggai, Zechariah, Malachi*. Vol. 2 of *The Twelve Prophets*, ed. D. W. Cotter. Berit Olam. Liturgical Press, 2000.

Unger, M. *Zechariah*. Zondervan, 1963.

Webb, B. G. *The Message of Zechariah*. InterVarsity, 2003.

Wolters, A. "Confessional Criticism and the Night Visions of Zechariah." Pages 90–117 in *Renewing Biblical Interpretation*, ed. C. Bartholomew et al. SHS. Zondervan/Paternoster, 2000.

———. "Zechariah 14: A Dialogue with the History of Interpretation." *Mid-America Journal of Theology* 13 (2002): 39–56.

———. "Zechariah 14 and Biblical Theology: Patristic and Contemporary Case Studies." In *Out of Egypt*, ed. C. Bartholomew et al. SHS. Zondervan/Paternoster, 2004.

36

Malachi

MIGNON R. JACOBS

The superscription (1:1) of the book identifies it as an oracle or *massa'* attributed to *mal'aki,* "my messenger/angel." The apparent simplicity of these assertions conceals the debates about the nature of the book and the identity of the one typically called Malachi. It also anticipates issues about the status and place of the book in the prophetic corpus and OT canon. In the Hebrew version, it is the last of the Book of the Twelve or Minor Prophets as well as the final book of *Nevi'im,* the "Prophets," the second section of the Hebrew Bible. It thus directly precedes the book of Psalms in the *Ketubim,* "Writings," the third section of the Hebrew Bible. In most English versions, it appears as the last book of the prophetic literature and of the OT, directly preceding the NT (some have the Apocrypha between OT and NT). Most often, the prophetic activity is dated to the fifth-century-BCE context of the Persian period.

History of Interpretation

While there are several notable issues in its interpretative history, the recurrent issues are the structure of the book and the identification of its genre that defines its organization; the function and place of 4:3–6 (3:21–24

MT); and the independent status of the book. These issues build on those of the church fathers. In particular, Tertullian (*Marc.* 4.8.1) observed the placement of the book as a representation of a transition from old to new covenant. Origen (*Comm. Jo.* 2:17; 6:13) saw Mal. 4:2–6 (3:20–24 MT) as the foreshadowing of John the Baptist and Jesus Christ (cf. Hill).

Internal Structure and Genre

The first decades of the twentieth century responded to the nineteenth-century classification of Malachi as prose (Torrey), with some affirming this classification (Smith) and others seeing it as largely poetic (Nowack). Most today affirm the prosaic nature of the book and the presence of question-answer schema as a characteristic feature. Thus, the characteristic format consists of (1) an assertion (e.g., 1:2a), and (2) a schema formed by a question (e.g., 1:2b) and an answer/response (e.g., 1:2c–5). Pfeiffer introduced this interpretative trend when he categorized the book as prophetic disputation and thus demonstrated his perspective that the book is constituted by one genre. Accordingly, he identifies the macrounits—1:2–5; 1:6–2:9; 2:10–16; 2:17–3:5; 3:6–12; 3:13–4:3 (3:13–21 MT), further noting that 4:4–6 (3:22–24 MT) is generically different from the rest. Inasmuch as its literary form is other than the prophetic disputation and its content is new, 4:4–6 is further classified as an additional rather than an integral part of the book.

While Petersen follows Pfeiffer's lead in asserting a common generic form, he denies that a tripartite structure forms the basic six units. First and foremost, he identifies the book as one of three oracles in the Zechariah–Malachi section of the Book of the Twelve (Zech. 9–11; 12–14). He proposes that the macrounits represent dialogues further identified as "diatribe-like discourses" comparable to Hellenistic diatribe. Petersen further identifies 4:4–6 (3:22–24 MT) as an epilogue that together with Hos. 14:9 (v. 10 MT) is an element of demarcation and a link between the Book of the Twelve and the rest of the Hebrew Bible canon (cf. Hill).

Like Pfeiffer, O'Brien tried to identify common macrounits that exhibit the same generic features and are reflective of the genre. On the other hand, she differs from Pfeiffer in the macrounits and in categorizing the genre of these units and the book as covenant lawsuit with its distinctive parts. She names prologue (1:1–5), accusations (1:6–2:9; 2:17–3:5; 3:6–12; 3:13–4:3 [3:13–21 MT]), admonition (4:4 [3:22 MT]), and an ultimatum (4:5–6 [3:23–24 MT]).

Lescow observes that the form and function of the text are products of the redaction process that transformed the original Torah speeches for didactic and homiletic purposes (e.g., 1:6–2:9). He takes the question-answer schema as an interchange between the prophet and the one(s) inquiring about a teaching. As to 4:4–6 (3:22–24 MT), he sees it as an appendix or conclusion of the prophetic corpus.

Floyd differentiates between stylistic and generic uniformity, further recognizing the various functions of generically similar units (e.g., 1:10b–14; 2:8–12). He challenges Pfeiffer and others and identifies two macrounits, a superscription (1:1) and the main body, categorized as *massa'* (oracle, 1:1, referring to 1:2–4:6 [3:24 MT]), which further consists of an introduction/prophetic disputation (1:2–5) and exhortation (1:6–4:6). As to the microunits, Floyd notes two units: the first looks at the "cultic corruption," addressing both the priests and the people (1:6–2:16); the second, showing the change from corrupt practices, is addressed to the people (2:17–4:6 [3:24 MT]).

Canonical Place

The first perspective is Malachi's interdependence on Zechariah, evidenced by the presence of the term *massa'* (oracle) in both Malachi (1:1) and Zechariah (9:1a; 12:1; e.g., Petersen; Mason). The second perspective is that Malachi's interdependence includes both Haggai and Zechariah—the latter corpus unified by its representation of the restoration community (e.g., Pierce; Lescow; Hill). With these two perspectives, the place of the book is also represented by the function of 4:4–6 as the conclusion of the Book of the Twelve and the *Nevi'im*—the prophetic corpus. In a third perspective, Floyd asserts the independent status of Malachi with 4:4–6 seen as an integral part of the microunit 2:17–4:6. It is best to read them as a unit and also as an example of God's interaction with the covenant community to address its concerns about God's love and what that entails for its practices.

Content and Theological Concerns

The fundamental message is God's love for Israel and Israel's response to that love. The book affirms that Israel's practices reflect its love for God. Through the question-and-answer schema, it challenges Israel to understand this and live accordingly. Consequently, the book encompasses several concerns, with multiple dimensions.

Malachi looks at various themes addressed elsewhere in the OT and in doing so suggests that there is an ongoing need to clarify God's requirement for the covenant community. It affirms that being the people of God carries responsibilities that encompass both correct understanding of God's requirements and aligning one's life with them. In particular, it holds the priests accountable for failure to uphold the covenant. Some of the concerns of Psalms and Proverbs concerning God's regard for the wicked (e.g., Pss. 37; 73; Prov. 10) and God's silence in the face of suffering reverberate through Malachi (cf. Ps. 37). These recurring themes signal the perpetual nature of the struggle to make sense of life in the midst of faith in God and the human responsibility to obey God.

God's Love

Israel's understanding of God's love was challenged by the experience of judgment. God's declaration of love for Israel addresses Israel's challenge for proof of that love in light of the turmoil that the restoration community suffered. Consequently, God highlighted love for Israel by contrasting two persons (Jacob, Esau) and the nations that ensued from them (Israel, Edom). The text echoes the Gen. 25:19–26 account of Jacob and Esau, where the choice between the brothers is noted without the stated criteria for the selection of who will serve whom. On the one hand, God loves (*'ahab*) Jacob/Israel and hates (*sane'*) Esau/Edom. God behaves consistently as seen in his covenant with Israel and preservation of Israel as compared to his resolution to destroy Edom and ensure its perpetual demise (1:2–5).

Tithe and Offering

The matter of the tithe and the offerings (*hamma'aser wehatterumah*) addresses the apparent misfortunes of the community (3:8). As a corrective, the people are admonished to stop robbing (*qaba'*) God by giving God the entire tithe (*ma'aser*; cf. Gen. 14:20; 28:18–22; Lev. 27:30–32; Num. 18:21–32; Deut. 14:22–29; Neh. 13:10–12). Several kinds of tithes are indicated: The general tithes of the produce of the land and livestock are designated for the Levites (Lev. 27:30–32; Num. 18:21). The tithe of the produce is annual and seasonal (Deut. 14:22–27). The third-year tithe is designated for the underprivileged (Deut. 14:28–29; cf. Hill; Petersen). Like Mal. 3:10, so also Num. 18:21–32 refers to the entire tithe (cf. Deut. 14:28) and stipulates that it be used to sustain the Levites, who are further required to present to God an offering (*terumah*) of the tithe that they receive. The pairing of the tithes and the offerings (*hamma'aser wehatterumah*) contributes to distinguishing the two (cf. Deut. 12:6, 11; 2 Chron. 31:12). Thus, Hill asserts that the offering (*terumah*) is a gift; others see the offering as a tithe of the tithe (*ma'aser*) or a tithe tax (Num. 18:26; Neh. 10:38; cf. Petersen; Glazier-McDonald).

Divorce

Malachi 2:16 declares that God hates (*sane'*) divorce but does not explain why. It has been interpreted as figurative language representative of the unfaithfulness in the covenant relationship. Some who render a literal interpretation concede that the intermarriage and divorce are the result of the priests' misteachings (cf. Hill). Others note various social and religious consequences of divorce as the reason for God's response. Among the reasons is the apostasy resulting from intermarriage with the foreign women (Ezra 9–10; Neh. 13).

In these cases, the prohibition against Israel's intermarriage with the daughters of other nations is a preventative measure against breaking the covenant with God (cf. Exod. 34:15–16; Deut. 7:3–4). When seen in the intertextual framework of the OT, Mal. 2:16 challenges the Deut. 24:1–4 representation of divorce as a recognized practice within the community (cf. Deut. 22:13–19, 28–29). Within the context of Mal. 2, God's response seems to be generated by the same force that underlies God's displeasure with other practices in the community (e.g., the sacrifices, tithing). In each of these instances, there is a greater ramification of the behavior than a misconstrued teaching. Rather, the practices are as much a detriment to the community as they are offensive to God.

Priests and Sacrifices

The priests are addressed as those who know torah and thus are able to discern and render sound teachings. Even so, they are also presented as deviating from God's requirement (e.g., 2:6–9). For example, God requires sacrifices that meet a specified standard (cf. animal sacrifice, Lev. 22:18–25; firstborn sacrifice, Deut. 15:19–23). Malachi 1:8 represents the unacceptable nature of the sacrifice as including blind, lame, blemished animals (cf. Deut. 15:21), which the priests were offering to God. They are challenged to keep the covenant by honoring God. The contrast is between their concern to please their rulers and the lack of regard for their Deity. Furthermore, their actions depict a disruption of a normative behavior within a relationship; as such, their utter disrespect for the Deity is highlighted.

God's Justice

Fundamentally, the issues in 2:17–3:5 are retribution and theodicy. Why do evildoers prosper? Why does God tolerate evil rather than punish it? While the lament attests to inquiries about God's justice (*mishpat*) and lack of response (cf. Pss. 13:1–3; 22:1; 74:1), there is also intertextual support for the belief in God's justice and response (Isa. 30:18–20). The book of Malachi challenges the character of God to respond in judgment to the evil (*ra'*; 2:17). In calling into question whether or not God is just, the community may have questioned (sarcastically or genuinely) whether God regards evil (*ra'*) as good (*tob*). This attitude culminates in the perception of God's silence as a lack of judgment, as an overall lack of concern about the practices in the community, and as endorsement of evil (cf. Hab. 1:2–3, 12–13).

Hermeneutical Challenges

The challenges raised here concern the declarations or perspectives within the text that lead to multivalent positions within contemporary settings. These challenges are represented as questions meriting further consideration and reflecting the need to trust God in the midst of life's complexities, without the error of trying to control God or reduce God to ways of being that only conform to one's expectations.

God's Love

God's love and hate represent God's choice and capacity for both. In Mal. 1:2–5 God's hate is a mechanism for demonstrating the particularities of love for Israel. If nothing else, the hermeneutical challenge is to recognize that just as Israel had no choice in being chosen as the object of God's love, so Edom had no choice in being the object of God's hate (cf. Rom. 9:11–14). The quandary is that God's ways in choosing whom to love and hate are complex at best. Having God's love does not exclude one from punishment but is the reason for God's particular response to the covenant community, either to defer or to expedite punishment, and in some cases to use punishment as a form of discipline. Thus, Malachi reminds Israel that God's discipline is a manifestation of love (cf. Deut. 8:5; Pss. 38:2; 94:12; Jer. 31:18; Heb. 12:6, 10). On the other hand, not every form of suffering is either punishment for sin or discipline. Most take for granted that God spoke a word of confirmation to Israel about God's love. However, that God loves the world will remain a paradox for those who continue to experience suffering without such a verifiable confirmation that they are favored by God, that they are not rejected by God and thus experience God's hate. They wonder if God is concerned about their suffering and will rescue them because of the universality of God's love and concern for all.

Tithing and Blessing

Two aspects of the tithe are noteworthy. First, the purpose of the tithe is variously represented in the OT. The tithe was used to maintain the temple and its personnel and to provide for the underprivileged of the community. Do the designated purposes in the OT obligate the same purposes in modern settings?

Second, the relationship of the tithe to blessings and curses is a complex matter. While the text suggests that there is a relationship, the danger of asserting the numerical quantity and the assurance of that relationship must be met by a caveat. Prosperity is not necessarily a sign of righteous living since evildoers are sometimes prosperous while the righteous endure adversity. Is the relationship between tithing and blessings extended to everyone who tithes? Is there a quantitative requirement that ensures the receipt of positive returns? Are all required to give regardless of their economic resources and obligations? The challenge that the modern reader must face is that everyone addressed in the text should tithe. This is not a prescription for becoming wealthy by obligating God. Even with the observation that God responds to obedience and tithing in particular, the larger significance of this is that God is in control of the resources. That control entails that God may or may not respond according to a mathematical calculation. Fundamentally, the tithe is a response to God's love and not a way of winning that love.

Divorce

Within the OT, divorce is presented as a normative practice, used to address various marital circumstances, including the dissatisfaction of a husband with his wife (Deut. 24:1–4; cf. 22:13–19, 28–29), or a solution to intermarriage (cf. Ezra 9–10; Neh. 13:23–31). Does God hate all divorces? If so, does God hate them equally, regardless of the reasons for divorce? The OT context indicates that some divorces are sanctioned (Deut. 24:1–4) but that in other cases it is not an option (22:29). If the resulting circumstances are the reasons for God's hatred of divorce, would God's response differ based on different resulting circumstances? Whether or not one can justify or condemn modern divorces on the basis of this multivalent perspective, the inescapable consequences of divorce remain. God responds to divorces because they bear evil consequences for the community and reflect violation of commitments. The OT context also sanctions remarriage after divorce but regulates who may enter marriage with a divorced woman without viewing it as adultery (cf. Lev. 21:7, 14; Deut. 24:3–4; Ezek. 44:22 vis-à-vis Matt. 5:32; Luke 16:18).

Bibliography

Bosshard, E., and R. Kratz. "Maleachi im Zwölfprophetenbuch." *BN* 52 (1990): 27–46.

Dumbrell, W. "Malachi and the Ezra-Nehemiah Reforms." *RTR* 35 (1976): 42–52.

Floyd, M. *Minor Prophets, Part 2*. FOTL 22. Eerdmans, 2000.

Glazier-McDonald, B. *Malachi*. SBLDS 98. Scholars Press, 1987.

Hill, A. *Malachi*. AB 25D. Doubleday, 1998.

Hugenberger, G. *Marriage as Covenant*. VTSup 52. Brill, 1994.

Lescow, T. *Das Buch Maleachi*. Calwer, 1993.

Mason, R. *The Books of Haggai, Zechariah, and Malachi*. CBC. Cambridge University Press, 1977.

Nowack, W. *Die kleinen Propheten*. Vandenhoeck & Ruprecht, 1922.

O'Brien, J. *Priest and Levite in Malachi*. SBLDS 121. Scholars Press, 1990.

Petersen, D. *Zechariah 9–14 and Malachi*. OTL. Westminster John Knox, 1995.

Pfeiffer, E. "Die Disputationsworte im Buche Maleachi." *EvT* 19 (1959): 546–68.

Pierce, R. "Literary Connectors and a Haggai-Zechariah-Malachi Corpus." *JETS* 27 (1984): 277–89.

Smith, J. M. P. *A Critical and Exegetical Commentary on Haggai, Zechariah, Malachi and Jonah*. ICC. T&T Clark, 1912.

Snyman, S. "Antitheses in Malachi 1,2–5." *ZAW* 98 (1986): 436–38.

Torrey, C. C. "The Prophecy of Malachi." *JBL* 17 (1898): 1–15.

Verhoef, P. *Haggai and Malachi*. NICOT. Eerdmans, 1987.

Wendland, E. "Linear and Concentric Patterns in Malachi." *BT* 36 (1985): 108–21.

Scripture Index

Genesis

1 34, 39
1–3 177, 183
1–11 30, 31, 32, 33, 60, 61, 153, 161–1, 165
1:1 31, 33, 171
1:1–2:3 33
1:1–2:4 54
1:2 35
1:9 35
1:26 34
1:26–28 239
1:27 39
1:28 34, 35, 43
2 38, 39
2–4 32
2:4 32
2:4–11:26 33, 34
2:21–25 35
2:24 39
3 39, 191
3–11 35, 36
3:8 37
3:15 33, 35, 40
3:18 35
3:19 35, 39
4 35, 37, 38, 128
4:1–16 37
4:24 145
5 31, 32
5:1 32
6–9 31, 49
6:5 50
6:5–6 35
6:5–13 49
6:8 49
6:9 32, 37
6:11 35, 37

6:13 35, 37
6:22 50
8 38
8:1 35, 49
8:17 35
8:20 49
8:21 35, 49, 50
9:1 35
9:7 35
9:20–21 35
9:20–27 33
10 292
10:1 32
11 31, 292
11:1–9 35
11:10 32
11:27 32
11:27–50:26 33
12 36, 60, 280
12–25 33
12–50 36
12:1 36
12:1–3 33, 36, 109, 160, 266
12:2 36, 43
12:2–3 48, 135
12:3 33, 36, 40, 165
12:7 36
12:10–20 36
12:20–13:3 38
13:8–10 37
13:14–17 36
13:15 36
13:15–16 36
13:16 37
14:15–24 36
14:20 308
15 60, 106
15:2–4 280

15:5 37
15:7 134
15:7–21 74
15:16 88
17 60
17:1 37
17:4–6 36
17:4–13 36
17:7 78
18:18 36
19 37, 98
20:1–18 36
20:17–18 36
21:1–7 36
21:22–24 36
21:22–33 36
22 38, 47
22:16–18 37
22:18 36, 37
23:1–20 36
24 107
24:15–28 38
25–33 35, 37
25–35 33
25:12 32
25:19 32
25:19–26 308
25:21 36
26:3 74
26:17–33 37
26:24 50
28:1–22 36
28:18–22 308
29:1–14 38
30:1 36
30:16 106
30:18 106
33 40
33:4 37

33:19 36
34:1–35:5 36
36 32
36:1 32
37 35
37–50 32, 37
37:2 32
39:3–23 36
39:10 144
40:20 144
41:35 144
41:37 144
41:42 144
41:50–52 135
43:14 144
47:13–25 36
49 34, 74
50 40
50:20–21 37
50:24 37

Exodus

1 72
1–19 52
1:1–2:22 43
1:7 43
1:13–14 50
2 38
2:23–7:7 44
2:24 46
3 42
3:6–22 38
3:7–8 44
3:9–10 44
3:11–4:12 44
3:13–15 44
3:14 44, 49
3:17 134

4:13–14   44
5:1–23   44
6:2–8   46, 74
7:8–11:10   45
9:4   45
9:14–16   45
9:26   45
12:1–15:21   45
12:2–6   134
12:49   73
14:31   47
15   86, 199, 288
15:18   164
15:22–18:27   46
16   46
16:1–3   46
16:4–5   46
16:6–12   46
16:13–14   46
16:15   46
16:16–18   46
16:19–21   46
16:22–30   46
16:31–36   46
17:1–7   46
19–24   46, 49
19:4   42
19:4–6   46
19:5–6   43, 135
19:9   47
19:10–15   47
19:16–19   47
19:19–20   47
19:21–24   47
19:21–20:1   47
19:24   47
20   42
20:1–Num. 10:10   52
20:8–11   34
20:18–19   47
20:20   47
20:22   47
21–23   47
21:2–6   50
22:13   260
22:21–24   281
22:26   260
23:20–33   84
24:1   47
24:2   47
24:3   47
24:4–8   47
24:9–11   47
24:12   73
24:15–16   50
24:15–18   47
25–31   48

25:17–22   48
25:22   48
25:31–40   48
29:20–21   47
29:38–46   48
32   60
32–34   48, 49, 297
32:1–6   48
32:7–10   48, 49
32:9   50
32:10   48
32:10–14   48
32:21–24   48
33:1   134
33:3   50
33:5   50
33:11   49, 84
33:11–20   48
33:12   49
33:12–18   49
33:19   49
33:20   49
33:21–23   49
34:6   169
34:6–7   49, 283
34:7   49
34:9   50
34:15–16   309
35–40   50, 297
35:4–36:7   50
39:32–43   50
40:16   50
40:34   50

Leviticus

1–7   52, 53, 55
1–10   55
1:1   55
1:1–17   55
1:1–2:16   58
2:1–16   56
3:1–17   56, 58
4:1–5:13   56, 58
5:14–6:7   56, 58
7:1   73
8   56
8–10   56
9   56
9:7   57
11   52, 53, 55
11–16   56
12   55
12:3   52
13–15   55
14:34–53   56
15:19–20   53

16   55, 56
16:2–14   57
17–26   53, 56, 57
18   39, 55
18–20   55
18:24–30   57
19   52
19:2   55, 56
19:18   52
20   39
20:23   88
21   55
21:7   311
21:14   311
22:18–25   309
23   57
23–25   55
23:22   281
23:23–43   57
23:42   57
24:20   56
25:1–7   57
25:8–12   241
25:55   50
26   217, 296
26:3–13   298
26:27–39   57
26:27–45   241
27   55
27:30–32   308

Numbers

1   59, 64
1:1   59
1:1–10:10   59
1:46   61
4:1–15   84
5–10   61
10:11–22:1   59
10:11–36:13   52
10:29–12:15   63
11   46
11:25–29   254
13–14   84, 86
15–16   61
15:30   56
15:32–36   61
17   61
18–19   61
18:21   308
18:21–32   308
18:26   308
19:14   73
20   60
20:2–13   46
20:14–21   63

21:4–9   63
21:12–32   63
22:2–25:5   63
22:2–36:13   59
25   60
26   59, 60, 64
26:51   61
27   60
27:1–11   61
27:12–23   84
28–30   61
34:17   84
35   61
36   61

Deuteronomy

1–3   62
1–11   77
1:1–5   72, 73
1:3   73, 75, 78
1:5   73
1:6–8   72
1:8   79
1:9–15   80
1:9–3:29   72
1:30–33   77
1:45   77
3:12–17   86
3:23–29   84, 85
4:1   75
4:1–4   62
4:1–8   72, 78
4:2   75, 88
4:6–8   69, 78
4:7   77
4:9   96
4:9–12   93, 99
4:9–13   44
4:9–31   77, 78
4:9–32   72
4:13   75
4:20   69
4:21   79
4:24   77, 79
4:24–25   79
4:25–28   80
4:26   79
4:26–31   72
4:28   79
4:30   62
4:31   77, 80, 99, 100
4:32–36   77
4:32–38   78
4:32–39   77
4:32–40   72, 78, 96
4:35   74

4:37 72, 77
4:39 74
5 68
5:1 71
5:1–22 77
5:7–21 73
5:9 77
5:14 34
5:22 75
5:29 79
5:31 88
6:3–4 71
6:4 72, 77
6:4–5 69
6:4–9 79
6:5 68, 219
6:5–19 72
6:10–15 77
6:15 77
6:20–25 69, 77, 78, 79
6:25 78
7:1 228
7:1–6 57
7:1–26 72
7:2–5 80
7:3–4 309
7:6 77, 78
7:6–8 72, 78
7:7–8 77
7:9 77
7:11–16 80
7:13 77
7:17–24 77
7:21 77
8:5 78, 310
8:7–14 77
8:15–16 77
8:17–20 80
9:1 71
9:1–23 78
9:1–24 80
9:3 77, 79
9:4–5 88
9:4–6 217
9:4–7 90
9:6 62
10:1–4 75
10:1–9 75
10:2 75
10:12–13 79
10:12–21 69
10:12–11:1 72, 79
10:15 69, 77
10:16 217
10:16–20 78
10:16–21 69
10:17 77

10:18 77
11 79
11:1 68
11:8–15 80
11:12 79
11:13 68
11:16–17 80
11:24 85
12 68, 76
12–26 69, 77
12:1–16:15 73
12:2–3 80
12:5 77
12:6 308
12:11 308
12:29–32 88
13:3 68
14:1 78
14:2 69, 78
14:22–27 70, 308
14:22–29 308
14:28 308
14:28–29 308
15 281
15:19–23 309
15:21 309
16:18 80, 87
16:18–18:22 77, 80, 81
17:14–20 81, 88, 96,
      99, 114
17:14–18:22 80
17:15 77
17:18 68
17:18–20 87
17:19 72
18:2 87
18:5 77
18:15 68
18:15–18 86
18:21–22 115
18:22 273
19–25 73
19:18 68
19:34 68
20:3 71
20:16–18 86
21:5 77
22 39
22:8 74
22:13–19 309, 311
22:28–29 309, 311
22:29 311
23:3–6 105
23:5 77
24:1–4 309, 311
24:3–4 311
26:5–9 70

26:16–19 77, 78, 79
26:18 78
26:18–19 69
26:19 78
27 84
27–28 296
27:1–10 73
28 76, 79, 217
28:1–14 80, 296
28:1–29:1 73
28:9 78
28:15–26 80
28:61 84
28:64–68 297
29–30 78
29:1 72
29:10–13 72
29:14–30:1 79
29:20 MT 73
29:21 73
30 76, 296
30:1 217
30:1–5 80
30:1–10 62, 72, 80, 297
30:3–5 217
30:6 68, 69
30:6–9 79
30:6–10 79
30:11–20 79
30:19 79
31:1–8 84
31:7 85
31:9 71
31:9–13 71
31:14–32:47 62
31:16–21 79
31:17 77
31:23 84
31:26 84
31:28 79
32:3 77
32:4 77
32:5–6 78
32:14–27 79
32:18 78
32:21 77
32:39 77
32:51 77
33 288
33:5 80
33:10 73
33:26 77
33:27 77
34 38
34:1–12 73
34:9 84
238:1–14 298

Joshua
1:1 85
1:1–9 84
1:1–5:12 85, 86
1:4 85
1:5 85
1:6 85
1:6–9 88
1:7 50
1:7–8 73, 85, 87
1:7–9 84
1:8 73
2 86, 89
2:14 86
3–4 86
4:10 84
5:10–12 86
5:13–12:24 85, 86
6:17 89
6:21 86
6:25 135
8:30–35 73, 84
8:31 76
9 89
9:15 86
9:18 86
11:23 85, 86
12 88
12:7–24 86
13:1 85, 86, 89
13:1–21:45 85, 87
14:3–4 87
15:6 85
15:63 86
16:10 86
17:12 86
18:1 87
21 87
21:44–45 85
22 87, 89
22:1–24:33 85
23 76
23:2 86, 87, 88
23:6 88
24 74, 76, 83, 87
24:19 89
24:25 88
24:25–26 86
24:26 88
24:27–31 99

Judges
1 96
1:1 86
1:1–2 96, 98
1:1–2:5 92

1:2–20   93, 96, 98
1:19   96
1:21   98
1:21–36   96
2:1–4   99
2:6–9   99
2:6–10   93, 99
2:6–16:31   92
2:10   96
2:11   96
2:16–19   97
2:17   97
2:18–19   100
2:19   97
2:20–23   93
3:1–6   93
3:7–11   96
3:7–16:31   96
3:11   97, 99
3:30   99
4:15–28   99
5   288
5:31   99
6:7–10   99
6:11   97
6:13   93, 97
6:25   97
7–8   93
8:28   99
8:33   97
9   93
10:16   97
11:32–40   94
12   99
17–18   97, 106
17–21   92, 96, 116
17:6   93, 96, 98
18:1   93, 96, 98
18:30–31   97
19   93, 98
19–21   97, 106
19:1   93, 96, 98
20   98
20:18   98
21:25   93, 96, 98, 116
28   99
29:2–4   97
30:6   97

Ruth

1:4   107
1:6   104, 106
1:8   103, 108
1:8–9   106
1:16   107
1:20–21   106

1:22   107
2   105, 106
2–3   103
2:2   107
2:6   107
2:8   107
2:8–16   107
2:10   107
2:11   108
2:11–12   102, 106
2:19–20   106
2:20   103, 108
2:21   107
3   106, 108
3:9   108
3:10   103, 106, 108
3:10–11   106
4   105, 107, 108
4:5   103, 107
4:10   103, 107
4:11–12   106
4:13   104, 106, 107
4:13–17   108, 135
4:14–15   102, 106
4:15   108
4:18–22   108

1 Samuel

2:1–10   114
2:7   107
2:10   117
2:28   114
2:31   114
2:31–36   115
3:1   115
3:4   114
3:11–14   115
3:19–4:1   115
4:1–7:1   112
4:11   115
8   112, 166
8–15   113
8:10   116
8:18–20   114
9:1–10:16   112
9:16   115
9:27   116
10:1–9   115
10:3–8   116
10:17–27   112
10:18–19   116
10:24   114
11   112
12   76, 112
12:8–12   93

12:13–15   113
12:19   114
12:24–25   113
13–14   112
13:14   114
15   112, 144
15:2–3   116
15:17–19   116
15:22   278
15:23   116
15:26   115
15:28   114
16:1   114
16:12   115
16:13   114
16:14   114
16:14–2 Sam 5   112
16:18   117
16:23   117
18:10   117
22:10   116
22:18–19   115
23:2   116
23:4   116
27:6   116
28   115
28:6–7   116
30:8   116
31   115
31:6   116

2 Samuel

2:1   116
2:8–5:10   98
5–10   114
5:1–3   115
5:6–10   96
5:6–14   115
5:17–25   96, 115
5:19   116
5:23   116
6   112
6:1–23   115
6:21   114, 116
7   60, 123, 166, 298
7:4–5   116
7:8   114
7:11–16   115
7:16   115
8–23   124
8:1–14   115
8:15–18   115
9   115
9–20   112, 113
11–20   115

11:21   93
12:1   116
12:1–7   105
12:10–12   116
13–20   116
21–24   112, 113, 114
22:1–51   117
22:2–51   114
22:51   117
23:1   117
23:1–7   114, 117
23:3–4   114
23:5   115
24   117
24:11–12   116
24:13   116
24:15   116
24:18   116

1 Kings

1–2   112
1–11   122
2:2–4   73
2:4   116
2:12   115
3   121
3:14   116
4   119, 121
5–6   121
5–7   297
5:5   116
6   115
6–7   119, 121
6:2   134
6:36   134
7:1–12   121
7:13–9:9   121
8   76, 119, 297
8:10–11   50
8:25   116
8:44–53   121
8:46–53   217
9:3–10   121
9:4–5   116
11   119
11:1–13   121
11:6   116
11:13   50
11:38   116
13:2   122
14:8   116
17   122
17–2 Kings 11   122
18   119, 120, 122
22:19–38   122

2 Kings

5:20–27   122
13:21   122
14:3   116
14:6   73
15:3   116
16:5   205
17   119, 120, 297
17–25   123
17:19–20   217
18:3   116
18:13–20:19   205
18:22   120
18:32–35   120
19   119
19:10–12   120
19:18   120
19:18–19   120
20:16–19   123
21   124
22–23   69
22:2   116
22:8   73
22:11   73
22:17   120
23:25   73
23:25–27   123
24:14   293
25   60, 217
25:12   293
25:27–30   298

1 Chronicles

1–9   125, 128, 129
3:17–24   125
6:14   134
9:2–34   126
10–21   116
10–2 Chron 9   128
11:1   129
11:1–4   129
13–16   129
13:1–4   129
13:5–6   129
13:8–12   129
15:3   129
16:3   129
17:3–14   128
18–20   124, 129
21   117
21:25   129
22–29   129
28:5   129
28:6   129
28:9   130

28:10   129
28:19   129
29:1   129
29:20–25   129

2 Chronicles

1–9   129
1:2   129
7:8   129
7:9–10   57
7:12–22   128
7:14   127, 130
9:30   129
10–28   128
10:16   129
11:3   129
11:13   129
12:1   129
12:5–8   130
13   129
13:4–12   129, 130
15:1–15   130
15:3   73
16:7–9   130
19:8   73
20:15–17   130
24:20–22   128
26:22   205
29–36   128
30:6–9   130
31:12   308
32:1–26   205
32:25–26   205
32:31   205
32:32   205
33   124
34–35   69
34:14   73
34:15   73
35:25   222
36:15–16   130
36:20–21   241
36:21   57, 216
36:22–23   127

Ezra

1–2   296
1–6   137, 140
1:1   136, 140, 216
1:1–4   136, 138
1:5–Neh 7:73   138
1:7–11   134
1:11   134
2   134

2:2   137
2:68   134
3:3   134
3:5   57
4:6–23   132
5:15   134
6:1–12   136
6:3–4   134
6:7   134
6:14   136
6:14–15   136
6:16   134
6:17   134
6:18   134, 138
6:22   135
7   132
7–10   132, 137, 140
7:1   134, 140
7:6   138
7:9   134
7:10   73
7:26   140
7:27   136, 140
8   134
8:31   134
8:35   134
9–10   309, 311
9:8–9   135, 140
9:10–14   135
9:11   57
10   135, 140
16:21   134

Nehemiah

1–7   140
1–12   141
1:1   137, 140
2:1   140
8–10   139
8–12   139, 140
8:1   138
8:1–13:31   138
8:14   138
8:14–15   57
9:22–37   93
9:36–37   140
10:29   138
10:38   308
11   139
13   140, 309
13:1   138
13:6   141
13:6–31   141
13:10–12   308
13:23–31   311

Esther

1:1–8:17   143
1:3   144
1:10–12   146
1:21   144
2:3   144
2:21–23   146
3   143
3:4   144
3:10   144
4:13–14   144
4:14   145
4:16   144
5:14   146
6:5   146
7:9–10   146
8   143
8:2   144
9:1–17   146
9:1–10:3   143

Job

1–2   148, 153
1:1   151, 153
1:6–12   154
1:8   151
1:9   150, 155
2:1–6   154
2:3   151
3–31   151
4:17   151
5:7   151
5:12–13   154
5:17–27   151
6:4   151
7:20–21   151
8:3–7   151
9:5–10   155
9:32–35   151
10:1–2   151
10:3   155
10:8–12   155
10:18   155
11:6   151
11:13–16   151
12:7–10   155
13:3   151
13:15   151
13:15–19   151
13:21   151
13:22–24   151
14:7–12   155
14:15   151
14:18–19   155
16:11–14   151
16:18–22   151

19:23–27   148, 151
19:25–27   151
23:10–16   151
24:5   155
24:19   155
26:5–14   155
28   149, 151, 155
28:28   151
29–31   151
31   151
31:1   155
31:9   155
31:24–25   155
31:26–28   155
31:29   155
31:35   151
32–37   151
34:3   151
34:5–6   151
34:9   151
34:35–37   151
35:7   154
35:16   151
36:27–37:24   155
38–39   155
38–41   152, 153, 154
38:1–38   154
38:8–10   176
38:8–11   154
38:26–27   155
38:39–40   155
38:39–39:30   154
39:1   155
39:13–14   149
39:13–16   155
39:19–25   155
40–41   154
41:11   154
42:2–6   152
42:3   152
42:5   152
42:6   152
42:7–8   150, 151, 152
42:8–10   152
42:10–15   155
42:10–17   152

Psalms

1   73, 76, 159, 160, 161
1–2   159, 162, 165
1–3   163
1–72   161
1:1   161, 164
1:1–2   159, 161, 163, 164
1:2   159, 166

1:5   159
1:5–6   161
1:6   163
2   160, 161, 164, 166, 167
2:1–2   161
2:2   158, 160, 166
2:7   166
2:8–9   164
2:8–12   163
2:12   161
3   117, 161, 162
3–72   161
3:1   161
3:1–2   161
3:2   161
3:7   161, 163
3:8   161
5:7   169
5:10   163
6:1   168
6:4   169
7   117
7:1   161
7:12–16   163
9:5–6   163
9:8   163
10:4   161
10:6   161
10:11   161
10:13   161
11:1   161
11:6   163
12   163
12:3–4   163
12:5   163
13:1–2   161
13:1–3   310
13:3–4   161
13:5   169
13:5–6   161
14:6   161
16:1   161
17:7   161, 169
18   117, 158
18:2   161
18:30   161
19   76
19:7–14   73
20   158
21   158
22   158, 167
22:1   153, 167, 310
22:24   167, 168
22:26   167
22:27   167
22:29   167

22:31   167
23:6   169
25:7   169
25:10   169
26:3   169
30–39   158
31   167
31:1–2   161
31:5   162, 167
31:14–15   162
31:16   169
31:19   161
31:21–22   168
32   158, 168
33:5   169
33:18   169
34   117
34:8   161
34:8–12   76
34:18   168
34:22   161
36:5   169
37   308
37:11   166
38:1   168
38:2   310
40:10–11   169
40:17   163
44   163
45   158
51   117, 168
51:1   169
52   117
54   117
56   117
57   117
57:3   169
58   163
59   117
60   117
61:7   169
63   117
63:3   169
66:1   165
68   288
69   158, 167
71:1–7   160
72   158, 161, 164, 166
72:1–4   160
72:1–7   160
72:2   160
72:3   160
72:4   160, 161
72:5–6   160
72:7   160
72:8   160, 303
72:8–11   160

72:12   160
72:12–13   160
72:12–14   160
72:13   160
72:14   160
72:15–17   160
72:16   160
72:17   160, 161
73   308
73:1–15   161
73:11   161
74:1   310
77   288
78   62, 99
78:54–72   93
78:56–64   99
78:65–72   99
82   164, 166
83   163
83:9–12   93
85:10   169
86:15   169
89   158, 164, 165, 166
89:14   169
89:38   164
89:38–51   164
89:51   164
90–106   164
93   160, 162, 164, 165, 166
93:1   160
94:12   310
95–99   160, 162, 164, 165, 166
95:3   160
96–99   166
96:1   166
96:7   160
96:10   160, 166
96:11–12   160
96:13   160
97:1   160, 166
97:2   160
97:6   160
97:11   160
97:12   160
98:1   166
98:2   160
98:6   160
98:7–8   160
98:9   160
99:1   160, 166
99:4   160
100   162
100:1   165
100:3   162
100:4   162

100:5   169
103:8   169
103:11   169
103:17   169
104   39
104:9   176
105   39, 62
106   39, 62
106:1   169
106:34–46   93
107:1   169
107:8   169
107:15   169
107:21   169
107:31   169
107:43   169
109   163
109:31   163, 168
110   158
111:10   76
113–118   164
115:1   169
115:4–8   79
117:1   165
117:2   169
118   167
118:1–4   169
118:25–26   167
118:29   169
119   73, 76, 164
119:44–45   51
120–134   164
127:3   106
130   168
130:4   49
132   158
136:1–26   169
137   163
137:8–9   163
138:2   169
139   163
140:12   163, 168
142   117
144   158
149   164, 165
149:2   164
149:5   164
149:7–9   164
149:9   164
150:6   162, 165

Proverbs

1–9   173, 175, 176, 177
1:1–7   173
1:2–7   173
1:3   173

1:6   173
1:7   173
1:20–33   175
2:16–19   175
3:9–10   153
3:19–20   152, 175
5:3–6   175
5:8   175
5:15–19   175
5:15–20   176
7:24–27   175
8   172, 176
8:1–9:6   175
8:9   173
8:15–16   173
8:22   171, 172
8:22–31   152, 175
8:29   176
8:30   171
8:35   175
9:1–6   175
9:1–18   175
9:10   173, 182
9:13–18   175
10   308
10–15   173, 175
10–29   172, 173, 175, 177
10–30   175
10:1   172
10:3   172
10:27–32   153
11:1   173, 175
12:10   177
12:10–11   175
12:25   175
14:10   175
14:13   175
14:31   173, 177
14:34   173
16–29   173, 175
16:1–15   173
16:10–15   175
16:11   175
16:11–13   173
17:3   175
17:17   174
17:17–18   174
17:18   174
17:27–28   174
18:22   175
22:17–20   172
22:17–23:14   172
24:15–16   153
24:23   172
25   175
25:1   172

25:11   173
25:18   173
26:4–5   153, 172, 174
26:7   173
27:8   173
27:14   173
28–29   175
28:5   173
28:8–9   173
28:19   175
29:4   173
29:7   173
29:12   173
29:14   173
30   173
30:1   172
31   173
31:1   172
31:1–9   173
31:10   105
31:10–31   173, 175
31:30   173

Ecclesiastes

1:2   182
1:3   184
1:13   182
2:3   182
11:8–10   182
12:1–8   183
12:8   182

Song of Songs

1:2–4   187
1:13   187, 188
2:7   191
3:5   191
5:2–6:3   191, 192
6:13   189
8:4   191
8:6   191

Isaiah

1   198
1–3   198
1–11   201
1–33   201
1–39   196, 206, 207
1:1   198
1:1–2:4   199
1:2   199, 208
1:2–31   199
1:4   208
1:8   202

1:9   205
1:9–10   204
1:10   73
1:11   278
1:12–15   58
1:17   278, 279
1:21   166
1:26   93, 204
1:27   166, 208
2:1   198
2:1–4   199, 208
2:1–5   199
2:1–6   195
2:2–4   166, 205, 279
2:3   204, 208
2:6–4:1   199
2:11–12   199, 208
2:13–15   207
2:17   199, 208
3:9   204
4:1   195
4:2–4   195
4:2–6   199, 204, 265, 296
4:6   200
4:16–22   207
5:1–7   200
5:1–30   199
5:3   199
5:4–6   208
5:7   166
5:8–25   209
5:15–16   208
5:18–30   204
5:19   208
5:24   73
6   199, 202
6–8   199
6:5   201, 208
6:9   205, 208
6:9–10   205
7   207
7–8   199, 200, 201
7–11   199, 200
7:1   205
7:3   199
7:4   199, 209
7:9   199, 209
7:11   199
7:11–13   199
7:14   195, 196, 199, 205, 207, 208
7:17   204
7:20   208
8   241
8:7–8   199
8:8–9   208

8:12–13   209
8:14   199, 205, 208
8:14–15   241
8:15   199
8:17   205
8:20   73
8:22   199
9   195, 199, 207
9–11   199, 201
9:1–2   205
9:1–7   281
9:2   208
9:2–7   298
9:3   200
9:4   93, 204
9:6–7   205
9:7   166, 207
10:1–4   209
10:1–19   265
10:5   208
10:5–15   283
10:10–11   208
10:12   208
10:12–14   280
10:20–22   208, 279
10:22   204
10:22–23   205
10:24   209
10:24–27   199
10:26   93, 204
10:27   195
11   195, 199, 207
11:1   207
11:1–2   117
11:1–5   205
11:1–9   281, 298
11:2   207
11:2–3   209
11:5   207
11:6   195
11:10   205
11:11   208, 279
11:16   203, 204, 208
12   199, 201
12:2   200, 209
13   280
13–23   196, 197, 199,
   200, 201, 206
13:1   198
13:1–14:23   200, 296
13:19   204
14   206, 241
14:12–15   206
14:28–17:14   199
14:32   200
16:1   195
16:5   195, 205

17–33   200
17:12–14   200
18–21   199
18:7   200
19:16   209
19:23   203
21:6   288
22:1–14   200
22:13   205
24   200
24–25   200
24–27   196, 197, 200,
   201
24:5–6   204
24:10   200
24:12   200
24:14–16   200
24:18   204
24:20   200
24:21–22   200
24:23   200, 208
25:1–5   200
25:2   200
25:3   200
25:4   200
25:6   208
25:6–8   200, 266
25:8   205
25:9   209
25:9–12   200
25:10–11   201
25:10–12   200
26–27   200
26:1   200, 209
26:1–19   200
26:2–4   200
26:3–4   209
26:5   200
26:5–6   200
26:8   209
26:12–13   209
26:14   200
26:15   200
26:16   200
26:17–18   209
26:19–27:1   200
26:21   200
27:1   200, 208
27:2–5   200
27:3   200, 208
27:9   205
27:10   200
27:13   200
28   241
28–33   199, 200, 201
28:1   200
28:5   195

28:11–12   205
28:13   199
28:16   199, 200, 205,
   209
28:16–17   208
28:17–29   199
28:21   204, 208
29:1   204
29:1–15   200
29:9–10   201, 208
29:10   205
29:13   205
29:14   205
29:18   201, 208
29:22   204
30:1   200
30:1–2   201
30:9   73
30:10–11   208
30:15   201
30:18–20   310
30:32   208
31:1   200
31:8   201
32   207
32–33   201
32:1   166, 201, 205
32:3–4   201, 208
32:15–20   205
32:16–17   166
32:17   201
33   207
33:1   200
33:2   209
33:6   209
33:17   201
33:22   201, 208
33:23   208
33:24   205
34   201, 283
34–35   196, 201, 202
34–66   198, 201
34:8   201
34:9   201
34:10   201
34:11   208
34:13   201
35   201, 296
35:4   201, 209
35:5–6   208
35:6   195, 201
35:7   201
35:8   201, 208
36–38   201
36–39   195, 196, 197,
   198, 199, 201, 202,
   205

36:2   199
36:14–20   208
37   241
37:1   199
37:6   199, 209
37:21–38   202
37:26   201
37:30   199, 201
37:31–32   279
37:32   201
37:33–37   208
37:35   204
38   202
38:5   204
38:5–6   202
38:7   199
38:9–20   205
38:22   199
39   202
39:1   200
39:5–7   200, 202
40   198, 202
40–48   202
40–55   134, 166, 196,
   201
40–66   196, 206, 207
40:3   205, 208
40:3–4   205
40:6–8   105
40:9   209
40:11   208
40:13   205
40:26   204
41   203
41:2   203
41:8   39, 204
41:8–10   204
41:10   209
41:13–14   209
41:25   203
42   203
42:1   207
42:1–3   205
42:1–9   166
42:2–3   203
42:3–4   207
42:4   205
42:5   204
42:6   203, 207
42:6–7   203
42:7   208
42:10   166
42:13   208
42:14   208
42:16   208
42:18–20   203, 208
42:24–25   204

43–44   203
43:1   203, 209
43:5   209
43:8   208
43:10   195, 209
43:14   203, 280
43:14–21   204
43:15   208
43:19   208
43:20–21   205
43:22–24   278
43:24   279
44:2   209
44:6   203, 208
44:8   209
44:9–10   208
44:15   208
44:17   208
44:18   208
44:22–24   203
44:24–45:25   203
44:28   203
44:28–45:1   296
45:1   203
45:4   203
45:5–6   208
45:7   204
45:12   204
45:18   204
45:21   205
45:22–23   208
45:23   205
46–47   203
46:1–4   203
46:10–11   208
46:13   203
48:19   204
48:20   203
48:20–21   204
48:22   202
49–57   202, 203
49:1   203
49:1–6   166
49:1–13   203
49:6   135, 203, 205
49:6–7   208
49:7   207
49:8   205, 207
49:8–9   203
49:11   208
49:14–50:3   203
49:18   205
49:18–21   204
50:4–11   203
50:10   209
51:1–2   204
51:1–52:12   203

51:3   204
51:4–7   205
51:7   73, 209
51:9   208
51:9–10   204
51:12   209
52:5   205
52:7   166, 205, 284
52:11   205
52:11–12   204
52:13–53:12   195, 203,
    242
52:15   205
53   203, 207
53:1   205, 209
53:1–6   209
53:3   196
53:4   205
53:7–8   205
53:9   205
53:10   203
53:12   205, 207
54   203
54–66   203
54:1   205
54:1–3   204
54:4   209
54:5   208
54:9   204
54:9–10   204
54:13   205
54:14   209
55:1   203
55:3   204, 205, 207
55:6–8   203, 208
55:12–13   204
56   198
56–57   203
56–58   208
56–66   196
56:1–8   204
56:3–8   135
56:7   205
57:11   209
57:14   208
57:16   204
57:21   202
58–66   202
58:1   203
58:8   203
58:11   208
59:7–8   205
59:9–15   209
59:10   208
59:12–13   204
59:15–19   204
59:17   201, 208

59:19   203, 209
59:20   204
59:20–21   205
60   204
60–62   297
60:1–2   203
60:7   203
60:9   203
60:13   203
60:19   203
60:21   203
61:1–2   205
61:1–3   204, 207
61:2   201
61:2–3   195
61:3   203
61:6   203
61:7   204
61:8   205
61:8–9   204
61:9   204
61:10   203
62   265
62:2   203
62:3   203
62:4–5   204
62:6–7   48
62:10   208
62:11   205
62:12   204
63–6   199
63:1–6   204, 208
63:4   201
63:7–64:12   204
63:9–13   204
63:15–64:12   209
63:16   204
64:4   205
64:8   208
65:1–2   205
65:9   204
65:17–25   204
66:1–2   205
66:11–12   203
66:18–19   203
66:18–23   204
66:19–21   208
66:24   199, 202, 203,
    204

Jeremiah

1:1   135
1:1–19   213
1:5   216
2   214, 218
2:1   192

2:1–7   62
2:1–6:30   213
2:19–23   207
3:14   218
3:14–18   213, 214
4:4   217, 219
4:19–22   214
5:22   176
6:16   219
6:20   279
7:1–15   214, 218
7:1–20:18   213
7:5–7   281
7:16   214
8:22–9:3   214
8:22–9:9   214
11:3–4   217
11:11–20   214
11:14   214
11:18–23   212
12:1–6   212
15:1   214
15:10–14   212
15:15–21   212
15:19   213
16:2–4   214
16:14–15   214
17:14–18   212
18:18   73
18:18–23   212
18:19–23   280
20:7–12   212
20:14–18   212, 214
21:1–25:38   213
22   214
22:3   281
22:13–17   166
23:1–8   229, 298
23:5   117
23:5–6   214
24   214, 279
24:7   214
24:8–10   215
25   214
25:9–14   279
25:12–14   214
26:1–36:32   213
28   214
29:1–14   296
29:10   224
29:14   215
30–33   215, 265, 296,
    297
30:1–33:26   213
30:6   217
30:12–15   215
30:12–17   215

30:16–17 215
31:15 207
31:18 213, 310
31:31–34 80, 212, 215
31:33 219
31:34 278
31:38–40 215
32 215
32:17 215
32:21–22 215
32:27 215
32:39–40 212, 215
34 215
35–36 215
36:3 278
37–39 215
37:1–45:5 213
37:13–16 215
39 280
39:10 293
40:7 293
42:18–22 215
43 216
44:12–14 279
46–51 216
46:1–52:34 213
48:47 216
49:6 216
49:39 216
50 280
50–51 216, 283, 296
50:34 216
52 217

Lamentations

1:8 223
1:11 224
1:12 223
1:13 224
1:15 223
1:18 224
2:2 223, 224
2:14 223
2:17 223
3 222
3:25–33 223
3:43 224
4 222
4:20 223
5:22 224

Ezekiel

1–3 241
1–7 227
1:1–3 227

1:26–27 231
2:8–3:11 226
3 228
3:17–21 231
7:26 73
8–11 227
8–13 227
8:1 227
9–10 241
9:4 231
9:8 229
11:16 146
11:19 216
12:21–13:23 227
14 231
14–19 227
14:1 227
14:1–12 227
14:14 153
14:20 153
16 192, 226, 230, 285
16:60 80
17 230, 241
18 228, 231, 280
18:1–32 227
18:32 229
19 241
20 62
20–24 227
20:1 227
20:32–44 228
22:7 281
22:30 48
23 192, 226
24:15–27 227
25 227
25–32 227, 230
26–28 227
26–32 283
28 206
29–32 227
31 241
33 228
33:1–9 231
33:21 228
33:23–29 230
33:33 228
34 228, 229
34–48 227, 228, 234
34:1–24 231
34:20–24 298
34:23–24 228
34:25–31 80
35:1–36:15 228
36–37 296
36:16–38 228
37 226, 231, 233

37:1–14 226, 228
37:15–28 228
37:24 117
38–39 228
40–48 226, 228, 265,
   296, 297
43–48 229
43:7 228
44:1–3 231
44:22 311
47:1–12 254

Daniel

1 239, 240
1:1–2 239
1:2 239
2 237, 238
2:21 239
2:34 237
2:34–35 241
2:44 239
3 237, 240, 242
4 241
4:10–12 242
4:34–35 239
4:37 239
6 240
7 237, 238, 241
7–12 238, 240
7:1 237
7:9–10 236
7:9–14 239
7:13 236, 237, 241
7:18 241
7:21–22 239
7:22 241
7:27 241
8 237, 238, 241
8:13 239
8:14 238, 242
9 238, 241
9–11 239
9:2 216, 241
9:4–16 80
9:20–27 237
9:24–27 241
10 241
10:13 240
10:20–11:1 240
11 238
11–12 236
11:3 239
11:16 239
11:24–25 237
11:27 239
11:29 239

11:32 236
11:33 240, 242
11:33–34 236
11:36 239
11:36–45 238
11:40–45 241
11:45 239
12 242
12:1–3 236, 241
12:3 240, 242
12:10 236
12:12 237

Hosea

1 245
1–3 192, 244
1:1 246
1:2 248
1:9–10 246
2:1–5 248
2:7–8 249
2:9 273
2:14–15 62
2:15 247
2:16–17 62
2:16–18 207
2:19 248
2:23 246
3 244, 245
3:1–5 248
3:5 248
4–13 245, 246
4:2 248
4:6–9 248
4:10–13 249
4:16 248
5:4 248
5:7 249
5:13 248
6:1–6 249
6:2 246
6:6 248, 278
7 244
7:1 247, 248
7:8–12 248
9:7–9 248
9:9 93
9:11 248
10:9 93
11:1 247, 207
11:1–3 248
11:1–4 248
11:1–9 296
11:3 248
11:4 248

11:5   248
11:8–9   247
11:8–11   249
11:9   248
11:10–11   248
11:10–12   248
11:12   248
12   39
12:6   248
12:7–8   249
13:4–5   247
13:5   248
13:9–16   248
13:16   280
14   216, 245
14:1 MT   280
14:4   248
14:4–9   248, 249
14:9   246, 306
14:10 MT   306

Joel

1:1   251
1:1–14   253
1:3–2:5   259
1:4   251
1:5–7   251
1:6   251, 255
1:8–10   251
1:11–12   251
1:15–18   253
1:19   254
1:19–20   253
2:1   253, 255
2:1–11   253
2:2   253, 255
2:2–11   251, 253
2:3   252, 253
2:3–8   251
2:4–5   255
2:10   253, 254, 255
2:11   253, 255
2:13   254
2:13–14   283
2:16–20   251
2:18–27   253
2:19   253, 273
2:20   251, 252, 253
2:21–22   253
2:21–23   253
2:23   253
2:24   253
2:25   252
2:25–27   253
2:26   253
2:26–27   253, 254

2:27   253
2:28   253, 254
2:28–32   253, 255
2:29   252
2:31   254, 255
2:32   254, 255
3:1 MT   253, 254
3:1–2   254
3:1–5 MT   253, 255
3:1–16   254
3:2 MT   252
3:2–4   254
3:4   252
3:4 MT   254
3:4–8   252, 254
3:5 MT   254, 255
3:10   254
3:12   254
3:13   254, 255
3:14   254
3:15   254, 255
3:16   252, 254, 260
3:16–19   265
3:17   253, 254
3:18   254, 255
3:19   252
3:21   254
4:1–16 MT   254
4:2 MT   254
4:2–3 MT   254
4:4 MT   252
4:4–8 MT   252
4:10–13 MT   254
4:12 MT   254
4:14 MT   254
4:15 MT   254, 255
4:16 MT   252, 254, 260
4:17 MT   253, 254
4:18 MT   254, 255
4:19 MT   252
4:21 MT   254
8:11   258
9:6   258
9:11–12   258
45:4–8 MT   254

Amos

1–2   261
1:1   259
1:2   252, 259, 260
1:3–2:3   265
1:7   252
1:9   265
1:9–10   252
1:11   252
1:11–12   265, 273

2:6–16   259
2:8   260
2:9–10   259
3   260
3–6   260
3:1–2   259
3:2   45
3:3–8   260
3:8   258
3:9–11   260
3:12   260
4   260
4:4   258
4:4–5   259
4:6   258
4:6–12   260
4:13   258, 259
5:1–17   260
5:8–9   259
5:10–13   260
5:14   259
5:18–20   258, 259
5:18–27   260
5:21–23   259
5:21–24   58, 279
5:21–25   278
5:24   166
5:25–27   261
5:26–27   257
6   260
6:1–3   259
6:12   260
7:1–8:3   260
7:8   260
7:10–17   260
8:2   260
8:4–14   260
8:9   258
9:1–4   260
9:5–6   259
9:7   259
9:8–10   260
9:10   259
9:11   257
9:11–12   261
9:11–15   260, 261
9:12   273

Obadiah

1   264
2–10   264
2–18   264
3   265
3–4   264
4   264
8   264

9   264
10   265
11–12   265
11–14   265
12   265
13–14   265
15   265
15–21   265
17   265
18   264, 265
20   265
21   266

Jonah

1   270
1:14–16   270
2   270
3   270
3:9–10   283
3:9–4:4   283
3:10   270, 271
4   270
4:2   283
4:6   270
4:9   270

Micah

1–3   277
1:1–5:15   276
1:2–16   276
1:5   278
1:6–7   276
2–5   277
2:1–2   278
2:1–5:15   276
2:3   278
2:3–5   280
2:12–13   276, 279, 280
3:1   278
3:1–2   278
3:4   280
3:5–6   278
3:7   280
3:8   278
3:10–11   278
3:12   280
4–5   277
4:1–3   205
4:1–5:14   279
4:1–5:15   279
4:6–7   279
4:6–8   279, 280
4:10   276
4:10–11   280
5:2–5   117

5:6–7 MT   279
5:6–8 MT   279
5:7–8   279
5:7–8 MT   280
5:7–9   279
5:8 MT   279
5:8–9   280
5:9   279
6   278
6–7   277
6:1–8   276
6:1–7:6   277
6:1–7:20   276
6:6–8   278
6:7   278
6:8   108, 279
6:9–7:20   276
7:1–7   281
7:7–20   277
7:18   278, 283
7:18–20   276, 278, 279, 280
7:19   278
24:2–7   280
24:8   280
29:17   280
44:12–14   280

Nahum

1   283
1:1   282
1:2–8   282
1:7–2:1   283
1:9–10   282
1:11   282
1:12–14   282
1:14–2:1   284
1:15   282, 284
2:1–10   282
2:11–12   282
2:13   282
3   282
3:1–4   282
3:5–7   283
3:8–12   283
3:13–17   283
3:18–19   283

Habakkuk

1–2   289
1:2–3   310
1:2–4   286
1:4   288
1:5   288
1:5–11   286, 287

1:12–13   310
1:12–17   260, 286, 287
1:13   40
1:41   288
2   287
2:1   286, 288
2:1–20   296
2:2–3   287
2:2–5   286
2:2–20   286
2:3   288
2:4   286, 288, 289
2:5   287
2:6–20   287
2:13   287
2:17   287
3   286, 287, 288, 289
3:2   287
3:3–7   287
3:4–5   287
3:6–20   287
3:8–15   287
3:13–15   287
3:14   287
3:16   287
3:17–19   287
3:20   287

Zephaniah

1–8   295
1:1–2:3   291
1:2–3   291
1:2–18   292
1:5   292
1:14   293
1:18   291
2   292
2:1–3   292
2:3   291, 294
2:4   292
2:4–15   294
2:4–3:8   291
2:5–11   292
2:11   291
2:12   292
2:12–15   292
2:13–15   292
3   292
3:1–7   292
3:6–7   292
3:8   291
3:8–13   292
3:9   292
3:9–20   291
3:12   291
3:14–20   292
3:15   292

Haggai

1:1   296, 297
1:2–6   297
1:2–11   297
1:2–15   296
1:6   296
1:8   297
1:9   296
1:12–14   297
1:13–14   297
2:1–19   297
2:4–5   297
2:5   297
2:6–8   297
2:9   297
2:10–14   298
2:15–19   298
2:20–23   298
2:23   298

Zechariah

1–6   300
1:4   303
1:16   302
1:16–17   302
1:21   302
2:9   302
2:10   302
2:11   302
2:12   302
2:15 MT   302
3:8   303
5:1   135
6:7–8   302
6:12–13   303
6:14   135
7–8   300
7:3–5   223
7:7   303
7:12   303
8:1–5   302
8:12–13   302
8:20–23   135, 302
9–11   306
9–14   300, 301
9:1   307
9:1–7   302
9:8   302
9:9–12   303
9:10   303
9:12   302
9:16–17   302
10:6   302
11:3   302
11:4–16   302
11:6   302

12–14   306
12:1   307
12:1–2   303
12:3–4   302
12:9   302
12:10–13:1   303
13:1   254
13:7–9   303
13:8–9   302
14   301
14:1–2   302
14:3   302
14:3–9   254
14:12   302
14:16   302

Malachi

1:1   305, 307
1:1–5   306
1:1–9   278
1:2   306
1:2–5   280, 306, 307, 308, 310
1:2–4:6   307
1:6–2:9   306, 307
1:6–2:16   307
1:6–4:6   307
1:8   309
1:10–14   307
1:13   278
2   309
2:6   73
2:6–9   309
2:8–12   307
2:9   73
2:10–16   306
2:16   309
2:17   310
2:17–3:5   306, 309
2:17–4:6   307
3:5   281
3:6–12   306
3:8   308
3:10   308
3:13–21 MT   306
3:13–4:3   306
3:20–24 MT   306
3:21–24 MT   305–6
3:22 MT   306
3:22–24 MT   306, 307
3:23–24 MT   306
3:24 MT   307
4:2–6   306
4:3–6   305
4:4   306
4:4–6   76, 306, 307
4:5–6   306

Baruch

2:7–10   140

2 Esdras

1:22–23   62
11–12   237
13   237
14:44–46   106

Additions to Esther

13:15   146
13:16   147
14:5   146
16:16   147

2 Maccabees

1:10–2:18   140

Wisdom of Ben Sira

24:23   172
46:11–12   93
48:17–25   194
48:22   195
48:23–24   195

Matthew

1   109, 207
1–2   207
1:1   117
1:20–23   207
4:17   166
5:3   166
5:3–11   166
5:5   166
5:16   174
5:17   75, 166
5:20   166
5:32   311
6:1   174
6:10   163
6:33   294
7:1   174
7:6   174
9:13   246
11:9   68
12   274
12:7   246
12:39–41   273
12:40   268
12:41   271
16:4   273
16:21   247

17:23   247
19:5   39
21:5   303
21:9   117
22:34–40   81
24:21   255
24:29   255
24:42   255
25:34–40   108
26:26–28   217
26:31   303
27:9   301
27:9–10   303
27:46   153, 167

Mark

1:11   166
1:15   166
4:29   255
4:35–41   154
5:25–34   53
8:34–35   169
10:3   68
10:23   293
11:9   167
12:19   68
14:22–24   217
14:27   303
15:34   167

Luke

1:32   117
4:25–27   122
9:22   247
10:7–19   206
11   274
11:29–32   273
11:30   274
11:51   128
12:48   45
16:18   311
20:18   241
20:28   68
22:20   80
23:46   167
24:44   76

John

1:1–4   154
1:1–18   177
1:14   100
1:21   68
1:25   68
3:14   63
3:36   288

5:45   68
6:14   68
6:54   217
7:40   68
7:42   117
8:39   230
9:28   68
12:15   303
13–16   74
19:37   303

Acts

2:17–21   255
2:25–36   117
2:38–39   255
2:39   255
7:36   63
7:41–43   261
7:45–47   94
13   288
13:19–20   94
15:13–18   261
22:16   255

Romans

1–3   61
1:1   50
1:3   109, 117
1:17   288
1:18–20   177
1:18–23   230
2:14–15   177
2:28–29   69
3   39
4   39
5   39
6:23   229
7   39
7:4–9   69
7:12   69
7:14–25   218
8   255
8:14   246
8:20   183
9:6–9   280
9:8–16   230
9:11–14   280, 310
9:25–26   246
10:6–8   68
10:12–15   255
10:13   255
10:15   284
10:19   68
11:8   68
11:27   217
11:28   255

11:35   154
12:1–12   81
12:2   22
12:19   68
13:1–5   90
13:8–10   69
15:11   165
15:16   255

1 Corinthians

3:19   154
5:7–8   45
5:13   68
6:20   177
8:6   68
9:9   68
10:3–14   63
10:16   217
11:25   80, 217

2 Corinthians

3:6   69
8:9   294

Galatians

2:16   288
3:10–25   69
3:11–12   288
3:13   68
3:29   230
4:9   26
4:24–31   230
5:1   51
5:13   51
6:2   81, 174
6:5   174
11:4   174

Ephesians

3:19   49
5:19   157
5:21–33   192
6:2–3   68
6:15   284

Philippians

2:5–8   100

Colossians

1:15–20   177
1:15–23   154
1:20   230
3:16   157

1 Thessalonians

5:1–11   255

2 Thessalonians

2:3–12   288

2 Timothy

3:1–5   279
4:3   281

Hebrews

1:3   100
2:17–18   57
3–4   63
3:1–6   57
4:8–11   83
4:15   57
5:3   57

5:7–8   57, 153
8:1–2   57
8:8–13   80, 217
9:13–14   57
9:15   57, 80, 217
9:25–26   57
10:16–17   217
10:38   288
11   94, 101
11:17–22   39
11:32   94
11:32–34   94
12:6   310
12:10   310
12:24   80, 217

James

1:9–11   293
2:5–6   293

2:6–7   261
2:21–23   39
5:1–6   261, 293
5:11   154

1 Peter

2:9   69
4:17   230
5:6–10   154

2 Peter

3:9   288

1 John

1:1–2   100
1:9   278
4:7–12   108
5:10–12   288

Revelation

5:5   117
5:11–14   154
6:12–13   255
6:17   255
8:6   255
8:12   255
9:7–9   255
12:7–9   206
13:1–4   241
13:5   242
14:15   255
17–18   283
19:6–8   192
19:15   255
21–22   154, 177
21:1–22:5   39
21:22–23   154
22:1   255

Subject Index

Aaron, 48, 56
Aaronic Priesthood, 55, 56
Abel, 35, 38, 128
Abiathar, 116
Abijah, 129, 130
Abimelech, 93
Abraham, 160, 165
  as agent of reconciliation, 37
  call of, 36, 77, 146
  covenant with, 43, 60, 78, 80,
    230, 266
  expulsion from Egypt, 38
  in Genesis, 33
  incarnation of blessing, 33
  in Isaiah, 204
  as model of faith, 39, 47, 60, 94
  as second Adam figure, 36
Abravanel, Don Isaac, 188
Achan, 86, 89
acquired intellect, 187
acrostic poems in Lamentations, 223
Acsah, 95
Active Intellect, 187
Acts, book of, 94, 205, 261, 288
Adam, 33, 35, 124, 191–92
adultery, 53, 192, 229, 245–46, 247,
  311
advent texts, 207
adversity, 311
African-American spirituals, 232
Agag, 144
Age of Criticism, 269
Ahab, 120, 122, 123
'ahab (he loved), 72
Ahasuerus (king of Persia), 139, 142,
  143, 146
Ahaz (king of Judah), 198
Ahaziah, 123
Ahimelech, 116
Ai, 84
Alexandrian school, 258

allegorical interpretation, 62, 83, 148,
    188, 232, 300
  of Ecclesiastes, 179
  of Ezekiel, 232
  of Song of Songs, 186–88
Amaziah, 260
Amos, book of
  authorship of, 259
  canonical context, 260–61
  history of interpretation, 257–58
  message of, 259–60
  modern perspectives on, 258–59
  monotheism and, 258
  oracle against foreign nations,
    261–62
  prophetic genre and, 257
  salvation oracle, 261
  social injustice and, 257
  theology of, 258, 261–62
ancient beliefs about gods, 39
Andrew of St. Victor, 196, 232
angels, 240
Anselm of Laon, 231
anthological interpretation, 189
anthropological interpretation, 54
antichrist, 231, 233, 237, 238, 241
Antioch, 288
Antiochene period, 238
Antioch school, 258
Antiochus Epiphanes, 237, 238
anti-Semitism, 143, 268, 269
apocalypticism, 238
apocalyptic millennialism, 238
Apocrypha, 62, 305
apostasy, 309
Aqiba, Rabbi, 186–87
Aquila, 191
Arian controversy, 172
Arithmoi, 59
ark of the covenant, 48, 114
arrogance, 288

Artaxerxes (king of Persia), 136, 139,
  142, 146
Asherah, 120
asqinah meter, 223
Assyria, 120, 129, 188, 201, 245, 252
Assyrian Empire, 286
Astruc, 30
Athaliah, 122, 123
atonement, 56, 207
Atrahasis epic, 31, 34, 35
attachments, 179, 218–19
Augustine of Hippo, 158, 172, 268,
  289
'awen (wickedness), 278
'awon (iniquity), 278

Baal, 120, 122
Baba Batra, 195
Babylon, 188, 201, 252
  conquest of Jerusalem, 202
  defeat of, 127, 223
  deportation to, 127
Babylonian Exile, 140, 164
Babylonian Talmud, 105, 106, 133
Bamidmar (in the wilderness), 59
Barak, 94
Barberini manuscript, 288
'bd (slave/servant), 50
Beatitudes, the, 166
Behemoth, 151, 154
Belshazzar, 240, 242
Ben Asher family of Masoretes, 105
Bengel, Johan Albrecht, 27
Ben Hayyim manuscripts, 105
Benjamin, 98, 129
Ben Sirach, Yeshua, 93
Bernard of Clairvaux, 188
Bethlehem, 106
Bible, 49
biblical authority, 269
biblical criticism, 19

biblical interpretation, 22, 24
biblical theology, 21
Bildad, 151
bishops, 231
bless and blessing, 65, 76
    of Abraham and descendants,
        36, 60
    covenantal blessings, 73, 208
    of David's reign, 115, 117
    Genesis and, 33
    Jerusalem and, 204
    loss of, 127
    on the nations, 161, 165, 195
    obedience and, 99, 121, 130
    pentateuchal blessings, 261
    in Ruth, 106, 108
    tithing and, 311
    of Yahweh, 296, 298
bless (*barakh*), 33
blood, 47
Boaz, 102, 104, 107
body and spirit, 191
Book of Common Prayer, 50
Book of Moses, 138
Book of the Events of the Days, The
    (Chronicles), 124
Book of the Torah, 71
Book of the Twelve, 264, 273, 276,
    283, 305
Booths, Festival of, 56
boundaries, 175–76
Branch, the, 303
Bunyan, John, 18
burning bush, 44, 48
burnt offerings, 55

Cain, 35, 38
Caleb, 79
Calvin, John, 112, 143, 149, 238
    on Deuteronomic law, 69
    on Job, 149
    on Joel, 251, 252
    on Jonah, 268
    on Psalms, 158, 169
Canaan, 36, 74, 88–89
canon sense, 25
catholic sensibility, 25
Chaucer, Geoffrey, 172
cherubim, 48
Child, Brevard, 239, 259
Chilion, 102
Christ
    Adam and, 30, 39
    birth of, 237
    death deals with sin, 230
    female Wisdom, 172
    judgment and redemption and, 46
    lamentations of, 153
    law and, 75
    Moses' serpent as image of, 63
    natures of, 231
    Passover and, 45
    Proverbs and, 177
    sacrifice and, 53
    See also Jesus

Christian apostasy, 63
Christian canon, 105
Christian interpretation, 74, 93,
    132, 187
Christianity, 63
Christian nations, 87
Christians, 280
Christian theology, 46, 176
Christian worship, 289
Christos, 166
Chronicles, books of
    "All Israel" theme, 129
    authorship of, 124, 126
    canonical context, 127–28
    dating of, 126
    Deuteronomic influence on, 76
    and Ezra-Nehemiah, 125, 126
    genealogies, 125, 128
    historical reliability of, 125
    Jeremiah and, 216
    message of, 126–27
    retribution, 130
    Samuel and Kings and, 125
    structure of, 128
    theology of, 125, 128–30
    worship in, 127–28
Chrysostom, John, 148, 195
church, 80
church and state, 133
church fathers, 20
church history, 20
Church of England, 133
church offices, 231
city-lament genre, 223
civic law vs. theological law, 69
class struggles, 277
clean and unclean, 55
common grace, 176
community, 77, 78, 140, 254
Community Rule, 236
compassion, 92, 248, 272. *See also*
    deliverance
confession, 56, 224
confessional criticism, 22
*Conjectures on the Memoires Used
    by Moses to Compile Genesis*
    (Astruc), 30
conquest generation, 59, 63
consumer cultures, 249
conversion, 107–8
Council of Chalcedon, 231
covenant, 298
    Abraham and, 60, 78
    breaking of, 48
    David and, 114–17, 125, 207,
        296, 298
    Ezekiel and, 229–30
    Hosea and, 246–47
    instruction in, 271
    Israel and, 55, 67, 71–81, 146, 208
    Jesus and, 57
    keeping of, 95–100
    Moses and, 218
    nature of, 72

renewal at Shechem, 83, 87, 88
Sinai and, 46–47, 297
unfaithfulness and, 100
covenantal relationships, 36
covenantal theology, 100
covenant fidelity, 72, 92
covenant lawsuit, 306
creation
    doctrine of, 30, 183
    God's purpose in, 239
    of human beings, 34
    in Isaiah, 204
    myths of, 31, 34
    presence of Wisdom at, 152
    renewal of, 253–55
    theology of, 153, 155
    violence in, 35
critical interpretation, 63
cross, 68, 101, 231
cult-functional approach, 158–59
cultic interpretation, 190
cultural revitalization model, 138
Cultural Transformation Phase, 139
Cushite dynasty, 292
Cyril of Alexandria, 187, 195, 258,
    289
Cyrus (king of Persia), 124, 127, 136,
    204, 223
Cyrus Edict, 127, 132, 296

Daniel, book of
    authorship and dating, 238–39
    canonical context, 240–42
    history of interpretation, 237–39
    human and divine faithfulness,
        239–40
    human and divine sovereignty, 239
    idolatry and, 240
    message of, 239–40
    New Testament and, 241–42
    Old Testament and, 216, 241
    theology of, 242
darash (care), 79
Darby, J. N., 238
Darius (king of Persia), 136
Darwin, Charles, 31
Davidic covenant, 298
David (king of Israel), 94
    census of, 116–17
    Christ and, 111
    genealogy of, 102, 105
    Isaiah and, 204
    Jerusalem cult and, 116
    leadership and, 93, 96
    Moabite ancestry of, 103, 105
    psalms and, 117
    sin and punishment of, 113
    as Yahweh's chosen king, 114
Day of Atonement, 55, 56
Day of the Lord, 252–53, 255, 265,
    293
Day of Yahweh, 291
dead, contact with, 53
Dead Sea Scrolls, 125, 144, 194

death, 35
Deborah, 95
Decalogue, the, 75
Delitzsch, Franz, 189
deliverance, 77, 100, 288. *See also* compassion
desire, 192, 287
Deuteronomic Code, 73
Deuteronomic History, 112
Deuteronomic source, 76
Deuteronomic theology, 99, 100, 224
Deuteronomic torah, 75
deutero-nomion, 68
Deuteronomistic History, 70, 76, 84, 94, 99, 112–13
Deuteronomy, book of
  authorship of, 68, 70
  as Book of the Torah, 73
  canonicity of, 75–77
  Christian loss of message, 71
  covenant curses in, 76
  covenant relationship in, 78
  dating of, 70–71
  Decalogue and, 68
  Deuteronomistic History and, 70
  implications of the covenant, 74
  inclusion in Torah, 73
  influence on Chronicles and Ezra-Nehemiah, 76
  land theology, 79
  message of, 71–75
  name theology in, 70
  Old Testament and, 73
  origins of, 69–70
  overall theme of, 77
  prophetic preaching in, 72–73
  Proverbs and, 76
  reading/hearing in, 72
  sources, 69–70
  structure of, 72
  theology of, 77
  title of, 68
  truth and, 74
  understanding, 74–75
Deutero-Zechariah, 301, 302
de Wette, William, 125
Diaspora Jews, 144
didachē, 73
Didache, 289
didaskalia, 73
Didymus the Blind, 300, 301
dietary laws, 52
discipline, 310
disloyalty, 229–30
disobedience, 64, 99, 114, 130, 165
dispensational movement, 238, 301
divided kingdom, 121
divine authorship, 23
divine election (*bakhar*, choose), 77
divine judgment. *See* judgment
divine presence, 47
divine providence, 104
Divine Warrior, the, 204
divorce, 135, 309, 311

documentary approach to pentateuchal studies, 69–70
double-meaning exegesis, 206
doulos (servant/slave), 50
Duhm, Bernhard, 196

early Christian interpretation, 143
  of Amos, 263
  of Ezekiel, 231
  of Job, 148
  of Jonah, 268
  narrative theology of, 30
  purity laws and, 52–53
  symbolism in, 30
early critical interpretation, 158
early modern interpretation, 301
Easter liturgy, 289
Eastern churches, 143, 145
'ebed (servant), 50, 207
Ebeling, Gerhard, 20
Ecclesiastes, book of
  authorship, 180
  canonical context of, 182
  fall and, 39
  genre and structure, 180
  gospels and, 183
  history of interpretation, 179–81
  Job and, 183
  joy in, 179, 182
  meaning and, 183
  message of, 181–83
  poetics of, 182
  Proverbs and, 183
  structure of, 181
  theme of, 180–81
  theology of, 183–84
  voices in, 181
ecological issues, 155
economics, 249
ecumenical consensus, 16
Edom, 263, 308
Edwards, Jonathon, 94
Egypt, 188, 245
Egyptian Hallel, 164
Egyptian Teaching of Amenemope, 172
election, 45, 77–78, 293
Eliezer of Beaugency, 231
Elihu, 149
Elijah, 120, 121, 122, 123, 127
Elimelech, 102, 107
Eliphaz, 151
Elisha, 121
'Elleh Haddebarim ("These are the Words"), 68
Elohim, 270
Elohistic (E) source, 30, 32
empiricism, 182, 184
Enarrations on the Psalm (Augustine), 158
Enlightenment, the, 30, 69, 172
Ephraim, 98, 106
Ephraim the Syrian, 231
epistemology, 184

Erasmus, 172
Esau, 265, 308
eschatological interpretation, 111, 231
eschatological visions, 233
eschatology, 238, 279, 288
2 Esdras, 191
Esther, book of
  anti-Semitism in, 143
  canonical context of, 144–45
  God's involvement in daily life, 153
  historiography vs. fiction, 143
  history of interpretation, 142–44
  message of, 144
  morality of, 145
  reversals in, 143
  secular tone of, 146
  theology of, 145–47
Esther Rabbah, 142
ethics, 42
ethnicity and inclusion, 107–8
Eucharist, 179
Eusebius of Caesarea, 195
Eve, 35, 191–92
evil, 40, 163, 253, 278
exclusivism, 272
exile, 127, 134, 140, 229
exodus, 204, 288
Exodus, book of
  burning bush story, 44
  Egyptian perspective, 45
  genres in, 43
  God's self-revelation in, 42
  historicity of, 43
  mercy seat, 48
  Passover texts, 45
  Sabbath in, 46
  servitude and freedom in, 50
  tabernacle, 48, 50
  Ten Commandments given, 47
  violence in, 44
  wilderness narratives, 46
  women in, 43–44
exodus generation, 59, 60, 62, 63
Ezekiel, book of
  argument of, 226–29
  audience, 226
  authorship of, 232
  canonical context, 229–30
  covenant, 80
  dating of, 232
  dry bones vision, 226, 228
  God, aspects of, 229
  interpretation of, 230–33
  idolatry and false prophecy, 233
  Israel's religious rebellions, 62
  Jeremiah and, 229
  Jews under thirty and, 231
  major themes, 226–29
  Moses and, 229
  New Testament and, 229
  postexilic community and, 230
  power and, 233
  premillennialism and, 233

prophecies of, 227–28
sexually charged language in, 226
spiritual and political restoration
in, 234
structure and genres of, 228
throne-chariot vision, 230–31
Ezra, 127
as compiler of Pentateuch, 30
as father of Judaism, 133
Ezra, book of
authorship of, 133
canonical context of, 134–35
chronology of, 135–36
genealogies in, 134
historical-critical issues in, 133–34
history of interpretation, 132–33
Jeremiah and, 216
message of, 133–34
thematic ordering of, 140
theology of, 135–36
See also Nehemiah, book of
Ezra-Nehemiah, 76, 132. See also
Ezra, book of; Nehemiah,
book of

faith, 39, 113, 287, 288, 289
faithfulness, 49, 239–40, 287, 289
faithlessness, 48
fall, the, 30, 191–92
false attachments, 218
false prophets, 284
fear of God, 47
Feast of Booths, 71
Feast of Purim, 143, 145
Feast of Tabernacles, 56
Feast of Weeks, 56, 105
female friendship, 108
feminist interpretation, 95, 144,
232, 245
fertility, 104, 106, 245
feuds, 37
fifth kingdom, 238
fifth monarchy men, 238
final-form literary approaches, 113,
150
fire, 44
First Isaiah, 196, 201
Five Books of Moses, 68
flood, the, 292
floods, 35
flood story, 31, 35, 39, 204
Florilegium, 236
folly, 175
foreign land, 292
foreign wives, 119, 135, 309
forgiveness, 37, 40, 56, 247, 278
form criticism, 23, 54, 84, 158–59,
177, 180, 295–96
of Amos, 258, 259
and Obadiah, 263
"former prophets," 303
fourth kingdom, 237–38
Franciscans, 237
fratricide, 35, 37

Fretheim, Terence, 165
friendship, 174

Gad, 116
Garden of Eden, 34–35, 36, 39,
191–92
Genesis, book of
Babylonian thought and, 34
bless and blessing in, 33
canonical context, 37–39
chronology of, 30
covenant relationship, 36
creation in, 39
dating of, 31
Exodus and Deuteronomy and, 38
fall, the, 35
flood, the, 35
forgiveness in, 40
Garden of Eden, 36
Hexaemeron (six days of
creation), 33–34
interpretation of, 29–32
Jewish readers of, 32
Joseph narratives in, 144
judgment in, 39
land, 33, 36
message of, 32
monotheism in, 39
New Testament and, 38
Noah in, 35
patriarchal stories, 39
promises in, 36
Protohistory, 34–35
reconciliation in, 40
Sabbath as goal of creation, 34
sacrifice in, 38
seed or offspring (zeraʿ), 33
sexes, relationships between, 39
sinfulness, 35, 39
sources of, 30
structure of, 32–33
theology of, 39–40
Tower of Babel, 35
genres, 23, 43, 223, 238, 269
Gentiles, 61, 103, 165, 261, 266, 269
German Empire, 237
German Peasants' Revolt, 238
Gerstenberger, Erhard, 159
Gibeah, 93, 98, 106
Gibeon, 89
Gibeonites, 86
Gideon, 94, 97
Gilgal, 84
Gilgamesh tablet, 11, 31, 35
Glossa ordinaria, 172, 174
God, 56
access to, 47
anger of, 44, 214
blessings of, 121, 127
Christ and, 153
coming kingdom of, 303
compassion of, 92
concern for humanity, 39
cross as symbol, 230

dependence on, 55
empathy of, 214
faithfulness of, 61
fear of, 47
grace of, 49, 77
hidden, 146
Israel and, 134, 168, 247, 307
judgment of, 121, 214
mystery of, 44, 57
power of, 167–68
presence of, 160
promises of, 46
relationship with, 248–49
requirements of, 278, 281, 307–8
selectivity of, 280
silence of, 224, 308
sin and, 40
sovereignty of, 34, 39, 120, 154,
166, 167, 229–30, 233, 302
transcendence of, 240
universality of, 146, 155, 160, 208
wrath of, 293
See also Yahweh
God's discipline, 310
God's hate, 310
God's justice, 309–10
God's love, 310–11
golden calf, 48
Gomer, 244, 245
Gomorrah, 204
grace, 49, 50, 168, 176, 216, 272, 302
grain offerings, 56
Greece, 238, 240
greed, 287, 289
Gregory of Nyssa, 47
Gregory the Great, 148–49, 206, 231
Grotius, Hugo, 238, 301
Guide to the Perplexed, The
(Maimonides), 149
guilt offerings, 56
Gunkel, Hermann, 54, 158, 180
Gutiérrez, Gustavo, 150

Habakkuk, book of
argument of the book, 286–87
canonical context, 287–88
interpretation of, 288–89
modern church and, 289
haggadah (illustrative narrative commentary), 62
Haggai, book of
authorship of, 295–96
Davidic covenant and renewed
blessing, 298
fulfilled prophecy in, 296
interpretation of, 295–96
temple and renewed community,
297–98
Haimo of Auxerre, 285
halakic (legal) interpretation, 62
Haman, the Agagite, 142, 143, 144,
146
Hananiah, 214
Hannah, 114

hattorah hazz'ot (this torah), 73
hayah (to be), 44
hebel hebalim (vanity of
    vanities), 182
hebel (vanity), 180, 182, 183
Hebrew Bible, 61, 62, 144
Hebrew Canon, 105, 127, 144, 240
Hebrews, book of, 63, 94, 100, 205,
    217–18, 288
Hebron, 98
Hellenism, 62, 306
henotheism, 265
hermeneutics, 17
Herodotus, 143
Hexateuch, 70, 84
Hezekiah (king of Judah), 128, 130,
    195, 198, 205, 207
high places, 120
Hippolytus, 187, 231, 237
Hippolytus of Rome, 289
historical criticism, 17, 138, 149, 198,
    232, 244, 263, 277, 284, 295, 301
    and Amos, 261
    and Ecclesiastes, 180, 181
    and Isaiah, 194
    and Job, 149
    and Obadiah, 263
Hittite treaty documents, 71, 72
Holiness Code, 53
holistic intrepretation, 232
Holy Spirit, 100, 253–54, 255
homiletical exegesis (*derash*), 62
honor roll of faith, 94
hope, 278, 279–80
Hosea, book of
    Amos and, 246
    canonical context, 246–47
    Deuteronomic influence on, 76
    feminist interpretations of, 245
    God, nature of, 246
    imagery in, 244, 248
    incarnational trends in, 218
    interpretation of, 244–45
    marriage metaphors, 247, 248
    message of, 245–46
    requirements of relationship, 248–49
    sexual imagery in, 244, 247
    theology of, 247
    wilderness and, 62
hubris, 242
humanity, 39
human love, 190
human piety, 155
Hus, Jan, 237
hyponone (perseverance), 154

Ibn Ezra, Abraham, 196
idolatry, 55, 195, 208
    in Amos, 246
    in book of Judges, 97
    in Daniel, 240
    exodus generation and, 60
    freedom from, 90
    in Hosea, 246

sin and, 99
imaginative typological interpreta-
    tions, 111
Immanuel, 208
imperialism, 283
incest, 56
individualism, 212, 219
injustice, 168, 208, 278, 281, 283,
    286, 289
    consequences of, 163
    in Israel, 260
inner-biblical exegesis, 128
insiders, 89
integrity, 49
intellect, types of, 187
intermarriage, 309
intertestamental literature, 140
intertextuality, 238
intimacy, 190, 191, 192
intratextual reading, 24
'ir'az (strong city), 200
irony, 182
Isaac, 37, 38
Isaiah, book of
    authorship of, 195, 196–97, 206
    canonical context of, 204–6
    as Christian Scripture, 207
    christological emphases in patristic
        interpretation, 195
    climax of, 202
    dating of, 196, 200
    as "Fifth Gospel," 194
    focus on Zion/Jerusalem, 198, 200
    foundational use in other biblical
        books, 205–6
    Hezekiah narrative, 198
    historicity of, 196–97
    history and eschatology in, 198
    history of interpretation, 194–97
    Immanuel text, 207
    influence on New Testament,
        205–6
    little apocalypse, 201
    major themes in, 200, 202–3
    message of, 197–204
    messianic texts in, 206–7
    oracles concerning foreign
        nations, 199–200, 206
    parallels with Micah and
        Jeremiah, 205
    portrayals of rupture and transfor-
        mation, 204–5
    prophetic thought in, 198, 207–8
    Servant Songs, 197
    structure of, 198, 199
    theocentric focus of, 208
    theological categories in, 206
    theological transitions in, 201
    theology of, 206–9
    unifying elements in, 197
    woe oracles, 200–201
    Zion and, 93
Ish-Bosheth, 98
Isidore of Seville, 231

Islam, 237
Israel, 80, 308
    claim to land, 32, 89
    Canaanites and, 88–89
    deliverance from Egypt, 50
    Deuteronomy and, 80
    identity of, 89, 90
    idolatry of, 62
    infidelity of, 79
    as model for the nations, 45
    monarchy and, 81
    origins of, 37
    as people of God, 42
    physical and spiritual aspects of,
        79, 80
    response to God's law, 307
    sinfulness of, 61, 135, 246, 259
    slavery of, 100, 139
    Ten Commandments and, 47
    theocracy and, 80

Jacob, 33, 265, 308
Jael, 95
James, Epistle of, 52, 261
Japhet, 126
Jebusites, 96
Jehoiachin (king of Judah), 123, 298
Jehoram, 123
Jephthah, 94
Jephthah's daughter, 95
Jeremiah, book of
    Book of Consolation, 213, 215
    canonical context, 216–18
    Deuteronomic influence on, 76, 217
    Deuteronomistic interpretation,
        212
    false objects of trust, 218
    genres, 211
    incarnation and, 216, 218
    interpretation of, 211–13
    Isaiah and, 216
    Kings and, 217
    Lamentations and, 105
    message of, 213–16
    new covenant, 80, 211, 215–18
    New Testament and, 217–18
    Oracles against the Nations
        (OAN), 213
    personal piety and, 212
    themes of, 214–16
    theological issues, 212–13, 218–19
Jericho, 84, 86
Jeroboam (king of Israel), 106,
    129, 245
Jeroboam II (king of Israel), 246
Jerome, 105, 124, 148, 187, 195, 231,
    289, 300
    on Amos, 258
    on Daniel, 231
    on Ezra-Nehemiah, 133
    on Jonah, 268
Jerusalem, 302
    fall of, 57, 127, 215
    Isaiah and, 198, 208

restoration of, 204
temple of, 50
worship in, 70
Jesus, 306
    Beatitudes of, 166
    as bringer of kingdom and eternal
        peace, 100
    contradictory sayings of, 174–75
    covenant and, 57, 217
    Deuteronomy and, 68
    eschatology and, 68
    faithfulness of, 100
    Gentiles and, 122
    incarnation of, 75
    Jonah and, 268
    kingly power of, 295
    Leviticus and, 52
    marriage and, 39
    Melchizedek and, 57
    Messiah, 207
    miracles of, 122
    Moses and, 57
    passion of, 167
    resurrection of, 247
    Sermon on the Mount, 171
    sinlessness of, 57
    as Son of Man, 242
    suffering of, 167
    titles of, 166
    See also Christ
Jewish exclusivism, 272
Jewish interpretation, 53, 93
Jewish liturgy, 289
Jewish national identity, 93
Jewish people, 146
Jewish theology, 49
Jezebel, 120, 123
Joash, 122, 123
Job, book of
    canonical context, 152–54
    creation theology in, 155
    Elihu speeches, 151–52
    false trails in, 151
    interpretation of, 148–50
    Job as Christ figure, 149
    message of, 150–52
    New Testament and, 154
    Satan and, 151, 154
    settings of, 152
    suffering in, 149
    theology of, 154–56
    trust and, 148
Joel, book of
    canonical context, 252
    dating of, 251
    eschatology and, 253
    imagery in, 253
    locust plague, 251–52, 252–53
    message of, 252–55
    new creation and, 254–55
    New Testament and, 255
    theological and literary unity
        of, 252
Johannine literature, 231

John, Gospel of, 63
John the Baptist, 127, 306
Johoiakim (king of Judah), 215
Jonah, book of
    audience, 270
    canonical contributions, 273–74
    God, names of, 270
    interpretation and, 268–70
    Jews and, 268
    parallelism in, 270–71
    Nahum and, 283
    structure of, 270
    theological message of, 269, 270–73
Jordan River, 86, 89
Josephus, 105, 144–45, 191, 230, 237
Joshua, 79
    Christ and, 83
    conquest of Canaan, 36, 86
    courage of, 85
    death of, 96
    Isaiah and, 204
    Josiah and, 84
    precritical Christian interpreta-
        tion of, 83
    succession of, 60
    Torah and, 73, 86, 87
Joshua, book of
    allegorical readings of, 83
    archaeological evidence, 85
    conquest and, 85, 86
    dating of, 84–85
    Deuteronomy and, 84
    historicity of, 84–85
    history of interpretation, 83–85
    Israel and, 83–84
    land, division of, 86–87
    message of, 85–87
    metaphorical understanding of, 89
    modern literary readings of, 85
    sociological readings of, 85
    theology of, 87–90
Josiah (king of Judah), 70, 80, 120,
    122, 207, 293–94
Jotham (king of Judah), 198
joy, 179, 182, 183, 253
jubilee cycles, 241
Judah, 129, 245, 279
    Canaanites and, 98
    fall of, 215
    Isaiah and, 198
    kings of, 128
    leadership of, 93, 96
    survival of, 120
Judaism, 63
Judges, book of
    canonical function of, 98–99
    dating of, 97, 99
    Deuteronomistic History and, 94
    feminist interpretation of, 95
    interpretation of, 93–95
    Israel requires Judean king, 97
    kingship and, 99
    message of, 95–98
    prophetic role of, 97

purpose of, 96
Ruth and, 105
setting of, 98
theology of, 92, 100–101
judgment, 130, 254, 261, 278, 279–80,
    292, 302
judgment-salvation pattern, 216–17,
    218
judicial power, 117
Julian of Toledo, 284
justice, 55, 165, 245, 248–49, 278

Kadesh Barnea, 60
Kenaz, 93
Ketubim (Writings), 105, 305
khatta'ah (sin), 278
khazon (vision), 198, 264
kherem (ban of destruction), 89
khesed (kindness), 102–3, 108
khesed (steadfast love), 169
khokmah, 182
Khomesh happequddim ("the fifth of
    the census totals"), 59
khoshek (darkness), 208
khuqqim (statutes), 75
Kimhi, David, 231
Kingdom of God, 303
king of Israel, 77, 81, 160
Kings, Books of
    genre of, 119
    Messiah and, 122
    themes in, 119, 122–23
    theology of, 120–21
kings, southern, 120
kingship, 96
kingship, theology of, 96, 99, 116–17
knowledge, 22, 173
Koheleth (K). See Qoholeth

Lady Folly, 175
Lady Wisdom, 172, 175
Lady Zion, 223
Lamech, 35, 37, 145
Lamentations, book of
    authorship, 222
    canonical context, 221
    dating of, 221–22
    early church responses to, 223
    form and genre, 222–23
    interpretation, 223–24
    Jeremiah and, 105
    liturgical use of, 223
    national suffering and, 224
lament genre, 223
land, 77, 297
    in covenant lawsuit context, 99
    faithfulness and, 80
    Genesis and, 33
    of inheritance, 99
    Joshua's conquest of, 85
    loss of, 97
    possession of, 88
    restoration of, 72, 80, 219
    theology of, 79–80, 99
    Torah and, 88

Latin America, 262
Latin Vulgate, 105
Latter Prophets, the, 240
"Learned Psalmography, The," 158
lepers, 55
Leviathan, 151, 154
Levi ben Gershom, 187
levirate marriage, 103, 104, 107
Levites, 70, 87, 125, 129, 308
Levite's concubine, 95
Levitical laws of purity, 53, 55
Levitical priests, 77, 127
Leviticus, book of
    canonical status of, 57
    conception of God in, 55
    dietary laws in, 53, 54
    Holiness Code, 53, 55, 56
    holiness of God, 57
    implications of, 56
    incest, 56
    Jesus as interpreter, 52
    Jewish family in, 53
    legalism and ritualism in, 53
    message of, 55–56
    priestly purity in, 53
    purity laws, 53
    relevance of, 54
    revenge and lex talionis, 56
    Sabbath years and, 5
    sacrifices, 55–56, 57
    sources of, 53
lex talionis (law of the talon or claw),
    56, 254
liberation theology, 45, 150, 262
limits, 55, 175–76
Literal Exposition of Job, The
    (Aquinas), 149
literal interpretation (peshat), 62, 179
literary criticism, 17, 54, 244, 252
literary source-critical interpreta-
    tion, 112
Lives of the Prophets, The, 93
Logoi (Words), 68
Lord of Hosts, 199
lots, 143
love, 168, 186, 190
love and sexuality, 191–92. See also
    sexuality
loving-kindness, 108
Luke, Gospel of, 205, 241
Luther, Martin, 143, 145, 238, 293
    on Daniel, 237
    on Deuteronomic laws, 69
    on Job, 149
    on Joel, 252
    on Jonah, 268
    on Psalms, 157, 158, 165
    works-righteousness, 69

Maccabean period, 232, 301
macrostructural models, 198
Mahlon, 102, 103
Maimonides, 53, 149
Malachi, book of
    canonical placement, 307
    content and theology, 307–10

dating of, 305
hermeneutical challenges, 310–11
interpretation of, 305–7
structure and genre, 305–6
mal'aki (my messenger/angel), 305
Manasseh, 124, 232
Marcionism, 71
Marduka, 143
Mark, Gospel of, 166
marriage, 53, 189, 192
    mixed, 103, 125, 132–33, 135, 309
marriage metaphors, 247, 248
Martyrdom and Ascension of
    Isaiah, The, 195
Mary, Virgin, 231, 293
mashiakh (anointed), 117, 158
maskil (teaching official), 236
Masoretes, Ben Asher family of, 105
Masoretic text of Samuel, 125
massa' (oracle), 305, 307
mataiotes (frustration, futility), 183
material intellect, 187
Matthew, Gospel of, 166, 205, 207,
    246
Mays, James L., 159, 162
medieval exegesis, 111, 149, 196, 252
medieval Jewish commentaries, 171
Megillot, 105, 106, 222
Melanchthon, Philipp, 171
Melchizedek, 56, 57
Melito, 191
Mephibosheth, 114
mercy, 49, 247
mercy seat, 48
Mesha, 89
Mesopotamian literature, 172, 223
Messiah, 122, 127, 158, 166, 195, 303
messianism, 117
metanarratives, 242
metaphorical interpretation, 45, 258
Micah, book of
    authenticity of, 277
    genres, 277
    interpretation of, 276–78
    judgment and hope in, 278
    theological concerns, 278–79
Micah (Zvi), 277
Micaiah, 122
Midian, 93
midrashim, 171
Midrash Sifre, 62
military powers, 289
Miller, William, 238
Minor Prophets, 251, 252, 293, 305
miracles, 121
Mishnah, 125, 194
mishneh hattorah ("a copy of the
    Torah"), 68
mishpakhah (family), 278
mishpatim (ordinances), 75
mishpat (justice), 164, 309–10
mixed marriage, 103, 125, 132–33,
    135, 309
Moab, 60, 201

Moabite Stone, 89
monarchy in Israel, 111, 114, 128
monotheism, 38, 103, 265
Moralia in Job (Gregory the Great),
    148
morality, 55
Mordecai, 143, 144, 145, 146
Moses
    access to God, 47
    authority of, 47
    authorship of Genesis, 30
    biographical information of, 38
    called to be prophet, 44
    and covenant promises, 38, 72
    faithfulness of, 48, 49
    intercessory role of, 48, 49, 74
    and Pharaoh, 44, 45
    psalm attributed to, 164
    Song of the Sea, 164
    succeeded by Book of the Law, 86
Mowinckel, Sigmund, 158
Muhammad, 238
multicritical interpretation, 277
Müntzer, Thomas, 238
mutuality, 190
mysterium tremendum et fascinans,
    44, 57
mystical-allegorical interpretation,
    258

Naaman the Syrian, 122
nagid (leader), 115
Nahum, book of
    argument of the book, 282–83
    authorship, 284
    canonical context, 283–84
    hermeneutical challenges, 279–81
    interpretation of, 284
    modern church and, 285
Nahum the Elkoshite, 282–85
nakhalah (grant), 79
name theology, 70
Naomi, 102, 103, 104, 107
naqam (to inflict just punishment vs.
    to take revenge), 145
Nathan, 115, 116
natural theology, 176
nature, 22
nature cults, 245
nature of God, 38
Near East, ancient
    acrostic poems in, 223
    conquest accounts, 84
    cultures, 188
    images and symbols in, 48
    law codes, 73
    literary conventions, 71, 176
    literary parallels to Job, 149
    religious war conventions, 89
    royal-cultic ideologies, 71
    treaty forms, 72
    wisdom, 172
Nebuchadnezzer II (king of Babylo-
    nia), 127, 134, 229–30, 240

Nehemiah, book of
  canonical context of, 139
  chronology of, 138
  historical-critical issues, 138
  interpretation of, 137–39
  structure of, 138
  theology of, 140–41
  See also Ezra, book of
Neo-Assyrian Empire, 284
Neoplatonic philosophy, 189
Nero, 238
Nevi'im (Prophets), 305
new covenant, 212–18, 295
"New Criticism," 180
nihilism, 184
Nineveh, 31, 270–73, 282–85
Noah, 33, 35, 38, 49
nomos, 73
northern kingdom, 120, 128, 129, 279
Numbers, book of
  authorship, 63–64
  canonical context, 60–61
  censuses, 59, 60
  Christian focus on, 63
  genres of, 62
  holiness, 61
  Israel's purity, 61
  Jewish focus on, 63
  Jews and Gentiles rebel, 61
  modern Biblical scholarship, 63–64
  post-Sinai context, 46
  ritual and legal material in, 61, 62
  setting of, 59
  structure, 63
  theology of, 61–63
  titles of, 59
  two-source theory, 63
  wilderness narratives, 46
Numeri, 59

Obadiah, book of
  authorship and dating, 263
  Day of the Lord, 265
  hatred of neighbor, 265
  human pride, 264–65
  prophecy and divine revelation, 264
  setting and genre, 263
  themes in, 264
Obed, 102, 105
obedience, 296
  Abraham as model of, 39
  blessing for, 99, 130
  freedom and, 50
  God and, 47, 78–79
  Israel tested in wilderness, 46
  love and, 168
  Moses and, 50, 72
  Noah and, 50
  salvation and, 79
offerings, 308
Old Greek text, 288
On the Life of Moses (Philo), 62
oppressed church, 294

oppression, 45–46, 50, 160, 262, 277, 282, 294
Origen, 187, 206, 231, 237, 306
  on Amos, 258
  on Isaiah, 195
  Scripture interpretation and, 53
Origin of the Species (Darwin), 31
'or (light), 208
Ornan's threshing floor, 129
Othniel, 96

palistrophic patterns, 228
paqad (divine visitation), 200
parody in ancient literature, 269
pasha (rebels), 199, 203
passion narratives, 167
passion texts, 207
Passover, 45, 56, 86
pastoral theology, 183–84
patriarchs, 32, 36
patristic exegesis, 111, 195, 252, 300
patristic theology, 30
Paul, Epistles of, 165, 288
  Christ and, 39, 50
  Christian freedom, 50
  contradictions in, 174–75
  definition of true Jew, 69
  exodus generation and Christian apostasy, 63
  Ezekiel and, 231
  Hosea and, 246
  law of love, 69
  Moses and, 68, 76
  parts of, 77
  salvation in, 68
  sin and, 39
peace offerings, 56
peace (*shalom*), 160, 165
Pentateuch, 36, 53, 67, 138
Pentecost, 105, 293
Peor, 60
Persian Empire, 136, 143, 144, 145, 240
Persian period, 125, 135, 305
personal/historical interpretation, 158
pesha' (crime/transgression), 278.
Peter, epistles of, 69
Pharaoh, 44
Philistines, 96, 114
Philo of Alexandria, 62, 230
Pilgrim's Progress (Bunyan), 188
political power, 117
political theology, 117
politics, 114
polygamy, 189
polytheism, 34, 265
poor, the, 160, 262, 293
pope, 237, 238
post-Enlightenment exposition of Jonah, 268
postexilic prophecy, 166
postmodern interpretation, 19–20, 242

postmodernism, 184
poverty, 293
power, 113, 114, 167–68, 230, 233, 281, 293
praise, 161–62, 253
prayer, 48, 53, 106, 156, 161–63, 211–12
precritical interpretation, 16, 63, 132–33, 137, 158
premillennialism, 233
Presenter, the (P), 181
pride, 200, 208, 228, 230, 233, 264
Priestly Code, 127
Priestly (P) source, 30, 32, 63, 76
priests, 50, 248, 308, 309
Primary History, 59, 60
process theology, 155
profane, 55
Prolegomena to the History of Israel (Wellhausen), 30
prophecy, 125, 166, 198, 227–28, 264
prophetic disputation, 306
prophetic movement, 122
prosperity, 311
Proverbs, book of
  canonical context, 176–77
  church and, 177
  contradictions in, 174
  genres in, 172–73, 176–77
  interpretation of, 171–72
  message of, 172–76
  purpose of, 173–74
  range of topics, 175
  salvation history in, 176–77
  theology of, 177
  wisdom books and, 171
Psalms, book of
  canonical context, 165–67
  cultic prototypes, 158
  dating of, 158, 162
  Deuteronomic influences on, 76
  enthronement psalms, 160, 162, 166
  exile and aftermath, 164
  God in, 168–69
  Hymn to a Valiant Woman, 173
  interpretation of, 157–59
  message of, 159–65
  Psalms of Ascents, 164
  psalms of lament or complaint, 161
  psalms of vengeance, 163
  refuge as central theme, 161
  torah and, 166
  theological perspectives of, 164, 167–69
  types of psalms, 158
Psalter, 127
Pseudo-Philo, 93
psychoanalytical interpretation, 232
Ptolemies, 126
punishment, 168, 260, 292
Purim, 143
Puritan tradition, 232

qanah (begot), 172
qiryat-tohu (ruined city), 200
Qoheleth ("preacher" or "teacher"), 181, 182, 183, 184
Qumran, 125, 230, 257, 288

ra'ah (destruction/discomfort), 270
rabbinic interpretation, 252
rabbis, 53
racial purity, 135
Rad, G. von, 172
ra' (evil), 278, 310
Rahab, 86, 89
Rashi, 62, 142, 231, 252
reading genres, 23
reading/hearing, 71
Rebekah, 107
reconciliation, 37, 40
redaction criticism, 258, 259, 295
redemption, 40, 289
Reed Sea, 86
Reformation, 145, 172, 179, 232, 268, 301
Reformation exegesis, 112
Reformed theologians, 168
Reformers, the, 30, 69, 83, 94, 149
Rehoboam (king of Judah), 123, 129
relationship, 248–49
religion, 133, 214, 218, 219
religiosity, 214, 218, 245, 281
religious individualism, 212
remarriage, 311
remnant, 279, 292, 293, 294
remnant (*she'erith*), 278, 279
renewal, 297
repentance, 127, 247, 261, 272, 293
responsibility, 224, 248
rest, 114
restoration, 283, 293
restored temple, 295
retribution, 279–80, 309–10
retribution, doctrine of, 121, 125, 150, 153, 168
retributive anger, 284
retributive paradox, 182
revelation, 264
Revelation, book of, 39, 205, 231, 234, 241
revenge, 56
reversal motifs, 107
rhetorical criticism, 159, 197, 261
right behavior, 248–49
righteousness, 78, 81, 165, 175, 248–49, 288
River Ahava, 134
Rogers, Richard, 94
Roman Catholic church, 69
Roman Empire, 238, 289
Romans, book of, 205, 246
Rome, 237
Rupert of Deuz, 232
Ruth, book of
    authorship of, 108
    canonical context of, 105–6

ethnicity and inclusion, 103, 107–8
fertility and, 106
formalist-folklorist approach to, 104
God and, 153
interpretation of, 102–5
Judges and, 105
levirate marriage and, 105, 107
Moabite ancestry of, 103
placement in Christian canon, 105
placement in Hebrew canon, 105–6
purpose of book, 102–5
salvation history and, 106
theological aspects of, 106–9
Ruth Rabbah (Ze'ira), 102

Sabbath, 34, 46, 125
Sabbath years, 57
sabbatical years, 241
sacrifices, 309
    Christ and, 53
    Exodus and, 48–49
    forms of, 55–56
    life changes and, 249
    Pentateuch and, 38
    salvation and, 52
    sin and, 56
salvation
    circumcision and, 52
    gift of, 68, 203
    history, 176, 239, 242
    sacrifice and, 52
salvation-historical interpretation, 258
salvation oracle, 261
Samaria, 276
Samson, 94
Samuel, books of
    Ark Narrative, 112
    attitudes in, 112
    authorship of, 112
    dating of, 112
    genres in, 112–13
    History of David's Rise, 112
    interpretation of, 111–14
    message of, 114–15
    structure of, 113
    themes in, 114–16
    theology of, 117–18
Sarah, 160, 165
Satan, the, 149, 151, 154, 206, 233, 289
Saul, 106, 113, 114
scapegoats, 56
Second Isaiah, 196, 201
Second Temple period, 93
Sefer Devarim ("Book of Words"), 67–68
sefer hattorah ("Book of the Instruction"), 73
segullah (possession), 78
Seleucids, 126
Sennacherib, 120, 202, 208
Sennacherib's Annals, 202

sensuality, 190
Septuagint, 142
Sermon on the Mount, 171
Sermons on 2 Samuel (Calvin), 112
Servant of God, 203
servant texts in Isaiah, 207
seven-branch lampstand, 48
sexual imagery, 247
sexuality, 175–76, 189, 190, 191–92
sexual relations, 55
sexual violence against women, 284
shalom (peace), 160, 165
shapat (judgment), 160
shapat (justice), 159
Shechem, 87
Shema, 69
Shiloh, 87, 114
shobabim (faithless), 218
shub (return/repent), 218
shub (turning), 215
Shulammite, the, 189
silence, 163, 224, 308
Similitudes (Parables) of Enoch, 236
sin, 175, 277, 278, 310
    effects of, 122, 229
    Genesis and, 35
    Israel and, 249
    land and, 229
    pride and, 264
    seriousness of, 248
Sinai, 46
Sinai covenant, 297
sin offerings, 56
slave trade, 265
Smith, G. A., 31
social justice, 260, 261, 278
social responsibility, 248–49
socioeconomic factors, 233
sociological criticism, 17, 54
Sodom, 39, 204
solidarity, 278
Solomon (king of Israel), 116, 119–20, 121, 123, 187
Solomon's temple, 56, 76, 121, 129, 134
Song of Songs
    canonicity, 191
    genres, 188
    interpretation of, 186–90
    marriage metaphor in, 192
    message of, 189
    Passover and, 105
    targum to, 187
    theology of, 190, 191–92
Song of the Sea, 164
Son of Man, 236, 241, 242
source criticism, 68, 179
southern kingdom, 279
speech-act theory, 261
Spinoza, Baruch, 30
spiritual adultery, 247
spirituality, 42, 177, 189, 191
stubbornness, 213
submission to Yahweh, 292
suffering, 151, 167, 168, 286, 310

Suffering Servant, 242, 303
Sumer, 188
Sumerian King List, 31
supersessionism, 268
symbolism, 30
syncretism, 294
synergy, 240
Synoptic Gospels, 166, 241
Syrian liturgy, 289
Syrus, Ephraim, 300

tabernacle, 48, 50, 55
Tabernacles, Feast of, 56
Talmud, 125, 144, 172, 237, 257–58
Targum of Ezekiel, 231
Tehillim (praises), 162
telos (outcome), 154
temple, 297
    destruction of, 53, 56, 127
    in Jerusalem, 50
    rebuilding of, 134, 140
    symbolism of, 128
Ten Commandments, 47
Tenebrae services, 223
Tennes revolt, 126
Ten Principles, 75
Tertullian, 191, 206, 231, 289, 306
text-critical interpretation, 125
text criticism, 277
text genres, 23
theocracy, 113, 117
theodicy, 150, 260, 309–10
Theodore of Mopsuestia, 188, 258, 300
Theodoret of Cyrus, 188, 195, 231, 258, 289
theological criticism, 21
theological interpretation, 16, 26
theophany, 288
Things Omitted, the, 124
Third Isaiah, 196, 197
third-year tithe, 308
Thomas Aquinas, 149
Tishah-b'Ab liturgy, 223
tithes, 308, 311
tob (good), 310
To Biblion ton Logon ("The Book of Words"), 68
To Deutoronomion ("Second Law"), 68
Torah, 67, 88, 172, 179, 230, 260–61
    as Law or Instruction, 38
    as moral and ritual constitution, 42

obedience to, 50
    as a response to salvation, 68
torah, 75, 159, 215, 288
    to teach (yarah), 73
Torat Mosheh (Law of Moses), 76
Tower of Babel, 35, 39
Tractatus theologico-politicus (Spinoza), 30
tradition criticism, 258
Transjordan, 60, 87
Treier, D. J., 15n1
Trinity, the, 195
trust, 283
tsadaq (righteousness), 159
tsedaqah (righteousness), 78, 81
twelve tribes, 37, 129
two-source theory, 63, 75

unclean, 55
underprivileged, 308
unfaithfulness, 245, 309
unrighteousness, 168
Ussher, Archbishop, 31
Uzziah (king of Judah), 198, 245

Vanhoozer, K. J., 16, 24
vanity, 179
Vashti (queen of Persia), 146
vengeance, 145, 163
victimization, 163
Victorinus of Petovium, 195
violence, 35, 90, 163, 286, 287, 289
Vulgate, 127

Wallace, A. F. C., 138
war, 90
War Scroll, 236
wealth, 293
Weeks, Feast of, 56
well-being offerings, 56
Wellhausen, Julius, 30
Western churches, 145, 294
Wetzstein, J. G., 189
wickedness, 175, 288
Wicked Tenants, parable of, 241
Wildberger, Hans, 206
wilderness, 62
wine, 287
Wisdom, 172, 173, 175
Wisdom in Israel (Rad), 172
Wisdom literature in Old Testament, 181

women, 55, 103, 108, 144
works-righteousness, 69
worship implements, 55
worship, language of, 286
wrath, 293
Writings, the, 240
wrongdoers, 277

Xerxes (king of Persia), 139, 142, 143

Yahweh
    compassion of, 72
    covenant with Abraham, 60
    Israel and, 42, 45, 77–78, 88, 266
    Jesus and, 75
    justice and, 265
    name of, 44
    nations and, 254
    nature of, 44
    providence of, 107
    relationship and, 77, 203
    as tribal or national deity, 45, 245
    torah and, 42
    See also God
Yahweh-Elohim, 270
Yahwist (J) source, 30, 32, 63
yarah (to teach), 73

Zaraphath, widow of, 122
Zechariah, 126, 128
Zechariah, book of
    authorship and dating, 301
    canonical context, 303
    interpretation of, 300–302
    message of the text, 302
    structure, 301
    theological significance, 303
Zedekiah (king of Judah), 215, 229–30
Ze'ira, Rabbi, 102
Zephaniah, book of
    argument of the book, 291–92
    canonical context of, 292–93
    interpretation of, 293–94
    modern church and, 294
    structure, 291–92
Zerubbabel, 295, 298
Zion, 252, 265, 266
Zophar, 151
Zvi, Ben, 277